Missing the Revolution

cumulative social science that is not utterly isolated from the other human sciences.

Missing's perspective is not just that we need both the social and biological sciences but that they are so intertwined that the one without the other is at best incomplete; at worst, in error. It comes at a point in history when many social scientists seem to be defining their interests and identities in *opposition* to the biological (Bauerlein, 2001), and at a time when much of the debate seems to involve the torching of conveniently constructed straw houses in which no one ever really lived (see Kurzban & Haselton, this volume). *Missing* presents some applications of evolutionary psychology (and related approaches) in a manner intended to illustrate their relevance to current concerns of social scientists. It hopes to be a bridge. Its goal is to persuade social scientists to put aside preconceptions and think about the likely links between what they are doing and what evolutionists are doing. That is, after all, what is happening both for the general reading public and in most non–social science academic disciplines. First, though, what Darwinian field are we talking about?

2. What Field Are We Talking About?

There is no single term for those applying Darwinian theories of evolution to human behavior, and no clear consensus about how, precisely, this perspective is to be applied. The terms "human behavioral ecology," "sociobiology," "evolutionary psychology," "Darwinian psychology," and even "selfish gene theory" are in current use, though many evolutionists (particularly evolutionary biologists and some psychologists) find no need to apply a distinctive term to themselves or to their work because, for them, evolution is mainstream. The supply of labels is not endless but can seem so: Iver Mysterud (2004) found 57 appellations that deal with what he considers "humans and modern evolutionary theory" (p. 107). To use my own work as an example of the fluidity of labels, in 1973 the term I used was "Darwinian psychological anthropology," in 1974 it was "biosocial anthropology," in 1980 it was "human ethology," in 1989 "sociobiology," in 1992 "evolutionary psychology," in 1994 "evolutionary psychological anthropology." Mysterud (p. 107) quotes Alexander's (1987) hope that labels such as "sociobiology" will "melt away" because they lead to "artificial subdisciplines" associated with particular individuals or points of view and so impede the integration of biological arguments into the human sciences in general. Alexander is no doubt right, but for the moment labels seem to be a necessary evil.

For this volume I will again favor "evolutionary psychology" because it clearly indicates that the goal is not to focus on individual or population differences but on human nature as a product of biological evolution. But note that the title of evolutionary psychology's first major edited volume was "Evolutionary Psychology and *the Generation of Culture*" (Barkow, Cosmides, & Tooby, 1992)—there was never any intention to make the field just one more kind of psychology. In the present context I will use "evolutionary psychology" rather inclusively and often in conjunction with "sociobiology." I will also use "human nature" as synonymous with "human evolved psychology." However, many of the contributors to this volume would definitely not call themselves evolutionary psychologists. Most but not all, I believe, would accept that *evolutionary psychology is the infrastructure of culture and society*. (This last phrase, abbreviated as "EPICS," was the original working title for this volume.)

3. An Insurgent Biology and What the Public Reads

In a *New York Times* review of David Buss's (2000) *The Dangerous Passion*, Courtney Weaver writes: "Is Darwin replacing Freud as the spokesman for a millennium? Judging from the recent publication by evolutionary scientists of decidedly politically incorrect theories, it certainly seems that way" (Weaver, 2000). Yes, and however belatedly, Darwin is replacing not only Freud but perhaps Marx and Max Weber as well, for the reading public, as the source of insight into human nature and society.

If physics was the preeminent field of most of the twentieth century, biology is queen of the first part of the twenty-first. Parsing the human genome was only the opening round, with proteomics (the study of the proteins produced by the genes) likely to compete with space weaponry in scope of funding requirements. The media are filled with stories of cloning and of the genetic engineering of food crops, while biomedicine promises imminent cures for a host of illnesses. Explainers of biology such as Helen Fisher (1992, 1999, 2004), Helena Cronin (1992), Richard Dawkins (1976, 1989, 1996a, 1996b, 1996c, 2000, 2003; Dawkins & Dennett, 1999), Richard Wrangham (Wrangham & Peterson, 1996; Wrangham, McGrew, de Waal, & Heltne, 1994), and the late Stephen Jay Gould (e.g., Gould, 1989, 1995, 2002) regularly find their work on the bestseller list, as do those who, like Michael S. Gazzaniga (1992, 2000), Jean-Pierre Changeux (1997, 2004), Changeux and Riocoeur (2000), Edelman and Changeux (2000), Antonio Damasio (1995, 2000, 2003), Daniel Dennett (1995, 1997, 2003), Oliver Sacks (1990, 1995a, 1995b), and Steven Pinker (1993, 1997, 2002), explain to the reading public how the brain and its mind work. The heroes of our time are not the anthropologists who study our own species, as Margaret Mead did, but those who, like Jane Goodall (1990) and Dian

Fossey (1983), have studied nonhuman primates. *Science*, the journal of the American Association for the Advancement of Science, allocates far more space to biology and biomedicine than it does to any other fields. In psychiatry, Freud has moved to the margins, and a powerful pharmacopeia has situated disorders not in the spirit or mind but in the brain and the biochemistry. Literature, music, the arts, film, and journalism are being revealed as structures that rest on a base of biology and evolution, thanks to thinkers and researchers such as Joseph Carroll (1994); Hank Davis (Davis & McLeod, 2003; Davis & Javor, 2004); Ellen Dissanayake (1992, 2000); Pamela Shoemaker (1996); Nils Wallin, Bjorn Merker, and Steven Brown (Wallin, Merker, & Brown, 2000); Robert Storey (1996); and Karl Grammar and Eckart Voland (Grammar & Voland, 2003). In the media, not nuclear war but bioterrorism and bioweaponry take pride of place among our fears. For better or worse, we live in the Age of Biology.

Academic disciplines have responded to the "evolution revolution" with varying degrees of engagement and incorporation (as [incompletely] summarized in Sidebar 1.1, "The Response of Disciplines"), just as they did in the past with Marxism, psychoanalysis, and feminism. Strangely, though, sociology and

---

Sidebar 1.1. The Response of Disciplines

Academic disciplines have engaged in various ways with the developments in evolutionary theory. This sidebar is intended to be illustrative rather than exhaustive, its point being that the evolutionary revolution is omnipresent except for mainstream sociology and social-cultural anthropology.

a. Political Science

Political science has, since 1980, boasted the Association for Politics and the Life Sciences, a group whose meetings and journal include a strong evolutionary stream. Major books in the field include Schubert and Masters's (1991) edited collection *Primate Politics*, Masters's (1989) *The Nature of Politics*, and Rubin's (2002) *Darwinian Politics*. Courses in what is sometimes referred to as "biopolitics" include discussions of evolutionary psychology, sociobiology, and primate behavior along with other relevant biological topics such as the new reproductive strategies.

b. Economics

Many economists are interested in evolutionary approaches to their discipline, resulting in, for example, the *Journal of Bioeconomics*. Peter Koslowski's (1999) *Sociobiology and Economics* presents a good overview of the evolution revolution in economics. There is widespread interest in game theory, with emphasis on mathematical models of the Prisoner's Dilemma type common in evolutionary biology and economics. This interest is reflected in, for example, Larry Samuelson's (1997) *Evolutionary Games and Equilibrium Selection*, Jurgen W. Weibull's (1995) *Evolutionary Game Theory*, and Herbert Gintis's (2000) *Game Theory Evolving*. Economists are also interested in the evolutionary nature of human self-interest, particularly with regard to contract behavior (e.g., Brian Skyrms's [1996] *Evolution of the Social Contract* and Peyton H. Young's [2001] *Individual Strategy and Social Structure: An Evolutionary Theory of Institutions*). The contrast between the traditional rational choice assumption of classical economics and the heuristics and decision-rules approach favored by evolutionary psychologists has provoked much intellectual interest.*

c. Law

The field of law enjoys a growing number of analyses of the implications of evolutionary psychology for its domain. For example, there is Roger D. Masters and Margaret Gruter's (1992) *The Sense of Justice: Biological Foundations of Law*; John H. Beckstrom's (1993) *Darwinism Applied: Evolutionary Paths to Social Goals*; and Kingsley R. Browne's (1998) *Divided Labours: An Evolutionary View of Women at Work* and (2002) *Biology at Work: Rethinking Sexual Equality*. These analyses have considerable importance not just for law but for sociology and for women's studies. Each year, the conferences of The Society for Evolutionary Analysis and the Law bring evolutionary and legal thought together.

d. Psychiatry, Medicine, and Nutrition

Aside from psychology, the field that perhaps has most engaged with evolutionary psychology and sociobiology is psychiatry. Evolutionary psychiatry is a burgeoning field. A few representative titles might include Stevens and Price's

(1996) *Evolutionary Psychiatry;* McGuire and Troisi's (1998) *Darwinian Psychiatry;* Bruce Charleton's (2000) *Psychiatry and the Human Condition;* Gilbert, McGuire, and Bailey's (2000) *Evolutionary Psychotherapy;* and Glantz and Pearce's (1989) *Exiles from Eden: Psychotherapy from an Evolutionary Perspective.* Any social scientist with a focus on "deviant" behavior or mental health needs to keep abreast of this exciting work.

(Nonpsychiatric) medicine and nutrition are also being influenced by evolutionary thought, particularly (though not exclusively) by "mismatch" or "discrepancy" theory— the premise that many of our ills (social, psychological, and physical) are due to the distance between our current environment and the environments in which we evolved and to which we presumably remain adapted. Good entries to this field would be Trevathan, Smith, and McKenna's (1999) collection, *Evolutionary Medicine;* or Nesse and Williams's (1994) *Why We Get Sick.* Eaton et al. (1994) will be of special interest to those concerned with the health of women, with special reference to cancer of the breast, ovary, and endometrium. A recurring theme of this field is that physicians have often misunderstood the body's adaptive response to disease (e.g., by taking the body's raised temperature and decreased iron levels in response to infection as illness to be treated rather than as adaptive defense); or have pathologized evolved prophylactic mechanisms such as (according to Profet [1992, 1993]) menstruation and pregnancy ("morning") sickness. In nutrition, Eaton, Shostak, and Konner's (1988) *The Paleolithic Prescription* remains a good popular introduction to using the likely diet of our ancestors as a guide to healthy eating. More recently, Loren Cordain (2001) has provided a similar argument and guide. (These authors are primarily scientific researchers rather than popularizers). The underlying assumption of these works is that our bodies are still adapted to the diet of our forager/hunting-gathering ancestors, rather than to the very high carbohydrate diet prevalent since the beginning of agriculture. Evolutionists (and others) argue that we are very poorly adapted to our current industrial diet of highly processed foods.

e. The Humanities and Philosophy

The humanities—literature and the arts—have not disregarded the evolution revolution. See, for example, Joseph

Carroll's (1994) *Evolution and Literary Theory;* Robert
Storey's (1996) *Mimesis and the Human Animal;* Cooke
and Turner's (1999) *Biopoetics;* Wallin, Merker, and
Brown's edited volume (2000) *The Origins of Music;* and
Ellen Dissanayake's (2000) *Art and Intimacy: How the Arts
Began.* Grammar and Voland's *Evolutionary Aesthetics*
(Grammar & Voland, 2003) replaces the mysteriousness of
judgments of beauty with Darwinian analysis.

Philosophers have long been deeply involved with evolutionary theory, often criticizing, often supporting, often
utilizing. The relevant literature is vast, but three illustrative works would be the huge tome edited by Hull and
Ruse (1998), *Philosophy of Biology;* Daniel Dennett's
(1995) *Darwin's Dangerous Idea;* and Larry Arnhart's
(1998) *Darwinian Natural Right: The Biological Ethics
of Human Nature.*

f. Management

In 1999, the journal *Managerial & Decision Economics* published a special, evolution-oriented issue titled "Management and Human Nature," while Nigel Nicholson's (2000)
*Executive Instinct: Managing the Human Animal in the Infor-
mation Age* explains the basics of evolutionary psychology
to the business community.

To summarize this sidebar, a multitude of fields are engaging with evolutionary psychology and the evolutionary
perspective in general, leaving the social sciences lagging
behind.

*My thanks to James Bryan for his helpful suggestions contained in a
personal communication dated August 31, 2001.

social-cultural anthropology have largely ignored the new perspective, for
the most part summarily dismissing it, occasionally attacking it in passing,
or, more usefully if less frequently, treating controversies over applying
Darwin to the human sciences as interesting sociological phenomena to be
analyzed (e.g., Segerstråle [2000] and this volume). Pierre van den Berghe
(1990) and Lee Ellis (1996) have described the reaction of social scientists
to evolutionary approaches to human behavior as "biophobia." But let us
separate sociology from social-cultural anthropology, for a moment.

Despite mainstream sociology's largely dismissive and negative reaction to "naturalizing" human beings and societies, there are a number of sociologists who have begun to take an evolutionary approach to the subject matter of their discipline: Bernd Baldus's and Anthony Walsh's respective chapters in this volume attest to this interest (though their approaches and conclusions are very different). Lee Ellis and Anthony Walsh's (2000) monumental *Criminology: A Global Perspective* is strongly influenced by evolutionary thinking. Martin Daly and Margo Wilson's (1988) *Homicide* has proven to be an enduring classic in both evolutionary psychology and criminology. Pierre van den Berghe has been a pioneer in applying biological evolution to sociology, and his (1979) insightful *Human Family Systems* and (1981) *The Ethnic Phenomenon* should have made of sociologists early adopters of evolution, had it not been for the barriers discussed below. Other sociologists who use the evolutionary paradigm at least in part include Stephen K. Sanderson and his important (2001) work, *The Evolution of Sociality*, William Gary Runciman's *The Social Animal* (1998) and *The Origins of Social Institutions* (2001), and Joseph Lopreato and Timothy Crippen's (1999) *Crisis in Sociology: The Need for Darwin*. Mainstream or "textbook" sociology, however, continues to pay scant and often negative attention to the evolution revolution (Machalek and Martin 2004).

Social-cultural anthropology has probably been even more resistant to evolution than has sociology. This may be because anthropology's disciplinary organization has had an unanticipatedly compartmentalizing effect on evolutionary thought. In the past, particularly in the United States, anthropology followed a "four-square" model consisting of social-cultural anthropology, anthropological archaeology, anthropological linguistics, and physical/biological anthropology. Though most anthropologists would specialize in just one of these areas, basic training in the discipline involved all. However, in recent decades the subfields have drifted apart, and increasingly their members read different journals, attend different meetings, and have different colleagues. In addition, many new subfields have developed within anthropology, so that the American Anthropological Society is now a federation of sections: "General anthropology" has become a residual category of membership for the temerarious, the courageous souls who scorn to escape the flood of journals and meetings by sheltering within a more narrow specialization. Thus it is that most social-cultural anthropologists automatically relegate to one of the physical/biological or archaeological subfields anything to do with "sociobiology" or evolution, including the evolution of human behavior and even the application of evolutionary perspectives to culture and current social phenomena. (Though not myself a biological anthropologist, for example, I found long ago that the only anthropologists who read my evolution-oriented work were the biological anthropologists, regardless of what audience I thought I was addressing.) The old fourfold model of anthropology essentially functions today not to integrate, as it once did, but to compartmentalize: social-cultural anthropologists routinely react to anything evolutionary as "biological anthropology, not my field, nothing to do with me or my work" (when they do not react with various nefarious stereotypes, discussed below).

However, there are perhaps three groups of anthropologists who have taken an explicitly evolutionary approach and who at least in times past would probably have been part of the social-cultural subdiscipline.[4] The first of these is the human behavioral ecologists, whose work Lee Cronk discusses in this volume. Many of these anthropologists, however, no longer identify with mainstream social-cultural anthropology, which by and large ignores them. In part, this is probably because behavioral ecologists see themselves as applying evolutionary biology to the human species and therefore doing "science," while many social-cultural anthropologists appear to see such efforts as mere "scientism."[5]

There has been a split within anthropology between those who think of themselves as doing "scientific" anthropology, with concerns about data, hypotheses, and objectivity; and those who see anthropology as largely a political and moral exercise sharing far more with the humanities than with the natural sciences.[6] Perhaps the most visible fallout of this dispute was the splitting of Stanford University's Department of Anthropology, in 1998–1999, into two separate administrative, degree-conferring units, one called the Department of Anthropological Sciences and the other the Department of Cultural and Social Anthropology. Though the two units overlap heavily in subject matter, one sees anthropology as a science, the other as part of the humanities. The split does not follow the boundaries of the four subfields. Traditionally, anthropology was both science and humanities—for many of us, having a foot in both camps was part of its appeal—but today there are strong pressures to dissociate. In the context of evolutionary psychology and sociobiology there is irony here, because, as we have seen, the humanities, but not the humanities-influenced social sciences, are to a reasonable extent engaging with Darwinian thought.

The second group of (nonbiological/nonarchaeological) anthropologists who have been hospitable to the evolutionary perspective consists primarily of those influenced by the cognitive sciences and who also tend to find it useful to view culture as particulate (the particles having various terms, with some adopting Richard Dawkins's [1976] term, "meme"). One thinks of the important analysis of the nature of religion being done by Pascal Boyer (1993, 1994a, 1994b, 2000, 2001) and by Scott Atran (2002), as well as Atran's insights into categorization (1998, 1999); and of Francisco Gil-White's (2001) analysis of ethnicity. Dan Sperber's (1994, 1996) conception of culture as an "epidemiology of representations," too, is informed by evolutionary and psychological perspectives. (Oddly, some social-cultural anthropologists seem to be respectful of some of these evolutionary efforts while being scornfully dismissive of evolutionary psychology per se.)

Finally, there is the important work of Peter Richerson and Robert Boyd on gene-culture coevolution. These authors view culture and genes as interacting systems of inheritance. Their approach is exemplified by their (2004) *Not by Genes Alone: How Culture Transformed Human Evolution.* (One of their many original ideas, that of the "work-around," will be discussed below in the context of "an evolutionarily informed praxis.")[7]

4. Sources of Intolerance for the Darwinian Gaze

Why are so many social-cultural anthropologists so scornful of evolutionary psychology and sociobiology? Whence comes this impulse to stick one's finger in the Darwinian eye whenever it dares to gaze at human behavior? The sources are (at least) five: First, there is the horrifying history of past and present misuse of biology in social science and in social policy. Second, there is the deeply embedded dominance of two strands of Cartesian thought in the social sciences: the fixed idea that there is a huge gulf between humans and other animals; and the belief that body and mind are separate rather than one and the same, which makes possible the implicit belief that biological evolution has to do with the body rather than the mind. Third, there is the Durkheimian fallacy, the idea that collectivities can share representations in ways somehow independent of the psychology of individuals, and its more recent adjunct that when such sociological determinism becomes insupportable then the protean concept of "agency" is all the psychology that need be added. Fourth, there is the nineteenth-century utopianism of Marx, with his romantic idea that if we can only get our mode of production and system of social relations right, all social inequality will be abolished and human nature will be perfected (or at least, greatly improved). Fifth, there is the idealistic belief that the social sciences have a mission, a moral mission, to oppose oppression and inequality wherever it is found, and the unexamined assumption that an evolutionary approach is somehow irrelevant or even opposed to that mission.

a. Misuse

We all know that the bad biology of the past has led to genuinely evil efforts, from selective sterilization to wholesale genocide: hellish policies have been conducted in the name of eugenics and of "racial" purification. The horror of these atrocities, culminating in the Holocaust, led to a wholesale repudiation of this pseudobiology and determinism and to a reshaping and

redefinition of sociology and social-cultural anthropology as antibiologi-
cal fields. Of course, current evolutionary thought is light-years away
from that horrifying pseudobiology, but that is no guarantor against its
appropriation and misuse. Demagogues and would-be demagogues from
all parts of the political spectrum are opportunistic and use and misuse
whatever they can (e.g., David Duke's [1998] irrelevant and misleading in-
vocation of sociobiology in his *My Awakening*). But the attempted appropriation of biology for political purposes does not contaminate it for other
use: Shakespeare[8] points out that "the devil can cite Scripture for his purpose," but this has not led the Christian world to abandon its Bible. Neither
Pol Pot nor Stalin led to worldwide rejection of Marxism.

b. Humans First! Cartesian Social Science Resists Evolution

Ptolemy may be dead, but his spirit lives on. Yes, Copernicus was right
and the Earth is not the centre of the universe; yes, we have learned to
denounce the claims of racism and patriarchy and we struggle against the
ethnocentrism that lurks within us, but no, species-centrism, that last and
most pervasive of all the centrisms, still seems self-evidently right to many
people. Even some who consider themselves prejudice-free may speak
(and more importantly, *think*) of "humans and animals" rather than "humans and other animals." Once, Descartes could preach that it was our
souls that separated us from all other living things, making of them mere
robots but of ourselves aspirers to the angelic; today's discourse has evolved,
for now our separateness and superiority are due not to our *esprit* but to our
culture: applicable as the theories of the evolutionary biologists may be to
the sex of the praying mantis, the alarm calls of marmots, the plumage of
the peacock, and the parenting habits of the mouth-breeding cichlid,
surely they are irrelevant to the complexities of human culture and society, divorced as these are from the genes and instincts that control the
actions of all others save ourselves. Surely, too, those who trespass by seeking to apply evolutionary psychology to our species and our societies must
have dark motives: perhaps they seek to reduce glorious humankind to
mere animal status or, even worse, to support the manipulations of eu-
genicists and the claims of racists. Much of the opposition to applying evolution to human behavior stems from this deeply conservative, even reactionary impulse to maintain the mysteriousness of human behavior and, at
all costs, to keep a chasm between ourselves and the rest of "Creation." Social scientists and creationists are often strange allies in the campaign to
continue to exclude human behavior and society from the natural world.
What unites them is their Cartesianism.

Cartesian thinking makes evolutionary psychology appear exculpatory. When we argue that there is an evolved underpinning beneath even the most despicable of human acts, even rape and torture, are we really excusing such behavior while pretending to condemn it? Evolutionists often find it difficult to convince critics that their accounts are in no way exculpatory. Perhaps this lack of communication is also Descartes's fault, for most of us (and virtually all social scientists) remain mired in his insistence on a mind-body split. In our society, we tend to construct the mind as an essence, a self or soul or awareness that is the executive responsible for controlling the body. The body in turn is seen as being responsible for supporting and maintaining the mind, the self. But how can the mind be expected to maintain responsible control when the body fails it? Our legal systems, reflecting our Cartesian folk psychology, do not always expect it to. The mind's control is believed to weaken when the body (never the mind!) produces powerful emotions, or when the body suffers from physical or mental illness, or when the body's use of alcohol or other drugs prevents it from providing the mind with proper support. Given this folk psychology, legal responsibility can be mitigated by bodily failings. But what does all this have to do with anger against evolutionists?

In our folk psychology, it is the body and not the mind that is the product of evolution. Thus, if I argue that males use violence and even rape to gain reproductive advantage, and have been selected to do so, I am heard as arguing that this is another instance of seeking to excuse criminal behavior on the grounds that it is a fault of the body, a failing, and that the mind, that impalpable Cartesian essence, cannot be expected to control so imperfect a body. This defense elicits even more anger than claiming alcohol use as mitigation in cases of, say, vehicular homicide, because while drunkards can sober up, men cannot stop being male: to invoke evolution and crime in the same paragraph is likely to be read as "you can never blame men for their violence." Add to this misunderstanding the faulty assumption that "biological" means "fixed or rigid," and I am heard as saying that not only are men violent criminals and rapists, not only can they not be blamed for it because their behavior is a product of evolution, but nothing can be done about it because it is biological. Well, that argument certainly is enraging. It is also stupid. The misunderstanding is a product of our (usually unexamined) Cartesian folk psychology.

The argument that I read most evolutionary psychologists as actually making begins with a non-Cartesian tack: there is no separate physical body and spiritual mind; there is nobody there but you. The brain consists of various mechanisms of varying degrees of generality and specificity. As they operate, we experience. It may be that self-consciousness is part of that experience because our species has been selected for complex, predictive cognitive maps of the social behavior of others and of ourselves (or our selves) (Barkow, 1989; see Damasio, 2000, for an essentially similar but neurologically based approach to the problem of consciousness and self).[9] Be that as it may, we do have a brain that is amazingly able to understand and to influence others but which nevertheless remains an organ of the body, not a separate spirit or essence. One of the evolved attributes of the body of a young human male, as Fessler (this volume) discusses, is the capacity for a flash of rage. It is no more good or bad than, say, the ability to store extra calories as adipose tissue—both capabilities are products of evolution that in some environments have adaptive and in others deadly consequences; both are at times unwelcome, but neither is utterly uncontrollable. Fessler is no more excusing male anger by pointing to its evolutionary roots than a physiologist is advocating obesity when discussing the formerly adaptive aspects of lipid metabolism.

c. A Durkheimian Fallacy

But how do we integrate a social science theory with the evolutionary and psychological when the theorist expressly denies having made any psychological or biological assumptions? There is, after all, a long tradition, associated in sociology with Emile Durkheim and in social anthropology with A. R. Radcliffe-Brown, which demands that one explain the social in terms of the social. From this perspective, any recourse to the psychological or biological is an incriminating reductionism that renders one's identity as a genuine social scientist suspect. Historically, this disciplinary firewall helped to protect the nascent disciplines of sociology and social-cultural anthropology from the racist pseudobiology and pseudopsychology that reigned during their early years. It also, not coincidently, made the new fields distinct from their neighbors, permitting them to claim in their own right authority from the public and resources from the academy. This convenient barrier against "reductionism" still serves its turf/resources protection function, which is probably why it continues to be staunchly defended. Unfortunately, however, it also serves to "protect" sociology and sociocultural anthropology from profiting from the massive advances made in recent years in biology and psychology.

It is not logically defensible to claim a Durkheimian disjunction (rather than continuity) between the social and the psychological/biological. How can human motives and emotions, the ways in which we bond with others, our jealousies and competitions—social-culturally constructed though these be—not have their roots in our biopsychology, our evolved human nature? Claudia Strauss and Naomi Quinn (1997, pp. 12–47) patiently deconstruct the myth that one can talk about the social—about social representations and selves and surfaces and emotions and even shared schemata—without being psychological. They explicate the confusions found in theoreticians from Clifford Geertz (both early and late) to Judith Butler and Pierre Bourdieu and Michel Foucault, confusions that arise because representations that are "external" or "public" necessarily have an internal (psychological) counterpart: if they are not instantiated in the brain, then where—the ether? Some schemata are more motivating than others, and psychology is necessary to understand this; however socially constructed emotions may be, they seem to have a core that is much the same in society after society; public ideas are also private ideas and under-standings; and so forth. For social behavior to take place, for meanings to be inferred and identities to be negotiated, the human brain must be at work—there are thoughts, perceptions, strategies, ideas, and emotions in play. While much is public, much is not. But even that which is public must be represented in the human brain, because where else can social knowl-edge exist? Cultural transmission is only a metaphor, what Strauss and Quinn refer to as the "fax" model. No direct transmission from brain to brain takes place, only inference (Sperber, 1996) involving complex evolved mechanisms.

Does the sociological concept of *agency* solve the problem of the Durkheimian fallacy? "Agency" is the term social scientists use to recognize that there is such a thing as human volition and choice and not just deter-ministic structure. One can argue that it is a useful abridgment that per-mits social scientists to get on with their work without having to go into psychological detail. One could also argue that social scientists should *not* be "getting on" with their work without, for example, first studying the well-developed literature in psychology and economics on decision-making (e.g., Gigerenzer, 2000; Kahneman & Tversky, 2000). Certainly, using "agency" can function to maintain an aura of the mysteriousness about human choice. Sociologist Bernd Baldus (this volume) argues that evolu-tionary psychology should be criticized for neglecting agency, which he sees as a major source of the variation in human behavior.

d. Objections From the "Cultural Left"

It is odd that by far the harshest critics of the application of Darwinian thought to human beings have come from what Segerstråle (this volume, 2000) refers to as the "cultural Left": after all, as she explains, evolution-ists have been in the past and frequently today are themselves in fact often politically to the left. Segerstråle concludes that the dispute, by and large, is a sort of leftover from the 1970s. Some on the Left, both past and present, she explains, have understood that if there is no such thing as a biologically based human nature, then totalitarian dictators can indeed succeed in re-creating humanity according to their own designs, as both Stalin and Hitler (among others) sought to do. However, Marx did teach and his more fundamentalist followers still believe that social inequality is the cause of most of the evils of human nature, and that we are a perfectable species: once social inequality has ended, the improved human nature that results will not restore it. For those of this faith, arguing for a highly complex evolved psychology is worthy only of anathema.

But if being on the Left has the core meaning of espousing a set of values having to do with equity and dignity, as the noted ethicist Peter Singer (2000) argues, then the Left needs a solid theory of human nature in order to achieve its goals. As we will see, evolutionary psychology may provide not just theory but a potential praxis for social activists.

e. Social Science as Moral Mission

Many social scientists see their work as a sort of moral mission—first and foremost, help the oppressed and protect our world. Very often, these individuals do estimable work both as serious scholars and as partisans of the public interest (e.g., the research and writing of anthropologist Nancy Scheper-Hughes on the trade in human organs (Delmonico et al., 2002; Scheper-Hughes, 1998, 1999, 2000). From their perspective, would not a focus on evolutionary psychology—a field whose goal is the accumulation of knowledge of human nature and society and which emphasizes past adaptations—draw attention away from the social inequality and oppression that are the proximate causes of human suffering? Would not a social science concern with our evolved psychology be at the expense of understanding and exposing the far more immediate cause of so much human pain, the unequal distribution of wealth and power?

Consider that the field of medical epidemiology, which some of us may naively imagine to epitomize benignity, has been strongly attacked by moral mission social scientists. The deservedly eminent medical anthropologist Paul Farmer (1998), for example, criticizes epidemiology for focusing on individuals rather than on political economy and transnational factors. He approvingly quotes (p. 103) McMichael's (1995) portrayal of that field as "oriented to explaining and quantifying the bobbing of corks on the surface waters, while largely disregarding the stronger undercurrents that determine where, on average, the cluster of corks ends up along the shoreline of risk." So, individual cases of disease are corks while political/economic forces are the currents, and epidemiologists focus only on corks while ignoring currents. What would a Farmer or McMichael make of evolutionary psychology, with its focus not even on the cork but on what is happening within the cork and on the cork's conjectural evolutionary history? Surely, for the moral mission sociologist or anthropologist, advising social scientists to engage with evolutionary psychology must appear akin to urging firefighters to take a break from the current conflagration in order to study pyromancy.

But that analogy is utterly false: a more apt comparison would be advising firefighters to study the principles of combustion in order to help prevent and more effectively extinguish fires. Evolutionary psychology is an essential aspect of understanding the problems our species faces and finding solutions to them. This is emphatically not because evolutionary thought is some kind of moral guide (as some scholars hope and as others fear): we cannot derive morality from biology.[10] But we can use evolutionary psychology as a tool in analyzing how capitalist systems function and why social problems, inequality in particular, *recur*. With the aid of social scientists, evolutionary psychology can lead to an *evolutionary praxis* (Barkow, 2003). Let us table that important possibility for the second time, for the moment, while we return to the topic of what evolutionary psychology is and is not.

5. What Evolutionary Psychology Is and What It Is Not

What is a gene?[11] A gene is not a recipe book—it is closer to being one of the ingredients in the stew. Perhaps the gene is the meat—no one denies the importance of the DNA—but it is not some kind of executive, or master plan, or anything like a blueprint. Information in a fertilized egg is *generated*, produced by cascades of interactions of mind-boggling complexity, with other factors, particularly the makeup of the mother-supplied machinery in which the gene finds itself, equally sine qua non. The gene-first approach—whether the conceptual gene used by the mathematics of population genetics or the distributed but physical gene of genomics—does have its virtues. But the misleading image of an executive gene, single-codonly able to cause disease or talent, has captured the popular imagination and helped to generate funding for gene-centered research. This approach has also drawn some thoughtful criticism. Nelkin and Lindee (1995) show how the gene is often presented as a sort of secular soul, the essence that ultimately determines individual behavior. The views of developmental systems theorists such as Griffiths and Gray (1994) and Oyama (1991, 2000) are in sharp contrast, seeing the gene as one ingredient among many. Evelyn Fox Keller (1999) goes so far as to write that "The history of genetic programs bears the conspicuous marks of a history of discourse and power" (p. 289). Despite such criticism, the gene-first assumption currently prevails. One hears people saying not "she has the gift for that" but "she has the gene for that."[12] This essentialistic/deterministic view feeds into biophobia because it presents the gene as the controlling CEO responsible for everything—including our most horrifying behaviors. If genes are so powerful then they must be dangerous, they are destiny: the fault, dear Brutus, lies not in our stars but in our genes! But though the myth of the executive gene[13] contributes to the anger social scientists often express when presented with evolutionary accounts of human behavior, in fact evolutionary psychologists do not usually study genes or genetics, and genes have but a small place in the present volume.

a. Genes Versus Mechanisms?

Between genes and behavior lie the mechanisms. Evolutionary psychology says little about genes[14] but much about these mechanisms.[15] (Some evolutionary psychologists at times do not seem to understand this, and it would be very good to set a moratorium on their talking about genes when it is mechanisms that are the real subject.) Presumably, the constellations of genes underlying our evolved mechanisms are the product of evolution, but the focus of the evolutionary psychologist is not on the DNA but on the adaptive problems our ancestors faced and the mechanisms that may have evolved in response to them (e.g., mechanisms that may protect one from being cheated in social exchange or aid in mate selection or helped to distinguish kin from non-kin). Theories of mechanisms need to be compatible with genetics and evolutionary biology in general, of course, but (in line with vertically integrated thinking, discussed below) cannot be reduced to individual genes. The ontological status of the mechanism construct and its relationship to neurobiology is a controversial one, but that debate *is* about ontology and ontogeny, not genetics.

Perhaps evolutionists themselves bear some responsibility for not emphasizing sufficiently mechanisms and the "distance between genes and culture" (Barkow, 1984). As has already been pointed out, most of the talk about "genes for behavior" has simply been metonymy on the part of theorists concerned with developing general theories of evolution and adaptation rather than theories of specific mechanisms. However, by not making it clear that there *must* be some kind of mechanisms involved, overly elliptical evolutionary exposition—or the hurriedly read accounts of some journalists—may give the reader the impression that genes are intended as some kind of executive replacement for complex theories rather than as components in a multilevel explanation of the behavior in question. We have already seen that privileging the gene and DNA has been attacked by developmental systems theorists who criticize even the idea of genetic "transmission" of traits, instead arguing that the genes are simply one of the sets of components involved in the construction of an organism. So long as it is accepted that the behavioral traits of an organism are indeed shaped by natural selection, there is no need for the social scientist *qua* social scientist to be concerned with arguments over the molecular biology of reproduction, including the precise definition and role of the gene. It is not even clear that the social scientist need be overly concerned with the details of the arguments over *mechanisms* (e.g., the "cheater-detection" mechanism posited by Leda Cosmides and John Tooby [Cosmides & Tooby, 1989, 1992, 2001]). We do not need to understand the biological bases of the mechanisms in order to understand their social consequences.

b. Mechanisms Both Constrain and Enable

Our culturally patterned behavior is both enabled and constrained by a panoply of evolved mechanisms that are just barely beginning to be understood (Barkow, 1989). Evolved mechanisms are useful heuristic devices, and we take them for granted when we talk about how our how bodies function. There are evolved physiological mechanisms to regulate our temperature and our caloric intake and our blood sugar level and our sexuality and so forth. These mechanisms are not in contrast to adaptation by natural selection; rather, they are its products. The challenge to biological evolution has been to select a single set of genes that can keep the organism adapted within a broad range of circumstances; and genes[16] that reliably produce mechanisms to do this are the solution. They permit the organism to adjust to the vicissitudes of environment within its own lifetime. Our immune systems respond even to novel disease organisms, our digestive systems can absorb nourishment from a vast array of foods (even unfamiliar ones), our pattern of physical strength and coordination improves with the particular demands we put on our bodies, and so forth. In similar fashion, the broad array of central nervous system and endocrinological mechanisms responsible for regulating our social behavior permit us to function across a very wide variety of ecological and cultural settings. These mechanisms *are* our evolved psychology, our human nature, and they permit the huge amount of variation in behavior typical of our species both within and across societies. So effective are these mechanisms that their operation is invisible to many social scientists, who imagine that the environment and "culture," unaided, have somehow alone shaped and patterned both the rich diversities and the enduring commonalities of human history. If all our social worlds are but a stage, evolutionary psychologists study the machinery backstage, the evolved mechanisms. They unpack the black box of human nature. There is no reason to imagine that the mechanisms of the central nervous system are any less complex than those of other bodily systems. Just as a shared set of digestive mechanisms both enable and constrain the diverse diets of human populations, so do a comparable set of behavioral mechanisms enable and constrain our social-cultural behavior. (Such, at least, is the guiding assumption of evolutionary psychology.)

It is evolutionary psychology's focus on the mechanisms that makes it *infrastructural* to understanding social action and the social sciences. The emphasis is *not* on the genes.

6. Evolved Mechanisms and Culture

Textbook after textbook informs the student that we human beings adapt to different ecological settings through *culture*, while animal species do so through genetic change. This commonplace observation tells us little because it leaves out evolved mechanisms. The behavior of one species differs from that of another because their evolved mechanisms are different. Ours have been designed by evolution to adapt us to a cultural environment. ("Culture" is defined below.)

Some evolved psychological mechanisms involve what can loosely be termed "learning." One can learn from one's own experience (individual learning) and from the experience of others (social learning). When a species becomes capable of a sufficient degree of social learning, a new possibility arises: local populations may develop pools of shared information that is communicated both within and across generations. The total pool of such information associated with a particular population can be termed a *culture*. In this sense of culture it is quite common among social animals, including whales and dolphins (Rendell & Whitehead, 2001). Our own species is hypercultural (Barkow, 2000), so heavily dependent on total immersion in a vast information pool that our central nervous system requires it to develop properly (Geertz, 1962, 1973).

The informational items comprising human cultures go by many names, including: ideas, beliefs, traits, instructions, representations, schemata, and (for those who like near-rhymes) "memes." The same or similar particles of information may occur in many different pools that, in any case, usually overlap with one another; the population(s) with which a pool is associated may be distributed rather than tied to limited geographic regions. A single individual may participate in more than one pool, given that pools are properties of populations and the same individual may be counted in multiple populations (there are many ways in which to define a population). The structure of information pools depends upon the brains of individuals at one level and upon the social organization of its population(s) on the other (i.e., some castes or professions may specialize in certain kinds of information) and is not a property of the pool itself. Note that this informational approach to the culture concept avoids the various criticisms leveled at it during the 1980s and 1990s by critics such as James Clifford and George E. Marcus

(1986) and Lila Abu-Lughod (1991). An evolutionary view of culture is not essentialistic, does not promote the exoticizing of the other, and does not confuse people with geography. At the same time, there is nothing of A. L. Kroeber's (1917) "superorganic" in it, either, and it is not a reified causal entity. It is, however, applicable to a globalizing world in which both people and information travel constantly. (For a broad introduction to the idea of culture as particulate, see the interesting collection edited by Robert Aunger [2000]. Aunger [1999] has also published a thoughtful defense of the culture concept itself. Cronk [this volume] discusses some approaches evolutionists have taken to culture, as do Janicki and Krebs [1998]. Though evolutionists often have different conceptions of culture, there does appear to be a consensus that it is informational and at least somewhat particulate in nature.)

From the culture-is-a-pool-of-particulates perspective, culture above all is something that people *use*. In doing so we both shape and are shaped by the information pools in which we swim. The cultural pool is also (to change metaphors) an "arena for conflict" (Barkow, 1983, 1989, 1994) in which we seek to add informational items in our own interest and change or delete items which are not. In recent years, many ethnographers have emphasized a particular kind of cultural information, that associated with discourse and text. However, many informational items, though they may profoundly influence our worldviews, our posture and gait and choice of comfort foods and what we expect from a friend, are not textual in nature (Spiro, 1996).

This great dependence on culture is a very risky business, from an evolutionary perspective. Our brains are full of evolved mechanisms that manage that risk. Here is a thought experiment: Imagine that our evolved psychology really is Malinowskian (in the sense of Malinowski's [1944] *A Scientific Theory of Culture*), basically a few drives tied to an empty sponge that absorbs culture like water until it is time for it to be squeezed out again for the next generation. Culture is thus static. Now, imagine an isolated population with a pool of this static information that, however, at the outset perfectly fits the local environment. But time passes and environments alter: fisheries get depleted, climates change, ecologies go through successions; at the same time, individuals introduce inaccurate information into the pool in pursuit of their own interests, while errors in transmission of information inevitably occur (Barkow, 1989). Eventually, a great deal of useless and even harmful information accumulates in the local cultural pool. Perhaps even worse, for lack of new information and revision of old, opportunities involving potential foodstuffs and innovative technologies and economic organization are missed, so that the environment is now being exploited ineffectively. For such a population of cultural sponges, one of two things will happen: either a crisis will drive it to extinction/

absorption by a rival group; or natural selection will occur against such heavy reliance on culture. Such selection could conceivably favor individual learning at the expense of cultural capacity. Most likely, however, there would be selection for the ability to test socially transmitted informational items, to challenge them, revise them, add to them and delete them. Individuals with these abilities would out-reproduce others. The population would develop various evolved mechanisms permitting people to edit and revise information. Individuals would be editors of the cultures in which they participated, so the information pools would be kept reasonably up-to-date.

It is doubtful that our ancestors were ever sponges but there is no doubt that we have evolved considerable ability to revise and edit culture (Barkow, 1989). We do it constantly, as we "rebel" emotionally as adolescents, rebel politically as adults; or when we scan the practices of disparate groups for interesting innovations. Above all, in searching for prestige we may either maintain or revise our culture. We seem to pay preferential attention to the high-in-status, learning more from them than from others (Barkow, 1976; Chance and Larsen, 1976; Boyd and Richerson, 1985). In small-scale societies, this mechanism would probably have spread the skills of the more successful cultivators, foragers, hunters and tool-makers; today it is a wild card leading to a proliferation of rock-star wannabees.

7. We Are All Social Constructionists: So What?

Social scientists almost universally accept some form of *social construction-ism*, the belief that rather than our living in a readily knowable "out there" reality, we dwell in a world that is socially constructed, constructed by our experience with others, and validated consensually and communally (Berger & Luckmann, 1966).[17] This belief makes sociologists and social-cultural anthropologists leery of large claims to truth ("metanarratives") and allegations of objectivity (Bauerlein, 2001). Social-cultural anthropologists in particular are more likely to be comfortable with local, contingent, non-absolute, and situated partial knowledges (as in the elucidation of "lived experience" and in interpretive approaches to ethnography) than with broad explanatory frameworks (such as Darwinism). To speak of "objective" knowledge strikes the social constructionist as embarrassingly naive. Indeed, social constructionist sociologists of science have spent much effort in debunking the claims to objectivity of "science" and arguing that scientific "truth" is in fact a socially constructed "truth claim," the product of social and political processes, a partial truth (e.g., many of the readings in Biagioli [1999] and in Jasanoff, Markle, Petersen, & Pinch [2001], as well as Latour & Salk [1986]). Social constructionism has become a badge of in-group membership, for many social scientists, in spite of both mild (e.g., Hacking, 1999) and scathing (Bauerlein, 2001) philosophical criticism of their use of the approach. If you are a sociologist or social-cultural anthropologist today, you must be a social constructionist.

a. Evolutionary Psychology Requires Social Constructionism

The nonradical social constructionism typical of the social sciences is not only compatible with evolutionary psychology, it is required by it. Our species has a hypertrophied cultural capacity, an immense dependence on socially "transmitted" information. *That we socially construct our realities is an inevitable concomitant of that reliance.* A culture-bearing species, one that like ours depends primarily on socially transmitted information pools for adaptation to local conditions, must also evolve mechanisms permitting and even requiring social construction—how else could individuals adjust to local reality, that is, to the different constructions of different cultural informational pools? Social construction is thus not an alternative to a biological account of human behavior; properly understood, it *is* a biological account, a major aspect of our evolved psychology (cf. Campbell, this volume). Like other biological traits, social construction is both enabled and constrained by our bodies, in this case the organ known as the brain and its various evolved mechanisms.

Let us take, as an example of how multilevel, vertically integrated social science explanation can work, Catherine Lutz's (1988) insightful analysis of the social construction of emotions on the Micronesian atoll of Ifaluk. Her argument for the uniqueness of local conceptions of emotions is incompatible with the assumption that our *English-language labels* represent a universal core of evolved emotions. But her work *is* entirely compatible with the argument that our English-language emotions are just as socially constructed as are those of Micronesia. Her work is also compatible with the strong evidence that there are indeed basic emotions and that they play a major role in the regulation of behavior and share a very similar neurophysiological basis among primates (and many other mammals) (Barkow, 1997; Damasio, 1999, 2000; Ekman & Davidson, 1995; Lane, Nadel, & Ahern, 2000) in general.[18] In effect, evolutionary psychology provides the equivalent of themes and ethnography the local socially constructed variations of human emotions.[19] An evolutionary perspective adds to Lutz's work: It frames it in a broad context and acknowledges the physical basis and evolutionary history of the emotions, but it takes nothing away from Lutz's insights and interpretations of Ifaluk society and the role played there by socially constructed emotions.

Understanding the evolutionary bases of social constructionism prevents the "anything goes" approach that Campbell (this volume) criticizes (particularly with regard to gender). Unconstrained social construction would obviously be maladaptive. Those with brains that constructed realities in which there was no need for the individual to gather or to hunt or to assess abilities realistically against those of competitors were presumably less likely to become our ancestors than were those who had some respect for physical reality. Natural selection should, logically, have provided some constraints on social construction: where are they? Elsewhere (1989), I have argued that two of these constraints may have been our alleged tendencies, as adolescents, to rebel against established authority and ideas, and to attend to and learn preferentially from the high-in-status. Adolescents everywhere strive to find a place for themselves, and often may question established ideas and practices. They also reevaluate local status hierarchies and seem to imitate those whom they perceive to be high in relative standing. It is possible (though obviously very difficult to establish empirically) that these tendencies would have tended to keep culture constructions from moving too far from physical reality. Note that these mechanisms, if mechanisms they are, seem to be weak and imperfect. Cultural editing has been studied in rather desultory ways by social scientists under rubrics such as "popular memory," "authenticity," "the invention of tradition" (Hobsbawm & Ranger, 1992), "revitalization movements" (Wallace, 1970), and religious and ideological change in general. The topic calls for the perspectives of evolved psychology and the notion of culture as an arena for (informational) conflict, and in the future is likely to be a significant focus within anthropology.

8. Are Human Behavior and Culture Normally Adaptive?

If our evolved mechanisms evolved in the first place to solve adaptation problems, does this mean that human behavior, especially the behavior patterned by our social institutions, is normally adaptive? Do we tend to act so as to enhance our genetic fitness? Not necessarily. Evolutionary wisdom is past wisdom, adaptation to previous environments, and the ways in which our current environments are both different from and similar to those of our ancestors is a question whose theoretical importance is matched only by the extent to which it has been underresearched! We are not our ancestors, and in today's range of human environments, with their often vast scale compared to the small bands of our predecessors, evolved mechanisms may play novel roles with little direct connection to adaptation and biological fitness. After all, in an age of contraception we may still maximize copulatory opportunity but not the reproductive success at the heart of biological evolution. Advertisers use our evolved mechanisms in myriad ways remote from genetic fitness as they seek to associate their products with sex and status, and the preferential-attention-to-the-high-in-status mechanism today has quite odd effects, producing a plethora of rock-star wannabees and children of peasant farmers who wish to grow up to be Jet Li. For evolution-minded social scientists, the interesting questions are not about gene frequencies but about (for example) the mechanisms that presumably underlie political behavior and generate social class—or gossip (Barkow, 1992) and sensational news (Davis & McLeod, 2003; Shoemaker, 1996). (Note that in Cronk's chapter in this volume, he describes his field of behavioral ecology as one in which the question of whether people are following adaptive strategies is paramount and the evolved mechanisms are of secondary interest. The approach he describes contrasts with the evolutionary-psychology-is-infrastructure approach being promoted here. Both perspectives, of course, are valid and, as he indicates, ultimately compatible and even convergent.)[20]

Can culturally patterned behavior be maladaptive, either in the technical sense of reducing genetic fitness or the everyday sense of reducing health and well-being? The answer is yes, for both senses. Maladaptation is possible for a variety of reasons that can only be telegraphed, here. First, organisms are never perfect biological machines, so that any adaptation may have some maladaptive consequences (e.g., monkeys fall from trees at times but living in trees is still on the whole adaptive; our cultural dependency is like the monkey's arboreal adaptation—usually adaptive but not always). Second, as "mismatch theory" argues, we are adapted to past but not necessarily to current environments. Third, culture is an arena for informational/belief conflict, and we can often be persuaded to follow a strategy that is in someone's fitness interests but not necessarily our own. (Believe me, buy my snake oil, religion, political party, etc. It will solve all your problems.) Fourth, we make mistakes and teach them to others ("high-impact aerobics, the great health discovery"). Fifth, some particles of cultural information ("memes") arguably are like viruses, spreading at the expense of their hosts, ourselves (e.g., certain religious ideas, according to Richard Dawkins [2003]).[21]

9. Psychic Unity, Essentialism, and Human Nature

Evolutionary psychologists argue that our shared evolved mechanisms make for the psychic unity of our species, our human nature. Is this belief a form of essentialism? Contrary to some (e.g., DeLamater & Hyde, 1998), evolutionary psychologists and other evolutionists are not essentialists.

Evolutionists do not ordinarily speak of canine nature or cervid nature or human nature (as I do). Instead, they speak descriptively of "species-typical characteristics," thereby recognizing that a species generally has no one defining trait but, rather, a cluster of traits in which no single one is necessarily crucial. The concept of species-typicality is rather similar to that of disease syndrome, where the overall pattern rather than a single feature is the defining quality. Human nature is not (let us hope) a disease syndrome, but it, too, refers to a cluster of traits rather than a universal essence. Of course, the precise mixture of components of any individual's psychology will be unique; given that the underlying mechanisms evolved to permit great flexibility in behavior, we expect considerable individual and group differences. (And as behavior geneticists point out, we do differ genetically from one another, as well. See Segal & Bouchard, 1999, for a study of the complexities of heredity and environment in connection with twins.)

Many social scientists follow Marx in believing that "human nature" is merely a reflex of society and of history (e.g., Geertz, 1973; Gramsci, 1957; Sahlins, 1976). A strict acceptance of this position requires a rejection of evolutionary psychology and an embracing of the Cartesian divide between humans and other animals, with economic systems replacing the Cartesian soul. However, in academia extreme positions tend to be constructed by opponents taking advantage of how easy it is to ignite straw. In practice, social science and evolutionary disputes about human nature today are often simple figure-and-ground problems. If one comes to the study of our species from a background in animal behavior and neuroendocrinology, then the notion that human nature is anything but biological is bizarre: there are demonstrable differences at the levels of DNA, gross morphology, and neural organization between ourselves and other species; surely, to the biologically oriented, our nature is human because of those differences. After all, human beings share so much in terms of both individual and collective behavior, compared even to our closest relatives, the apes (cf. Rodseth and Novak, this volume). But if one's background is limited to sociology or ethnography, then it is the differences among human groups that are salient, and explanations of these differences surely must have to do with history and environment and economics, not biology. But both the evolutionist's distal and the ethnographer's proximal perspectives are entirely valid (and in the spirit of vertical integration, discussed below, should always yield very different but mutually compatible theories and data; wherever apparent incompatibilities are detected, these should be generating research). Unfortunately, the ugly history of biology in the social sciences and "biological determinist" stereotyping can make it difficult for the social scientist to appreciate the evolutionist's perception of our species. At the same time, the social-cultural anthropologists whose work is readily accepted by evolutionary psychologists are primarily those who concentrate on universals, whether underlying or overt. The name at the top of this short list is probably that of Donald Brown (1991), who has ably described the universals of human societies. (Social-cultural anthropology's old documentation-of-difference project has obscured the essential similarities among human societies—careers in ethnography are not made by the highlighting of similarities. But to be fair, many similarities with their own home culture are likely to be invisible to ethnographers, so that they perforce write only about what they see: the differences.)

10. Vertical Integration

Evolutionary psychology partakes of the notion of vertical or compatible integration (Barkow, 1989; Cosmides, Tooby, & Barkow, 1992; Walsh, this volume). The "integration" is of the modest kind found in the natural sciences. For example, chemistry is compatible with the laws of physics, but in no practical way can chemistry be reduced to physics. Biology is compatible with chemistry as well as with physics, but no one in their right mind would attempt to reduce the functioning of the pancreas or the succession of forest ecologies to chemistry alone. However, a biologist who described processes incompatible with chemistry or a chemist who claimed to have discovered reactions that violated the laws of physics would be considered a crank. The natural sciences follow the compatibility rule, meaning that apparent incompatibilities with current consensus in related disciplines are considered to be indicators of error in one field or the other and a justification for further research. Much of the steady, cumulative progress of the natural sciences is a product of the compatibility rule. Much of the chaos in the human sciences, the changes in fashion that some social scientists optimistically consider progress,[22] and the strong current tendency to join the humanities and abandon the goals of a social science entirely, reflect the confusions brought about by the lack of a compatibility rule.

Unlike natural scientists, social and behavioral theorists typically ignore explanations at other levels of organization, or, worse, treat them as competitors! Thus, even in the twenty-first century most social scientists still usually write about a phenomenon—violent assault, monogamy, whatever—as if it were primarily a matter *either* of biology *or* of environment/culture (see Kurzban & Haselton, this volume, for further discussion). But vertical integration emphasizes the systematic search for compatibilities and incompatibilities among the multiple levels of explanation required to account for the complexities of human social life, and a forsaking of dated dichotomies such as "nature vs. nurture" and "mind vs. body" and "culture vs. biology." What evolutionists are asking is only that sociology and social-cultural anthropological accounts be *compatible* with what we think we know of human evolution and psychology: that is all. Incompatibilities indicate errors at one level or the other and must drive research. The aim is never to *replace* sociology or anthropology with psychology and biology, and certainly not to create a social science comparable to axiomatic physics, with its elegant, intricate aspirations to mathematical lawfulness and predictability.

Our accounts of human psychology must be compatible with our understanding of human evolution, but psychology cannot be *reduced* to evolutionary biology. The social sciences and psychology must be mutually compatible, but the social sciences cannot *become* psychology. Reduction is foolish because different levels of organization have emergent properties, properties that cannot be readily predicted from lower levels. Thus, our complex evolved psychology has characteristics—such as consciousness, self-deception, and so forth—in no way predictable from Charles Darwin's theory of natural selection, prescient though Darwin was. Similarly, the social organization of states or the impact of the automobile on cityscapes cannot be reduced to or predicted from psychology or biology. But when social scientists do explain such phenomena, they inevitably make psychological assumptions (*pace* Emile Durkheim), assumptions that need to be assessed for compatibility with the current consensus in psychology and human evolution. If a social science theory implies a psychological trait that appears to be impossible in the light of biological evolution, then this is an indicator of a problem point, a place on which to focus attention, because either the social science theory is in error or the fault lies in psychology and evolutionary theory (or perhaps both are in error). Even when we find that some social practices do indeed enhance genetic fitness (as the behavioral ecologists discussed in Cronk's contribution to this volume often do), that does not somehow cancel the necessity and validity of the disciplines of psychology, history, and sociology.

Abandoning the intellectually sloppy habit of making implicit and unexamined psychological assumptions will come at a price. We will have to be even more careful than at present not to bury our psychology in personifications (as when "society" or "culture" *causes* behaviour) or in protean concepts such as "embodiment," "patriarchy," "agency," or "power." A move toward making our assumptions explicit, while leading to much greater clarity and substance in theorizing, may be at the expense of some of the magnificent *display prose* that has come to be so admired by many social scientists, whose hermeneutics permit them to appreciate the aesthetic interplay of the hybridized potentialities of pastiches of multivocalic subjectivities. Striving for a sentence to instantiate a single meaning may seem retrogressive, for some, but vertical integration requires it. If your words may have many meanings, they can certainly be played with, but the profusion of potential significances makes it impossible to apply the compatibility rule. The goal of impressing the reader with one's complex brilliance may have replaced that of building cumulative understanding. (Those who have built their careers upon their mastery of richly dense, multiplexly abstract social theory will face a problem of translation into prose that permits the identification of implicit assumptions. No doubt there will be competing translations.)

Of course, there are evolutionary psychologists, too, who forget or ignore the compatibility rule. Far from being an excuse for social scientists to do the same, such lapses are best viewed as an opportunity for sociologists and social-cultural anthropologists to criticize evolutionary psychology in a constructive rather than dismissive manner. (Social scientists are also needed to protect psychologists, including evolutionary psychologists, from their tendency to generalize to the human species on the basis of research done on undergraduates in one or two countries.)

11. Vertical Integration and the Social Sciences

What vertical integration and evolutionary psychology do for the social sciences is threefold: (1) they permit culling of impossible theories while identifying areas where further research and thought are needed; (2) they permit a practical if strictly limited approach to the often-sought unification of the life sciences with the social sciences; and (3) they can reveal serious deficiencies in academic programs and training.

(1) Culling and Hidden Assumptions

The first decade of this century is a fertile time for the social sciences, with a thousand flowers blooming . . . along with a dismaying number of weeds. Social scientists often think of career success in terms of founding a personal school of thought, complete with partisans and critics and neologisms. Training consists not of studying a sequence of topics (e.g., molecular biology, genomics, medical implications of genomics, etc.) but of great individualistic, relatively unintegrated thinkers (e.g., Karl Marx, Max Weber, Emile Durkheim, Talcott Parsons, Jürgen Habermas, Michel Foucault, Pierre Bourdieu, Judith Butler, G. H. Mead, Anthony Giddens, Bruno Latour, etc.). How do we weed this overgrown garden by getting rid of at least the weakest theoretical approaches? The compatibility requirement of vertical integration suggests one way. Are the psychological/biological assumptions made by the theory compatible with what we believe about our evolution and psychology? After all, a theory involving chemistry that violated physics' requirement for conservation of matter and energy would be readily discarded. A theory in social-cultural anthropology or in sociology that incorporated assumptions that are impossible in terms of modern biology and psychology should at the least be considered suspect. For example, suppose our implicit or explicit assumption is that human females and males are psychologically identical except for matters directly touching on reproductive physiology. As we see from Campbell's contribution to this volume, this assumption is incompatible with an immense amount of psychological (and also neuroendocrinological) research. It is also incompatible with evolutionary biology, where we learn that sex differences in the amount of investment needed to reproduce, as well as differences in the variability of reproductive success, always (in every species studied) lead to differences in reproductive strategies and therefore behavior.

(2) Vertical Integration Cannot Fully Unify the Social and Life Sciences

Evolutionary psychology with its commitment to vertical integration seeks to retie Latour's (1993, pp. 1–8) "gordian knot" but fails. Latour argues that modern thinkers have developed "three distinct approaches to talking about our world: naturalization, socialization and deconstruction" (p. 5). He chooses the work of E. O. Wilson as emblematic of the first perspective, the "naturalizers"; Pierre Bourdieu is taken as emblematic of the second, the "socializers" or "sociopolitical" (the latter is my own term); and Jacques Derrida as emblematic of the third, the discourse analyzers. The naturalizers view the world in terms of the biological—the sociopolitical and the text/ discourse disappear in the sense that they are disregarded. The socializers speak of society and power but, for them, both the biological and the textual/discursive vanish. For the analysts of discourse, both the sociopolitical and any claims for a "real" world disappear. Indeed, for those concerned with the analysis of discourse, "to believe in the existence of brain neurons or power plays would betray enormous naïveté" (p. 6). The problem with these three modes of analysis, Latour explains, is not their lack of power but their inability to be combined, their mutual exclusivity.

An evolutionary approach is clearly a naturalizing one—the goal of evolutionary approaches to the human sciences is, after all, to put our own species back into the natural world. But Latour does not appreciate the inclusive nature of the naturalistic perspective. True, if the human sciences are to be naturalized, then contemporary sociology and social-cultural anthropology must pass through the culling process of compatibility with adjacent fields, but most of the familiar landscape would remain. We have already seen that social constructionism survives handily, and Foucauldian ideas of power can certainly be linked to the evolutionist's conception of power as the ability to influence the behavior of others in one's own (genetic) self-interest. Much in Marxism and even classical economics can and should be rethought in terms of a more sophisticated evolutionary psychology in which people have multiple, shifting goals that do not reduce to greed. Much of deconstructionism and discourse analysis is readily compatible with the evolutionist's insistence that communication evolved as a way to influence the behavior of others in one's own interest, rather than to convey some kind of truth for its own sake. The culled social sciences would still be recognizable as the social sciences but with new clarity and compatibility and a tendency for ordered understandings to accumulate rather than for fashions to shift.

Vertical/compatible integration is an intellectually much less ambitious goal than the total ending of dichotomies for which Latour (1993) calls in *We Have Never Been Modern*—for followers of Latour and other philosopher/anthropologists, its very simplicity will make it unacceptable.[23] The approach is also far more modest than the "jumping together" of explanations espoused by E. O. Wilson (1998) in his *Consilience*. I am sympathetic to the goals of these authors and aware that for true unifiers vertical integration can be no more than a first step. But it is a step we have not yet taken.

Will an evolutionarily informed, vertically integrated social science resemble the natural sciences?[24] Perhaps it should not. The eminent biologist (and critic of sociobiology) Richard Lewontin (1995, p. 28) warns: "Each domain of phenomena has its characteristic grain of knowability. Biology is not physics, because organisms are such complex physical objects, and sociology is not biology because human societies are made by self-conscious organisms. By pretending to a kind of knowledge that it cannot achieve, social science can only engender the scorn of natural scientists and the cynicism of humanists." In similar fashion, sociologist of science Bent Flyvbjerg (2001, p. 166) urges us "to drop the fruitless efforts to emulate natural science's success in producing cumulative and predictive theory; this approach simply does not work in the social sciences." True enough, axiomatic physics makes a poor model for the social sciences, but the pronouncements of Lewontin[25] and especially Flyvbjerg seem remarkably premature given that few social scientists have ever attempted vertical integration. Human science theory needs to be evaluated in terms of compatibility with adjacent levels of analysis. I suspect that the eventual result will probably be a lot closer to the multilevel, multidisciplinary field of natural history and to plant and animal ecology than to chemistry or physics: but in the end, all sciences are unique, and other fields have only limited applicability as models. (Adopting the formalisms of the natural sciences without their vertical integration produced the kind of foolishness in which academic psychology, for much of the twentieth century, ruled consciousness out of its subject matter in order to be more "scientific," straitjacketing itself by tailoring its theories to fit its conception of "scientific" methodology.)

(3) Training Social Scientists

A third practical implication of vertical integration has to do with the training of students. The notion of a biologist who understands no chemistry or a chemist who knows no physics is a nonsensical idea; yet training in social science requires scant acquaintance with psychology and none at all with biology, especially evolutionary biology! As Donald T. Campbell (1969) once pointed out, it is unproductive for academics to seek to clone themselves. In the social sciences, however, we strive to duplicate in our successors ancient academic boundaries while too often inculcating in them disciplinary ethnocentrism and intolerance, carefully excluding the neighbors as sources of insight.[26] Ending the parochialism and insularity of the social sciences does not mean that our students must begin by becoming biologists and psychologists, however, any more than biologists must begin by becoming chemists. They are expected to know the basics of related fields but this requirement stops far short of full multidisciplinarity. Basic evolutionary biology and psychology are actually quite simple. Students weaned on postmodernism and its privileging of display prose often find evolutionary psychology startlingly straightforward.

12. An Evolutionarily Informed Praxis and an Evolutionary Analysis of Capitalism

a. Evolutionary Psychology Is Infrastructural to Society and Culture

How can evolutionary psychology/sociobiology aid in one of the great tasks of today's social science, the analysis and critique of a globalizing, postcolonial world under assault by neoliberal ideology? Let us begin with a simple example: the evolutionary analysis of "globesity," the obesity pandemic.

We know that we evolved in environments in which the scarce nutrients were often salt, fat, and (because it is an indicator of the ripeness and thus nutritional value of fruit) sweetness. Our ancestors in part became our ancestors because they were the ones who could detect and then prefer these valuable nutrients. Offspring resemble their parents, taught Darwin, and we resemble our ancestors in prizing fat and salt and sweet. In the modern era, the manufacturers of industrial foods have taken full advantage of our evolved chemical-detection/preference mechanisms by producing foodstuffs super-rich in fat, salt, and sugar. We love them, we rush to buy products rich in them, we eat far more of them than our bodies require or even can safely process: and so food-processing plants and corporate capitalism flourish. Unfortunately, their success is based on a large proportion of the population ingesting too many of these nutrients and too little of others, resulting in ill health (particularly obesity and its frequent sequelae, type 2 diabetes and cardiovascular disease). (See Sidebar 1.1 for further discussion of and references to the mismatch between our industrial diet and the diet to which our bodies are adapted.)

There are parallels between commercially successful industrial foods and commercially successful mass media. Our attentional mechanisms draw our focus, willy-nilly, to what for our ancestors would have been adaptation-relevant information. The weather, physical danger from any source, scarce resources—these topics readily capture our attention. But we are a social species and apparently evolved in an environment featuring strong social competition (Mithen, 1996). As a result, much of the apparently adaptation-relevant information that pricks up our ears is social information such as sexual activity, change in others' reputation for honesty; alteration in health, strength, or relative standing; creation and demise of friendships/alliances, birth and death; and so forth. We constantly exchange such information, often distorting it so that it is in our self-interest or the interest of relatives and friends (cf. Buss & Dedden, 1990; McAndrew & Milenkovic, 2002). We call this phenomenon "gossip" (Barkow, 1992). A careful study of 200 years of newspapers shows that these are also the kinds of topics that we want to read about (Davis & McLeod, 2003).

Commercially successful Hollywood and Bollywood movies also focus on these topics (Hejl, Kammer, & Uhl, in preparation). We seem to automatically yet avidly attend to gossiplike information about, for example, the reputations and sexual activities of fictional high-status individuals or of actual celebrities who, however, are for no practical purpose members of our communities. Just as industrial food manufacturers exploit our evolved sense of taste, other corporations exploit our evolved attentional mechanisms to sell us newspapers, movies, and other media. Whether this flood of often fictitious information is actually harmful has not yet been clearly established, but it certainly is profitable for the interests producing it.

This is not the place in which to develop a full theory of the media exploitation of the brain's attentional triggers: the topic is illustrative of the point that the evolutionary perspective helps us understand the infrastructure of modern society and readily generates substantial research programs with great relevance for social-cultural anthropologists and sociologists. Anyone interested in "globalization" will find that Darwin is a good place to begin in understanding how multinational corporations can be so successful in creating demand for their products worldwide. Evolution is always a good place to begin but—remembering the lessons of vertical integration—seldom a good place to end.

The infrastructural role of our evolved psychology is hardly limited to film and food. For example, in the 1970s, in the city of Maradi in Niger, I undertook a study based on the premise that human beings, as we grow older, learn to substitute symbolic prestige criteria for the relatively agonistic dominance hierarchies of young children and of other primates. I found, in Maradi, that those shut out of other paths to high relative standing by the ruling government *fonctionnaires* were turning to Islam. They were also delegitimating status-claims of the French-language-educated élites, creating a powerful resurgence of religion (Barkow, 1975). A project that began with theories of primate social hierarchies moved, in vertically integrated fashion, to a study of religion. One conclusion of the study was that was that some prestige strategies have the emergent result of generating socioeconomic development, while other strategies have primarily political and ideological or religious impacts. Peoples who seek prestige primarily in terms of display or of religious learning are less likely to prosper economically than those who seek prestige through the long-term accumulation of resources, including skills and education. As usual, this evolutionary perspective complements, rather than invalidates, existing theories of development. Once again, an evolutionary perspective proved infrastructural and integrative with respect to social science theory.

Are there political orders that work well because of their match with our evolved psychology, and others that fail for lack of such a match? Francis Fukuyama (2002, p. 106) argues that "contemporary capitalist liberal democratic institutions have been successful because they are grounded in assumptions about human nature that are far more realistic than those of their competitors." This assertion begs for detailed and vertically integrated analyses of the specific social institutions he has in mind and the way in which our evolved psychology underlies each, both for societies he categorizes as successful and those he considers unsuccessful. Of course, clear definitions and a historical perspective are crucial for any such generalizations about whole societies, but here is a research project worthy of our efforts.

There are various other pockets of evolutionary perspective in human science research, as is discussed in Sidebar 1.1 and earlier in the context of sociologists and social-cultural anthropologists who are not in the mainstream because they are Darwinian. These quick references and brief discussions are meant only to be suggestive: a full, vertically integrated explication of the relationships between our evolved psychology and modern societies and socioeconomic systems will require nothing less than the participation of engaged social scientists!

b. An Evolutionary Praxis and the Return of the Reformed

The great weakness of the Marxist and Marxian critique of capitalism and struggle against oppression is their failure to predict the recurrence of inequality. History shows that after the revolution comes . . . another revolution. Social problems recur, with each set of solutions leading to new problems, while slow reforms often only palliate. There is a cliché that youthful Marxist idealism gets replaced with middle-aged conservatism, a veer to the political Right. Perhaps this is because the middle-aged have experienced the return of the reformed, that is, the restoration of old problems in new guise, the endless recurrence of social inequality, of people wanting more resources and respect for themselves and their children and their friends than they want for others. The old aristocrats and capitalists are overthrown only to be replaced by a "new class"—in the case of Soviet Communism, by the *nomenklatura* or bureaucratic élite (Djilas, 1957). Such phenomena are generally discussed in moral terms, that is, in terms of betrayal. Unfortunately, moral condemnation, no matter how well deserved, does not make for adequate social theory. It is the evolutionary perspective that can provide not only a framework for analysis but at least a hope of effective praxis.

Social stratification is a reflex of the evolutionary fact that people do want more for their own children than they want for the children of others (Barkow, 1992; Tiger & Shepher, 1975): ideologically based efforts to create social systems that ignore this evolutionary reality, as in the early Israeli kibbuttzim, fail. In evolutionary terms, this is a no-brainer: Offspring resemble their parents, and we are the children of those who did more for their own children and other kin than they did for others because by doing so they had more surviving children and other relatives than did those others. Once human societies became relatively sedentary and it became possible for us to leave rank and wealth to our children, we did so (Barkow, 1992). But biology is not destiny unless we ignore it (Barkow, 2003). An anti-nepotistic, meritocratic ideology makes for far better-qualified administrators than does a favor-your-children-and-other-relatives ethic. It also directly counters our evolved psychology.[27] Fortunately, by using our practical awareness of human nature when we design bureaucracies, we can *work around* our tendency toward nepotism. We can try to make sure that the system rewards those who are not nepotistic and punishes those who are. Constant vigilance will still be needed because we are indeed working around human nature and also because one aspect of that nature is our tendency to believe that rules and even moral principles apply only to others rather than to ourselves; but relatively non-nepotistic bureaucracies can and do exist. Wise social planners and designers of bureaucracies are constantly taking our evolved psychology into account, sometimes working with it and other times *working around* it.

The term "work around" comes from the work of evolutionists Peter Richerson and Robert Boyd (1999, 2001). How do we explain the Wehrmacht, the Germany military forces of 1935–1945, when we obviously did not evolve to risk our lives on behalf of non-kin strangers running a murderously aggressive modern state? Richerson and Boyd analyzed how the German officer corps *worked around* our evolved psychology, manipulating it to create an evolutionarily unanticipated social institution whose effects had nothing to do with genetic fitness (and which, in fact, was no doubt maladaptive for a large proportion of its participants, particularly those who were killed!). Our species's evolved psychology is well adapted to mutual defense on a local level, and given external threat we bond tightly on the basis of kinship and community and their markers, such as accent, rallying around a leader who takes the role of a senior relative.[28] The German military's work-around involved: (1) organizing the army in terms of units of men from the same region who shared a local dialect; (2) training officers to look after the men and to take responsibility for their welfare; and (3) promoting strong bonding among the men and between enlisted men and officers.

Military organization is hardly unique in having an evolutionary psychology infrastructure: We could move from social institution to social institution and for each one identify the underlying evolutionary psychology. This claim seems particularly plausible in connection with the advertising and marketing industries, but there are no institutions without motivated individuals, and the study of those motivations ultimately leads to a study of our evolved psychology. Capitalism itself (as was previously suggested) involves a complex work-around of mechanisms having to do with social standing, reputation, and resource control. The work-around concept helps move us from evolutionary biology's concerns with genetic fitness and the evolutionary psychologist's focus on individual-level evolved mechanisms to the social scientist's emphasis on society and culture. Work-arounds simply are the way in which Boyd and Richerson chose to talk about how history has channeled the expression of our evolved psychology. Note that work-arounds do not ordinarily arise from a sophisticated understanding of Darwin but out of experience and insight with what works, in the real world, and probably also from a group-level selection process. That is, organizations and even nations arise and dissolve in a (nonbiological) Darwinian process. We mostly get to know and study only the successful societies, so it would be surprising if we did not find that they utilized numerous effective work-arounds. For example, societies with non-nepotistic civil services are probably more likely to endure, historically (all things being equal), than those with in which bureaucratic advancement is more a matter of kinship than merit.

An *evolutionarily informed praxis* would look much like deliberately designed work-arounds (Barkow, 2003). Could we develop a work-around to correct the industrial food problem previously discussed? We could and we should. Perhaps the attend-preferentially-to-the-high-in-status mechanism previously discussed could be enlisted: high-status individuals would be presented as disdaining some industrial food products in favor of more healthy foods. Perhaps the ethnocentrism response could be harnessed if we taught children to associate fat, sweet, and salty foods with out-group membership. Linking healthy foods to having a competitive edge would be a likely tactic, as would associating them with sexual attractiveness.

Do we really need evolutionary psychology to develop ideas that, frankly, would not win novelty awards from the advertising industry? Not necessarily. Elsewhere (Barkow, 1994), I have described evolutionary psychology as "Granny's psychology" because so much of its content is intuitively valid. Evolutionary psychologists argue that human intelligence is primarily social, having evolved largely to solve the problems of social living. This means that we are the products of selection for expertise in dealing with other people. If so, then by now most of the possible insights into the operation of our minds and societies must already have been figured out (probably by the ancient Greeks!). We should therefore expect that evolutionary psychology strategies will frequently elicit an "I already knew that" response. Of course, the reward structure of academia strongly privileges the unexpected and implausible assertion (e.g., we can learn about human intelligence by studying rats while ignoring the contents of consciousness), and there is a culture in the human sciences of devaluing the familiar. It is as if the response to Newton's theories of gravity had been, "Nothing new here; I already was aware that apples fall down and not up." But if evolutionary psychology has any validity, then most if its findings should be consistent with our lived experience. And if it is not, then we have not an evolutionary praxis but an evolutionary paradox.

The only person I know who has deliberately attempted to follow an evolutionary praxis is activist and columnist Amy Alkon. In a poster presented at Rutgers University during the June 2002 meetings of the Human Behavior and Evolution Society, she described how she used evolutionary psychology in a campaign against sport-utility vehicles.[29] The shaming techniques she exploited would not startle any experienced environmental activist. They make considerable intuitive sense and are also excellent evolutionary psychology (since shaming involves lowering the other's status, and status, for evolutionists, has much to do with access to both social and physical resources ultimately linked to genetic fitness).

Evolutionary psychology does not produce magic bullets for the guns of social activism, but it remains useful. It teaches us what is likely to work and why. It reminds us that we as social activists and moral mission social scientists are also human, subject to the same temptations of self-deception and desire for status and advantage for our children as the rest of the world, and therefore we are at risk of being the successors of the current oppressors. It especially teaches us that the claim to moral superiority is just another kind of claim to status. An evolutionary perspective provides an intellectual framework considerably more sophisticated than the "good guys vs. bad guys" mindset into which even the brightest activists risk falling. And it reminds us that both we and Granny probably believe in a lot of silly things, so that putting our beliefs in the form of hypotheses and throwing them into the bearpit of research and controversy in evolutionary psychology is wiser than assuming that our intuitions are always correct (e.g., does shaming really lower status, and did Amy Alkon's tactics effectively lower status, and in whose eyes?—these are researchable questions). Finally, it could turn out that some evolutionary insights are indeed genuinely novel.[30]

Still, an evolutionary praxis will often simply frame the familiar in terms of the Darwinian metanarrative. Just that is satisfying for some of us and should not be objectionable to the rest. The point is that evolution and activism are definitely mutually compatible, and the association is likely to strengthen the latter. The "moral mission" social scientists previously referred to will find the evolutionary approach largely comfortable (except, perhaps, for the reflexivity aspect of it; examining one's own motives and actions is always disquieting and can be embarrassing).

13. Darwinism as a Metanarrative

Human beings apprehend the world through stories, and stories about stories, and the Darwinian metanarrative is one of the greatest stories about stories ever told. For the human sciences, it serves two purposes. One of these is to provide a framework which "makes sense" to researchers, which permits us to put human and nonhuman behaviors and societies in a framework meaningful to ourselves and our students and readers. Is the framework objectively true? That kind of question no longer has meaning. Does it have competition, in its power and comprehensiveness? Marxism and neo-Marxism leave out the natural world and are thus not competitors—only the world's great religions are comparable in scope. Do we need powerful, integrating metanarratives? Postmodernists would say no, for the postmodernist stance is skepticism toward all grand theory (Lyotard, 1984), all "totalizing" metanarratives. One could argue that postmodernism is itself a metanarrative, an argument whose only point is that all or at least most of us seem to need some kind of broad framework to understand the universe, even if that framework involves the organized denial of that need. For many of us, Darwin seems to work, constantly giving us the feeling of "now that makes sense." For those for whom a Darwinian framework does not work, that fact provides license for thoughtful criticism and a reason to seek to develop alternative frameworks leading to alternative predictions and definitions of data, but it is certainly not grounds for contemptuous dismissal.

Regardless of whether the evolutionary framework provides some kind of cognitive satisfaction, of "fitting together" for any particular individual, it serves its second human science purpose for everyone: it is an incredibly powerful generator of theories and hypotheses. These must be tested and debated, alternatives considered, and so forth, in the usual business of science. The so-called adaptationist program is about generating hypotheses and theory; it is first and foremost a heuristic stance. Only secondarily, because it is also a satisfying metanarrative for many, need its theories and data and plain stories be linked to other Darwinian stories in a grand narrative. And always, the compatibility requirement is a rigorous test of what can be retained and what must be rethought, a requirement largely lacking in non-science metanarratives.

One can be deeply skeptical of the Darwinian metanarrative while still seeking to understand and use it. Non-Marxists can and do read Marx and use his insights. Non-Christians may learn from that religion. Non-evolutionists may find much of value in Darwin and in the Darwinian perspective shared by evolutionary psychology and sociobiology. Of course, if they know nothing of these fields but the parodies produced by critics, then they will indeed wonder what the fuss is about. But because so much of the intellectual life of our period of history is heavily influenced by Darwin, they miss much. For social scientists, who have largely been among the missing, they risk seeing their fields marginalized (Ellis, 1996; Lopreato & Crippen, 1999).

Of course, for many evolutionists, Darwinism is not a "metanarrative," it is simply the truth, and those who reject it are the heathen, the infidels, the out-group. Enthusiastic evolutionists do at times forget about vertical integration, they do at times overgeneralize from data from a single society, and they do at times create stories about past adaptive advantage that serve only to account for current results rather than to generate new hypotheses: In short, they do, at times, need and benefit from criticism. There is no good reason for such criticism to be vicious or belittling or disrespectful, however, even when it is badly needed.

The naturalizing project of the Darwinians has suffered badly from a *lack* of criticism, a lack of informed criticism from social scientists. Social scientists have no monopoly on expertise in human society and culture, true, but their knowledge of this subject is massive. Psychologists and biologists may present much theory and data on likely evolved mechanisms and human commonalties, but without informed criticism from sociologists and social-cultural anthropologists they may overlook even the need for theorizing differences and contingencies, for appreciating the role of social structure and economics—and history—in human action. If the work of sociologists and social anthropologists suffers from the Durkheimian fallacy, that of psychologists in particular can suffer from a slighting of levels of organization above that of the individual. But when evolutionary perspectives do encompass both the individual and the socioeconomic context, wonderful things happen. We get, for example, the previously cited accounts of the nature of religion from Boyer and Atran. We get Barbara Smuts's (1995) account of the origins of patriarchy. We get the beginnings of a coherent framework for understanding both human psychology and sociology. We get social science disciplines in which knowledge is cumulative and accessible across the island empires of competing frameworks. Possibly, just possibly, we get a reversal of the steadily growing marginalization of the social sciences.

14. Conclusions

The ethnographers of old were so self-absorbed with their own discipline and its conventions and fashions that they at times ignored the political revolutions around them, patiently reconstructing "timeless" ways of life that never existed. Today, most of their successors blithely ignore or dismiss the evolution-revolution going on all around them, endlessly identifying social injustices but not taking advantage of the new knowledge that sheds insight into their recurrence and just might provide a helpful praxis. From the humanities the social sciences borrow fashions like secondhand clothes, gaining useful garments—there can be real insights embedded within display prose, to be sure—but also often donning a set of vicious prejudices against empirical and quantitative work, against the idea of hypothesis-testing and the primacy of data, against Darwin and biology, and in favor of a literary style that often produces not precious metal but rough ore, with every reader perforce a refinery. The social sciences are not bankrupt, intellectually, but they have certainly lost massively in public esteem because, to change metaphors, they are constructing a plethora of interesting roofs and sometimes even walls but are ignoring the foundation of their work, which, if it is not to collapse, must take account of the evolved nature of our species and the findings of adjacent disciplines.

Because (as was discussed previously, and at greater length, in Barkow, 1989), we apparently evolved in terms of small groups that often competed against one another, we readily fall into such groupings today and seize on badges of group identity. Dress, hairstyle, language, and accent readily serve as such markers or badges (Irwin, 1987), as do ideologies and beliefs. Academia is full of the politics of small bands and coalitions battling against one another. Whenever we see a construction/belief held as beyond question, treated as so obvious that only idiots and enemies would challenge it, we should suspect that we are seeing a group-identity marker, a way of distinguishing between in-group and out-group members. So it is with the antievolutionary, antiscience, unexamined social constructionist stance so often held by sociologists and social-cultural anthropologists. It is an identity marker rather than a serious intellectual position because intellectual engagement with the evolution revolution is not there; its place has been taken by misconceptions and stereotypes. Note that the problem is not the critical stance of social scientists toward evolutionary psychology—both fields can only benefit from mutual criticism. It is the dismissal, the lack of engagement, that is so lamentable.[31]

Why should social scientist constructionists who reject the natural sciences' claims to objectivity and argue that science is only one way of knowing rush to embrace the evolutionists' assertions that in Darwin and evolutionary psychology and neuroscience lie the scientific (biological) bases for human society and culture? They will not, cannot, should not. Neither should they rush to dismiss. The Darwinian perspective is indeed only one way of knowing—but one so powerful and pervasive that in their scornful dismissal it is the social sciences themselves that are becoming marginalized! To repeat, one does not have to be a Marxist to be familiar with Marxism and to use some of its lessons—Marx is taught as a matter of course to students of social anthropology and sociology. So it should and perhaps eventually will be with Darwin and evolutionary psychology and sociobiology. The perspective may never come to dominate the social sciences, but it will be recognized as one requiring engagement rather than dismissal.

We need and will always need the engaged social scientist working within a moral mission. Their struggle will never end because the conditions they challenge are ultimately rooted in our evolved human nature. This is not a counsel of despair. True, individuals will always tend to seek their own self-interest, form coalitions and join groups, work to transmit their own advantages to their children at the expense of the children of others, see themselves as noble and good and their rivals as ignorant or evil, be prone to ethnocentrism and to feelings of moral superiority and self-righteous anger, and compete in the arena of culture to edit information in self-serving ways. Both individuals and collectivities that see themselves as lower in status and control of resources than others will periodically challenge their relative standing. Those in advantageous positions will continue to follow strategies to maintain their privilege, from military means to ideologies and religions that preach that the status quo is good for all and perhaps divinely sanctioned. There can be no enduring, unchanging utopia: always, there will be individuals and groups who can see changes that would benefit themselves and who will effortlessly convince themselves that the benefits of reform or revolution will accrue to all (and sometimes they will be right). Always, all sides will see themselves as "the good guys." If nothing else, each young generation will seek pride and place, challenging the existing order and those already well established in it, taking a critical stance toward received culture and editing it. All these strivings, even in the absence of other causes of change (e.g., environmental degradation, resource depletion, technological developments, population growth or decline, climate change) will mean that revisions and reversals and new constructions will always be there. Fukuyama (1992) notwithstanding, history will not end. The need to struggle against oppression is permanent because the notion of a perfected human nature is oxymoronic. (And as with "Granny's wisdom" [above], we knew that already, didn't we?)

None of this implies fatalism. Evolutionary psychology tells us that the game is endless, not that it is bootless. Capitalism can be a Marxist nightmare or a cornucopia, depending on the kinds of governments and laws we devise, and an evolutionist perspective on human nature and society merely reminds us that we have to work very hard and keep on working hard if we are to have sound laws and good governments. But this constant effort is the stuff of life, and as evolutionists would expect, in playing the game of life and politics we often experience great happiness, cooperate mightily, create magnificent works of art, and frequently act with much generosity and even nobility. It is our evolved human nature that permits all this. Evolutionary psychology is a recognition of our humanness, not, as some may fear, its denial. An understanding of evolutionary psychology is a license to struggle against the self-seeking tendencies we find in others and in ourselves and, if we so choose, to fight against social inequality and injustice, all the while taking a skeptical attitude toward the accounts and excuses of others for their actions—and for our own, when we turn the Darwinian gaze inward.

This volume asks the social scientist to become, not an uncritical convert and devotee, but at least an informed critic. Previous generations of sociocultural anthropologists and sociologists came to grips with Freud and with Marx; it is past time for the current generation to come to grips with Darwin.

15. Guide to This Book

The brief "bridging" passages that precede each of the four sections of this book are in effect continuations of this introduction. The chapters are illustrative of current evolutionary approaches but are too few to represent more than a sampling of ongoing work—a truly comprehensive overview of Darwinian perspectives in the human sciences would require a trilogy!

Notes

1. By "social scientists" I mean to include sociologists, social-cultural anthropologists, and any other individuals or groups comfortable with this umbrella appellation.

2. And if you happen to be a sociobiologist or evolutionary psychologist who thinks otherwise—or who writes as if you think otherwise—then it is especially good that you are reading this book.

3. See, for example, the angry scorn of Lancaster's (2004) commentary in *Anthropology News*, the newsletter of the American Anthropological Association. Lancaster presents evolutionary psychology as a proponent of the

"bioreductionism" that he quite correctly criticizes. One could make a good case, however, for evolutionary psychology being as much victim as perpetrator of "bioreductionism": By reducing the subtlety and sophistication of evolutionary psychology's arguments to silly statements about "genes" and "programming," Lancaster himself is a species of "bioreductionist."

4. I am omitting the major contributions made by archaeological anthropologists to understanding the evolution of human behavior because my focus is on social-cultural anthropology. I do not for a moment mean to slight such important work as, for example, Steven Mithen's (1996) *The Prehistory of Mind: The Cognitive Origins of Art, Religion and Science.*

5. "Scientism" usually refers to the belief that the "scientific method" is the only road to true knowledge. For most social scientists, there are various roads to knowledges (the plural is deliberate), and that of science is perhaps so weak as to be inapplicable to their subject matter. Note that my generalizations about social scientists are based on my own experience and reading—I know of no applicable survey research data.

6. See Kuznar (1996) for a defense of "scientific anthropology" against creationists and racists as well as Marxists and some feminists and postmodernists.

7. I am not sure how to categorize the Cambridge sociologist and evolutionist W. Gary Runciman (1998, 2001; Runciman, Maynard Smith, & Dunbar, 1996)—some people are simply individuals rather than schools of thought.

8. In *The Merchant of Venice*, act I, scene 3.

9. My argument was that we were selected for complex internal representations of others in order to predict their behavior. Such a system necessarily requires an internal representation of the organism itself in order to model the outcome of social interactions. Any organism with an internal representation of self experiences consciousness, with self-awareness the product of a sufficiently complex internal representation of self. This argument, while totally lacking in neurophysiological sophistication, has the virtue of being testable. See Barkow (1989) for the full discussion.

10. There is a huge literature on the relationship between biology and ethics. While Darwin is anything but a guide for proper behavior—there (arguably) never was a "social Darwinism," only a "social Spencerism"—evolution does have much to say about our "moral emotions" and sense of injustice and about the ways in which cooperation can often be the outcome of competition. For those who wish to explore this broad area, the reader edited by Katz (2000) is a good place to begin. Ridley's (1997) well-written work is likely to be of particular interest to social scientists concerned with altruism, cooperation, and the environment. Other relevant works include Alexander (1993), Arnhart (1998), Boehm (2000), De Waal (1996), McGuire (1992), Wilson (2002), and Wright (1994).

11. For excellent and highly readable answers to the questions of what genes and genomes are, see Ridley (2000). There are a variety of conceptions of the "gene," a term that itself seems to be evolving.

12. I have even heard, "He just doesn't have the *genes* for that." In that context, "genes" was apparently meant to be a euphemism for *cojones*.

13. Evolutionists must constantly battle against the idea of a superdeterministic gene. For recent skirmishes, see Dennett (2003) and Pinker (2002).

14. Segarstråle (this volume) suspects that this avoidance of genetics represents an effort on the part of evolutionary psychologists to avoid controversy, and this suspicion is shared by at least one behavior geneticist of my acquaintance. My own research interests do not involve genes, but perhaps Segarstråle is correct and this focus does reflect a desire for a quiet life. I doubt that, in my own case, but of course I cannot speak for others.

15. Otherwise well-informed critics such as Ehrlich and Feldman (2003), who see evolutionary psychologists as some kind of genetic reductionists, are very far off the mark because the field has little to do with genetics or genes. The debate in which such critics need to engage involves the nature, generality, limits, and of course ontological status of posited mechanisms and the claim that they constrain and enable the enormous diversity of human societies.

16. More properly, *polygenes*, groups of genes that work together to help produce a particular trait or mechanism.

17. *Social constructivists* differ from constructionists in focusing on the individual, psychological level (Gergen, 1994, p. 67), while *radical constructivists* (von Glasersfeld, 1991, 1995) are careful not to posit any kind of "objective" reality out there at all.

18. I am grateful to Dan Fessler for his insight into the relationship between Lutz's work and evolutionary psychology. Any misunderstandings are entirely my own, however.

19. For a more philosophical approach to reconciling social constructionist and evolutionary psychology, with particular reference to the nature of emotion and the work of Catherine Lutz (1988), see Mallon & Stitch (2000) and Stitch (1996). These authors see the dispute over local rather than core universal definitions of emotions as a misunderstanding about metaphysics.

20. See also Borgerhoff Mulder, Richerson, Thornhill, & Voland (1997) for a thorough discussion of the relationship between evolutionary psychology and human behavioral ecology.

21. For discussion of how maladaptive cultural traits can become established, see Aunger (2000), Barkow (1984, 1989, pp. 293–322), Edgerton (1992), Logan & Qirko (1996), Richerson & Boyd (2004), and Takahasi (1998, 1999).

22. Jack Goody (1982, p. 8) describes "the emergence of new sociological theory" as involving "the statement of opposition to the present establishment." He adds that "this process is often 'cyclical' and 'repetitive,' more rebellion than revolution" (drawing on Max Gluckman's distinction between rebellions as opposed to revolutions). Changes are more substitutions in approach than major changes in theory: "Rather than crystallizing

existing knowledge and offering a model for future experimental and intellectual work, such changes indicate any shift of emphasis between possibilities that lie permanently embedded in the analysis of sociological material." Goody disputes that sociology and social anthropology are cumulative fields, as opposed to cyclical fields, in which not so much theory as "approach" changes over time. An approach provides a "plan of attack," a general research strategy about what "to look for" (p. 7). Poststructuralists would no doubt disagree with Goody.

23. Complex ambiguity is the academic version of conspicuous consumption. Geoffrey Miller (2000) explains conspicuous consumption as a type of display behavior—items are frequently purchased by the wealthy not in spite of their cost but because of their cost. Similarly, in academia, obscure, convoluted, richly ambiguous theoreticians are often read not in spite of their difficulty but because of their difficulty. The ostensible payoff in conspicuous consumption is utility, and that in conspicuous display prose is intellectual insight, but in fact in both cases the payoff is primarily a claim to status by the purchaser/reader. The philosopher Bertrand Russell (1946) long ago demonstrated that the most abstruse of philosophical ideas could in fact be presented with great lucidity—but Russell was writing at a time when it was indeed clarity rather than its lack that earned prestige and publication.

24. O'Meara (1997) and the accompanying commentaries on his position make for a good entry to the debate within anthropology on this topic. As of this writing, there is no sign of a consensus emerging.

25. Lewontin has been a powerful critic of efforts to understand the behavior of our species in the light of evolutionary biology (see Segerstråle, [2000], this volume). While he appreciates that adopting an empty scientific formalism ("scientism") is not the solution to the problems of the social sciences, he would apparently not agree that the solution is making the assumptions of social scientists compatible with evolutionary biology and psychology. Few, however, have made the attempt.

26. For a discussion of the sociological processes in the social sciences that generate ignorance of and antipathy toward adjacent fields, see Barkow (1989, pp. 11–14). The structurally generated insularity of the social sciences is a significant factor in the movement of many social scientists to the humanities, in recent years. Without the power of the vertically integrated approach to winnow out impossible theory, and without the stimulation that comes from cross-species comparisons, the student of social science is faced with a bewildering variety of approaches and no easy way to differentiate among them except, to be sure, the political (that is, in terms of alliances and career interests, factors important in all fields).

27. In 1968, while living in a small Hausa village in northern Nigeria, I once attempted to explain to an ordinary farmer the idea that nepotism was something bad and civil service examinations good. I knew the precise instant when, in spite of my imperfect Hausa and the bizarreness of the idea, he had grasped what I was saying because he suddenly looked at me in shock.

His instant and amazed reproach was: "You would favor strangers over your own brothers?" It was clear that, for him, I was advocating a really unusual kind of immorality.

28. These evolved mechanisms underlie the ethnocentrism phenomenon, the tendency for human beings to readily form into in-groups that are likely to compete with out-groups for status and resources and to face external threat with increased in-group solidarity. For discussion of ethnocentrism and also of how we may have been selected for this cluster of traits, see (for example) Alexander (1979), Barkow (1989, 2000), Irwin (1987), LeVine & Campbell (1972), Reynolds, Falger, & Vine (1987), and Shaw & Wong (1988).

29. Amy Alkon, a journalist and syndicated columnist, placed cards on the windshields of SUVs parked on Los Angeles streets. The cards read (to quote from the account under her own byline that appeared in the *Los Angeles New Times* of April 11, 2002 (http://www.newtimesla.com/issues/2002-04-11/sidecar.html/1/index.html), and from the account in the *London Guardian* of April 16, 2002 (http://www.guardian.co.uk/Archive/Article/0,4273,4395102,00.html): "Road-hogging, gas-guzzling, air-fouling vulgarian! Clearly you have an extremely small penis or you wouldn't drive such a monstrosity. For the adequately endowed, there are hybrids or electrics. 310 798 1817." Dialing that telephone number would result in a voice saying, "Piggy, piggy, piggy. If you can afford one of those huge new SUVs you can afford something that doesn't suck all the air out of the planet and spit it back black. . . . It's really creepy that you drive that thing and I just wanted to let you know." Alkon (in a personal communication) explains that she pressed the evolutionary psychology buttons that she believes would create shame over driving an SUV because doing so meant that these drivers were using up more than their fair share of resources. Though her campaign is only a modest and simple beginning, and not necessarily the best possible strategy to achieve her end of protecting the environment, it does support the notion that an evolutionary praxis is possible. Presumably, more subtle techniques are possible.

30. For example, the study of sperm competition and its implications was quite unanticipated (e.g., Bellis & Baker, 1995; Birkhead, 2000; Low, 1999).

31. In part, though only in part, the larger context for the anti-evolution stance of the human sciences is that of the "science wars" of the turn of the twenty-first century. For an analysis of anti-biology and anti-evolutionism in the humanities, see McBride (1998).

References

Abu-Lughod, L. (1991). Writing against culture. In R. G. Fox (Ed.), *Recapturing Anthropology: Working in the Present* (pp. 137–162). Santa Fe, NM: SAR Press.

Alexander, R. D. (1979). *Darwinism and Human Affairs*. Seattle: University of Washington Press.

Alexander, R. D. (1987). *The Biology of Moral Systems*. New York: Aldine de Gruyter.

Alexander, R. D. (1993). Biological considerations in the analysis of morality. In M. H. Nitecki & D. V. Nitecki (Eds.), *Evolutionary Ethics*. Albany: SUNY Press.

Arnhart, L. (1998). *Darwinian Natural Right: The Biological Ethics of Human Nature*. Albany: SUNY Press.

Atran, S. (1998). Folk biology and the anthropology of science: Cognitive universals and cultural particulars. *Behavioral and Brain Sciences, 21*(4), 547–609.

Atran, S. (1999). The universal primacy of generic species in folkbiological taxonomy: Implications for human biological, cultural and scientific evolution. In R. A. Wilson (Ed.), *Species: New Interdisciplinary Essays* (pp. 231–261). Cambridge, MA: MIT Press.

Atran, S. (2002). *In Gods We Trust: The Evolutionary Landscape of Religion*. New York: Oxford University Press.

Aunger, R. (1999). Against idealism/contra consensus. *Current Anthropology, 40*(Supplement), S93–S101.

Aunger, R. (2000). *Darwinizing Culture: The Status of Memetics as a Science*. New York: Oxford University Press.

Barkow, J. H. (1975). Strategies for self-esteem and prestige in Maradi, Niger Republic. In T. R. Williams (Ed.), *Psychological Anthropology* (pp. 373–388). The Hague and Paris: Mouton.

Barkow, J. H. (1976). Attention structure and the evolution of human psychological characteristics. In M. R. A. Chance & R. R. Larsen (Eds.), *The Social Structure of Attention* (pp. 203–220). London and New York: Wiley.

Barkow, J. H. (1983). Begged questions in behavior and evolution. In G. Davey (Ed.), *Animal Models of Human Behavior* (pp. 205–222). Chichester and New York: John Wiley.

Barkow, J. H. (1984). The distance between genes and culture. *Journal of Anthropological Research, 37*, 367–379.

Barkow, J. H. (1989). *Darwin, Sex, and Status: Biological Approaches to Mind and Culture*. Toronto: University of Toronto Press.

Barkow, J. H. (1989). Overview. *Ethology and Sociobiology, 10*, 1–10.

Barkow, J. H. (1992). Beneath new culture is old psychology. In J. H. Barkow, L. Cosmides, & J. Tooby (Eds.), *The Adapted Mind: Evolutionary Psychology and the Generation of Culture* (pp. 626–637). New York: Oxford University Press.

Barkow, J. H. (1994). Evolutionary psychological anthropology. In P. K. Bock (Ed.), *Handbook of Psychological Anthropology* (pp. 121–138). Westport, CT: Greenwood.

Barkow, J. H. (1997). Happiness in evolutionary perspective. In N. L. Segal, G. E. Weisfeld, & C. C. Weisfeld (Eds.), *Uniting Psychology and*

Biology: Integrative Perspectives on Human Development (pp. 397–418). Washington, DC: American Psychological Association.

Barkow, J. H. (2000). Do extraterrestrials have sex (and intelligence)? In D. LeCroy & P. Moller (Eds.), *Evolutionary Perspectives on Human Reproductive Behavior* (Vol. 907, pp. 164–181). New York: Annals of the New York Academy of Sciences.

Barkow, J. H. (2003). Biology is destiny only if you ignore it. *World Futures*, forthcoming.

Barkow, J. H., Cosmides, L., & Tooby, J. (1992). *The Adapted Mind: Evolutionary Psychology and the Generation of Culture*. New York: Oxford University Press.

Barkow, J. H., et al. (2001). Social competition, social intelligence, and why the Bugis know more about cooking than about nutrition. *Origins of Social Institutions* (Vol. 110, pp. 119–147). London: British Academy.

Bauerlein, M. (2001). Social constructionism: Philosophy for the academic workplace. *Partisan Review*, 68(2).

Beckstrom, J. H. (1993). *Darwinism Applied: Evolutionary Paths to Social Goals*. Westport, CT: Greenwood.

Bellis, M. A., & Baker, R. R. (1995). *Human Sperm Competition: Copulation, Masturbation and Infidelity*. New York: Chapman & Hall.

Berger, P. L., & Luckmann, T. (1966). *The Social Construction of Reality*. London: Penguin.

Biagioli, M. (Ed.). (1999). *The Science Studies Reader*. New York: Routledge.

Birkhead, T. R. (2000). *Promiscuity: An Evolutionary History of Sperm Competition and Sexual Conflict*. Cambridge, MA: Harvard University Press.

Boehm, C. (2000). Conflict and the evolution of social control. In L. D. Katz (Ed.), *Evolutionary Origins of Morality: Cross-Disciplinary Perspectives* (pp. 79–101). Bowling Green, OH: Imprint Academic.

Borgerhoff Mulder, M., Richerson, P. J., Thornhill, N. W., & Voland, E. (1997). The place of behavioral ecological anthropology in evolutionary social science. In P. Weingart, S. D. Mitchell, P. J. Richerson, & S. Maasen (Eds.), *Human by Nature: Between Biology and the Social Sciences* (pp. 253–281). Mahwah, NJ: Lawrence Erlbaum.

Boyer, P. (1993). *Cognitive Aspects of Religious Symbolism*. Cambridge: Cambridge University Press.

Boyer, P. (1994a). Cognitive restraints on cultural representations: Natural ontologies and religious ideas. In L. A. Hirschfeld & S. A. Gelman (Eds.), *Mapping the Mind: Domain Specificity in Cognition and Culture*. Cambridge: Cambridge University Press.

Boyer, P. (1994b). *The Naturalness of Religious Ideas: A Cognitive Theory of Religion*. Los Angeles/Berkeley: University of California Press.

Boyer, P. (2000). Functional origins of religious concepts: Ontological and strategic selection in evolved minds. *Journal of the Royal Anthropological Institute*, 6(2), 195–214.

Boyer, P. (2001). *Religion Explained: The Evolutionary Origins of Religious Thought*. New York: Basic Books.

Brown, D. E. (1991). *Human Universals*. New York: McGraw-Hill.

Browne, K. (1998). *Divided Labours: An Evolutionary View of Women at Work*. London: Weidenfeld & Nicholson.

Browne, K. R. (2002). *Biology at Work: Rethinking Sexual Equality*. New Brunswick, NJ: Rutgers University Press.

Buss, D. (2000). *The Dangerous Passion: Why Jealousy Is as Necessary as Love and Sex*. New York: Free Press.

Buss, D. M., & Dedden, L. (1990). Derogation of competitors. *Journal of Social and Personal Relationships, 7*, 395–422.

Campbell, D. T. (1969). Ethnocentrism of disciplines and the fish-scale model of omniscience. In M. Sherif & C. W. Sherif (Eds.), *Interdisciplinary Relationships in the Social Sciences* (pp. 328–348). Chicago: Aldine.

Carroll, J. (1994). *Evolution and Literary Theory*. St. Louis: University of Missouri Press.

Chance, M. R. A., & Larsen, R. R. (Eds.). (1976). *The Social Structure of Attention*. London: Wiley.

Changeux, J.-P. (1997). *Neuronal Man*. Princeton, NJ: Princeton University Press.

Changeux, J.-P. (2004). *The Physiology of Truth: Neuroscience and Human Knowledge* (M. B. DeBevoise, Trans.). Cambridge, MA: Belknap Press of Harvard University Press.

Changeux, J.-P., & Ricoeur, P. (2000). *What Makes Us Think? A Neuroscientist and a Philosopher Argue about Ethics, Human Nature, and the Brain*. Princeton, NJ: Princeton University Press.

Charleton, B. (2000). *Psychiatry and the Human Condition*. Abingdon, UK: Radcliffe Medical Press.

Clifford, J., & Marcus, G. E. (1986). *Writing Culture: The Poetics and Politics of Ethnography*. Berkeley: University of California Press.

Cooke, B., & Turner, F. (1999). *Biopoetics: Evolutionary Explorations in the Arts*. Lexington, KY: ICUS.

Cordain, L. (2001). *The Paleo Diet: Lose Weight and Get Healthy by Eating the Food You Were Designed to Eat*. New York: John Wiley & Sons.

Cosmides, L., & Tooby, J. (1989). Evolutionary psychology and the generation of culture, II. Case study: A computational theory of social exchange. *Ethology and Sociobiology, 10*, 51–97.

Cosmides, L., & Tooby, J. (1992). Cognitive adaptations for social exchange. In J. H. Barkow, L. Cosmides, & J. Tooby (Eds.), *The Adapted Mind: Evolutionary Psychology and the Generation of Culture* (pp. 163–228). New York: Oxford University Press.

Cosmides, L., & Tooby, J. (2001). Evolutionary psychology: A primer.

Cosmides, L., Tooby, J., & Barkow, J. H. (1992). Introduction. In J. H. Barkow, L. Cosmides, & J. Tooby (Eds.), *The Adapted Mind. Evolutionary Psychology and the Generation of Culture* (pp. 3–15). New York: Oxford University Press.

Cronin, H. (1992). *The Ant and the Peacock: Altruism and Sexual Selection from Darwin to Today*. Cambridge: Cambridge University Press.

Daly, M., & Wilson, M. I. (1988). *Homicide*. New York: Aldine de Gruyter.

Damasio, A. R. (1995). *Descartes' Error: Emotion, Reason, and the Human Brain*. New York: Pan Macmillan.

Damasio, A. R. (1999). *The Feeling of What Happens: Body and Emotion in the Making of Consciousness*. New York: Harcourt Brace.

Damasio, A. R. (2000). *The Feeling of What Happens: Body and Emotion in the Making of Consciousness*. San Diego, CA: Harcourt/Harvest Books.

Damasio, A. R. (2003). *Looking for Spinoza: Joy, Sorrow, and the Feeling Brain*. New York: Harcourt.

Davis, H., & Javor, A. (2004). Religion, death and horror movies: Some striking evolutionary parallels. *Evolution and Cognition, 19*, 11–18.

Davis, H., & McLeod, S. L. (2003). Why humans value sensational news: An evolutionary perspective. *Evolution & Human Behavior, 24*, 208–216.

Dawkins, R. (1976). *The Selfish Gene*. Oxford: Oxford University Press.

Dawkins, R. (1982). *The Extended Phenotype: The Gene as the Unit of Selection*. Oxford and San Francisco: W. H. Freeman.

Dawkins, R. (1989). *The Selfish Gene* (2nd ed.). New York: Oxford University Press.

Dawkins, R. (1996a). *The Blind Watchmaker: Why the Evidence of Evolution Reveals a Universe without Design*. New York: W. W. Norton.

Dawkins, R. (1996b). *Climbing Mount Improbable*. New York: W. W. Norton.

Dawkins, R. (1996c). *River Out of Eden: A Darwinian View of Life*. New York: Basic Books.

Dawkins, R. (2000). *Unweaving the Rainbow: Science, Delusion and the Appetite for Wonder*. Boston: Houghton Mifflin.

Dawkins, R. (2003). *A Devil's Chaplain: Reflections on Hope, Lies, Science, and Love*. Boston: Houghton Mifflin.

Dawkins, R., & Dennett, D. C. (1999). *The Extended Phenotype: The Long Reach of the Gene* (2nd ed.). New York: Oxford University Press.

De Waal, F. (1996). *Good Natured: The Origins of Right and Wrong in Humans and Other Animals*. Cambridge, MA: Harvard University Press.

DeLamater, J. D., & Hyde, J. S. (1998). Essentialism vs. social constructionism in the study of human sexuality. *Journal of Sex Research, 35*(1), 10–18.

Delmonico, F. L., Arnold, R., Scheper-Hughes, N., Siminoff, L. A., Kahn, J., & Younger, S. J. (2002). Sounding board: Ethical incentives—not payment—for organ donation. *New England Journal of Medicine, 346*(25), 2002–2005.

Dennett, D. (1997). Consciousness in human and robot minds. In M. Ito, Y. Miyashita, & E. T. Rolls (Eds.), *Symposium on Cognition, Computation, and Consciousness*. Oxford: Oxford University Press.

Dennett, D. C. (1995). *Darwin's Dangerous Idea: Evolution and the Meanings of Life*. New York: Simon & Schuster.

Dennett, D. C. (2003). *Freedom Evolves*. New York: Viking.

Dissanayake, E. (1992). *Homo Aestheticus: Where Art Comes from and Why*. New York: Free Press.

Dissanayake, E. (2000). *Art and Intimacy: How the Arts Began*. Seattle: University of Washington Press.

Djilas, M. (1957). *The New Class: An Analysis of the Communist System*. New York: Praeger.

Duke, D. (1998). *My Awakening: A Path to Racial Understanding*. Covington, LA: Free Speech Books.

Eaton, S. B., Pike, M. C., Short, R. V., Lee, N. C., Trussell, J., Hatcher, R. A., Wood, J. W., Worthman, C. M., Jones, N. G. B., Konner, M. J., Hill, K. R., Bailey, R., & Hurtado, A. M. (1994). Women's reproductive cancers in evolutionary context. *Quarterly Review of Biology, 69*(3), 353–367.

Eaton, S. B., Shostak, M., & Konner, M. (1988). *The Paleolithic Prescription: A Program of Diet and Exercise and a Design for Living*. New York: Harper & Row.

Edelman, G. M., & Changeux, J.-P. (Eds.). (2000). *The Brain*. Somerset, NJ: Transaction.

Edgerton, R. B. (1992). *Sick Societies: Challenging the Myth of Primitive Harmony*. New York: Free Press.

Ehrlich, P., & Feldman, M. (2003). Genes and cultures: What creates our behavioral phenome? *Current Anthropology, 44*(1), 87–107.

Ekman, P., & Davidson, R. J. (Eds.). (1995). *The Nature of Emotion: Fundamental Questions*. New York: Oxford University Press.

Ellis, L. (1996). A discipline in peril: Sociology's future hinges on curing its biophobia. *American Sociologist, 27,* 21–41.

Ellis, L., & Walsh, A. (2000). *Criminology: A Global Perspective*. New York: Allyn & Bacon.

Farmer, P. (1998). Social inequalities and emerging infectious disease. In P. J. Brown (Ed.), *Understanding and Applying Medical Anthropology* (pp. 98–107). Mountain View, CA: Mayfield.

Fisher, H. (1999). *The First Sex: The Natural Talents of Women and How They Are Changing the World*. New York: Random House.

Fisher, H. E. (1992). *The Anatomy of Love: The Natural History of Monogamy, Adultery and Divorce*. New York: W. W. Norton.

Fisher, H. E. (2004). *Why We Love: The Nature and Chemistry of Romantic Love*. New York: Henry Holt.

Flyvbjerg, B. (2001). *Making Social Science Matter: Why Social Inquiry Fails and How It Can Succeed Again* (S. Sampson, Trans.). Cambridge: Cambridge University Press.

Fossey, D. (1983). *Gorillas in the Mist*. Boston: Houghton Mifflin.

Fukuyama, F. (1992). *The End of History and the Last Man*. New York: Free Press.

Fukuyama, F. (2002). *Our Posthuman Future: Consequences of the Biotechnology Revolution*. New York: Farrar, Straus & Giroux.

Gazzaniga, M. S. (1992). *Nature's Mind: The Biological Roots of Thinking, Emotions, Sexuality, Language, and Intelligence*. New York: Basic Books.

Gazzaniga, M. S. (2000). *The Mind's Past*. Berkeley: University of California Press.

Geertz, C. (1962). The growth of culture and the evolution of mind. In J. M. Scher (Ed.), *Theories of Mind*. Glencoe: Free Press.

Geertz, C. (1973). *The Interpretation of Cultures: Selected Essays*. New York: Basic Books.

Gergen, K. J. (1994). *Realities and Relationships: Soundings in Social Construction*. Cambridge, MA: Harvard University Press.

Gigerenzer, G. (2000). *Adaptive Thinking: Rationality in the Real World (Evolution and Cognition)*. Oxford: Oxford University Press.

Gilbert, P., McGuire, M. T., & Bailey, K. G. (2000). Evolutionary psychotherapy: Principles and outline. In P. Gilbert & K. G. Bailey (Eds.), *Genes on the Couch: Explorations in Evolutionary Psychotherapy* (pp. 3–27). New York: Brunner-Routledge.

Gil-White, F. J. (2001). Are ethnic groups biological "species" to the human brain? Essentialism in our cognition of some social categories. *Current Anthropology, 42*(4), 515–554.

Gintis, H. (2000). *Game Theory Evolving*. Princeton, NJ: Princeton University Press.

Glantz, K., & Pearce, J. K. (1989). *Exiles from Eden. Psychotherapy from an Evolutionary Perspective*. New York: W. W. Norton.

Goodall, J. (1990). *Through a Window: My Thirty Years with the Chimpanzees of Gombe*. Boston: Houghton Mifflin.

Goody, J. (1982). *Cooking, Cuisine and Class*. Cambridge: Cambridge University Press.

Gould, S. J. (1989). *Wonderful Life: The Burgess Shale and the Nature of History*. New York: W. W. Norton.

Gould, S. J. (1995). *Dinosaur in a Haystack: Reflections in Natural History*. New York: Harmony Books.

Gould, S. J. (2002). *The Structure of Evolutionary Theory*. Cambridge, MA: Harvard University Press.

Grammar, K., & Voland, E. (Eds.). (2003). *Evolutionary Aesthetics*. Berlin: Springer Verlag.

Gramsci, A. (1957). *The Modern Prince and Other Writings*. New York: International Press.

Griffiths, P. E., & Gray, R. D. (1994). Developmental systems and evolutionary explanation. *Journal of Philosophy, 91*(6), 277–304.

Hacking, I. (1999). *The Social Construction of What?* Cambridge, MA: Harvard University Press.

Hejl, P. M., Kammer, M., & Uhl, M. (In preparation). The really interesting stories are the old ones: Evolved interests in economically successful films from Hollywood and Bollywood. In J. H. Barkow & P. M. Hejl (Eds.), *You Can't Turn It Off: Media, Mind, and Evolution*. New York: Oxford University Press.

Hobsbawm, E., & Ranger, T. (Eds.). (1992). *The Invention of Tradition*. Cambridge: Cambridge University Press.

Hull, D. A., & Ruse, M. (1998). *The Philosophy of Biology (Oxford Readings in Philosophy)*. New York: Oxford University Press.

Irwin, C. J. (1987). A study of the evolution of ethnocentrism. In V. Reynolds, V. Falger, & I. Vine (Eds.), *The Sociobiology of Ethnocentrism: Evolutionary Dimensions of Xenophobia, Discrimination, Racism and Nationalism* (pp. 131–156). London and Sydney: Croom Helm.

Janicki, M. G., & Krebs, D. L. (1998). Evolutionary approaches to culture. In C. Crawford & D. L. Krebs (Eds.), *Handbook of Evolutionary Psychology: Ideas, Issues, and Applications* (pp. 163–210). Mahwah, NJ: Lawrence Erlbaum.

Jasanoff, S., Markle, G. E., Petersen, J. C., & Pinch, T. (2001). *Handbook of Science and Technology Studies*. Rev. ed. Thousand Oaks, CA: Sage.

Kahneman, D., & Tversky, A. (2000). *Choices, Values and Frames*. Cambridge: Cambridge University Press.

Katz, L. D. (2000). *Evolutionary Origins of Morality: Cross-Disciplinary Perspectives*. Exeter, UK: Imprint Academic.

Keller, E. F. (1999). Elusive locus of control in biological development: Genetic versus developmental programs. *Journal of Experimental Zoology (Mol Dev Evol), 285*, 283–290.

Koslowski, P. (1999). *Sociobiology and Economics: The Theory of Evolution in Biological and Economic Theory*. Berlin: Springer-Verlag.

Kroeber, A. L. (1917). The Superorganic. *American Anthropologist, 19*, 163–213.

Kuznar, L. (1996). *Reclaiming a Scientific Anthropology*. Walnut Creek, CA: AltaMira Press.

Laland, K. N., Odling-Smee, J., & Feldman, M. (2000). Niche construction, biological evolution and cultural change. *Behavioral and Brain Sciences, 23*, 131–146.

Laland, K. N., Odling-Smee, J., & Feldman, M. W. (2001). Cultural niche construction and human evolution. *Journal of Evolutionary Biology, 14*(1), 22–33.

Lancaster, R. N. (2004). The place of anthropology in a public culture reshaped by bioreductivism. *Anthropology News, 45*(3), 4–5.

Lane, R. D., Nadel, L., & Ahern, G. (Eds.). (2000). *Cognitive Neuroscience of Emotion*. New York: Oxford University Press.

Latour, B. (1993). *We Have Never Been Modern*. Cambridge, MA: Harvard University Press.

Latour, B., & Salk, J. (1986). *Laboratory Life: The Construction of Scientific Facts*. Princeton, NJ: Princeton University Press.

LeVine, R. A., & Campbell, D. T. (1972). *Ethnocentrism: Theories of Conflict, Ethnic Attitudes and Group Behavior*. New York: Wiley.

Lewontin, R. C. (1995). Sex, lies, and social science. *New York Review of Books, 28*.

Logan, M. H., & Qirko, H. N. (1996). An evolutionary perspective on maladaptive traits and cultural conformity. *American Journal of Human Biology, 8*(5), 615–629.

Lopreato, J., & Crippen, T. (1999). *Crisis in Sociology: The Need for Darwin*. Somerset, NJ: Transaction.

Low, B. (1999). *Why Sex Matters: A Darwinian Look at Human Behavior*. Princeton, NJ: Princeton University Press.

Lutz, C. A. (1988). *Unnatural Emotions: Everyday Sentiments on a Micronesian Atoll and Their Challenge to Western Theory*. Chicago: University of Chicago Press.

Lyotard, J.-F. (1984). *The Postmodern Condition: A Report on Knowledge* (G. Bennington & B. Massumi, Trans.). Minneapolis: University of Minnesota Press.

Machalek, R., & Martin, M. W. (2004). Sociology and the second Darwinian revolution: A metatheoretical analysis. *Sociological Theory* 22(3), 455–476.

Malinowski, B. (1944). *A Scientific Theory of Culture*. Chapel Hill: University of North Carolina Press.

Mallon, R., & Stich, S. P. (2000). The odd couple: The compatibility of social construction and evolutionary psychology. *Philosophy of Science*, 67(1), 133–154.

Masters, R. D. (1989). *The Nature of Politics*. New Haven, CT: Yale University Press.

Masters, R. D., & Gruter, M. (Eds.). (1992). *The Sense of Justice: Biological Foundations of Law* (Vol. 136). Newbury Park, CA: Sage.

McAndrew, F. T., & Milenkovic, M. A. (2002). Of tabloids and family secrets: The evolutionary psychology of gossip. *Journal of Applied Social Psychology*, 32(5), 1064–1082.

McBride, T. (1998). Why academic humanists resist contemporary Darwinism. *Human Ethology Bulletin, 13*(3), 6–8.

McGuire, M. T. (1992). Moralistic aggression, processing mechanisms, and the brain: Biological foundations of the sense of justice. In R. D. Masters & M. Gruter (Eds.), *The Sense of Justice: Biological Foundations of Law* (pp. 67–92). Newbury Park, CA: Sage.

McGuire, M. T., & Troisi, A. (1998). *Darwinian Psychiatry*. New York: Oxford University Press.

McMichael, A. (1995). The health of persons, populations and planets: Epidemiology comes full circle. *Epidemiology*, 6, 633–636.

Miller, G. (2000). *The Mating Mind: How Sexual Choice Shaped Human Nature*. New York: Doubleday.

Mithen, S. (1996). *The Prehistory of Mind: The Cognitive Origins of Art, Religion and Science*. London: Thames & Hudson.

Mysterud, I. (2004). One name for the evolutionary baby? A preliminary guide for everyone confused by the chaos of names. *Social Science Information Sur Les Sciences Sociales, 43*(1), 95–114.

Nelkin, D., & Lindee, M. S. (1995). *The DNA Mystique: The Gene as a Cultural Icon*. New York: Freeman.

Nesse, R., & Williams, G. (1994). *Why We Get Sick: The New Science of Darwinian Medicine*. New York: Times Books/Random House.

Nicholson, N. (2000). *Executive Instinct: Managing the Human Animal in the Information Age.* New York: Crown Business.

O'Meara, T. (1997). CA Forum on Theory in Anthropology: Causation and the struggle for a science of culture. *Current Anthropology, 38*(3), 399–418.

Oyama, S. (1991). Bodies and minds: Dualism in evolutionary theory. *Journal of Social Issues, 47*, 27–42.

Oyama, S. (2000). *Evolution's Eye: A Systems View of the Biology-Culture Divide (Science and Cultural Theory).* Durham, NC: Duke University Press.

Pinker, S. (1993). *The Language Instinct: How the Mind Creates Language.* New York: William Morrow.

Pinker, S. (1997). *How the Mind Works.* London: Penguin.

Pinker, S. (2002). *The Blank Slate: The Modern Denial of Human Nature.* New York: Viking.

Profet, M. (1992). Pregnancy sickness as adaptation: A deterrent to maternal ingestion of teratogens. In J. H. Barkow, L. Cosmides, & J. Tooby (Eds.), *The Adapted Mind: Evolutionary Psychology and the Generation of Culture* (pp. 327–365). New York: Oxford University Press.

Profet, M. (1993). Menstruation as a defense against pathogens transported by sperm. *Quarterly Review of Biology, 68*(3), 335–386.

Rendell, L., & Whitehead, H. (2001). Culture in whales and dolphins. *Behavioral and Brain Sciences, 24*, 309–382.

Reynolds, V., Falger, V., & Vine, I. (Eds.). (1987). *The Sociobiology of Ethnocentrism: Evolutionary Dimensions of Xenophobia, Discrimination, Racism and Nationalism.* London and Sydney: Croom Helm.

Richerson, P. J., & Boyd, R. (1999). Complex societies: The evolutionary origins of a crude superorganism. *Human Nature, 10*, 253–289.

Richerson, P. J., & Boyd, R. (2001). Institutional evolution in the Holocene: The rise of complex societies. In W. G. Runciman (Ed.), *The Origin of Human Social Institutions* (pp. 197–234). Proceedings of the British Academy, vol. 110. Oxford and New York: Oxford University Press.

Richerson, P. J., & Boyd, R. (2004). *Not by Genes Alone: How Culture Transformed Human Evolution.* Chicago: University of Chicago Press.

Ridley, M. (1997). *The Origins of Virtue: Human Instincts and the Evolution of Cooperation.* New York: Viking.

Ridley, M. (2000). *Genome: The Autobiography of a Species in 23 Chapters.* New York: HarperCollins.

Rubin, P. H. (2002). *Darwinian Politics: The Evolutionary Origin of Freedom.* New Brunswick, NJ: Rutgers University Press.

Runciman, W. G. (1998). *The Social Animal.* Hammersmith, London: HarperCollins.

Runciman, W. G. (Ed.). (2001). *The Origins of Human Social Institutions, Vol. 110.* London: British Academy.

Runciman, W. G., Maynard Smith, J., & Dunbar, R. I. M. (1996). *Evolution of Behaviour Patterns in Primates and Man. A Joint Discussion Meeting of the Royal Society and the British Academy.* Oxford: Published for the British Academy by Oxford University Press.

Russell, B. (1946). *The Problems of Philosophy*. Oxford: Oxford University Press.

Sacks, O. W. (1990). *Awakenings*. New York: HarperPerennial.

Sacks, O. W. (1995a). *An Anthropologist on Mars: Seven Paradoxical Tales*. New York: Knopf.

Sacks, O. W. (1995b). *The Man Who Mistook His Wife for a Hat and Other Clinical Tales*. New York: Summit Books.

Sahlins, M. D. (1976). *Culture and Practical Reason*. Chicago: University of Chicago Press.

Samuelson, L. (1997). *Evolutionary Games and Equilibrium Selection*. Cambridge, MA: MIT Press.

Sanderson, S. K. (2001). *The Evolution of Human Sociality: A Darwinian Conflict Perspective*. Lanham, MD: Rowman & Littlefield.

Scheper-Hughes, N. (1998). Truth and rumor on the organ trail. *Natural History, 107*(8), 48–57.

Scheper-Hughes, N. (1999). One previous owner. *New Scientist, 164*(2217), 48–49.

Scheper-Hughes, N. (2000). The global traffic in human organs. *Current Anthropology, 41*(2), 191–224.

Schubert, G., & Masters, R. D. (1991). *Primate Politics*. Carbondale: Southern Illinois University Press.

Segal, N. L., & Bouchard, T. J. (1999). *Entwined Lives: Twins and What They Tell Us about Human Behavior*. New York: Penguin Putnam.

Segerstråle, U. (2000). *Defenders of the Truth: The Battle for Science in the Sociobiology Debate and Beyond*. New York: Oxford University Press.

Shaw, R. P., & Wong, Y. (1988). *Genetic Seeds of Warfare: Evolution, Nationalism, and Patriotism*. Boston: Unwin Hyman.

Shoemaker, P. J. (1996). Hardwired for news: Using biological and cultural evolution to explain the surveillance function. *Journal of Communication, 46*(3), 32–47.

Singer, P. (2000). *A Darwinian Left: Politics, Evolution, and Cooperation*. New Haven, CT: Yale University Press.

Skyrms, B. (1996). *Evolution of the Social Contract*. Cambridge: Cambridge University Press.

Smuts, B. (1995). The evolutionary origins of patriarchy. *Human Nature, 6*(1), 1–32.

Sperber, D. (1994). The modularity of thought and the epidemiology of representations. In L. Hirschfeld & S. Gelman (Eds.), *Mapping the Mind*. Cambridge: Cambridge University Press.

Sperber, D. (1996). *Explaining Culture: A Naturalistic Approach*. Oxford: Blackwell.

Spiro, M. E. (1996). Narcissus in Asia. *Ethos, 24*(1), 165–191.

Stevens, A., & Price, J. (1996). *Evolutionary Psychiatry: A New Beginning*. London and New York: Routledge.

Stitch, S. (1996). *Deconstructing the Mind*. New York: Oxford University Press.

Storey, R. (1996). *Mimesis and the Human Animal: On the Biogenetic Foundations of Literary Representation.* Evanston, IL: Northwestern University Press.

Strauss, C., & Quinn, N. (1997). *A Cognitive Theory of Cultural Meaning.* Cambridge: Cambridge University Press.

Takahasi, K. (1998). Evolution of transmission bias in cultural inheritance. *Journal of Theoretical Biology, 190*(2), 147–159.

Takahasi, K. (1999). Theoretical aspects of the mode of transmission in cultural inheritance. *Theoretical Population Biology, 55*(2), 208–225.

Tiger, L., & Shepher, J. (1975). *Women in the Kibbutz.* New York: Harcourt Brace Jovanovich.

Trevathan, W. R., Smith, E. O., & McKenna, J. J. (Eds.). (1999). *Evolutionary Medicine.* New York: Oxford University Press.

Van den Berghe, P. (1979). *Human Family Systems: An Evolutionary View.* New York: Elsevier.

Van den Berghe, P. (1981). *The Ethnic Phenomenon.* New York: Elsevier.

Van den Berghe, P. (1990). Why most sociologists don't (and won't) think evolutionarily. *Sociological Forum, 5,* 173–186.

Vandermassen, G. (2005). *Who's Afraid of Charles Darwin? Debating Feminism and Evolutionary Theory.* Lanham, MD: Rowman & Littlefield.

Von Glasersfeld, E. (1991). Knowing without metaphysics: Aspects of the radical constructivist position. In F. Steier (Ed.), *Research and Reflexivity* (pp. 12–29). London: Sage.

Von Glasersfeld, E. (1995). *Radical Constructivism: A Way of Knowing and Learning.* London: Falmer Press.

Wallace, A. F. C. (1970). *Culture and Personality* (2nd ed.). New York: Random House.

Wallin, N. L., Merker, B., & Brown, S. (Eds.). (2000). *The Origins of Music.* Cambridge, MA: MIT Press.

Weaver, C. (2000). Heartburn. *New York Times* on the Web. Retrieved Feb. 13, 2000, from http://www.nytimes.com/books/00/02/13/reviews/000213.13weavert.html

Weibull, J. W. (1995). *Evolutionary Game Theory.* Cambridge, MA: MIT Press.

Wilson, D. S. (2002). *Darwin's Cathedral: Evolution, Religion, and the Nature of Society.* Chicago: University of Chicago Press.

Wilson, E. O. (1998). *Consilience: The Unity of Knowledge.* New York: Knopf.

Wrangham, R., & Peterson, D. (1996). *Demonic Males: Apes and the Origins of Human Violence.* Boston: Houghton Mifflin.

Wrangham, R. W., McGrew, W. C., de Waal, F. B. M., & Heltne, P. G. (1994). *Chimpanzee Cultures.* Cambridge, MA: Harvard University Press.

Wright, R. (1994). *The Moral Animal: The New Science of Evolutionary Psychology.* New York: Pantheon.

Young, P. H. (2001). *Individual Strategy and Social Structure: An Evolutionary Theory of Institutions.* Princeton, NJ: Princeton University Press.

PART I

Gender

Anne Campbell's chapter represents a feminist evolutionary psychologist reaching out her hand to feminist social constructionists. Her message to other feminists is similar to that of Peter Singer's message to Marxists (discussed in the Introduction): your mistaken beliefs about biology are getting in the way of your major goals. Campbell shows how the concept of social construction, taken to an extreme, is as intellectually untenable as the idea that we can analyze discourses that privilege hegemonic interests while simultaneously ignoring the attitudes, beliefs, and other representations that the hegemonic interests are seeking to influence! Underlying what most social scientists today refer to as "gender differences" to emphasize their social constructionist nature are sex differences, population differences between males and females that reflect the evolutionary history of our species. Campbell's strong feminism is reflected in her final section, in which she calls for a removal of all constraints so that we can see whether the evolutionary psychologists are right—and, in the process, achieve social justice for women. (For additional discussion of evolution and feminist theory, see Griet Vandermassen's recent monograph, *Who's Afraid of Charles Darwin? Debating Feminism and Evolutionary Theory* [2005]. Vandermassen, like Campbell, finds considerable compatibility between feminism and evolutionary psychology.)

Daniel Fessler begins by explaining why our species should have been selected for the male "flash" of anger, how it apparently would have been quite adaptive in earlier environments and why it should be more marked in males than in females, and how other species have evolved equivalent behaviors under similar circumstances. He goes on to explain the hormonal bases of the flash of anger, and how childhood experience shapes that flash. Then he shows how, in some environments (e.g., pastoralism), it continues to be valuable even today, while in environments in which success and even survival itself depends on cooperation, there is a strong and explicit socialization and social pressure to control anger at all times. Fessler's is an example of a vertically integrated account (discussed in the Introduction): compatible explanations at multiple levels (in this case, the evolutionary, hormonal, psychological, and ecological) are presented in ways that emphasize their complementarity, rather than the usual academic approach of privileging one disciplinary or subdisciplinary level and type of explanation while treating other types of explanation as competing or at best ancillary. Fessler could have discussed the flash of anger in terms of serotonin metabolism and then derided "sociological" accounts, or he might have presented the evolutionary psychology analysis in isolation, ignoring cross-cultural variability. Instead, he shows how varying accounts are complementary and strengthen one another. His inclusiveness and comfort with integrated explanation represents the direction the social sciences must take if they are to escape their current ghettoization and regain public respect.

2   Feminism and Evolutionary Psychology

Anne Campbell

Feminism is a social movement and political program aimed at ameliorating the position of women in society. This is a goal endorsed by women and men from a variety of backgrounds—including a very large number of evolutionary psychologists. They have written at length about practices such as patriarchy, men's proprietary attitudes toward women, wife abuse, the sexual double standard, the importance of female competition, and the devaluing of mothering (e.g., Dickemann, 1997; Hrdy, 1999; Jolly, 1999; Gowaty, 1997; Smuts, 1995; Wilson & Daly, 1992). Nonetheless, for many feminists in the social sciences, evolutionary psychologists are still seen as the enemy. One important reason for this lies with fundamental differences, not about the desirability of social change, but about if and where the causes of gender differences can be found.

As feminism has matured, it has also diversified. Although as many as nine different "feminisms" have been identified (Percy, 1998; Rosser, 1997), academic feminists can be broadly trichotomized into *social constructionists* (who reject scientific method as it is usually understood) and liberals (who accept scientific method but seek to redress the past androcentrism of the topics studied and conclusions reached). Liberals in turn can be further split into those who see gender differences as a result of cultural practices (*environmental liberals*) and those who believe that a full understanding must encompass a recognition of the role of natural and sexual selection (*evolutionary liberals*).

In this chapter, I want to do three things: I will consider the light that has been shed on our understanding of gender differences first, by social constructionists and second, by environmental liberals. In both cases, I will highlight points of divergence and potential convergence with evolutionary approaches. (Because of my own disciplinary background, many of the stances and studies to which I refer are drawn from the psychological literature. Nonetheless, the positions that I discuss—interpretative and discursive analysis of gender, the enculturation of the child into his or her gender role, the division of labor in society as reproducing gender relations—are familiar ones in other social science disciplines.) Finally, I will directly address the criticisms of evolutionary psychology made by social constructionist and environmental liberal feminists and question the "illusory correlation" that has been promulgated between explanation and ideology.

Social Constructionists and Gender

A paradoxically positivistic study by Unger (1996) confirms the fact that most self-identified feminists reject traditional views of science. She developed a 40-item unipolar scale to measure epistemological preference for positivism versus constructionism. In a sample of U.S. college students, she found no gender or race differences. She did find that women enrolled in feminist courses and women who considered themselves to be actively involved in feminist groups had significantly higher scores on constructionism. Feminist psychologists who were leaders of the Psychology of Women Division of the American Psychological Association had "the most constructionist epistemology I have ever measured" (Unger, 1996, p. 171). They were particularly high on items that involved rejection of biological causality and of the value of science for solving human problems. (Although Unger's sample focused on psychologists, there is every reason to suppose that feminists in other social science disciplines would have produced similar results; see Farnham, 1987; Haraway, 1988; Harding, 1986, 1987). These two areas form part of a feminist epistemology, the essence of which is captured by Keller (1985, p. 9) in her statement "the logical extension of the personal as political is the scientific as personal."

Social Constructionism and Epistemology

In Table 2.1, I have tried to summarize the arguments adduced against positivism and in favor of social constructionism by social scientists from a variety of disciplines (Burman, 1990; Burr, 1998; Clifford & Marcus, 1986; Oakley, 1981; Strathern, 1987; Visweswaran, 1994; Wilkinson, 1986, 1996).

Table 2.1 Positivist and Feminist Constructionist Paradigms Compared

Relationships

Detachment	→	Emotional engagement/empathy
Objectivity	→	Subjectivity
Distance	→	Intersubjectivity
Sex differences	→	Individual differences between women

Politics

Political neutrality	→	Overtly stated political (feminist) position
Disinterest	→	Commitment
Knowledge for society	→	Personal development for researcher, empowerment for women
Psychology	→	Antipsychology

Methods

Seeks universal laws	→	Seeks socially and historically situated subjectivities
Transcendent nature of truth	→	Provisional and changing subjectivities
Research quality judged by validity criteria, e.g., control of confounding. variables, replicability, generalizability	→	Research quality judged against experiential resonance, researcher's ideology, ability to improve women's lives

At least three broad areas of concern are woven together into this alternative paradigm: relationships, politics, and methods.

First, at an interpersonal level, constructionist feminists seek to obliterate boundaries between the researcher and the researched in order to remove (or at least disguise) differential power in the relationship. This springs in part from an appreciation of women's greater connectedness to others, variously called communion (Bakan, 1966), expressiveness (Spence, Helmreich, & Stapp, 1974) and femininity (Bem, 1974), and from a rejection of masculine interpersonal detachment, which is seen as quasi-pathological:

> A science that advertises itself as revealing a reality in which subject and object are unmistakably distinct may perhaps offer special comfort to those who, as individuals (be they male or female) retain particular anxiety about the loss of autonomy. . . . The attempt to delineate absolutely between self and other represents a miscarriage of development, or at the very least "a development that has somehow gone too far." (Keller, 1985, pp. 90, 101)

Women's "natural" empathy is seen not as an obstacle to impartial observation but rather as an asset that affords them a different "way of knowing" (Belenky, Clinchy, Goldberger, & Tarule, 1986). This empathy is endorsed even in the nonhuman sciences; "If you want to understand about a tumour, you've got to be a tumour" (Goodfield, 1981, p. 213). Allied to this is an orientation toward the idiographic or at least an avoidance of generalization: Each woman is unique, and sweeping statements about women in general or classes of women are viewed with suspicion.

The second strand of thought is an explicit acknowledgment of the political nature of feminist research (Cole & Phillips, 1995). Its aim is to improve the lives of women ("The information-gathering purpose of research thus takes second place to a facilitative and liberatory one" [Burr, 1998, p. 139]), rather than to serve existing patriarchal institutions. Because no firm line is drawn between the researcher and the researched, the fruits of feminist research benefit the former as much as the latter ("Inquiry, as I have portrayed it, is an uncertain, vulnerable process with immense potential for personal growth and intellectual creativity" [Marshall, 1986, p. 208]). It is clear that the feminist political agenda takes precedence over "malestream" social science. Psychologist Celia Kitzinger (1990, pp. 121–122) is blunt in her denouncement: "Having identified psychology as incompatible with feminism because of its refusal to deal with political realities, and its pretence at objectivity, feminists with a professional involvement in the discipline then sought to redefine and harness psychology for the feminist cause." In extremis, this has lead to the wholesale rejection of psychology as conflicting with feminist ideology: "The antipsychology approach [which grants all psychological data and theories a severely limited validity, or even rejects them completely] is the one which I shall argue offers most to feminist psychology" (Squire, 1990, p. 79).

Third, and stemming from the previous two concerns, there is a postmodern rejection of the possibility of objective truths and causal relations and consequently of "grand" theories. The researcher should aim to document the lived experience of women as it is told to her, but in so doing she must avoid the trap of thinking that she has privileged access to the internal lives of the participants: "The aim of the analysis is not to reveal what the person truly thinks or feels . . . but to identify the discourses, representations and ideologies which are flowing through a person's talk in order to theorize how our representations of ourselves are linked to inequalities and power relations" (Burr, 1998, p. 142). Discourses are the tools that construct facts and interpret experience. Because discourses are historically and socially bound, no general statements can be made about the nature of women's experiences. Because facts about human behavior do not have an independent existence, the traditional means by which positivistic scientists establish and check them become not only irrelevant but burdensome: "Many researchers use qualitative methods positivistically, trying to pin down and constrain their data into incontestable, replicable, generalized, detached truths. This approach limits the method's potential and burdens qualitative research with inappropriate criteria of validity" (Marshall, 1986, p. 194). Instead, research should be judged by: (1) qualities of the researcher such as "reflexivity" (the capacity to reflect upon the interaction between her own value judgments and the research material) or political convictions ("only those whose 'consciousness has been raised' in relation to feminism can do feminist research" [Wilkinson, 1986, p. 17]); (2) the ability of the research to change and improve women's lives (Jayaratne, 1983); and (3) the extent to which the findings resonate with or confirm other women's experience, including that of the researcher ("One hallmark of feminist research . . . seems to be the investigator's continual testing of the plausibility of work against her own experience" [Parlee, 1979, p. 130]).

Discourses of Patriarchy

Gender, for social constructionists, is effectively removed from the human mind and instead allowed to float freely in an insubstantial ether as a "social construction," "situated discourse," or "interpretative repertoire." To give a flavor of their approach to gender differences, I quote from one of the most frequently cited writers of this genre (Hollway, 1984, pp. 227–228):

> Hence recurrent day-to-day practices and meanings through which they acquire their effectivity may contribute to the maintenance of gender difference (reproduction without a hyphen) or to its modification (the production of modified meanings of gender leading to changed practices). . . . I am interested in theorising the practices and meanings which re-produce gendered subjectivity (what psychologists would call gender identity). . . . Gender differentiated meanings (and thus the positions differentially available in discourse) account for the content of gender difference.

In this article, Hollway goes on to explain how different discourses about sexuality locate women and men in relation to one another. She writes of the "discourse" of the stronger male sex drive, the "discourse" of the Madonna-whore distinction, and the permissive "discourse" which appeared to (but did not) liberate women's sexuality.

In discourse analysis, the question of whether the social world that people construct in dialogue might have any basis in fact is rarely addressed. But this would seem to be a key question. Before assuming that cultural forces have shaped adherence to a pluralistic fiction about sex differences (and without denying that this can happen, as I will later discuss), it might be useful to examine whether people's discourses are in fact reasonable approximations to the state of the world. If they are, then men's sex drive should be stronger—and it is (Oliver & Hyde, 1993). Women should experience a reputation cost if they gain a reputation for promiscuity—and they do (Cashdan, 1996). Women should find casual sexual liaisons less satisfactory than men—and they do (Townsend, Kline, & Wasserman, 1995). In Hollway's examples, then, the term "discourse" seems to describe the way in which human experience is represented in everyday talk between people.

This question of whether ideas that are promulgated through discourse are veridical is one that constructionists finesse because they reject the methods by which "facts" and "truth" are established. But in a crucial way, their avoidance of this question places them in a very awkward position in relation to their aims of both representing women's experiences and improving women's lives. Constructionists' analyses of women's experiences are negotiable, provisional, and subjective "glosses" of women's negotiable, provisional, and subjective discourse about themselves. Since there is no "self," aside from its situated constitution in text, it makes no sense to lay claim to "accuracy" in any description of women's lives since the term is meaningless without a criterion for factuality. In addition, if there are no facts (encapsulated in Derrida's famous dictum "There is nothing outside the text"), then constructionists are forced to concede that men's historical oppression of women, the suffering of abused wives, and working women's inability to break through the glass ceiling are not facts but situated social constructions.

Most social constructionists do not in reality subscribe to such an extreme position. They acknowledge the existence of a material physical world, parts of which we can accurately access through our senses. They implicitly accept that the "invisible" portion of the physical world is governed by general laws that allow humans to do such things as exploit electricity and create nuclear fusion. In the realm of the biological, most accept that pathogens exist and can be fought by the body's natural immune system and with synthetic antibiotics. Facts about the brain, the organ that runs the mind, also seems to be generally accepted: most would agree that brain damage can cause selective impairment of functioning and that drugs which alleviate mental illness work by altering the chemical balance of neurotransmission. Skepticism about empiricism and the status of "facts" seems to be reserved chiefly for matters of the mind and, within that arena, facts about the social world (experiences, preferences, opinions) seem to be treated especially skeptically. "Facts" that have been established by traditional empirical methods (e.g., women's dissatisfaction with positivism) are often accepted when they concur with feminist aims. But when faced with uncomfortable empirical findings that indicate unwanted gender differences (of the kind I mentioned above in attitudes or preferences about sexual relations), a frequent response is to query the "flawed" empirical method that was used to generate them.

But pointing to the wrong-headed political agenda of the researcher misses the point that the responses came from ordinary members of the public who have no particular ideological axe to grind. Certainly bias can be introduced by the way questions are posed and by the interaction between researcher and participant, but increasingly meta-analytic and meta-ethnographic conclusions are based on dozens, often hundreds, of studies whereby error, being random, is canceled out. If we do not accord research participants the right to have their voices heard, even when their responses depart from our own ideological or theory-driven preferences, we do them a gross disservice by privileging the researchers' selective interpretation of their views over their own voices. When research participants tell us uncomfortable truths, our aim should not be to select, edit, dilute, or prejudge them as products of false consciousness or unresolved conflicts. Traditional empirical method may not be perfect, but it has the advantage of being a self-correcting system that allows every research participant to make a difference. By being open, clear, and nonselective in how data is collected and analyzed, we make replication possible so that errors can be uncovered and corrected.

Social constructionists not only refuse to seriously address the possibility of a social reality beyond the text (that may or may not be accurately represented in discourse) but are equally reluctant to consider the origins of everyday discourses. If the stronger male sex drive *is* a collective fiction, then where did it originate? Which sex benefits from it? Why is it not disconfirmed by thousands of women's own experience? At what age and how do young people acquire it? These are, we are told, illegitimate "mechanical" questions:

> But to assume the mechanical reproduction of discourse requires asking how it got to be like that in the first place. And that question is in danger of throwing theory back into answers according to the terms of biological, Oedipal or social and economic determinisms. (Hollway, 1984, pp. 238–239)

Because constructionist feminists reject determinism of any sort, they are reluctant to invoke causes, and without causes there is no basis for theory construction in the traditional sense. A theory is usually taken to be a higher-order explanation from which local hypotheses can be derived and tested. The term "feminist theory" often amounts to some variant of the declaration that women have been and continue to be oppressed by men, which is an observation rather than an explanation. Aside from socialist and Marxist feminists, who postulate an economic cause in the form of capitalism, most feminist perspectives do not ask why or in what domains men should seek to dominate women but turn their attention to the means by which gender relations are reproduced across generations (discourse, socialization, unconscious conflicts, etc.). Gender discourse becomes an autonomous, sui generis abstraction, irreducible to the people who carry it. The "how" question is addressed at the expense of the "why" question.

Evolutionary Approaches to Patriarchy

Evolutionary psychology seeks to explain the origins and functions of men's oppression of women in a way that carries with it a specification of the particular domains in which it would be advantageous to men to control them. It is in this arena that evolutionary feminists have been particularly vocal in drawing attention both to the gender inequalities that we share with other mammals and to the peculiarly lopsided power relations seen in our own species.

At the biological heart of sex differences lies anisogamy—the vastly unequal size (and consequent energetic cost) of gametes contributed by male and female in sexual reproduction. As Williams (1996, p. 118) points out, anisogamy marks the start of male exploitation of females. "When egg-producers reproduce, they must bear the entire nutritional burden of nurturing the offspring. By contrast, the sperm-makers reproduce for free. A sperm is not a contribution to the next generation; it is a claim on contributions put into the egg by another individual. Males of most species make no investments in the next generation, but merely compete with one another for the opportunity to exploit investments made by females." When combined with internal fertilization, the stage is set for an even greater inequality in parental investment for two main reasons. First, the cost to the female of abandoning the embryo or newborn is far greater than to the male. At any given point in time she has made the greater commitment to the offspring (in terms of time and energy) and will suffer a higher replacement cost if she deserts it (all the more true in humans, where her reproductive future is truncated by menopause). Second, internal fertilization introduces uncertainty about paternity. While a female need never doubt that the offspring to which she gives birth is her own, males must entertain the possibility of cuckoldry. The degree of paternal care depends, across species, on the male's certainty that he is the biological father. Doubt reduces the likelihood of male investment and leaves the mother "holding the baby." For these reasons, in over 90% of mammals, it is the female who exclusively cares for the young. As primates, humans are remarkable on three counts. First, they must cope with a very protracted period of infant dependency. Babies are born, biologically speaking, about nine months prematurely so that the huge cranium can pass through the pelvis—a channel that could not grow larger without compromising the mother's bipedal locomotion. Sexual maturity is

not attained for 12 to 14 years because an extensive learning period is required to master the complexity of the social environment that humans
must navigate. Second, humans display a very high degree of paternal care
relative to other primates. Men did not elect this route as a favor to
women—selection does not favor strategies that selflessly benefit others at a
net cost to the donor. Polygyny (men taking multiple mates) can offer huge
reproductive benefits to a man, but the sheer mathematics of the situation
mean that a high proportion of the less desirable will fail to reproduce at
all—and may not even survive the intense degree of male competition that
polygyny engenders. The prizes are high, but the odds are strongly stacked
against winning. For most men, it would be more advantageous to remain
with one woman and increase the likelihood of their joint offspring surviving than to court multiple women whose offspring had a low survival probability for lack of male investment. Third, human males are also notable for
the degree of control that they exercise over their mates. These three facts
are not unconnected. The high and protracted dependence of young growing humans means that they benefit from care by both parents. These long-
term costs are only likely to be met by males who have high levels of paternal
certainty. That certainty requires close mate guarding of female partners.

These fundamental facts lie at the heart of evolutionary feminist theories of the emergence of patriarchy in human societies (Campbell, 2002;
Gowaty, 1992; Hrdy, 1997; Smuts, 1995). In the ancestral environment in
which humans evolved, women (unlike most primate females) emigrated
from their natal group, weakening their bonds with kin. In these hunter-
gatherer societies, women gathered most of the calories consumed by local
foraging. They were relatively free from resource dependence on men, and
in such societies today, women have considerable latitude to establish and
end sexual relationships as they see fit (Shostak, 1990).

A mere 10,000 years ago (perhaps only a tenth of the period during
which *Homo sapiens* has existed) came agriculture and animal husbandry.
Not only diet and lifestyle but the very structure of societies began to
change. Women no longer foraged in independent sorties with their children
but were confined to the local fields or to the home. It became easier for men
to monitor and control their whereabouts. At the same time, as men made
a greater contribution to women's food supply, they became increasingly
concerned with controlling women's sexuality in order to ensure their own
paternal certainty. Evolutionary feminists have been in the forefront of cat-
aloging the extreme and repugnant measures to which men will go to
achieve this end. Even today women in some societies must cover themselves from head to foot to deter the possibility of arousing male interest. In
others, women may not leave their home without supervision. Even today,
infibulation (vaginal suturing) is still used to ensure women's virginity at
marriage and clitoridectomy to eliminate the possibility of their seeking

sexual pleasure (Dickemann, 1997). Until this century, in many countries, adultery was a crime that was defined exclusively in terms of the marital status of the woman involved (Daly & Wilson, 1988). The very term derived from the notion of diluting or diminishing—and what was diminished was paternal certainty.

And as women came to depend more and more on the resources provided by males, it became increasingly risky to resist male control. Under agriculture, wealth differentials between men increased because surplus resources could be stored and traded—unlike the day-to-day, hand-to-mouth existence of hunter-gatherer peoples. So differences in status and power among men became more marked. In these circumstances the value of cooperation between women was reduced because each woman could do better by competing for the best male than by creating alliances with other unrelated women. Women's own kin colluded in this by bartering their infant daughters' futures, supporting surgical interventions and medical examinations to ensure their virginity, and even murdering those who engaged in premarital sex. Martin Daly and Margo Wilson (1988) have documented how custom and law around the world have until quite recently accepted the right of a man to use violence to protect his exclusive access to his wife's sexuality. In Texas until 1974, a killing was justified (and hence subject to no criminal sanction) when it was committed by a man who had found his wife in flagrante delicto. Even where the killing is subject to criminal penalty, Western law since 1803 considers a man in this situation guilty of the lesser crime of manslaughter, rather than murder, because of the high degree of provocation involved (despite the fact that during this same period, a woman who killed a persistently abusive husband was not considered to have been provoked [Campbell, 1993]). The vast majority of cases of spousal homicide and abuse derive from men's attempts to control their wife's sexuality (Wilson, Daly, & Scheib, 1997). The possibility of infidelity is read into any independent action on her part—from spending too long talking to a man at a party to expressing a desire to attend college or take a job. The attentive concern that a woman appreciated early in the relationship reveals itself to be, or escalates into, an obsessive tyranny. So extreme can this become that a man, after being abandoned, may hunt down and kill his ex-wife before taking his own life. She has become a chattel, a piece of property (Wilson & Daly, 1992). If he cannot have her, nobody will.

So evolutionary feminists locate patriarchy initially in the reproductive interests of males under conditions of uncertain paternity and protracted paternal investment. Superimposed upon and enhancing these biological factors came the cultural developments of agriculture and industrialization, which increased the wealth differentials between men and thus decreased the potential for female solidarity. But note that this does not amount to saying, as some socialist feminists have, that capitalism causes patriarchy. A cursory historical analysis shows that patriarchy is as evident in feudal and agricultural societies as in capitalist societies. Exaggerated wealth differentials between men arising from any cause will enhance the benefits of women attempting to "marry up" rather than establishing strong female coalitions—as long as women are forced into economic dependence on men.

Discourse, Deception, and Evolutionary Psychology

With some trepidation, I would offer the following encapsulation of the social constructionist agenda. First, it is concerned with versions or interpretations of reality that are constructed through language. Second, it is concerned with how these versions of reality are used strategically to enforce and contest power at both a macro-social level (by institutions such as governments and media [e.g., Henriques, Hollway, Urwin, Venn, & Walkerdine, 1984]) and at a micro-social, interpersonal level (to warrant, blame, excuse, and so on [Edwards & Potter, 1992]). For feminist constructionists, the chief focus of interest is in how these processes shape our understanding and experience of gender. Can we find any points of commonality between these interests and those of evolutionary psychology, a discipline often characterized by outsiders as a fundamentally biological and behavioral one?

Many evolutionary theorists acknowledge that "purely biological models will not be able to supply a full account of human behavior without references to cultural processes" (Janicki & Krebs, 1998, p. 202). For evolutionists, culture is *shared* knowledge—knowledge that has not arisen through the interaction of innate modules and the environment (e.g., our universal tendency to break the electromagnetic spectrum into discrete and consensual categories called colors) nor by individual trial-and-error learning and insight (an individual primate's discovery that sweet potatoes immersed in water are less gritty when eaten). Writing, reading, computer literacy, driving cars, and eating with cutlery are all cultural in this sense. The evolution, transmission, and selection of socially acquired knowledge (in the form of representations, memes, or semantic memory nodes) has been at the heart of a number of evolutionary formulations (e.g., Barkow, 1989; Boyd & Richerson, 1985; Dawkins, 1989; Durham, 1991; Janicki & Krebs, 1998; Lumsden & Wilson, 1981; Tooby & Cosmides, 1992). All agree that the capacity for social learning evolved because its superiority over individual trial-and-error learning brought fitness benefits. Individual learning is specific, costly, and potentially dangerous, while social learning is generalizable, cheap, and safe. Technical knowledge can be passed on by simple observation and imitation, and much work has addressed these capacities in our own and other primate species. Many motor skills that are vital for survival can be acquired in this way.

But humans are able to do far more than merely imitate behavior. When an apprentice watches a carpenter constructing a piece of furniture, she does not copy her obvious mistakes. The observer does not assume that hitting one's thumb with the hammer is an integral part of the production process (Dawkins, 1999). What allows the observer to understand the real goals of the carpenter? To open up the problem more widely, what allows us to understand the beliefs and desires of others and to comprehend the intentionality of their behavior? Tooby and Cosmides (1992, p. 118) use the term "epidemiological culture" to describe the process whereby "observation and interaction between the source and the observer cause inferential mechanisms in the observer to recreate the representations or regulatory elements in his or her own psychological architecture." This inferential mechanism has received considerable scrutiny in recent years under the term "theory of mind." Developmentally, theory of mind starts with belief-desire reasoning from manifest behavior, in the form "Sally is looking in the box because she *believes* her toy is there and she *wants* to find it" (Whiten, 1991). From there children progress to second-order and then third-order reasoning ("Sally [or Ann] *knows* that Peter *thinks* that Sally *believes* that the toy she wants is in the box").

The concept has been of special interest to evolutionary psychologists, who have argued that its universal, untutored appearance (at about the age of four), independence from intelligence, and capacity for selective impairment strongly suggests an evolved information-processing module (Anderson, 1983; Baron-Cohen, 1997). The fitness advantages of such a module are proposed to result from the highly social living arrangements of primate species. The ability to read the mind of others allows for the appraisal of others' beliefs, the prediction of their likely behavior, and the consequent possibility of tactical manipulation (Byrne & Whiten, 1988; Dunbar, 1993; Humphrey, 1976; Jolly, 1966). Through the deliberate misrepresentation of one's own or others' beliefs or desires, third parties can be led to behave in ways congruent with these "engineered" false beliefs. In language and mind reading, we find the basic building blocks of dialectical social construction: a piece of discourse alerts a listener to the internal representation held by the speaker, and in understanding this, she is in a position to manipulate it.

Deception is common in the animal world, evident in both mimicry and camouflage. The fitness advantages of deception are clear. However, the kinds of deception practiced by humans are of another kind in that they are neither morphological nor long-standing and can be deployed at a linguistic and therefore representational level. Social constructionists address how language is used to create versions of reality that are advantageous to the communicator. Some of these versions of reality are tactically deceptive in the sense that they are not veridical and may work to the disadvantage of the receiver.

At a societal level, social constructionists are concerned with how powerful groups transmit and sustain versions of reality that are congenial to the maintenance of their power. Many beliefs that have historically been held about gender (e.g., education will interfere with women's childbearing capabilities, women's superego is weaker than men's) effectively oppose women's own fitness interests (their ability to garner resources independently or to make their own moral decisions). Durham (1991) calls these beliefs "oppositional" memes and proposes that they most often result from imposition by the powerful. This chimes very directly with the analysis offered by feminist evolutionary psychologists in terms of men's control over resources needed by women and their consequent ability to impose unilaterally advantageous memes. Barbara Smuts (1995) suggests that with the advent of language a new weapon became available to men in their control of women. Language could be used to develop myths and ideologies that legitimated their power. Patricia Gowaty (1992, p. 237) writes of "society-wide lies that foster sexist oppression" in the context of male control of females' reproductive opportunities and independent access to resources.

But where evolutionary psychology moves into the arena of deceptive communication, it also takes on the need to establish truth as an anchor point. If a man believes that women have poor spatial skills and communicates this belief to his wife, then no deception has occurred even if his premise is incorrect. His choice to "disclose" this fact to her might well be tactical and manipulative, but it is not deceptive. If, however, he knows the truth to be otherwise, then his communication is deceptive. This draws attention firmly to the state of mind of the communicator and specifically to representational thought—versions of the world that exist in the minds of people prior to their expression in language. Constructionists are eager to avoid reducing discourse (which they see as an emergent property of social talk) to a psychological construct. Researchers are admonished to avoid any tendency to reduce discursive findings to properties of individual people (i.e., as reflecting "cognitivist" internal models of the world):

> Discourse analysis has eschewed any form of cognitive reductionism, any explanation which treats linguistic behavior as a product of mental entities or processes, whether it is based around social representations or some other cognitive furniture such as attitudes, beliefs, goals or wants. The concern is firmly with language use; the way accounts are constructed and different functions. (Potter & Wetherell, 1987, p. 157)

Clearly, the notion of representations causes considerable discomfort to discourse analysts. For them social talk cannot reflect (accurately or deceptively) the speaker's internal working model of the world, for no such thing exists. Paradoxically, while they champion the view that people employ language manipulatively (i.e., to their own power advantage), they refuse to acknowledge the existence of the very thing that the speaker aims to manipulate—the representation held by the other party. Constructionist writing often leaves the reader with the feeling that understanding and meaning exist in a superorganic, hermeneutic universe (in a way that echoes anthropologists' treatment of culture) but never in the mind of any one person. This being the case, representations cannot guide or inform an individual's actions—either to manipulate or deceive. More moderate constructionists do not reject the notion of a mind that harbors and transmits ideas, but they do not see it as a useful avenue of social psychological study. Cognitivism, for them, is in danger of subsuming the social within the individual.

For evolutionary psychologists, however, the first step in understanding the dialectics of manipulation is to establish what beliefs reside in the minds of the parties involved and to what extent they map on to reality. Where they are suggestive of tactical manipulation, we have to ask to whose benefit they work.

Environmental Liberal Approaches to the Study of Gender

Liberal feminists share the goal of improving women's opportunities, though they do not reject empirical methods and the concept of cause. But the causes they identify are proximate and external. Proximate, in the sense that their concern is not with why gender differences exist (in terms of the wider evolutionary picture) but with how they are sustained and transmitted across generations. External, in the sense that the creation of male and female preferences, styles, and behaviors is assumed to stem from outside the child in the forces of socialization that transmit gender-appropriate behavior. Although the Standard Social Science Model as described by Tooby and Cosmides (1992) has been criticized as something of a caricature (Holcombe, 1998; H. Rose, 2000), it is perhaps nowhere more manifest than in social and developmental psychologists' accounts of sex differences.

Shaping Gender

Socialization explanations of sex differences are built on the foundation of the tabula rasa infant shaped, rewarded, and punished until it conforms to societal demands for sex-appropriate behavior. They first took shape in the era of behaviorist learning theory. The account was a simple one; parents treat boys and girls differently, reinforcing the correct behavior in each. Boys are encouraged to fight, climb trees, and play football. Girls are forced to wear dresses, play with dolls, and share. The "Baby X" paradigm was hailed as conclusive evidence of socialization differences (e.g., Will, Self, & Datan, 1976). A six-month-old baby was wrapped in a blue or a pink blanket, identified as a boy or a girl, then handed to a woman who was asked to look after it for a few minutes. When told it was a girl, the women more often offered the infant a doll in preference to other toys. Surely this showed that parents treat infants differently as a function of their biological sex?

But there was a problem. Despite many attempts at replication, the effect seemed even weaker than it had on first sight appeared (and recall the effect was found only for toy selection—there were no differences in social behavior to the infant). It was certainly not strong enough to support the whole edifice of sex differences (Stern & Karraker, 1989). And even if parents gave their children different toys, such a finding would be trivial unless it could be shown that the toys changed the child's subsequent behavior. But the real challenge came when Lytton and Romney (1991) collected from around the world 172 studies that had examined the way in which parents treat their sons and daughters. Considering them all together, the evidence for differential treatment was virtually nil. Parents did not differ in the amount of interaction with the child, the warmth they showed, their tendency to encourage either dependency or achievement, their restrictiveness, their use of discipline, their tendency to reason with the child, or the amount of aggression that they tolerated. There was one area that showed a difference. Parents tended to give their children sex-appropriate toys. But sex-differentiated toy preference has been found in infants from nine months of age (Campbell, Shirley, Heywood, & Crook, 2000). Children play more with sex-appropriate toys even when their parents do not specifically encourage them to do so (Caldera, Huston, & O'Brien, 1989). It is quite likely that parents are not using toys to turn their children into gender conformists but are simply responding to the child's own preferences.

Anyway, if parents' behavior toward their children was being guided by their desire for them to conform to traditional gender stereotypes than we would expect to find that the most sex-typed adults have the most sex-typed children. Yet studies find that there is no relationship between traditional household division of labor, parents' attitudes to sex-typing, their sex-typical activities, and their reactions to children's behavior on one hand and children's degree of sex-typing on the other (Maccoby, 1998).

Following these early views of the child shaped by selective reinforcement came social learning theory, which emphasized a hitherto neglected (but altogether central primate) capacity—imitation. This was co-opted into an explanation of sex differences by proposing that children selectively imitate their same-sex parent. Laboratory studies were done in which children were exposed to adult "models" performing a variety of novel behaviors. If social learning theorists were right, then the statistical analysis would show a significant interaction between sex-of-model and sex-of-child—girls would imitate women and boys would imitate men. Dozens of such studies failed to find such an effect (Huston, 1983; Maccoby & Jacklin, 1974). Perry and Bussey (1979) devised an ingenious experiment that avoided the pitfalls of the previous studies, where children had a one-off exposure to an adult model. They showed children a film of eight adults selecting a preferred fruit. In one condition all four men made one choice (e.g., orange), while all four women made another (e.g., apple). In another condition, three men and one woman chose an orange while three women and one man chose an apple. In another condition half the men chose oranges and half the women chose apples. They found that the extent to which children copied an adult preference depended upon the proportion of their sex that made that choice. In the first condition, there was a high degree of same-sex imitation, in the second a much smaller amount, and in the third, there was no significant difference between the girls and boys in their choices. What this suggested was that children were not slavishly imitating a same-sex adult but rather judging the appropriateness of a particular (in this case wholly arbitrary) preference on the basis of the proportion of male or female adults who made it. These results helped to make sense of previous work, which had already shown that children tended to imitate activities that they already knew to be sex-typed regardless of the sex of the model who was currently engaged in it (Barkley, Ullman, Otto, & Brecht, 1977). What was important was the child's internal working model of gender and behavior.

Understanding Gender

Many developmentalists had already rebelled against the thoroughly passive view of the child constructed by learning theory. Martin and Halverson (1981) argued that children have a natural tendency to think categorically. They form categories about all sorts of things, from animals to sports, and it would be surprising if they did not, very early in life, form categories of male and female. Once these categories are formed, all incoming information that is gender-related gets shunted into the correct binary slot, and over time a stereotype is built up about what males and females look like, do, and enjoy. It is this internal model or *gender schema*, not the surveillance of parents, which drives the child toward sex-appropriate behavior. At the very same time that this proposal was being offered for child development, Bem (1974) was proposing an identical scheme to explain adult differences in sex-typing. The degree to which we "type" information as gender-relevant is an individual difference variable. Women who strongly sex-type information become more stereotypically feminine than women who are less inclined to tag information with gender labels. The cognitive revolution had come to sex differences: it was not a matter of behavioral training, it was a matter of mental categorizing, organizing, and recalling.

But gender schema theory was so cognitive that it left no room for an adapted mind. The cracks inevitably began to appear. One problem was timing: sex differences in toy choice, play styles, activity levels, and aggression are found as early as two years of age (Brooks & Lewis, 1974; Fagot, 1991; Freedman, 1974; Howes, 1988; Kohnstamm, 1989; O'Brien & Huston, 1985; Roopnarine, 1986), but children are not able to correctly sort pictures of boys and girls into piles until their third year (Weinraub, Clements, Sockloff, Ethridge, & Myers, 1984). Children prefer sex-congruent toys *before* they are able to say whether the toy is more appropriate for a boy or a girl (Blakemore, LaRue, & Olejnik, 1979). They prefer to interact with members of their own sex and show sex differences in social behavior *before* they can label different behaviors as being more common among boys or girls (Serbin, Moller, Gulko, Powlishta, & Colburne, 1994; Smetana & Letourneau, 1984). Longitudinal studies confirm that sex-typed behavior does not wait upon gender labeling (Campbell, Shirley, & Candy, under review; Fagot & Leinbach, 1989; Trautner, 1992). A second problem was correspondence: even when children's gender stereotypes crystallize and peak at about seven years of age, there is no relationship between a child's gender knowledge and how sex-stereotypic their own behavior is (Serbin et al., 1994; Martin, 1994; Powlishta, 1995). Children seem to need neither the ability to discriminate the sexes nor an understanding of gender stereotypic behavior to show sex differences.

Yet, problematic as they were, stereotypes were also invoked to form the foundation for another explanation of sex differences—social role theory (Eagly, 1987). According to this formulation the division of labor in society, rather than the child's natural tendency to form categories, is the starting point for sex differences. Men occupy roles that require competitiveness, autonomy, and aggression. Women occupy roles that require nurturance, caring, and cooperation. These roles draw out of their occupants the commensurate qualities and skills. These in turn set up stereotypes that embody beliefs in the appropriateness of expected characteristics. "Expectancy confirming behaviour should be especially common when expectancies are broadly shared in a society, as is the case for the expectancies about women and men" (Eagly, 1987, p. 15). These expectancies are internalized, resulting in sex differences in both behavior and self-perception.

During the last twenty years there has been a significant change in the nature of women's labor, as women have moved into many arenas traditionally occupied by men. We might therefore expect to see a shift in both stereotypes and self-perceptions by men and women. No such shift has occurred (Helmreich, Spence, & Gibson, 1982; Lewin & Tragos, 1987;

Lueptow, 1985; Lueptow, Garovich, & Lueptow, 1995). Furthermore, we would expect to see a fair degree of cultural specificity, with "traditional" societies showing more marked stereotypes than more egalitarian ones. We do not (Williams & Best, 1982). Social role theory supposes that sex differences are responsive to stereotypes and hence that stereotypes should be more extreme and polarized than actual sex differences. They are not (Swim, 1994). We are left with the alternative suggestion that stereotypes are reasonably accurate assessments of the typical differences between men and women. Rather than stereotypes causing sex differences, the reverse is the case. If this is true, then we at least have a means of explaining the typical division of labor between the sexes (women elect to spend more time than men do in parenting activities). Although Eagly acknowledges that two biological factors (gestation and lactation in women, and size and strength in men) may be implicated in the division of labor, for her biology stops at the neck: "This viewpoint assumes that men and women have inherited the same evolved psychological dispositions" (Eagly & Wood, 1999, p. 224). While anisogamy may have forced the reproductive burden upon women, Eagly and Wood make the implausible argument that there has been no commensurate adaptation of their goals, strategies, or preferences.

Nobody can seriously doubt that environmental and cultural factors influence the expression of sex differences. But to acknowledge the impact of culture upon the surface structure of femininity is not to say that gender has no biological basis and that the nature of men and women is wholly constructed by society. The problem with such a position is that it fails to address the issue of why sex differences take the particular form that they do. If gender differences are arbitrary, it is a curious coincidence that they follow such a similar pattern around the world (Brown, 1991; Murdock, 1981). Even if sex differences were driven by differential parental treatment, we would still want to ask why a trait is considered more desirable for one sex than another. If they were driven by selective imitation, we would still want to ask why children might show an untutored interest in their own sex. If driven by gender schema, we would need to ask why sex-specific conformity is so attractive to children. If driven by the division of labor, we still need to explain the preference of men and women for agentic and expressive occupational roles. Liberal feminists explain the transmission of the status quo—but without asking where it came from.

Objections to Evolutionary Psychology

The Politics of Human Nature

The accusation that sits at the pinnacle of feminist constructionist objections to an evolutionarily-informed psychology is political—which comes as no surprise, given the avowedly political goals of their research. Once a discipline accepts the political motive of the researcher as a criterion for the quality of research produced, it becomes legitimate to apply the "politics" criteria to other disciplines also. With considerable honesty, Fausto-Sterling (1992, p. 212), for example, writes of the difficulty that she experiences in distinguishing between "science well done and science that is feminist." Hence politics looms large in criticism of evolutionary psychology, as the following quotes show:

> Sociobiology functions as a *political* theory and program. (Bleier, 1984, p. 46)

> Evolutionary psychology is not only a new science, it is a vision of morality and social order, a guide to moral behavior and *policy agendas.* (Nelkin, 2000, p. 20)

> The biological accounts of male-female difference and male dominance that have emerged since the mid–nineteenth century have merely used the language of science, rather than the language of religion, to rationalise and *legitimise the status quo.* (Bem, 1993, p. 6)

> Ought science to be seen as truth-telling, or as *politics by other means,* or can it be both things at the same time? (Fausto-Sterling, 1992, p. 58)

A long-standing, political goal of social science disciplines has been to deny any universal human nature (male or female), to emphasize cultural variability, and, in doing so, to deny any biological basis to behavior. The denial of human universals is central to the liberal agenda because of adherents' erroneous acceptance of the naturalistic fallacy and their mistaken belief that biology is destiny. If something is universal, it may reflect fundamental human nature, and if such a thing is biological, then attempts to ameliorate the status quo are doomed. This shaky reasoning underpins the enormous kudos given to anthropologists who return with reports of novel and bizarre behavior in exotic locations. Hoaxes such as Carlos Castaneda's dissertation on Don Juan or the discovery of the Tasaday (who were inventions of the Marcos government) were eagerly and, for many years, uncritically embraced. An anthropological challenge by Margaret Mead (1935) to the traditional equation of masculinity with aggression and femininity with gentleness was also welcomed (see Daly & Wilson, 1983). She conveniently found, within a hundred-mile area, three tribes in which these equations broke down: the Arapesh (both sexes gentle), the Mundugumor (both sexes aggressive), and the Tschambuli (sex role reversal). Since that time, her claims have been discredited by other researchers (see Freeman, 1983). Although she argues that both sexes are violent in the Mundugumor, the men express it by murder, rape, and head-hunting raids, while the women express it by serving tastier dishes to their husbands than their co-wives can.

Among the allegedly gentle Arapesh, young men were initiated into adulthood only after they had committed homicide. Among the sex-role-reversed Tschambuli, the makeup worn by men celebrates their killing of an enemy, and the aggressive women were frequently beaten by their gentle husbands.

It is hard to know what to make of Fausto-Sterling's (1992, p. 199) claim that "there is no single undisputed claim about universal human behavior (sexual or otherwise)." Presumably even the most ardent cultural relativist would accept that everywhere people live in societies, that they eat, sleep, and make love, and that women give birth and men do not. Some feminist biologists refuse to engage in any debate about the evolved nature of psychological sex differences by denying that two sexes even exist. Muldoon and Reilly (1998, p. 55) believe that "the objectivity of "hard science" in this area can be questioned, so much so that the biological definition of sex itself becomes untenable." They suggest that there is no biological basis for our belief in male and female as "dichotomous, mutually exclusive categories" (see also Bem, 1993). Notwithstanding these authors' uncertainty, most feminists accept that the vast majority of the population belongs to one of two biologically distinct sexes. Indeed, most feminists acknowledge that the reproductive differences between them are the result of evolution.

The problems seem to arise when we move from biological functioning of the body to the biological functioning of the brain—which are seen as quite unrelated (Bem, 1993). Though everywhere women are the principle caretakers of children, the fact that there may be variation in how that task is fulfilled leads some anthropologists to conclude that mothering is not universal (Moore, 1988). This is analogous to arguing that because people eat different food in different parts of the world, eating is not universal. Fortunately, Donald Brown (1991), trained in the standard ethnographic tradition, has documented the extent of human universals. Of special interest to the study of gender we find: binary distinctions between men and women, division of labor by sex, more child-care by women, more aggression and violence by men, and acknowledgment of different natures of men and women.

Even though the brain is the most expensive organ in the human body in terms of calorie consumption, even though feminists accept that hominid brain size itself was a result of natural selection, and even though the production of the very hormones that orchestrate bodily differences originate in the brain, many social science feminists reject the notion that evolution could have had an impact on the minds of the two sexes. Though successful reproduction is the reason for our existence today and though the sexes play vital and different roles in that process, they reject any notion that their minds may have been sculpted by millions of years of evolution to set different goals or pursue different strategies.

Biological Determinism

Political aversion to biology springs from the mistaken belief that genetically influenced traits are unalterable. For some feminists, evolutionary psychology is the pinnacle of genetic determinism—the (erroneous) belief that genes alone direct development and behavior. Take four examples culled from many dozen similar pronouncements:

> Sociobiologists argue that these strategies are given by biology and thus imply that they are *eternally fixed* features of human sexual relations. (Sayers, 1982, p. 60)

> By reducing human behaviour and complex social phenomenon to genes and to inherited and programmed mechanisms of neuronal firing, the message of the new Wilsonian Sociobiology becomes rapidly clear: we had better resign ourselves to the fact that the more unsavoury aspects of human behavior, like wars, racism, and class struggle, are *inevitable results of evolutionary adaptations based in our genes*. (Bleier, 1984, p. 15)

> Genetic explanations of sex differences in behaviour are part of a broader wave of opinion *denying the importance of social forces* in the development of human behaviour. (Rogers, 1999, p. 50)

> Evolutionary principles imply *genetic destiny*. They de-emphasise the influence of social circumstances, for there are natural limits constraining individuals. The moral? *No possible social system*, educational or nurturing plan *can change the status quo*. (Nelkin, 2000, p. 22)

I can assure you that it is far harder to find examples of evolutionary psychologists' allegations that genes are unaffected by environment than it is to find accusations of this caricature. Responsiveness to the environment is a quality of *all* living things—a fact taught in high school biology courses. Trees planted closely together must grow taller than their neighbors to reach the sun. Animals packed too closely together must either compete or disperse if they are to survive. Maternal aggression tracks gestation and lactation; it emerges and wanes in response to life history changes. If evolutionary psychologists were in fact alleging that humans are different from the rest of the natural world—insensitive to or immune from responding to environmental change—it would be bizarre indeed. Evolutionary theory asserts that natural selection operates *on* genes, but it operates *through* the phenotype, which is the product of genes and environments. It is individuals that live or die, out-reproduce their rivals or fail to.

When evolutionary theorists speak of interactions between genes and environment, they mean it in a genuinely bidirectional sense. When critics speak of genetic determinism, it is clear that they have in mind structural genes whose activity is largely unaffected by the environment. These are the Mendelian structures that give us blue eyes or long legs. But most genes are not structural but *regulator* genes that are able to interface with the environment, affecting the way our mind works. There is nothing mystical about this. Communication in the brain occurs chiefly between neurones, where chemical messengers—neurotransmitters—convey the information across the synaptic cleft. These neurotransmitters can communicate with the nucleus of the cell, the home of the regulator genes that manage the sensitivity of receptors and the production of enzymes that create neurotransmitters. The activation or deactivation of a variety of genes as a result of experience can create differences between people who began life with exactly the same genome. Post-traumatic stress disorder, a condition that has been studied in American war veterans, clearly shows this. Exposure to intense and prolonged stress causes intracellular genetic change that results in acute neurochemical hypersensitivity to the slightest threat (Niehoff, 1999).

But more mundane environmental experiences are necessary for the normal emergence of many species-typical adaptations. Absence of contact with a language-using community can severely disrupt the development of language; early close contact with a reliable caretaker is important for optimal socioemotional functioning; and the neural structure of the visual cortex depends upon the kinds of visual experiences to which the organism is exposed. In addition, the manifestation of some species-typical adaptations depends on contemporaneous environmental cues: for example, sexual jealousy may be a human universal, but it is activated only when people experience a deep attachment to an exclusive romantic partner and perceive (rightly or wrongly) a threat to that exclusivity.

Nor do all members of animal species respond to environmental contingencies in the same way. They possess alternative strategies. Some male fish pursue a "sneaker" strategy; dwarf males are small enough that they do not elicit concern from normal-sized males and in consequence are able to sneak up on females and fertilize their eggs. In our own species, men's choice of mating tactics depends on what women want and on men's ability to provide it (Gangestad & Simpson, 2000). In societies where assistance with provisioning is more crucial to infant survival, women prefer men who may be of lesser genetic quality but who can offer greater resource commitment. In societies with high pathogen loads, women look for signs of male physical symmetry as an index of their genetic quality and disease resistance that can be passed to offspring. Men's ability to meet women's facultative preferences depends on their own resources (physical symmetry and material). Early developmental events may be especially important in channeling individuals into different pathways by setting different expectations about the environment. Father-absent children, raised with the expectation that paternal investment is a statistically rare event, reach puberty earlier and are more likely to pursue short-term mating patterns (Belsky, Steinberg, & Draper, 1991). Despite some critics' assertion that evolutionary psychologists ignore humans' use of alternative tactics (Fausto-Sterling, 1997), one book alone (Low, 2000) documents hundreds of studies examining how environmental variables such as pathogen stress, social stratification, resource availability, matrilinearity, protein deficiency, group size, means of subsistence, religion, sex ratio, and climate affect strategy choice.

But we do more than adjust our behavior to the environment; we learn from it. This is advantageous for dealing with "generational deadtime," "a lag time that is an invariant feature of any system whose construction takes time and which is based on a set of instructions that cannot be continually updated" (Plotkin, 1994, p. 137). Learning is an ability that we share with many other species. At its most rudimentary, it may consist of little more than the acquired aversion to stimuli that have proved painful and an attraction to stimuli that are associated with pleasure. Nonetheless, this fundamental development allowed for the environment to shape behavior adaptively in the lifetime of an individual (if it did not get killed in the process). Phylogenetically later came the ability to learn from observation (an altogether safer tactic) and, in humans, the ability to use and transmit representations. This opened the way to even more efficient means of thinking (off-line thought experiments that helped us to avoid bad behavioral choices) and acquiring knowledge (through language and inferential mechanisms). This array of mechanisms allows us to produce novel responses to the environment.

Some have taken this to mean that learning has superceded genetics— that the "capacity for culture" means that humans are free to behave with unconstrained plasticity. Clearly they are not—we cannot learn to hear the range of sounds that dogs do or to swim for hours underwater. Furthermore, there are some things which we learn with ease and some which are acquired only after years of sustained practice and concentration. The former are often referred to as "innate," "hardwired," or "genetically canalized," such walking or our first language. The latter, skills such as playing the piano or solving algebra problems, are not devoid of a genetic basis (otherwise we could not do them at all) but are much more dependent on local environmental input. Evolutionary theorists see cultural learning as supplying a range of means that can be used in the service of evolved goals or fitness tokens (Barkow, 1989). Thus people everywhere seek sexual partners and perform parenting duties, but the means that they use to increase their attractiveness or to soothe a distressed baby may vary. Margo Wilson and her coworkers (1997, p. 433) perhaps put it best: " 'Biology' is the study of the attributes of living things, and only living things can be "social." So whence this idea of antithesis? . . . The irony is that developmentally, experientially and circumstantially contingent variation is precisely what evolution-minded theories of social phenomenon . . . are all about."

So far we have discussed objections that apply to any kind of biologism—from the assertion that prenatal hormones might shape the human brain, to the idea that genes might inform psychological development. But a further set of objections are aimed more directly at evolutionary explanations.

Reductionism

The first is that evolutionary psychology is both simplistic and reductionistic. Evolution is the process of selection that causes differential survival and reproduction of individuals as a function of their performance in a particular ecological niche. I can think of few other theories that can be expressed so succinctly. Yet pejorative accusations of "simplistic" notwithstanding, it is apparently not simple enough to escape misunderstanding (see Wright, 1996). Fausto-Sterling (1992), a biologist and vocal critic of evolutionary psychology, correctly explains the evolutionary premise that the sex that makes the lower parental investment (typically males) tends to display greater promiscuity in its mating habits. She then describes female promiscuity in phalaropes exclaiming, "You name your animal species and make your political point." The critical point that she misses is that in the phalarope it is the *male* not the female that makes the greater parental investment. Hence this example is entirely consistent with evolutionary theory and merely demonstrates what the theory has always argued—it is parental investment, not sex per se, that drives mating strategy.

The truly remarkable thing about evolution is that, although the theory itself is simple, it leads to highly varied and often counterintuitive hypotheses. An evolutionary analysis of incest developed by Westermark argued that people develop an aversion to later sexual contact with those with whom they spent their infancy and childhood years (normally siblings). One counterintuitive prediction was that children raised in kibbutzim should avoid marriage with their kindergarten peers despite their nonrelatedness. This prediction turns out to be true (Shepher, 1983). A different strand of evolutionary thought has been concerned with homogamy (the tendency for like to mate with like). Together these two pieces of work can explain the recent reports that siblings separated at birth and then reunited in adulthood tend (to their distress) to find one another sexually attractive. This seems to me to be simplicity at its best—a simple theory that is able to explain apparently unrelated and unexpected findings in the real world. There was a time when simplicity used to be called elegance and constituted one of the criteria for quality—if the data equally support two theories, then the simpler one was the better one.

The charge of reductionism comes in two forms. The first objects to the "reduction" of complex human behavior to the action of genes, and we have already discussed the fact that no serious evolutionary psychologist believes that genes can operate independently of the environment (although many feminists apparently fear that they may). The second highlights a failure to include the full range of variables that are needed to account for a given behavior. No scientist really wants this contrived simplicity, any more than her critics do. We would all love to offer complete theories that fully account for the range and diversity of human behavior. But reductionism is a necessary evil. It is a stepping stone that allows us to work toward the truth by first decomposing the explanation into its constituent elements. The complexity of human behavior means that these constituent elements are likely to span the range from the biological to cultural. This diversity calls for multidisciplinary coordination and integration. Cultural variables have to be compatible with what we know about interpersonal behavior (which gives rise to it). Interpersonal behavior in turn must be compatible with what we know about the human mind reading (which gives rise to it). Mind reading must be compatible with internal representational states, and so on. If (as many feminists prescribe) we refuse to decompose and take on the full complexity of a phenomenon as it appears in the real world, we are faced with an insurmountable problem. We can offer only a description and nothing more. We cannot generalize beyond the historical moment and the actors involved. Feminists, like gestalt psychologists, argue that the whole is more than the sum of the parts. If we wanted to remove or introduce variables to observe their effect, we would have "committed reductionism" in accepting the potential decomposability of the event. Now many feminists are happy to accept these limitations. But in so doing they become historians (not social scientists), describing (but not explaining) nongeneralizable and unique events by the use of a subjective interpretation (that is itself the product of a particular moment in history, geography, and culture).

Genes and Adaptations

Some feminists in the social sciences rely on their biologist colleagues to mount a finer-grained attack on evolutionary psychology. Many of these challenges have been lucidly described and defended by Waage and Gowaty (1997), but here I will briefly consider two.

The first is the "Show me the gene" argument, which maintains that we need not accept the hereditary basis of any trait until biologists locate the gene responsible. As I have just discussed, phenotypic behavior is not reducible to a gene; it depends upon incredibly complex cascades of interactions with the environment. We will never find a one-to-one relationship between a gene and a life history strategy (e.g., mature early and breed plentifully versus mature late and invest heavily) because all members of a species have the ability to take either route and the one that is selected is a function of environmental factors such as crowding, stress, status, and developmental experiences. Even discounting environmental effects, the biological (to say nothing of psychological) development of a single trait could not be a straightforward mapping exercise because of pleiotropy (where a single gene affects two or more apparently unrelated traits), polygenics (where a single trait is controlled by many genes), nonadditivity (where genes at different loci interact) and switch genes (higher-order genes control the action of many others). These complexities aside, evolutionary psychologists are not geneticists, and it is unreasonable to expect them to be. But this does not mean that psychologists must remain gagged until then. When we see universal complexities of psychological design that suggest an adaptation, it is reasonable to test such a proposal—just as alternative formulations (e.g., sex differences are absent where children possess no cognitive categories for male and female) are free to test theirs.

The next objection, championed by Gould (2000) and Fausto-Sterling (1997), is the "Prove it's an adaptation" argument. These critics accuse evolutionary psychology of being too free and easy in identifying aspects of human behavior as adaptations. We are rebuked for failing to consider factors other than natural selection that can result in change in the gene pool. Evolution is composed of two processes—natural selection and random genetic drift. As an antidote to "ultra-Darwinism," Gould (2000) and Steven Rose (2000) believe that we need to accord a greater role to the second of these. Crudely, if we accept the predominance of drift over selection, then humans got to be the way they are as a result of chance.

Drift works this way. Imagine a bag holding six white balls and six black balls, the colors corresponding to two different alleles in a gene pool (Majerus, Amos, & Hurst, 1996). Put in your hand and randomly select six balls to go into the next generation of the game. You pull out four white and two black. The population is now reset at a new value for allelic diversity. Next time around, you select two white and two black; the population drifts back to equilibrium. The random process provides a backdrop of rising and falling genetic noise upon which is imposed the directional force of natural selection. But there is a chance that on the second round you might have pulled out nothing but white balls. The white allele would have gone to fixation—as a result of chance deaths, not selection. When individuals die before reproduction, they take their genes with them, and this is as true when they die as a result of random misfortune (being struck by lightning) as when there is a genetic vulnerability (they are not resistant to a common pathogen).

The effects of drift are most pronounced in very small populations. Imagine a small group of individuals who migrate away from their community and become the "founders" of a new population. They might take with them a distribution of alleles that is not representative of the parent population—rarer alleles might even be absent altogether. A genetic bottleneck occurs when there is a sudden crash in population size (usually as a result of some catastrophic event): the remaining population is subject to the same "founder effects." So if *Homo sapiens* had been subject to a population crash (and there is reason to believe that we were), the gene pool might have been altered. But any disadvantageous trait that established itself from drift alone would rapidly be selected out, leaving the possibility that only neutral or beneficial traits were retained. More importantly, it is extremely unlikely that chance alone could generate a complex psychological adaptation. An adaptation, such as the eye, requires the activity of many genes harmoniously working to produce a functional design characterized by the coordination and cooperation of different submechanisms. The likelihood of this occurring by chance has been likened to the probability that a hurricane passing through a junkyard would assemble a functioning airplane. Though a single allele may reach fixation through genetic drift, it stretches the bounds of credulity to imagine that chance alone threw together the entire suite of genes needed to produce a brain with specific modules that acquire language, accurately infer others' mental states, recognize faces, and "automatically" detect facial symmetry.

But drift is not the only weapon that is wheeled out against evolutionary psychology. In addition to adaptations, natural selection also produces by-products. These are traits that are linked to adaptations but that serve no adaptive function in and of themselves. A light bulb is designed to emit light, but as a side effect it also produces heat, and the fact that bones are white is an artifact of their being made from calcium (Buss, Haselton, Shackelford, Bleske, & Wakefield, 1998). How can we be sure, Gould asks, that what appear to be adaptations are not in fact by-products? He suggests that language is a side effect of large brains (which were developed for some other function that he does not identify). In fact, by-products are identifiable by the fact that, by virtue of being merely carried along with an adaptation, they show no evidence of design complexity or of independent functionality (coordination with an environmental problem). Daisies may float as a side effect of their weight and surface-to-mass ratio (Dennett, 1995). But there is no evidence of this being an adaptation—they have not altered their means of photosynthesis to compensate for their leaves being submerged, and it is doubtful that flotation makes any difference to their reproductive success. Language, on the other hand, is a complexly crafted ability (so complex that it has taken linguists decades to decipher the universal deep structure) that enhances knowledge transfer. Its design and functionality make it a very unlikely candidate for being a by-product.

In essence, the response to the "prove it's an adaptation" position is a clear specification of how to recognize one. In establishing this, we can identify by-products as well as the adaptation on which they are free-loading. The requirements for considering a trait to be a putative adaptation, for me at least, are as follows:

1. It is present in all cultures at all times.
2. It emerges in relatively intact form at a predictable point in the life cycle.
3. It is manifest in response to a specific range of inputs.
4. It appears without specific tutoring.
5. It is resistant to modification attempts.
6. It is not a function of intelligence.
7. It shows evidence of special design (complexity, economy, efficiency, reliability, precision, functionality) in relation to an environmental problem.

If we take gender segregation in childhood as an example, we can see the seven following principles. (1) It appears cross-culturally (Omark, Omark, & Edelman, 1973; Whiting & Edwards, 1988). (2) It emerges in the third year of life (Howes, 1988), intensifies so that between the ages of 8 and 11 the median time spent with the opposite sex is zero (Gray & Feldman, 1997), and recedes in adolescence (Larson & Richard, 1991). (3) It depends on the presence of a critical mass of co-present, unrelated children (Harris, 1995). Children show less sex segregation with relatives or siblings (Maccoby, 1998). (4) It appears independent of parents' views about the desirability of mixed-sex or same-sex play (Maccoby, 1998). (5) Though it can be modified by reinforcement in the short term, once the reinforcement is withdrawn it reasserts itself (Serbin, Tonnick, & Sternglanz, 1977). (6) It does not appear to be more or less marked in children of different IQ. (7) Where the sexes are forced into close proximity in childhood, they subsequently reject one another as marriage partners (Shepher, 1983). Sex segregation operates to maintain distance from the opposite sex in childhood, rendering them as potential sexual partners at a later date (Bem, 1996). Given the serendipitous, coattailing nature of by-products, they are unable to meet these stringent criteria of an adaptation.

An adaptation is a structure, process, or behavior pattern that makes an organism more fit to survive and reproduce than other members of its species. Though the above criteria provide prime facie evidence of an adaptation, some have argued that our inability to time travel to the environment of evolutionary adaptedness (EEA) means that we can never "prove" which environmental problem the adaptation was designed to solve. On the characterization of the EEA, evolutionary psychologists are divided. Some "mismatch" theorists argue for important environmental changes in the last 100,000 years that can result in evolved adaptations currently producing maladaptive behavior. Others maintain that the very absence of epidemic levels of stress and pathology argues for the fact that we have constructed a world that matches, in most important respects, the environment in which we evolved (see Crawford, 1998). Some believe the dispute will be resolved by archaeological and anthropological evidence that will ultimately provide a clearer picture of our ancestral lifestyle. Others argue that the most-needed information—about psychological mechanisms underlying social practices such as cooperation, altruism, jealousy, mate choice, and cheat detection—does not fossilize (Hampton, 2000). Still others argue that we can work backward from the present because contemporary evidence of adaptations will allow us to reconstruct the nature of the EEA (Tooby & Cosmides, 1992). Gould (2000, p. 88) appears to agree with this latter position, arguing that we "must therefore try to infer causes from results—the standard procedure in any historical science, by the way, and not a special problem facing evolutionists." But we must go further. In the first instance we can generate accounts of the specific problem that was solved by a putative adaptation. If these are clearly specified, we can develop empirical tests of their adequacy. An adaptation (such as fever) designed to produce a particular beneficial outcome (parasite destruction) should occur when the body detects pathogens and not at other times. Psychological mechanisms like attachment should wane as the child reaches the age at which she has the social and motor skills to explore the world. If we have conserved a herding response to danger, we should prefer to be with others when we face threatening uncertainty. If guilt is an emotion signaling unpaid obligation, we can make clear predictions about the likelihood of altruism when it is aroused. If symmetry reflects good genes, then symmetrical people should be healthier as well as more attractive. The more novel the prediction, the more satisfying the empirical test. However, that should not debar us from explaining known facts about the world—a criticism uniquely leveled against evolutionary psychologists. All branches of psychology (as well as all other sciences) account for known facts—there is little point in generating an elegant theory of why working memory is limitless or how infants are able to do calculus. A good theory, in any discipline, explains what we know as well as correctly predicting what we do not yet know.

Conclusion

At the risk of stating the obvious, feminists of all persuasions aim to ameliorate the position of women in society. In the early years, there was a far more prescriptive agenda for women that emphasized the emulation of male attitudes, roles, and behavior. The happiness of women was supposed to be increased by their full participation in work, their rejection of the sexual double standard, the deferment or abandonment of motherhood as a confining role, and, in extremis, the rejection of heterosexual sex as a form of rape. Since that time, the tendency to tell women what they should want has declined in favor of a commitment to removing inequality (in, for example, wages, opportunities for promotion, social control, and law) and to opening up avenues of opportunity (higher education, childcare provision). This more liberal agenda rests on a moral commitment to maximizing happiness while not preaching a single route to women's fulfillment. In short, inequality should be removed in order to increase women's choices, but the choices that they make must lie beyond politics and legislation.

When constraints are removed, my bet is that we will not see a sea change in what women choose to do with their lives. My bet is that, all other things being equal, they will continue to work (as women always have despite some localized historical anomalies) and that they will seek ways to combine motherhood with that work (Hrdy, 1999). My guess is that they will prefer a long-term partner who contributes financially and emotionally to the lives of their joint children (Geary, 2000). As a sex, they will remain far behind men in their rates of violence and crime (Campbell, 1999), and will exceed them in their sensitivity to the emotional states of others (Hall, 1984). I may be mistaken. It could be that the removal of constraints will reveal a female nature utterly different from the one that has existed heretofore, showing that our notions of womanhood have been the result of imposed social constructions, stereotypes, and repressive socialization. Let's finish this social experiment, for the sake of justice, and find out.

References

Anderson, J. R. (1983). *The architecture of cognition.* Cambridge, MA: Harvard University Press.

Bakan, D. (1966). *The duality of human existence.* Boston: Beacon.

Barkley, A., Ullman, G., Otto, L., & Brecht, M. (1977). The effects of sex-typing and sex-appropriateness of modeled behavior on children's imitation. *Child Development, 48,* 721–725.

Barkow, J. (1989). *Darwin, sex and status: Biological approaches to mind and culture.* Toronto: University of Toronto Press.

Baron-Cohen, S. (1997). How to build a baby that can read minds: Cognitive mechanisms in mindreading. In S. Baron-Cohen (Ed.), *The maladapted mind: Classic readings in evolutionary psychopathology.* Hove: Psychology Press.

Belenky, M. F., Clinchy, B. M., Goldberger, N. R., & Tarule, J. M. (1986). *Women's ways of knowing.* New York: Basic Books.

Belsky, J., Steinberg, L., & Draper, P. (1991). Childhood experience, interpersonal development, and reproductive strategy: An evolutionary theory of socialization. *Child Development, 62,* 647–670.

Bem, D. J. (1996). Exotic becomes erotic: A developmental theory of sexual orientation. *Psychological Review, 103,* 320–335.

Bem, S. L. (1974). The measurement of psychological androgyny. *Journal of Consulting and Clinical Psychology, 42,* 155–162.

Bem, S. L. (1993). *Lenses of gender: Transforming the debate on sexual inequality.* New Haven, CT: Yale University Press.

Blakemore, J., LaRue, A., & Olejnik, A. (1979). Sex-appropriate toy preference and the ability to conceptualise toys as sex role related. *Developmental Psychology, 15,* 339–340.

Bleier, R. (1984). *Science and gender: A critique of biology and its theories on women.* New York: Pergamon.

Boyd, R., & Richerson, P. (1985). *Culture and the evolutionary process.* Chicago: University of Chicago Press.

Brooks, J., & Lewis, M. (1974). Attachment behavior in thirteen-month-old, opposite sex twins. *Child Development, 45,* 243–247.

Brown, D. E. (1991). *Human universals.* New York: McGraw-Hill.

Burman, E. (Ed.). (1990). *Feminists and psychological practice.* London: Sage.

Burr, V. (1998). *Gender and social psychology.* London: Routledge.

Buss, D. M., Haselton, M. G., Shackelford, T. K., Bleske, A. L., & Wakefield, J. C. (1998). Adaptations, exaptations and spandrels. *American Psychologist, 53,* 533–548.

Byrne, R. W., & Whiten, A. (1988). *Machiavellian intelligence: Social expertise and the evolution of intellect in monkeys, apes and humans.* Oxford: Oxford University Press.

Caldera, Y., Huston, A., & O'Brien, M. (1989). Social interactions and play patterns of parents and toddlers with feminine, masculine and neutral toys. *Child Development, 60,* 70–76.

Campbell, A. (1993). *Men, women and aggression.* New York: Basic Books.

Campbell, A. (1999). Staying alive: Evolution, culture and women's intrasexual aggression. *Behavioural and Brain Sciences, 22,* 203–214.

Campbell, A. (2002). *A mind of her own: The evolutionary psychology of women.* Oxford: Oxford University Press.

Campbell, A., Shirley, L., & Candy, J. (under review). A longitudinal study of gender-related cognition and behaviour.

Campbell, A., Shirley, L., Heywood, C., & Crook, C. (2000). Infants' visual preference for sex-congruent babies, children, toys and activities: A longitudinal study. *British Journal of Developmental Psychology, 18,* 479–498.

Cashdan, E. (1996). Women's mating strategies. *Evolutionary Anthropology, 5,* 134–143.

Clifford, J., & Marcus, G. (Eds.). (1986). *Writing culture.* Berkeley: University of California Press.

Cole, S., & Phillips, L. (1995). *Ethnographic feminisms: Essays in anthropology.* Montreal: McGill-Queens University Press.

Crawford, C. (1998). Environments and adaptations: Then and now. In C. Crawford & D. L. Krebs (Eds.), *Handbook of evolutionary psychology: Ideas, issues and applications.* Mahwah, NJ: Lawrence Erlbaum.

Daly, M., & Wilson, M. (1983). *Sex, evolution and behavior* (2nd ed.). Belmont, CA: Wadsworth.

Daly, M., & Wilson, M. (1988). *Homicide*. New York: Aldine de Gruyter.

Dawkins, R. (1989). *The selfish gene* (2nd ed.). Oxford: Oxford University Press.

Dawkins, R. (1999). Foreword. In S. Blackmore, *The meme machine*. Oxford: Oxford University Press.

Dennett, D. (1995). *Darwin's dangerous idea: Evolution and the meanings of life*. New York: Touchstone.

Dickemann, M. (1997). Paternal confidence and dowry competition: A biocultural analysis of purdah. In L. Betzig (Ed.), *Human nature: A critical reader*. Oxford: Oxford University Press.

Dunbar, R. I. M. (1993). Coevolution of neocortical size, group size and language in humans. *Behavioral and Brain Sciences, 16*, 681–694.

Durham, W. (1991). *Coevolutionary theory*. Stanford, CA: Stanford University Press.

Eagly, A. (1987). *Sex differences in social behavior: A social role interpretation*. Hillsdale, NJ: Lawrence Erlbaum.

Eagly, A., & Wood, W. (1999). The origins of sex differences: Evolved dispositions versus social roles. *Behavioral and Brain Sciences, 22*, 223–224.

Edwards, D., & Potter, J. (1992). *Discursive psychology*. London: Sage.

Fagot, B. (1991). Peer relations in boys and girls from two to seven. Paper presented at the biennial meeting of the Society for Research in Child Development, Seattle.

Fagot, B., & Leinbach, M. (1989). The young child's gender schema: Environmental input, internal organisation. *Child Development, 60*, 663–672.

Farnham, C. (Ed.). (1987). *The impact of feminist research in the academy*. Bloomington: Indiana University Press.

Fausto-Sterling, A. (1992). *Myths of gender: Biological theories about women and men* (2nd ed.). New York: Basic Books.

Fausto-Sterling, A. (1997). Beyond difference: A biologist's perspective. *Journal of Social Issues, 53*, 233–258.

Freedman, D. (1974). *Human infancy: An evolutionary perspective*. Hillsdale, NJ: Lawrence Erlbaum.

Freeman, D. (1983). *Margaret Mead and Samoa: The making and unmaking of an anthropological myth*. Cambridge, MA: Harvard University Press.

Gangestad, S., & Simpson, J. (2000). The evolution of human mating: Trade-offs and strategic pluralism. *Behavioral and Brain Sciences, 23*, 573–644.

Geary, D. (2000). Evolution and proximate expressions of human paternal investment. *Psychological Bulletin, 126*, 55–77.

Goodfield, J. (1981). *An imagined world*. New York: Harper and Row.

Gould, S. J. (2000). More things in heaven and earth. In H. Rose & S. Rose (Eds.), *Alas, poor Darwin: Arguments against evolutionary psychology*. London: Cape.

Gowaty, P. A. (1992). Evolutionary biology feminism. *Human Nature, 3*, 217–249.

Gowaty, P. A. (Ed.). (1997). *Feminism and evolutionary biology: Boundaries, intersections and frontiers*. New York: Chapman and Hall.

Gray, P., & Feldman, J. (1997). Patterns of age mixing and gender mixing among children and adolescents at an ungraded school. *Merrill Palmer Quarterly, 42*, 67–86.

Hall, J. A. (1984). *Nonverbal sex differences: Communication accuracy and expressive style.* Baltimore: Johns Hopkins University Press.

Hampton, S. J. (2000). Evolutionary social psychology, natural history and the history of ideas. PhD diss., Durham University.

Haraway, D. (1988). Situated knowledges: The science question in feminism as a site of discourse on the privilege of partial perspective. *Feminist Studies, 14*, 575–600.

Harding, S. (1986). *The science question in feminism.* Ithaca, NY: Cornell University Press.

Harding, S. (Ed.). (1987). *Feminism and methodology.* Bloomington: Indiana University Press.

Harris, J. R. (1995). Where is the child's environment? A group socialization theory of development. *Psychological Review, 102*, 458–489.

Helmreich, R., Spence, J., & Gibson, R. (1982). Sex role attitudes, 1972–1980. *Personality and Social Psychology Bulletin, 8*, 656–663.

Henriques, J., Hollway, W., Urwin, C., Venn, C., & Walkerdine, V. (Eds.). (1984). *Changing the subject: Psychology, social regulation and subjectivity.* London: Methuen.

Holcombe, H. R. (1998). Testing evolutionary hypotheses. In C. Crawford & D. L. Krebs (Eds.), *Handbook of evolutionary psychology: Ideas, issues and applications.* Mahwah, NJ: Lawrence Erlbaum.

Hollway, W. (1984). Gender difference and the production of subjectivity. In J. Henriques, W. Hollway, C. Urwin, C. Venn, & V. Walkerdine (Eds.), *Changing the subject: Psychology, social regulation and subjectivity.* London: Methuen.

Howes, C. (1988). Peer interaction of young children. *Monographs of the Society for Research in Child Development, serial number 217, 53*(1).

Hrdy, S. B. (1997). Raising Darwin's consciousness: Female sexuality and the prehominid origins of patriarchy. *Human Nature, 8*, 1–49.

Hrdy, S. B. (1999). *Mother Nature: Natural selection and the female of the species.* London: Chatto and Windus.

Humphrey, N. (1976). The social function of intellect. In P. P. G. Bateson & R. A. Hinde (Eds.), *Growing points in ethology.* Cambridge: Cambridge University Press.

Huston, A. (1983). Sex typing. In P. Mussen & M. Hetherington (Eds.), *Handbook of child psychology: Volume 4. Socialisation, personality and social behavior* (pp. 387–467). New York: Wiley.

Janicki, M., & Krebs, D. L. (1998). Evolutionary approaches to culture. In C. Crawford & D. L. Krebs (Eds.), *Handbook of evolutionary psychology: Ideas, issues and applications.* Mahwah, NJ: Lawrence Erlbaum.

Jayaratne, T. E. (1983). The value of quantitative methodology for feminist research. In G. Bowles & R. D. Klein (Eds.), *Theories of women's studies.* London: Routledge.

Jolly, A. (1966). Lemur social behaviour and primate intelligence. *Science, 153*, 501–506.

Jolly, A. (1999). *Lucy's legacy: Sex and intelligence in human evolution.* Cambridge, MA: Harvard University Press.

Keller, E. F. (1985). *Reflections on gender and science.* New Haven, CT: Yale University Press.

Kitzinger, C. (1990). Resisting the discipline. In E. Burman (Ed.), *Feminists and psychological practice.* London: Sage.

Kohnstamm, G. A. (1989). Temperament in childhood: Cross-cultural and sex differences. In G. A. Kohnstamm, J. E. Bates, & M. K. Rothbart (Eds.), *Temperament in childhood.* Chichester: Wiley.

Larson, R., & Richards, M. H. (1991). Daily companionship in late childhood and early adolescence: Changing developmental contexts. *Child Development, 62*, 284–300.

Lewin, M., & Tragos, L. (1987). Has the feminist movement influenced adolescent sex role attitudes? A reassessment after a quarter century. *Sex Roles, 16*, 125–135.

Low, B. S. (2000). *Why sex matters: A Darwinian look at human behavior.* Princeton, NJ: Princeton University Press.

Lueptow, L. (1985). Concepts of masculinity and femininity: 1974–1983. *Psychological Reports, 57*, 859–862.

Lueptow, L., Garovich, L., & Lueptow, M. B. (1995). The persistence of gender stereotypes in the face of changing sex roles: Evidence contrary to the socio-cultural model. *Ethology and Sociobiology, 16*, 509–530.

Lumsden, C., & Wilson, E. O. (1981). *Genes, minds and culture.* Cambridge, MA: Harvard University Press.

Lytton, H., & Romney, D. (1991). Parents' differential treatment of boys and girls: A meta-analysis. *Psychological Bulletin, 109*, 267–296.

Maccoby, E. E. (1998). *The two sexes: Growing up apart, coming together.* Cambridge, MA: Belknap Press of Harvard University Press.

Maccoby, E. E., & Jacklin, C. N. (1974). *The psychology of sex differences.* Stanford, CA: Stanford University Press.

Majerus, M., Amos, W., & Hurst, G. (1996). *Evolution: The four billion year war.* London: Longman.

Marshall, J. (1986). Exploring the experience of women managers: Toward rigour in qualitative methods. In S. Wilkinson (Ed.), *Feminist social psychology: Developing theory and practice.* Milton Keynes: Open University Press.

Martin, C. L. (1994). Cognitive influences on the development and maintenance of gender segregation. In C. Leaper (Ed.), *Childhood gender segregation: Causes and consequences.* San Francisco: Jossey Bass.

Martin, C. L., & Halverson, C. F. (1981). A schematic processing model of sex-typing and stereotyping in children. *Child Development, 52*, 1119–1134.

Mead, M. (1935). *Sex and temperament in three primitive societies.* New York: Morrow.

Moore, H. (1988). *Feminism and anthropology*. Cambridge: Polity Press.

Muldoon, O., & Reilly, J. (1998). Biology. In K. Trew & J. Kremer (Eds.), *Gender and psychology*. London: Arnold.

Murdock, G. P. (1981). *Atlas of world cultures*. Pittsburgh: University of Pittsburgh Press.

Nelkin, D. (2000). Less selfish than sacred? Genes and the religious impulse in evolutionary psychology. In H. Rose & S. Rose (Eds.), *Alas, poor Darwin: Arguments against evolutionary psychology*. London: Cape.

Niehoff, D. (1999). *The biology of violence*. New York: Free Press.

Oakley, A. (1981). Interviewing women: A contradiction in terms. In H. Roberts (Ed.), *Doing feminist research*. London: Routledge and Kegan Paul.

O'Brien, M., & Huston, A. C. (1985). Development of sex-typed lay behavior in toddlers. *Developmental Psychology, 21*, 866–871.

Oliver, M. B., & Hyde, J. S. (1993). Gender differences in sexuality: A meta-analysis. *Psychological Bulletin, 114*, 29–51.

Omark, D. R., Omark, M., & Edelman, M. (1973). Formation of dominance hierarchies in young children. In T. R. Williams (Ed.), *Psychological anthropology*. The Hague: Mouton.

Parlee, M. B. (1979). Psychology and women. *Signs: Journal of Women in Culture and Society, 5*, 121–133.

Percy, C. (1998). Feminism. In K. Trew & J. Kremer (Eds.), *Gender and psychology*. London: Arnold.

Perry, D., & Bussey, K. (1979). The social learning theory of sex differences: Imitation is alive and well. *Journal of Personality and Social Psychology, 37*, 1699–1712.

Plotkin, H. (1994). *Darwin machines and the nature of knowledge*. London: Penguin.

Potter, J., & Wetherell, M. (1987). *Discourse and social psychology: Beyond attitudes and behaviour*. London: Sage.

Powlishta, K. K. (1995). Intergroup processes in childhood: Social categorisation and sex-role development. *Developmental Psychology, 31*, 781–788.

Rogers, L. (1999). *Sexing the brain*. London: Weidenfeld and Nicholson.

Roopnarine, J. L. (1986). Mothers' and fathers' behaviors toward the toy play of infant sons and daughters. *Sex Roles, 14*, 59–68.

Rose, H. (2000). Colonising the social sciences? In H. Rose & S. Rose (Eds.), *Alas, poor Darwin: Arguments against evolutionary psychology*. London: Cape.

Rose, S. (2000). Escaping evolutionary psychology. In H. Rose & S. Rose (Eds.), *Alas, poor Darwin: Arguments against evolutionary psychology*. London: Cape.

Rosser, S. V. (1997). Possible implications of feminist theories for the study of evolution. In P. A. Gowaty (Ed.), *Feminism and evolutionary biology: Boundaries, intersections and frontiers*. New York: Chapman and Hall.

Sayers, J. (1982). *Biological politics: Feminist and anti-feminist perspectives.* London: Tavistock.

Serbin, L. A., Moller, L. C., Gulko, J., Powlishta, K. K., & Colburne, K. A. (1994). The emergence of gender segregation in toddler playgroups. In C. Leaper (Ed.), *Childhood gender segregation: Causes and consequences.* San Francisco: Jossey-Bass.

Serbin, L. A., Tonnick, I. J., & Sternglanz, S. H. (1977). Shaping cooperative cross-sex play. *Child Development, 48,* 924–929.

Shepher, J. (1983). *Incest: A biosocial approach.* New York: Academic Press.

Shostak, M. (1990). *Nisa: The life and words of a !Kung woman.* London: Earthscan.

Smetana, J. G., & Letourneau, K. J. (1984). Development of gender constancy and children's sex-typed free play behaviour. *Developmental Psychology, 20,* 691–696.

Smuts, B. B. (1995). The evolutionary origins of patriarchy. *Human Nature, 6,* 1–32.

Spence, J., Helmreich, R., & Stapp, J. (1974). The Personality Attributes Questionnaire: A measure of sex role stereotypes and masculinity-femininity. *Journal Supplement Abstract Service Catalog of Selected Documents in Psychology, 4,* 42(617).

Squire, C. (1990). Feminism as antipsychology: Learning and teaching in feminist psychology. In E. Burman (Ed.), *Feminists and psychological practice.* London: Sage.

Stern, M., & Karraker, K. H. (1989). Sex stereotyping of infants: A review of gender labeling studies. *Sex Roles, 20,* 501–522.

Strathern, A. (1987). Out of context: The persuasive fictions of anthropology. *Current Anthropology, 28,* 251–281.

Swim, J. (1994). Perceived versus meta-analytic effect sizes: An assessment of the accuracy of gender stereotypes. *Journal of Personality and Social Psychology, 66,* 21–36.

Tooby, J., & Cosmides, L. (1992). The psychological foundations of culture. In J. H. Barkow, L. Cosmides, & J. Tooby (Eds.), *The adapted mind: Evolutionary psychology and the generation of culture.* New York: Oxford University Press.

Townsend, J. M., Kline, J., & Wasserman, T. H. (1995). Low-investment copulation: Sex differences in motivation and emotional reaction. *Ethology and Sociobiology, 16,* 25–51.

Trautner, H. M. (1992). The development of sex-typing in children: A longitudinal analysis. *German Journal of Psychology, 16,* 183–199.

Unger, R. K. (1996). Using the master's tools: Epistemology and empiricism. In S. Wilkinson (Ed.), *Feminist social psychologies: International perspectives* (pp. 165–181). Milton Keynes, UK: Open University Press.

Visweswaran, K. (1994). *Fictions of feminist ethnography.* Minneapolis: University of Minnesota Press.

Waage, J. K., & Gowaty, P. A. (1997). Myths of genetic determinism. In P. A. Gowaty (Ed.), *Feminism and evolutionary biology: Boundaries, intersections and frontiers.* New York: Chapman and Hall.

Weinraub, M., Clements, L. P., Sockloff, A., Ethridge, T. E., & Myers, B. (1984). The development of sex role stereotypes in the third year: Relationships to gender labeling, gender identity, sex-typed toy preference and family characteristics. *Child Development, 55,* 1493–1503.

Whiten, A. (Ed.). (1991). *Natural theories of mind: Evolution, development and simulation of everyday mindreading.* Oxford: Blackwell.

Whiting, B. B., & Edwards, C. P. (1988). *Children of different worlds: The formation of social behavior.* Cambridge, MA: Harvard University Press.

Wilkinson, S. (1986). *Feminist social psychology: Developing theory and practice.* Milton Keynes: Open University Press.

Wilkinson, S. (Ed.). (1996). *Feminist social psychologies: International perspectives.* Buckingham: Open University Press.

Will, J. A., Self, P. A., & Datan, M. (1976). Maternal behavior and perceived sex of infant. *American Journal of Orthopsychiatry, 46,* 135–139.

Williams, G. C. (1996). *Plan and purpose in nature.* London: Phoenix.

Williams, J., & Best, D. (1982). *Measuring sex stereotypes: A thirty nation study.* Beverly Hills, CA: Sage.

Wilson, M., & Daly, M. (1992). The man who mistook his wife for a chattel. In J. H. Barkow, L. Cosmides, & J. Tooby (Eds.), *The adapted mind: Evolutionary psychology and the generation of culture.* New York: Oxford University Press.

Wilson, M., Daly, M., & Scheib, J. E. (1997). Femicide: An evolutionary psychological perspective. In P. A. Gowaty (Ed.), *Feminism and evolutionary biology: Boundaries, intersections and frontiers.* New York: Chapman and Hall.

Wright, R. (1996). The dissent of woman. *Demos, 10,* 18–24.

3 The Male Flash of Anger: Violent Response to Transgression as an Example of the Intersection of Evolved Psychology and Culture

Daniel M. T. Fessler

Scope of Inquiry

A great deal of scholarly attention has been devoted to three questions: why, in general, men are more violent than women; why some individuals are more violent than others; and why some societies are more violent than others. Traditionally, these questions have constituted contested turf in the struggle between explanations focusing on nature and those emphasizing nurture. However, like the other authors in this volume, I believe that evolutionary psychology can constitute the foundation for vertically integrated analyses that take account of multiple levels of causality (Barkow, 1989). In the following essay I will attempt to demonstrate that central questions in the study of violence are usefully addressed using multiple, mutually complementary forms of explanation.

At first glance, broad questions as to the causes of violence seem to be unanswerable, since specific instances can plausibly be explained by reference to factors as disparate as, say, the presence of attractive women in a bar or the rising price of crude oil. However, this wide variation is reduced if we adopt the position that (contrary to some popular portrayals) there are critical differences between spontaneous, face-to-face aggression and calculated, organized combat, particularly at the level of the nation-state. While in some instances powerful leaders may initiate international combat in response to interindividual events akin to those that lead to a barroom brawl, it is nevertheless likely that most large-scale wars are fought for other reasons. Moreover, in such warfare the soldiers doing the fighting lack personal conflicts with those whom they are directed to kill.[1] A useful first step in the investigation of violence is therefore to draw a distinction between events in which actors are spontaneously motivated to respond to the actions of a specific individual and those in which actors participate because of the influence of complex political institutions.[2] I will focus exclusively on the former. I take as a starting point the following observations: (a) subjective experience is importantly influenced by evolved predispositions; (b) subjective experience is an important locus of culture's influence on individuals; and (c) subjective experience is the source of raw materials in the creation of cultural ideas. In short, it is at the psychological level that evolutionary and cultural processes most importantly interdigitate.

The Evolution of Anger and Violent Response to Transgression

A wide variety of sources, from ethnographic accounts (cf. Gladwin & Sarason, 1953; Lee, 1993; Burbank, 1994; Chagnon, 1997; Otterbein, 2000) to police reports (see Daly & Wilson, 1988; also, Ghiglieri, 1999), suggest that in cases of spontaneous violent conflict, the emotion which English speakers label "anger" is a principal feature of the actors' subjective experiences.[3] Although there are important cross-cultural differences in both its eliciting conditions and its nuanced associations, it is likely that anger is one of the most universally identifiable emotions (Ekman, 1994; Haidt & Keltner, 1999). Moreover, while eliciting stimuli vary, many share a common theme: Notions of goals, rights, property, and even the definition of a person are culturally variable; but howsoever these things are defined, when they are transgressed, people react with anger. While it may take many forms, the most common behavioral outcome of anger is an attempt to inflict some kind of harm on the transgressor.

Often, when people are very angry, they act in ways that seem to make no sense to observers, or even to the actors themselves when reflecting on their behavior later—in English we speak of being "blinded by anger," while the Bengkulu of Sumatra with whom I worked metaphorically described the state as *kemasukan*, possession by an evil spirit. Inspection reveals that the "irrationality" of the angry person's behavior has two components: risk indifference and disproportionality. First, angry individuals may seek to inflict costs on transgressors that greatly outweigh the costs suffered as a result of the transgression—murderous assaults may stem from a disrespectful glance or gesture, or even a quick lane change on the freeway. Second, when attempting to inflict harm on the transgressor who elicited the emotion, the angry person often seems indifferent to the potential costs entailed by their actions. Actors may confront opponents who are much more power-ful than themselves, or may risk costly social sanctions ranging from ostra-cism to execution.

Generations of philosophers have dismissed anger, like other emotions, as a primitive mental state with no utility, a crude limitation that detracts from, rather than promotes, the individual's ability to cope with the world. However, evolutionary psychologists take a different approach, asking in-stead what adaptive function this feature could have performed in the past such that this capacity would have been uniformly selected for among our common ancestors. Consider first the utility of aggressive response to trans-gression, the behavioral outcome resulting from anger. Prompt responses that inflict high costs on the transgressor are likely to deter future transgres-sions, both from the original transgressor and, to the extent that others learn of the response, from other potential transgressors as well. Moreover, the greater the costs inflicted on the transgressor, the greater the resulting de-terrence effect (Daly & Wilson, 1988). Hence, while the reaction to trans-gression may seem disproportionate to the costs suffered as a result of the transgression, this inequality disappears when one considers the sum of the costs that would occur were future transgressions not deterred. Seen in this light, anger, the compelling desire to inflict significant harm on transgres-sors, is highly functional (see also Trivers, 1971; McGuire & Troisi, 1990; Edwards, 1999, pp. 140–141). Lastly, this functionality would have been es-pecially marked in the small-scale, face-to-face communities characteristic of most of our species' history, as reputations have much greater impact in such groups than they do in the mobile, largely anonymous social world of contemporary industrialized nation-states.

As lawmakers and insurance salespeople know only too well, in every-day thinking, immediate costs loom larger than future potential costs—people often choose not to wear seat belts or buy auto insurance because the costs (hassle, expense, etc.) are immediate, and these overshadow po-tential future costs (injury or liability resulting from an accident). Although responding to transgressions in an apparently disproportionate fashion may protect the actor from large potential future costs, it entails incurring more salient immediate costs, something that people would normally avoid. There is therefore great utility in a biasing mechanism that overcomes reticence to incur immediate costs, and anger serves exactly this purpose (Frank, 1988).

Developmental Pathways and the Calibration of Risk Sensitivity

In general, risk-taking behavior is adaptive when it is inversely proportional to the actor's future prospects: individuals who are likely to have a rosy fu-ture ahead of them should be averse to significant risks, while those who have poorer prospects should be more willing to gamble (as the song says, "If ya got nothin', ya got nothin' to lose") (Daly & Wilson, 1988). Moreover, no two individuals face exactly the same future prospects, and individuals are not born knowing their futures—experience is the only grounds for prognostication. Accordingly, we can expect that individuals should be equipped to use past experiences in order to assess their future prospects, and they should adjust their risk-taking behavior in light of this (ongoing) assessment. In otherwise healthy humans, highly traumatic experiences often produce a syndrome characterized by impulsiveness, aggressivity, and reduced serotonergic functioning (Southwick et al., 1999). Experimental modification of rearing conditions in a nonhuman primate model indicate that adverse early experiences result in subnormal levels of serotonin, a neurotransmitter implicated in impulsive risk-taking (Rosenblum et al., 1994; see also Higley & Linnoila, 1997). Similar patterns characterize boys raised in families characterized by frequent parental physical punishment and anger (Pine et al., 1996). Among incarcerated adult male violent offenders, recidivism is predicted by indices of low serotonin levels, and this in turn is correlated with a childhood history of paternal alcoholism and violence, paternal absence, and the presence of (presumably similarly aggressive) brothers in the home (Virkkunen et al., 1996).

The Origin of Sex Differences in the Response to Transgression

The greater the stakes to be won or lost in transgressions, the more important defensive measures become. In a (mildly) polygynous species such as our own, the variance in male reproductive success is greater than that in female reproductive success: that is, in the EEA, or environment of evolutionary adaptedness, the difference in the number of offspring between highly successful and highly unsuccessful men was larger than the corresponding difference among equivalent women. As a result, in our ancestral state, males had more at stake in defending against transgressions than did females.[4] Furthermore, unlike all other apes, human males often invest significantly in their mates and offspring. As a consequence, being cuckolded poses a grave threat to a man's fitness, for he risks wasting his investment on another man's genes. The advent of hominid paternal investment thus raised the potential costs of transgressions, further increasing the selective advantages of male psychological attributes that function to deter transgression (Wilson & Daly, 1992; Buss et al., 1992). Together, these factors are likely to have selected for a sex difference in the subjective response to transgression. Because the stakes to be won or lost in transgressions are likely to have been consistently higher for males than for females, it is plausible that se-

lection favored males who, in comparison with females, were both more easily and more dramatically blinded by anger. This psychological difference
corresponds with morphological differences, as the greater size and muscu-
larity of men is reasonably explained as the product of intrasexual selection
(i.e., men are in part designed for combat).[5] This combination of psychological and morphological differences corresponds with manifest differences
in behavior: around the globe, spontaneous murderous violence is largely the
domain of men (Daly & Wilson, 1988, 1990; Ghiglieri, 1999; Campbell, this
volume; Walsh, this volume).[6]

Culture, Information, and Behavior

Although the gender difference in homicidally violent responses to transgression bridges diverse cultures, there is enormous cross-cultural variation
in attitudes toward, and frequency of, male violence (cf. Ghiglieri, 1999).
To explain this more global variation, we begin by leaving considerations of
biological evolution behind for the moment and turn instead to the question
of cultural evolution. Because the concept of culture, always much debated,
has come under increasing scrutiny lately (cf. Aunger, 1999), it is necessary
to begin with a definition. Following Swartz and Jordan (1980), I take "culture" to be the sum of the morally forceful understandings acquired through
learning and shared with members of a learner's group, where such sharing
need not be universal but, on the contrary, is often distributed in a patterned
way across the population (see also Swartz, 1991). Culture is composed of
ideas varying greatly in specificity, from the meaning of an observable gesture, such as an erect middle finger, to the existence of an invisible property,
such as "honor." Similarly, while some ideas have overt moral connotations,
other forms of socially transmitted information may only exhibit moral force
at a far more subtle level—people care, for example, not only with whom
others conduct their sexual relationships, but also how they court, or even
how they tie their shoes. Clearly, much of the difference between "warlike"
societies and "peaceful" societies derives from the meaning attached to violence itself (cf. Robarchek & Robarchek, 1992). However, in keeping with
the position introduced at the beginning of this essay, I suggest that the reason that such meanings are deeply internalized by many of the members of
a given society is that they are congruent with more profound subjective experiences (see Spiro, 1997), experiences which are the product of the interaction between evolved propensities and acquired ideas.
  Evolutionary theorists frequently point out that selective processes
often give rise to proclivities rather than to iron-clad behavioral directives,
in large part because the former allow for fitness-enhancing adjustment
in light of local circumstances (cf. Belsky, 1999; Chisholm, 1999). This

inherent flexibility opens the door for cultural influence via two paths. First, by indirectly shaping the behavioral environment in which an individual matures, culture patterns the inputs processed by evolved calibration mechanisms, thereby increasing the likelihood that some evolved propensities will be enhanced, while others will be dampened. Of direct relevance here, culturally shaped parental attitudes and prescribed socialization practices are likely to interact with the serotonergic risk sensitivity mechanism described earlier, resulting in a partial patterning of the degree of impulsivity across members of a single culture-sharing group. Second, because human mental experience is profoundly shaped by socially acquired information, the process of enculturation can influence the subjective salience and motivational significance of different evolved propensities. In particular, both lexical labels and the organized, hierarchically embedded information structures called cultural schemas which accompany such labels provide individuals with cognitive tools that make it easier to anticipate, identify, and reflect on given types of mental events (D'Andrade, 1995). Such cultural marking, or *hypercognizing* (Levy, 1973), increases the impact of the labeled mental events. By the same token, the selective absence of cultural information regarding a given type of experience (*hypocognizing*, in Levy's terms) decreases its significance. Third, those subjective experiences that are culturally marked may be either pre- or proscribed, with the result that individuals may strive to prolong or curtail them, and may seek out or avoid circumstances that elicit them. Finally, it is important to recognize that, because cultural understandings are not uniformly distributed within a population, all three of these processes can lead to both similarities and differences between individuals within any one group. However, because individuals within a given society are often influenced by a larger number of the same understandings than are individuals in different societies, variation within societies is expected to be generally lower than variation between societies.

Culture and the Male Flash of Anger

I suspect that the male flash of anger, with its overwhelming subjective change and drastic behavioral outcome, is both sufficiently dramatic and sufficiently far-reaching in its social consequences as to preclude its ever being hypocognized—I would be greatly surprised if any culture were to be found to lack lexical labels for "anger," or to not contain cultural schemas describing the potential for aggressivity and risk-taking characteristic of men. However, a predicted absence of hypocognizing in no way means that we should expect uniformity in the manner and degree to which cultures influence both the experience and the manifestation of this evolved propensity. Quite the opposite is true, since, depending upon socioenvironmental circumstances, the male flash of anger can constitute either a vital asset or a perilous threat in patterned social relations.

If the male flash of anger is "designed" to diminish transgressions in the service of acquiring and maintaining control over a variety of economic and social resources, then it follows that three distinct considerations will affect the utility or importance of this psychological feature. First, the more easily that valuable resources can be appropriated, the more damaging any transgression is likely to be, and hence the more important it is to curtail transgressions. Second, the less that overarching social institutions protect actors from transgressions or allow them to seek redress, the greater the significance of those individual actions that curtail transgressions. Third, the less that actors depend on others in crucial political and economic endeavors, the less important it becomes to preserve social relationships, and hence the fewer the costs associated with aggressive responses to potential transgressions. Accordingly, we can expect that concepts or experiences associated with the male flash of anger will be both hypercognized and valorized in societies in which (a) vital resources are highly appropriateable, (b) little protection is provided for the individual, and (c) cooperation is not highly relevant to resource acquisition. While a definitive examination of this proposition awaits systematic ethnological comparison, the following cases illustrate prospective polar types on the spectrum of the world's cultures.

Nisbett and Cohen (1996) argue that the violent "culture of honor" characteristic of the U.S. American South and Southwest is a legacy passed down from the Scots-Irish immigrants who settled these regions. In contrast to the English farmers who settled the Northeast, the Scots-Irish were pastoralists. Unlike wheat or barley, cattle and sheep are mobile and can be easily taken away from their owner. Animals do not require the periodic, brief investment of large amounts of labor that make collective action valuable in planting or harvesting. Finally, the independence that pastoralism allows, combined with the mobility that pastoralism requires, constitutes an obstacle to the formation of complex overarching social institutions and diminishes the importance of dispute-resolution mechanisms. In short, pastoralism is often highly conducive to the hypercognizing of circumstances surrounding the male flash of anger (see also Goldschmidt, 1965; Edgerton, 1971).[7] The southern concept of "honor" can be thought of as a reified representation of a well-guarded individual, free of transgressions: "honor" is "slighted" or "offended" by "insult," and must then be "defended"—that is, transgressions elicit an aggressive response. Not surprisingly, it is men who are most often called upon for such defense, and it is men who seem most sensitive to questions of honor. Nisbett and Cohen present experimental evidence showing that transgressions elicit stronger physiological correlates of anger in southern men than in New Englanders. Hence, in this culturally constituted reality, it is not the male flash of anger per se that is elaborately hypercognized but, rather, the social integrity which that response protects, with the result that the male flash of anger is both more easily elicited and more violently acted upon.

Next, consider the "street" culture of North Philadelphia described by Anderson (1994). For the young men of the street, wealth and prestige are advertised in the form of jewelry and clothing, items that are easily taken by force. Money is acquired through activities that require only minimal social connections. Chaotic family lives, neighborhood entropy, and police apathy (or overt hostility) add up to an absence of mechanisms of social control. Here, the highest value is placed not on "honor" but on "respect," a reification of the behaviors that indicate an awareness of another's propensity to react violently to transgression: young men crave "respect" and are ferociously angry if they believe that others are questioning or testing their ability to respond to transgressions. Risk-taking and reputational conflict are an inherent part of daily life. Men who live to maturity either struggle to maintain the same degree of ferocity or essentially withdraw from male-male social competition; public space generally belongs to young men. Finally, childhood experiences are congruent with those of later life: Aggression within the family is overt, economic needs are inconsistently met, and family structure is highly labile. Hence, once again we find a cultural meaning system, functionally congruent with the socioenvironmental context, that enhances both the ease of elicitation and the behavioral intensity of the male flash of anger.

In contrast to the utility of the male flash of anger for societies in which individual defense against transgression is paramount, this same evolved propensity constitutes a significant hazard in societies where adverse circumstances both necessitate cooperation and entail vulnerability to revenge. Consider the Scandinavian-derived inhabitants of the Faeroe Islands, an isolated archipelago in the North Atlantic. As described by Gaffin (1995), the principal male economic activities consist of team fishing in turbulent waters, shepherding (which is communal due to frequent absences while fishing), and the harvesting of sea birds from steep sea cliffs. All of these endeavors put men in considerable danger, and many require cooperation. It is therefore not surprising that the Faeroe Islanders place a premium on the ability to avoid becoming angry. Indeed, this is a defining characteristic of proper adult masculine behavior. So central is this feature to the male ideal that Faeroe Island culture contains an elaborate schema concerning the type of man who fails in this regard. Villagers constantly taunt one another, testing each others' capacity to control anger. Men who fail such tests are pejoratively labeled and taunted at length, thereby repeatedly demonstrating both their own inability to conform to the cultural ideal and the explosive danger inherent in giving in to anger.

Perhaps the most complete psychocultural portrait of a society for which the male flash of anger constitutes a hazard is Briggs's (1970) study of the Utkuhikhalingmiut Eskimos (or Utku), tellingly titled *Never in Anger*. At the time of Briggs's research, Utku society consisted of 35 individuals, the only inhabitants in an arctic region of more than 35,000 square miles. This environment, characterized by extreme weather conditions and marked fluctuations in food availability, is arguably the primary determinant of a wide range of features of Utku culture. Importantly, although individual households are largely self-sufficient, social networks provide the only source of security in the event of misfortune or illness. In a small population subject to seasonal restrictions on mobility, open social conflict could seriously imperil an entire community. Moreover, because hunting and fishing activities require men to brave hazardous conditions alone or with a few partners, men are extremely vulnerable to retribution. Under these circumstances, it is understandable that for the Utku the sine qua non of maturity is emotional equanimity. Anger in particular is proscribed and elaborately hypercognized, importantly including a cultural schema in which angry thoughts are seen as having the power to magically harm others. By definition, individuals who openly experience and express anger are not adults, and men in particular are held to a stringent standard. As Briggs documents in great detail, Utku socialization practices reflect these ideals, as adults' interactions with children are characterized by a remarkable absence of aggression. Briggs also makes much of the warmth and intimacy of caretakers' behavior during early childhood. Although children display predictable resentment at the decrease in parental attention following the birth of a sibling, this fades away. Indeed, the overriding message of Utku childhood is that others care for one, one's needs will be met, and the world is a stable and predictable place. In short, Utku childhood typically involves experiences which indicate that the future is bright. As noted earlier, on both economic and neurophysiological grounds we can expect that impulsive risk-taking and aggressivity will be minimal under such circumstances, thus furthering the correspondence between cultural ideals and subjective experience.

Interindividual Variation and Cultural Evolution

Although marked differences in both behavior and ideation occur between groups, such differences do not preclude variation within the group. Intragroup variation can stem from a variety of causes, including (a) genetic variation in the propensity to anger (Cates et al., 1993), aggressivity (Vernon et al., 1999; Eley et al., 1999), and impulsivity (Hur & Bouchard, 1997; Seroczynski et al., 1999; Saudino et al., 1999); (b) variation in those life experiences, including both resource availability and exposure to parental anger, that contribute to the calibration of risk sensitivity; and (c) heterogeneity in the possession and/or interpretation of cultural understandings (cf. Aunger, 1999). In addition to internal heterogeneity, societies also exhibit change over time in shared understandings. Moreover, it is likely that these two phenomena, intragroup variation and cultural change, are causally linked.

The heterogeneity of motivational dispositions found within any given group at any given time may constitute a key element in the process of cultural change. Central cultural understandings may develop as a result of the social dynamics that emerge from the intersection of interindividual variation and local parameters of utility. Given some defining features of a local socioecological environment at a given moment in time, because of interindividual variation resulting from a combination of genetic differences, differing life experiences, and differing cultural schemas, a fraction of the population will possess patterns of emotions, inclinations, and other motivators that "fit" well (or, at least, better than others) with the demands of that environment. These individuals are likely to succeed where other individuals, possessing different motivational constellations, are likely to fail. However, because cultural information, unlike genetic information, can be transmitted horizontally, this initial partitioning of the population (in part) on genetic grounds will not persist. As soon as substantial differences in success become apparent, less successful members of the group will begin to strive to imitate the newly successful individuals (Boyd & Richerson, 1992). As a consequence, the locally adaptive behavior pattern will spread within the population. Public self-justification by those who achieve success, combined with a growing awareness of the increasingly normative pattern, will then lead individuals to create and promulgate schemas that both describe and prescribe these locally optimal behavioral features and the psychological orientations that underlie them. Over time, these schemas will become increasingly refined as people reflect on both their own subjective experiences and the pervasive behavioral patterns. In turn, cultural schemas will affect both subjective experience and the attractiveness of other, related ideas, including those concerning child-rearing practices. The net result is often the gradual creation of elaborate and somewhat integrated sets of ideational and behavioral patterns that differ substantially across groups.

As the case of the southern "culture of honor" demonstrates, integrated systems of belief and practice can be quite stable, sometimes even outliving the socioecological conditions that initially gave rise to them. However, while the general determinants of such stability are as yet unclear, it is nevertheless apparent that cultures can also change dramatically. The above reasoning suggests one factor that may facilitate substantial, and often rapid, cultural reconfiguration: In the event that a change occurs in the basic socioecological parameters within which a society operates, the existing inter-individual variation in endogenous motivational patterns will constitute a pool from which new patterns of thought and behavior can emerge (compare with Hollan, 2000). For example, as a combined result of the economic opportunities created by the introduction of the horse (and, later, the gun) and increasing attacks from neighboring groups, within a relatively short period of time a number of North American Indian societies, including the Cheyenne, the Arapaho, and the Teton Dakota, transformed from sedentary horticulturalists into nomadic hunter-gatherers. Dramatic modifications of the social structure reflected fundamental changes in the underlying value systems, as hereditary offices were largely replaced by a meritocracy based on individual performance in the male activities of hunting, raiding, and fighting (Oliver, 1962). Although we lack information on the interpersonal dynamics of those changes, it is likely that the temperaments which best suited the earlier social form differed substantially from those which best suited the later social form.[8]

Thus far I have stressed the functionality of cultural beliefs and practices. However, it is important to recognize that the feedback relationships between the demographic distribution of an idea and its cultural elaboration are such that change can sometimes carry societies down one-way paths that lead to increasing social disruption and disorganization or, at the very least, limit the growth of social complexity (cf. Edgerton, 1992). For example, there may be cases in which, independent of the initial socioecological costs or benefits of aggressivity, a critical mass of aggressive men achieves success. This could then lead to increasing valorization of violence, with the result that warfare becomes endemic and internal conflicts prevent groups from ever growing large enough to pacify their neighbors (cf. Chagnon, 1997). Conversely, the prior development of elaborately hypercognized concepts may limit a group's ability to adapt to changing circumstances (cf. Fessler, 1995). For example, a culturally entrenched fear of anger and aggressivity is likely to hinder groups that are faced with external competition, with the result that they are simply marginalized, assimilated, or killed (cf. Dentan, 1979). The lesson from these examples is that the internal dynamics that generate cultural change do not guarantee functionality at the group level, since change is frequently the product of the actions of individuals who may be self-interested, short-sighted, or both.

A striking feature of the transformations that occurred on the North American Plains is the remarkable convergence of cultural forms. The various Plains societies originally stemmed from groups possessing markedly different means of production (ranging from foraging to horticulture), different social structures (from egalitarian to hierarchical), and different attitudes toward violence (from valorization to abhorrence); but after only a few centuries, the Plains were populated by a relatively homogeneous set of nomadic hunter/warrior societies, a highly efficient form in the given socio-ecological setting (Oliver, 1962). Given that the social dynamics that generate cultural change are themselves undirected, and hence can conceivably produce a wide range of outcomes that differ markedly in their functionality at the level of the group, the convergent cultural evolution evident in the Plains case suggests that a process termed "cultural group selection" was at work. Essentially, this is a form of "survival of the fittest" at the level of both cultural information and the populations that hold, act on, and transmit that information.[9] The combination of the heterogeneity of the original forms that gave rise to Plains societies and the homogeneity of the resulting complex suggest that those sociocultural variants which did not lead to the locally optimal form were eliminated, displaced, or assimilated by those which did. By the same token, it is likely that the exquisite fit between the entailments of Faeroe Islander fishing or Utku foraging and the respective cultural conceptions of the male flash of anger is the product of cultural group selection—societies in which successive cultural changes have produced locally highly functional attitudes toward male anger and violence will ultimately outlive societies possessing less functional cultural schemas.

In conclusion, the case of the male flash of anger illustrates how evolutionary psychology and cultural anthropology provide complementary components in vertically integrated explanations of important human phenomena. Evolutionary approaches both shed light on the functionality of anger as a response to transgression and account for the age- and sex-biased distribution of violent risk-taking behavior. Evolutionary psychology also provides an ultimate explanation for the process whereby, via alterations that occur at the level of the neurotransmitter, childhood experience influences adult risk-taking propensities. In turn, culturally constituted socialization practices and interactional patterns shape childhood experience, inscribing culturally preferred responses to transgression on individual actors; these tacit lessons are further reinforced by overt morally weighted cultural schemas and lexicons. However, despite the redundancy of cultural mediation, intragroup variation in the response to transgression persists due to genetic variation, idiosyncratic life experiences, and incomplete sharing of cultural information. This variation constitutes the raw material for culture change, as some orientations will be more congruent than others with the demands of the current socioecological setting, and hence some individuals will be more likely to succeed and, thereafter, to be imitated. At a still larger scale, cultural group selection can occur when differing sociocultural systems come into contact with one another, as those systems that most successfully meet the challenges posed by the socioecological setting are most likely to prosper and spread. These processes explain why there is often an exquisite fit between the demands of the socioecological setting and the culturally shaped response to transgression. However, because optimality is relative to a given set of competing sociocultural systems, and because any given system is the product of unique and often random historical events, non- or even dysfunctional beliefs and practices may also persist, thus explaining the existence of societies that are mired in perpetual internecine warfare, or those that are so pacifistic that they are easily displaced by newly arrived competitors.

I thank Robert Boyd, Joseph Manson, Nicholas Blurton-Jones, Jerome Barkow, and Dov Cohen for productive discussions. Veronica Davidov provided research assistance.

Notes

1. For discussion of how culturally evolved institutions motivate participation in anonymous warfare by exploiting emotions that normally operate at the interpersonal level, see Richerson & Boyd (1999); also, see Feshbach (1994).

2. Large-scale violence directed at civilians, such as that which occurred in the Balkans or Rwanda, often seems to have a personal flavor, and survivors frequently report that they were acquainted with their assailants. The same is often true of raiding and warfare in traditional societies (cf. Chagnon, 1997). Accordingly, events such as these may be amenable to explanation in the framework discussed herein.

3. Elsewhere (Fessler, 2001) I have argued that "shame," which is intimately linked to "anger," is also a critical contributor to violent conflict.

4. Note that this should not be interpreted as meaning that females were not, or are not, both socially competitive and aggressively responsive to transgression. Rather, the difference between the sexes is one of degree, as males are expected to be generally willing to risk incurring substantially higher costs than females given the higher stakes involved.

5. This argument rests upon cross-species comparisons that reveal a positive correlation between sexual dimorphism (in both size and armaments) and degree of intrasexual competition, i.e., the higher the reproductive stakes, the more that male physiological resources are dedicated to combat (see Daly & Wilson, 1983; Plavcan & Van Schaik, 1997).

6. Note that this argument seeks to explain differences in the degree to which men and women put themselves and others at risk when they experience anger—the same economic logic selected for angry reactions in males and females, but the sex difference in costs and benefits resulted in greater aggressivity and greater indifference to risk as part of anger in males than in females. As a consequence, even in cultures which enhance the violent potential of female anger, we can expect women to generally resort to lethal violence less often than men (cf. Burbank, 1992).

7. Recent findings from Mongolia (F. Gil-White, personal communication) and Africa (R. McElreath, personal communication) call into

question the universality of the association between pastoralism and the male honor complex. I suspect, however, that pastoralist societies lacking an elaborate honor complex will possess overarching mechanisms of social control, such as age-grades that perform corporate functions in protecting property, which reduce or obviate the need for individual aggressive response to transgression.

8. By way of comparison, Tuzin (1989) has documented how changes in the socioecological context of the Ilahita Arapesh of Papua New Guinea led to a dramatic cultural revolution; significantly, these changes involved the meteoric rise of a man whose personality had previously relegated him to the sidelines of social life.

9. Though long implicit in anthropological theories, cultural group selection has only recently been examined in a rigorous fashion. See Soltis et al., 1995; Richerson & Boyd, 1998.

References

Anderson, Elijah. (1994). The code of the streets. *Atlantic Monthly 273*(5), 80–94.

Aunger, Robert. (1999). Against idealism/contra consensus. *Current Anthropology 40*(supplement), S93–S101.

Barkow, Jerome H. (1989). *Darwin, sex, and status: Biological approaches to mind and culture.* Toronto: University of Toronto Press.

Belsky, Jay. (1999). Modern evolutionary theory and patterns of attachment. In J. Cassidy & P. R. Shaver (Eds.), *Handbook of attachment: Theory, research, and clinical applications* (pp. 141–161). New York: Guilford.

Boyd, Robert, & Peter J. Richerson. (1992). Cultural inheritance and evolutionary ecology. In E. A. Smith & B. Winterhalder (Eds.), *Evolutionary ecology and human behavior* (pp. 61–92). Foundations of human behavior. New York: Aldine de Gruyter.

Briggs, Jean L. (1970). *Never in anger: Portrait of an Eskimo family.* Cambridge, MA: Harvard University Press.

Burbank, Victoria K. (1992). Sex, gender, and difference: Dimensions of aggression in an Australian Aboriginal community. *Human Nature 3*(3), 251–278.

Burbank, Victoria K. (1994). *Fighting women: Anger and aggression in Aboriginal Australia.* Berkeley: University of California Press.

Buss, David M., Randy J. Larsen, Drew Westen, & Jennifer Semmelroth. (1992). Sex differences in jealousy: Evolution, physiology, and psychology. *Psychological Science 3*(4), 251–255.

Cates, David S., B. K. Houston, C. R. Vavak, M. H. Crawford, & M. Uttley. (1993). Heritability of hostility-related emotions, attitudes, and behaviors. *Journal of Behavioral Medicine 16*(3), 237–256.

Chagnon, Napoleon A. (1997). *Yanomamö.* Fort Worth: Harcourt Brace College.

Chisholm, James S. (1999). *Death, hope, and sex: Steps to an evolutionary ecology of mind and morality*. Cambridge: Cambridge University Press.

Daly, Martin, & Margo Wilson. (1983). *Sex, evolution, and behavior*. Boston: Willard Grant Press.

Daly, Martin, & Margo Wilson. (1988). *Homicide*. New York: Aldine de Gruyter.

Daly, Martin, & Margo Wilson. (1990). Killing the competition: Female/female and male/male homicide. *Human Nature 1*(1), 81–107.

D'Andrade, Roy G. (1995). *The development of cognitive anthropology*. Cambridge: Cambridge University Press.

Dentan, Robert Knox. (1979). *The Semai: A nonviolent people of Malaya*. New York: Holt Rinehart and Winston.

Edgerton, Robert B. (1971). *The individual in cultural adaptation: A study of four East African peoples*. Berkeley: University of California Press.

Edgerton, Robert B. (1992). *Sick societies: Challenging the myth of primitive harmony*. New York: Free Press.

Edwards, David C. (1999). *Motivation and emotion: Evolutionary, physiological, cognitive, and social influences*. Thousand Oaks, CA: Sage.

Ekman, P. (1994). Strong evidence for universals in facial expressions: A reply to Russell's mistaken critique. *Psychological Bulletin 115*(2), 268–287.

Eley, Thalia C., Paul Lichenstein, & Jim Stevenson. (1999). Sex differences in the etiology of aggressive and nonaggressive antisocial behavior: Results from two twin studies. *Child Development 70*(1), 155–168.

Feshbach, Seymour. (1994). Nationalism, patriotism, and aggression: A clarification of functional differences. In L. R. Huesmann (Ed.), *Aggressive behavior: Current perspectives* (pp. 275–291). New York: Plenum.

Fessler, Daniel Marcel Thickstun. (1995). A small field with a lot of hornets: An exploration of shame, motivation, and social control. PhD dissertation, Department of Anthropology, University of California, San Diego.

Fessler, Daniel Marcel Thickstun. (2001). Emotions and cost/benefit assessment: The role of shame and self-esteem in risk taking. In R. Selten & G. Gigerenzer (Eds.), *Bounded rationality: The adaptive toolbox* (pp. 191–214). Cambridge, MA: MIT Press.

Frank, Robert H. (1988). *Passions within reason: The strategic role of the emotions*. New York: Norton.

Gaffin, Dennis. (1995). The production of emotion and social control: Taunting, anger, and the rukka in the Faeroe Islands. *Ethos 23*(2), 149–172.

Ghiglieri, Michael Patrick. (1999). *The dark side of man: Tracing the origins of male violence*. Reading, MA: Perseus Books.

Gladwin, Thomas, & Seymour Bernard Sarason. (1953). *Truk: Man in paradise*. New York: Wenner-Gren Foundation for Anthropological Research.

Goldschmidt, Walter. (1965). Theory and strategy in the study of cultural adaptability. *American Anthropologist 67*(2), 402–408.

Haidt, Jonathan, & Dacher Keltner. (1999). Culture and facial expression: Open-ended methods find more expressions and a gradient of recognition. *Cognition & Emotion 13*(3), 225–266.

Higley, J. D., & M. Linnoila. (1997). Low central nervous system serotonergic activity is traitlike and correlates with impulsive behavior: A non-human primate model investigating genetic and environmental influences on neurotransmission. In David M. Stoff & J. John Mann (Eds.), *The neurobiology of suicide: From the bench to the clinic* (pp. 39–56). New York: New York Academy of Sciences.

Hollan, Douglas. (2000). Constructivist models of mind, contemporary psychoanalysis, and the development of culture theory. *American Anthropologist 102*(3), 538–550.

Hur, Yoon-Mi, & Thomas J. Bouchard Jr. (1997). The genetic correlation between impulsivity and sensation seeking traits. *Behavior Genetics 27*(5), 455–463.

Lee, Richard B. (1993). *The Dobe Ju 'hoansi*. Fort Worth: Harcourt Brace College.

Levy, Robert I. (1973). *Tahitians: Mind and experience in the Society Islands*. Chicago: University of Chicago Press.

McGuire, Michael T., & Alfonso Troisi. (1990). Anger: An evolutionary view. In Robert Plutchik & Henry Kellerman (Eds.), *Emotion, psychopathology, and psychotherapy* (pp. 43–57). San Diego, CA: Academic Press.

Nisbett, Richard E., & Dov Cohen. (1996). *Culture of honor: The psychology of violence in the South*. Boulder, CO: Westview.

Oliver, Chad. (1962). *Ecology and cultural continuity as contributing factors in the social organization of the Plains Indians*. Berkeley: University of California Press.

Otterbein, Keith F. (2000). Five feuds: An analysis of homicides in eastern Kentucky in the late nineteenth century. *American Anthropologist 102*(2), 231–243.

Pine, Daniel S., G. A. Wasserman, J. Coplan, J. A. Fried, Y. Y. Huang, S. Kassir, L. Greenhill, D. Shaffer, & B. Parsons. (1996). Platelet serotonin 2A (5-HT-sub(2A)) receptor characteristics and parenting factors for boys at risk for delinquency: A preliminary report. *American Journal of Psychiatry 153*(4), 538–544.

Plavcan, J. Michael, & Carel P. Van Schaik. (1997). Intrasexual competition and body weight dimorphism in anthropoid primates. *American Journal of Physical Anthropology 103*(1), 37–68.

Richerson, Peter J., & Robert Boyd. (1998). The evolution of human ultrasociality. In I. Eibl-Eibesfeldt & F. K. Salter (Eds.), *Indoctrinability, ideology, and warfare: Evolutionary perspectives* (pp. 71–95). New York: Berghahn Books.

Richerson, Peter J., & Robert Boyd. (1999). The evolutionary dynamics of a crude super organism. *Human Nature 10*, 253–289.

Robarchek, Clayton A., & Carole J. Robarchek. (1992). Cultures of war and peace: A comparative study of Waorani and Semai. In J. Silverberg

& J. P. Gray (Eds.), *Aggression and peacefulness in humans and other primates* (pp. 189–213). New York: Oxford University Press.

Rosenblum, Leonard A., J. D. Coplan, S. Friedman, T. Bassoff, J. M. Gorman, & M. W. Andrews. (1994). Adverse early experiences affect noradrenergic and serotonergic functioning in adult primates. *Biological Psychiatry 35*(4), 221–227.

Saudino, Kimberly J., J. R. Gagne, J. Grant, A. Ibatoulina, T. Marytuina, I. Ravich-Scherbo, & K. Whitfield. (1999). Genetic and environmental influences on personality in adult Russian twins. *International Journal of Behavioral Development 23*(2), 375–389.

Seroczynski, Alesha D., C. S. Bergeman, & Emil F. Coccaro. (1999). Etiology of the impulsivity/aggression relationship: Genes or environment? *Psychiatry Research 86*(1), 41–57.

Soltis, Joseph, Robert Boyd, & Peter J. Richerson. (1995). Can group-functional behaviors evolve by cultural group selection? An empirical test. *Current Anthropology 36*(3), 473–494.

Southwick, S. M. (1999). Neurotransmitter alterations in PTSD: Catecholamines and serotonin. *Seminars in Clinical Neuropsychiatry 4*(4), 242–248.

Spiro, Melford E. (1997). *Gender ideology and psychological reality: An essay on cultural reproduction.* New Haven, CT: Yale University Press.

Swartz, Marc J. (1991). *The way the world is: Cultural processes and social relations among the Mombasa Swahili.* Berkeley: University of California Press.

Swartz, Marc J., & David K. Jordan. (1980). *Culture: The anthropological perspective.* New York: Wiley.

Trivers, Robert L. (1971). The evolution of reciprocal altruism. *Quarterly Review of Biology 46*(4), 35–57.

Tuzin, Donald. (1989). Visions, prophecies, and the rise of Christian Consciousness. In G. H. Herdt & M. Stephen (Eds.), *The religious imagination in New Guinea* (pp. 187–208). New Brunswick, NJ: Rutgers University Press.

Vernon, P. A., J. M. McCarthy, A. M. Johnson, K. L. Jang, & J. A. Harris. (1999). Individual differences in multiple dimensions of aggression: A univariate and multivariate genetic analysis. *Twin Research 2*(1), 16–21.

Virkkunen, Matti, M. Eggert, R. Rawlings, & M. Linnoila. (1996). A prospective follow-up study of alcoholic violent offenders and fire setters. *Archives of General Psychiatry 53*(6), 523–529.

Wilson, Margo, & Martin Daly. (1992). The man who mistook his wife for a chattel. In J. Barkow, L. Cosmides, & J. Tooby (Eds.), *The adapted mind: Evolutionary psychology and the generation of culture* (pp. 289–322). New York: Oxford University Press.

PART II

Controversies

Because the evolutionary perspective is perpetually under attack, many of the contributors to this volume find it necessary at least in passing to defend their work against the endless stream of accusations. To those engaged in the fray, the critics of evolutionary approaches to human nature and society are taking the role of the wolf in the tale of the three little pigs. In this version, however, the wolf helpfully builds the houses for the pigs himself, before commencing to huff and puff. As it turns out, he has built all three houses of straw. Though the critics of sociobiology include the eminent, their misstatements of sociobiology and evolutionary psychology have often been extreme (Segerstråle, this volume, 2000). Kurzban and Haselton's chapter constitutes a powerful and essential response to some of the various accusations made against evolutionists. Their response is especially necessary because the eminence of some of the critics has given their parodies credibility. Many social scientists seem to have (mis)learned what little they know of evolutionary approaches to human behavior and society from these critics.

As Ullica Segerstråle explains, to understand current controversies over evolutionary approaches to the human sciences, one must go back perhaps 30 years. After all, some of the attackers from that era are still with us, lobbing old ammunition against the new field of evolutionary psychology. Of course, in the current Age of Biology, fierce attacks against those who would naturalize our understanding of human behavior by placing it in the same framework that has so successfully been applied to other animal species seem a bit quaint and anachronistic. Segerstråle, a sociologist and long-term student of these disputes, provides an arms-length analysis that in part summarizes ideas developed at much greater length in her exhaustive study *Defenders of the Truth*.

References

Segerstråle, U. (2000). *Defenders of the Truth: The Battle for Science in the Sociobiology Debate and Beyond.* New York: Oxford University Press.

4 Evolutionary Explanation: Between Science and Values

Ullica Segerstråle

1. Suspicions About Biology and Behavior

Sociobiologists and more recently evolutionary biologists have sometimes been told that it is "evil" to pursue research on the biological foundations of human behavior. This is perplexing for evolutionary psychologists, who regard their discipline as deliberately avoiding sociobiological traps, because it concentrates on the makeup of the human mind, rather than on genetic tendencies for behavior. Evolutionary psychologists, like sociobiologists, behavioral ecologists, Darwinian anthropologists, and other related researchers, see themselves, just like other scientists, as engaged in a detached quest for knowledge and truth. But this has led to loud protests from many left-liberal scientists. At the same time, traditional social scientists are often skeptical of the new evolutionary approaches. Many, if not most, clues to these sentiments against research in the biological foundations of human behavior can be found by studying the sociobiology controversy.

In this chapter I will discuss the reasons why the evolutionary psychologists have not been able to satisfy the requirements of the critics of sociobiology. For that we will go to the basic oppositions in the sociobiology controversy. I will be analyzing the critics' overall beliefs and agenda, as manifested already in the sociobiology debate—and the IQ debate before that. Why was sociobiology seen as both scientifically and politically "incorrect" at the time? How did the critics demonstrate that sociobiology was "bad" science? What was E. O. Wilson's real aim with *Sociobiology?* What was the critics' own agenda? And why have the critics continued their attacks despite the efforts of evolutionary psychology to be politically correct? Has anything changed after more than a quarter century?

I will argue that the sociobiology debate, which has often been interpreted as a political controversy between conservative hereditarians and progressive culturalists (or environmentalists), in fact represented a clash between two total scientific-cum-moral worldviews. What was at stake was the nature of science and the moral responsibility of the scientist, especially when it came to "telling the truth" about the biological foundation of human nature. It was fundamentally a debate about the nature of evolutionary explanation of human behavior and what ought to count as "acceptable knowledge" at a particular time—a conflict with deep metaphysical underpinnings. Finally, the views and strategies of the participants in the debate reflected different beliefs in the relationship between science and values, and the merits of pursuing these together or apart. Rather than between traditional Left and Right, the dividing line went between a type of New Left academic activist and a traditional type of scientist.

2. Sociobiology and Its Enemies

The real attack on Wilson's book started in the fall of 1975 with a letter from the Sociobiology Study Group to the *New York Review of Books* (Allen et al., 1975). In that letter, *Sociobiology* was being connected to nazism and racism, and Wilson was said to support a conservative agenda by emphasizing the genetic underpinnings of human behavior. Actually, though Wilson's book was more than 500 pages long, only the last chapter was devoted to the human species. There he argued that a number of behaviors, including sex roles, aggression, altruism, and even moral and religious beliefs, could well have a biological basis. To boost this argument, he drew parallels to the behavior of other primates and invoked research on selected traits from behavioral genetics and twin studies, suggesting that additional traits may turn out to have a similar genetic foundation. The critics, however, argued that Wilson had no evidence and that his statements supported a biological determinist view of humans. For them, such a view implied that social inequality was "in our genes," which would make social measures to diminish inequality futile.

Wilson had defined sociobiology as "the systematic study of the biological basis of all social behavior." The idea was that, just like other features, behavior was undergoing evolution. His book was intended as an encyclopedia of all the new information about animal social behavior, both theories and empirical studies, that had accumulated over several decades. In this endeavor Wilson saw himself as continuing the work of the neo-Darwinian or

Modern Synthesis—the grand fusion of Mendelism and Darwinism, and its extension to a number of biological fields (systematics, paleontology, botany)—by incorporating the field of behavior. A number of theorists (William D. Hamilton, George C. Williams, Robert Trivers, George Price, John Maynard Smith) had shown that, just like morphological traits, behavior could evolve, and they had successfully applied the new field of population genetics (which expresses evolution as a change in gene frequencies of populations) to the area of social behavior.

The scientific breakthrough in sociobiology was the mathematical demonstration of the conditions under which altruism—a puzzle for Darwin—could actually evolve as a genetic trait among related individuals. Hamilton's key idea was shifting the focus from the individual organism to groups of relatives who shared genes. With the help of cost-benefit calculations and with an eye to the genetic relatedness between a donor and a recipient of an altruistic act, it now became possible to show that from a gene's point of view it made sense for a bird, say, to sacrifice itself by letting out an alarm call, if it in this way could save a (calculable) number of relatives.[1] Trivers (1971) later extended this to unrelated individuals with his notion of reciprocal altruism.

But what Wilson wanted to present as exciting new findings his critics declared to be "bad" and dangerous ideologically influenced science. And among his critics could be found two of Wilson's Harvard colleagues, Richard Lewontin and Stephen J. Gould, who were members of the Sociobiology Study Group, which had formed soon after Wilson's book was announced as news on the front page of the *New York Times* in late May 1975. This group organized many critical activities, starting with a letter in the *New York Review of Books* signed by a number of Boston-area academics. The high point of criticism was a sociobiology symposium at the 1978 meeting of the American Association for the Advancement of Science in Washington, DC, where a group of activists (from the antiracist group Committee Against Racism) chanted "Racist Wilson, you can't hide, we charge you with genocide!" whereupon two of them poured a pitcher of ice water on Wilson's neck, shouting, "Wilson, you are all wet!"

In 1975 the critics benefited from the political climate in which biological explanations of humans were taboo. This was a time when the liberal credo reigned. There was the spirit of the post–World War II UNESCO declaration stating that no evidence for racial differences existed, and the general agreement to restrict genetic explanations of humans to the field of medicine. This was also the time of postwar "environmentalism" (or, rather, culturalism); people like Margaret Mead in anthropology and B. F. Skinner in psychology were still held in high regard. And just before the sociobiology debate, as a warning for all, there had been the controversy about IQ around psychologist Arthur Jensen's (1969) suggestion that the 15-point difference

in measured IQ between whites and blacks could have a genetic explanation. Wilson had actually been careful with IQ and race in his book, and even
covered his back by citing Lewontin's (1972) discovery that variation between populations (races) is much smaller than variation within a population (race), a point that was widely regarded as undermining the usefulness
of race as a biological concept. But for the critics, that was not enough. What
mattered to them was the fact that Wilson had dared discuss biological underpinnings for human behavior at all. This is why he had to be forcefully
denounced as a "bad" scientist, both morally and scientifically.

In 1975 many believed the critics when it came to Wilson's political
motives. Very few ever read his book or asked about his actual agenda—or,
for that matter, about the critics' agenda.

3. The Political Nature of Sociobiology

According to the Sociobiology Study Group, Wilson's real aim was to promote a conservative political agenda by defending social inequality as a natural state of affairs. In fact, the members were so sure about the political
nature of Wilson's book that they challenged the readers of *Science* to see for
themselves, assuring them: "There is politics aplenty in *Sociobiology*, and we
who are its critics did not put it there" (Alper et al., 1976). Wilson himself
has steadfastly denied that he was considering these kinds of political consequences when he wrote his book. Wilson explained that his primary goal
was to provoke the social sciences into taking biology seriously (e.g., Wilson,
1981, 1991, 1994). Wilson saw (and sees) himself as a taboo breaker, and
that is what he was with *Sociobiology*. His provocation only succeeded
too well.

Wilson soon responded to his critics in kind, insisting that their criticism
of sociobiology was purely political, dismissing them as "tabula rasa Marxists." Wilson has persisted in this view till today, in various presentations and
publications (e.g., Wilson, 1995). With this, the terms of the debate were
set. Over the next quarter century the protagonists went on accusing each
other. Meanwhile, both parties used the controversy for furthering what I
call their moral-cum-scientific agendas.

What exactly did the critics mean when they said that *Sociobiology* was
political? It seems they relied solely on textual analysis, not on empirical
evidence. But clearly their interpretation was not the only possible one. In
1980 a quick overview of the actual politics of some leading sociobiologists
gave grounds for treating sociobiology as a movement closer to the Left than
the Right—even a communist conspiracy (van den Berghe, 1980). Historically, too, biological foundations have often been invoked by the Left
(e.g., the 1930s British leftist biologists, such as J. B. S. Haldane). Also, poli-

tically it is not obvious that a culturalist position is the better leftist alternative; one reason being that a socialist society needs a vision of human nature and the needs of humans (Chomsky in talk to Science for the People 1976). And if we try to find political connotations by examining the nature of sociobiological theory, it is not obvious that an atomist or individualist approach (such as used in sociobiological models) is conservative and a "holistic" perspective (hankered for by the critics) is progressive; individualist approaches can be radical (e.g., Rousseau) and holistic ones conservative (e.g., Durkheim) (Masters, 1982).

Finally, for left-wing academics at the time, joining the critics of sociobiology was not the only game in town. Several high-profile political activists, such as Noam Chomsky, Salvador Luria, and George Wald, did not join the Sociobiology Study Group. Chomsky disagreed with the group's attack on the study of human nature, Luria did not think sociobiology was a good enough cause for political mobilization, and Wald thought the Left should focus on better things, such as nuclear disarmament.

4. The Dangers of Bad Science

The members of Science for the People were genuinely convinced that sociobiology was, indeed, evil. (Of course, for academic activists, the fight against sociobiology was also a welcome cause to rally around after the IQ controversy.) The working logic of the critics is worth examining more closely. It involved a type of "cognitive coupling" between three things: bad science, ideological influences, and bad consequences. Moreover, there was a clear connection between the critics' criticism of sociobiology and their conception that "bad," and only "bad," science would be socially abused.

What, then, was "bad" science? It turned out to be the kind of science that the critics disliked: sociobiology, behavioral genetics, IQ research. Bad science was never the kind of science that the critics did themselves in their own labs. Bad science was science that involved working with models and statistics of various sorts, not science at the molecular, reductionist level. For many critics, the molecular level was where the "real" truth lay. Modeling would never really yield reliable, serious science—only objective-seeming, dangerous pseudoscience. This was Lewontin's (1975a) position. As Lewontin had already declared about those who studied cognitive traits, they "could not" be interested in genuine science, because real science had to do with the molecular level. Therefore they "must" be pursuing their research for ideological reasons—which could also explain the "shoddiness" of their science (Lewontin, 1975b).

In other words, in their zeal to combat "biological determinism," the opponents of sociobiology took a very strict view of what counted as "good science." From the critics' point of view, sociobiologists, psychometricians, and others were not allowed to operate with data or methods that the latter themselves considered acceptable (or that represented standard practice in their respective fields)! Note, however, that although the critics' stance might be called "molecular chauvinism," they did not adopt this view just so that they could outlaw sociobiology. There was indeed a profound scientific disagreement between molecularists and modelers in addition to the differences in their view about the dangers of bad science and the need for vigilantism. Even though one might argue that the critics had unrealistically strict standards for science, they did represent a possible scientific position, one that might be called a "hardliner" position. This position was not particularly Marxist. Rather, it was typical of reductionistically oriented experimental scientists in general (such as physicists, chemists, and molecular biologists): such scientists were often impatient with sociobiology (and with naturalist reasoning).

What was unusual, however, was the critics' view that it was a moral offense for their targets to publicly state their scientific convictions—because these beliefs were, from the critics' point of view, erroneous. This means that sociobiologists were attacked simply for opening their mouths. With this kind of belief machine in place, no wonder that the venerable naturalist tradition of "adaptive story-telling" in evolutionary biology was immediately transformed into support of the status quo as the best of all possible worlds—the purported conviction of "adaptationists."

Gould and Lewontin later moved on to a more scientific concern with "the adaptationist program" of sociobiology, but even so, they could not really let go of moral and political (or, in Lewontin's case, sneering) comments about the science or scientists that they were attacking. The guiding star for the critic collective was their shared belief in the intimate connection between (wrong) ideology, bad science, and dangerous social consequences.

5. A Police Officer's Task Is Not an Easy Lot

What, then, to do with all this bad science? It was not safe to have it around! So the critics appointed themselves weeders of bad science, debunking it as it was produced, so that this science would not be around to mislead the innocent layman and social policy makers. We then had a rather paradoxical situation of a new group of scientific workers, taking it upon themselves to weed out, in the name of public safety, what their colleagues had planted. These weeders trusted neither the scientific process to sort out good science from bad, nor the democratic process to reach sound decisions when it came to the uses of scientific knowledge. As a result, traditional scientists—

the "weed planters"—were cast in a strange role as evil scientists for just doing what they and their professional colleagues considered "normal science" in their own fields.

Where did the weeders get this negativistic style of reasoning? The beliefs of weeders often coincided with the New Left ideology and with the political tenets of the American 1960s student movement and peace movement. The American left-wing radicals had been influenced by the thinking of the European Critical School, which saw a power-elite manipulating the members of a mass society. Meanwhile, and ironically, the radical students in Europe adhered to a more traditional Marxist class analysis (Bouchier, 1977; Segerstråle 2000a, chap. 11). In other words, from a European Marxist point of view, most members of Science for the People could hardly be called "Marxists"; rather, they represented concerns typical of American radicalism. Wilson, meanwhile, used the blanket label "Marxist" for all his radical opponents.

A police officer's task is not an easy lot. Here is a trio of critics reflecting on the need for constant vigilance. The critics describe themselves as firefighters:

> Critics of biological determinism are like members of a fire brigade, constantly being called out in the middle of the night to put out the latest conflagration, always responding to immediate emergencies, but never with the leisure to draw up plans for a truly fireproof building. Now it is IQ and race, now criminal genes, now the biological inferiority of women, now the genetic fixity of human nature. All of these deterministic fires need to be doused with the cold water of reason before the entire neighborhood is in flames. Critics of determinism, then, seem to be doomed to constant nay-saying, while readers, audiences and students react with impatience to the perpetual negativity. (Lewontin, Rose, & Kamin, 1984, p. 266)

As part of their task as guardians of the innocent layman against bad science, Lewontin and his fellow-weeders further warned the public not to trust experts ("experts are servants of power, by and large" [Lewontin, 1975c]). In contrast, planters emphasized the possibility and desirability of objective scientific expertise (Wilson, 1977; Davis 1975, 1978, 1986). For them, the social responsibility of a scientist consisted in acting as an objective and rational authority for the public.

The two camps had completely different views of the best way of keeping science pure—that is, free from ideology. Take Bernard Davis, Wilson's Harvard ally and a scientific traditionalist. For him, Nazi science (just like Lysenkoism in the Soviet Union) was an example of what happens when scientific objectivity is abandoned to serve ideological causes. That is why science needed to be objective, and objectivity in science was, according to him, achievable. For the Sociobiology Study Group, again, Nazi science was the prime example of how bad, racist science led to bad consequences. Therefore, it was important to guard against bad science at any specific time; they noted especially that bad science may well be masquerading as objective-sounding biological claims about humans (which would then be used by evil politicians for discriminatory purposes). This is why the ideological underpinnings of objective-sounding, bad theories had to be found and exposed. (In a 1981 interview, Davis expressed sadness that he and the critics so profoundly disagreed about science, since they had equally good reason to abhor the Nazis. He explained the difference by the fact that they represented two different generations of Jewish academics.)

We see here how emphasizing or deemphasizing objectivity were actually alternative strategies for reaching the same goal of keeping science pure! Both sides in the sociobiology controversy were, in their own way, "defenders of the truth." At the same time, neither side acknowledged the possible scientific legitimacy of the other side's position. This situation appears quite typical in the world of science. In the sociobiology debate each participant believed that he himself was pursuing "good science" and the truth, while the opponent's incorrect position could obviously not be scientifically based and must therefore be explained by some bias interfering and clouding the Truth.

6. Wilson's Real Agenda

So far we have looked at the critics' interpretations of *Sociobiology*. What was it Wilson wanted to achieve with his book? His ambition can be described as a complex, combined moral and scientific agenda. At the most general level, *Sociobiology* was intended as a contribution to a larger cultural discourse about the problem of runaway technology. This was a problem stemming from the 1960s, raised again by Konrad Lorenz in his *On Aggression* (1966). Like Lorenz and the popular writers on human ethology and biocultural anthropology in the late 1960s and early 1970s (such as Robert Ardrey, Lionel Tiger, and Robin Fox), Wilson believed that mankind was in danger. Technological development was outrunning our capacity to cope. Culture was proceeding faster than evolution. Meanwhile humans were stuck with behavioral patterns that were once adaptive in an ancestral environment, but maladaptive in modern life. And as a biologist, Wilson was convinced that a culture that was fundamentally maladaptive would not prevail. This was why it was important for us to know the truth about human nature and to try to do something about this discrepancy between culture and nature. Finding out about human nature would help us understand the realistic range for social and cultural experimentation, and help with social planning. Wilson had no small goal: he wanted to save mankind.

Moreover—and this was something that served both his larger program and his more personal protest against the Church—Wilson hoped to biologize ethics. In this way, there would be no arbitrary moral rules imposed on us by "theologians." This had been Wilson's concern ever since he left the Southern Baptist Church as a teenager and became an evolutionist instead (see discussion in Segerstråle, 1986). For Wilson, morality was merely one of the many products of evolution, generated by 'epigenetic rules' and tailored to our particular human species nature (e.g., Ruse & Wilson, 1985; Wilson, 1980).[2]

There was no doubt that Wilson blatantly committed the so-called naturalistic fallacy, going from is to ought, and that is what the critics picked up on. Although Wilson sometimes equivocated on this point, it seems that for him there actually existed no naturalistic fallacy; it was his way of reasoning about man and nature. He saw "a genetically accurate and therefore completely fair code of ethics" as a rational alternative to the arbitrary and ungrounded teachings of religious leaders.[3] In 1982 he actually wrote that we ought to get rid of the is-ought distinction as soon as possible!

There is a profound misunderstanding of Wilson's ambitions, due to a "generation gap" of sorts. Both in his problem definition and his preferred biological paradigm, Wilson can be seen as being one academic generation "off" in relation to the critics. His liberal critics on the East Coast were far removed from this tradition of deriving values from nature (still represented by people like C. H. Waddington at the time of the sociobiology controversy, and earlier by Lorenz, Teilhard de Chardin, and others). They interpreted Wilson's value statements as his championing a political program instead.

Scientifically, *Sociobiology* was Wilson's great attempt to extend the Modern Synthesis to the field of behavior, using the mathematical formulae and methods of population genetics (augmented with ecological and other considerations). It seems that early on he hoped to capture the very trajectory of mankind in this way, using evolutionary biology as a substitute for divine prophecy (see Segerstråle, 1986). Philosophically, a grand ambition of Wilson's was to unite the social and natural sciences. He believed that sociobiology, the most mathematized area of evolutionary biology, would be central in this effort. The solution was to make the social sciences scientific (here he meant partly putting them on a quantitative statistical basis, employing population genetic formulae similar to the kinetic gas laws in physics). But Wilson had not asked the social sciences what they themselves thought about this. Vehemently resisting such promised "cannibalization," sociologists and anthropologists became immediately suspicious of sociobiology.

7. Raiders of the Lost Ark: Gould and Lewontin

Let us take a closer look at Gould and Lewontin's moral-cum-scientific agenda. Gould and Lewontin had early on joined forces with Science for the People's Sociobiology Study Group and were thus participating in the overall campaign against sociobiology. Later, they turned their interest to a scientific critique of what they called "the adaptationist program" in evolutionary biology, of which sociobiology was seen as a prime example. Their famous paper "The Spandrels of San Marco and the Panglossian Paradigm: A Critique of the Adaptationist Programme" (Gould & Lewontin, 1979) accused evolutionists of trying to demonstrate that every trait of every animal, including its behavior, was perfectly adapted. Adaptationists were just like Dr. Pangloss in Candide: they believed that this was the best of all possible worlds. The point with using the architectural notion of spandrels was to demonstrate that pan-adaptationism does not hold up: a trait may have come about as a by-product of evolution acting on something else, just like four "spandrels" are automatically created by two arches crossing in the ceiling of San Marco in Venice.[4]

Gould and Lewontin's paper in turn triggered protests from the so-called adaptationists (who objected to being so classified). Dawkins (1982) pointed out that the assumption that a feature was adaptative was simply a research tool, not a belief! He thought it "unfair" to equate modern adaptationism with naive perfectionism in the style of Dr. Pangloss, because despite the claims of Gould and Lewontin (1979), "there are many kinds of adaptive, indeed Panglossian, explanations which would be ruled out by the modern adaptationists" (Dawkins, 1982, p. 50). Maynard Smith calmly observed that the aim of using an adaptationist explanatory framework was not to demonstrate that nature optimizes, but rather to test particular hypotheses (Maynard Smith, 1978).

For the critics of sociobiology, the possibility that an adaptationist framework was a research heuristic never even arose. They had from the very beginning treated adaptation as a political conspiracy. Already in their first letter the Sociobiology Study Group charged that "for Wilson, what exists is adaptive, what is adaptive is good, therefore what exists is good," and "It is a deeply conservative politics, not an understanding of modern evolutionary theory that leads one to see the wonderful operation of adaptation in every feature of human social organization" (Allen et al., 1975). It was this position that Gould and Lewontin later spelled out in more scientific detail. No wonder the Spandrels paper was widely regarded as a politically motivated attack on sociobiology (e.g., Queller, 1995).

But Gould later seemed to imply that he and Lewontin in fact used the politically loaded sociobiology controversy as a mere vehicle for what they really desired: a serious scientific consideration of alternatives to adaptation!

This is what Gould told a meeting for Science for the People in the spring of 1984:

> We opened up the debate by taking a strong position. We took a defin-
> itive stand in order to open up the debate to scientific criticism. Until
> there is some legitimacy for expressing contrary opinions, scientists will
> shut up. A scientist will reason: "If I say this, they will accuse me of
> something unbiological." (Gould, spoken comment)

On this view, Gould's and Lewontin's political involvement with sociobiology would have been a strategic maneuver aiming at gaining a later hear-
ing for their basically scientific arguments against adaptation! In other words,
Gould and Lewontin were using the sociobiology debate as a Trojan horse
to create legitimacy for an unpopular scientific idea that might easily be
rejected out of hand. Using political scandal to capture the scientific community's interest, they raided the lost ark of existing anti-adaptationist
arguments while coming up with additional ones themselves.

8. Taking the Bull by the Horns, Sticking One's Head in the Sand, or What? Coping With Values in Evolutionary Biology

But just like Wilson, Gould and Lewontin were pursuing a complex, combined moral and scientific agenda. Inside their scientific objection to adaptationism there was hidden another Trojan horse: a moral/political concern.
If everything is optimally adapted, there is no point in changing society. But
if you instead of adaptation emphasize discontinuity, contingency, and
chance, you indicate that in a radically new environment new types of individuals will flourish. It is not a question of the selection of the fittest; everybody gets a chance. Lewontin (whose anti-adaptationism preceded Gould's)
had found an apt biblical quote (from Ecclesiastes) to illustrate their position: "The race is not to the swift, nor yet bread to the wise . . . but time and
chance happeneth to them all" (Lewontin, 1981a).

On this view, Gould's continuous search for theoretical alternatives to
the adaptationist program can be seen as one long argument for social reform and social justice. Punctuated equilibria was his (and Eldredge's) first
dent in the adaptationist bulwark: long periods of gradualism and adaptation
were interrupted by unpredictable events, which could even give rise to new
species (Eldredge & Gould, 1972; Gould & Eldredge, 1977). Later Gould
emphasized chance and contingency even more, arguing, for instance, that
in the Cambrian explosion many different phyla existed that later went ex-
tinct. The organisms that humans come from are traceable to only a single

one of these simple organisms. In other words, humankind may never have come about. We came here entirely by chance. Gould also protested against the idea that evolution has a direction (going, for instance, toward greater complexity). Some simple organisms are perfectly well adapted, he noted, and in some cases evolution has even gone one step backward rather than forward! He suggested making the humble bacteria the biological model species (Gould, 1992, 1994).

Lewontin, unlike Gould, does not have an alternative scientific theory to offer. Rather, he is promoting a philosophical research program, where organisms are seen as subject and object, wholes as implying parts and parts as implying wholes, and other types of dialectical ways of looking at reality (e.g., Lewontin, 1981b, Levins & Lewontin, 1985).[5]

Gould and Lewontin's overall strategy, then, seems to have been to develop those kinds of scientific arguments which, if taken as social belief and if acted upon, will conceivably have politically desirable social implications (e.g., everybody getting their chance). They are simply taking the nasty social-implications bull by the horns by providing "correct" science for the people. (I am not implying that they do not believe in what they say. Actually, I believe that it is typical for leading American participants in the sociobiology controversy to combine genuine belief with strategic considerations, all the while establishing multiple links between science and values. They thus are able to do everything simultaneously, including pursue their political impulses within science. These scientists could be classified as "super-optimizers.")

Interestingly, Wilson, too, has pursued a similar agenda of "politically correct" science, at least part of the time. For instance, already in *Sociobiology* he played down the significance of IQ and dismissed race as a useful biological concept. In his next book (Wilson, 1978), he discussed "the cardinal value of the survival of the human gene pool" and the need for genetic diversity. He also argued for universal human rights, "because we are mammals," and even observed that "the long-term consequence of inequity will always be visibly dangerous." He topped this off by advocating a more liberal sexual morality and defending homosexuality as socially useful. All this was based on the values that he saw as connected to facts from evolutionary biology. And note that, in blatant contrast to the critics' accusations, the social implications Wilson derived from his own theories were always liberal.

One problem with predicting the social consequences of certain scientific claims is, of course, that people may not agree about one's assessment (as we saw with many of Wilson's suggestions); in addition, one may simply be factually wrong. Finally, the facts themselves may change over time as science develops, and the social meaning of the facts may change with a changing social climate.

When it comes to coping with facts and values, and the social implications of science, the dividing line does not go neatly between the sociobiological and the critical camp. Instead, we have scientists who believe in
keeping scientific and moral truth apart and scientists who regard it as desirable and/or necessary to pursue scientific and moral/political truth together. This line often coincided with the Atlantic divide.[6]

As we have seen, the American protagonists in the sociobiology debate
followed various types of normative strategies, pursuing science and values
together (deriving values from science, criticizing undesirable science,
putting science in the direct service of values by producing "politically correct" science, and so on). In contrast, the participants from the United King-
dom typically coped by adopting the exact opposite strategy: a strictly
objectivist one, striving to keep science and values apart (e.g., Dawkins and
Maynard Smith). (There was a good precedent for such a stance, going all
the way back to "Darwin's bulldog," Thomas Henry Huxley [1898], who
hoped that the perceived message of evolution could be counteracted by
education and culture.)[7]

Wilson, although clearly normative when involved with his moral-
cum-scientific agenda or when writing in a visionary style, shifted into an objectivist mode when writing as a scientist (or defending sociobiology against
political critics). In other words, Wilson had two hats, and it was not always
clear which one he was putting on. (Incidentally, one problem with the in-
famous last chapter of *Sociobiology* may exactly have been the mixing of
these modes).

There are obviously arguments to make in favor of both strategies for
evolutionary biologists, the normative and the objectivist one. What is interesting is that the strategies seem to be based on different images of the audience for evolutionary ideas. The normative alternative is utility-oriented,
based on the belief that evolutionary biological claims will directly affect
the actions of people or policy makers, in the short or the long run. It sees
evolutionary biology as a type of applied science. In contrast, the objectivist alternative is connected to a vision of evolutionary biology as pure
science: knowledge that does not necessarily have consequences, mere
wonder at the workings of nature. We have here two different underlying
visions of science (which presumably also have their different sociopolitical correlates).

But if we ask what people in general will typically believe, it may be
that it is the critics of sociobiology who have the more realistic assessment.
People will jump to conclusions based on even tentative knowledge. And
they may, indeed, take scientific facts (even tentative ones) as a guide for
values, unless they have other, stronger belief systems in place (say, systems
that say that scientific facts have no bearing whatsoever on the social
value of human beings). Huxley's belief in education as counteracting

undesirable types of reasoning is competing with our existing social psychological biases and tendencies.

9. The Rise of Evolutionary Psychology

More than a quarter century has passed since the beginning of the sociobiology debate. The "environmentalist" or culturalist paradigm that used to be so prevalent has come under increasing attack. Anthropology, with its emphasis on cultural differences, got into hot water with Derek Freeman's attack on Margaret Mead's study of adolescence in Samoa and the reevaluation of similar case studies of cultural peculiarities. What is being stressed now, instead, is human universals, to an extent that would have been unfathomed some 25 years ago. The mind is in, and cognitive science is riding high, broadening the definition of science in a way that adherents to the 1950s and 1960s behaviorist paradigm could not have imagined. Primate studies, too, have changed: we are now far away from the "killer apes" of the 1960s. The emphasis is not on aggression and territoriality but instead on moral behavior (see, e.g., de Waal, 1996, 2001). Clearly, if chimpanzees have such good features, it is easier to acknowledge that they are our cousins. The same goes for language. Research on chimpanzee language resumed after the controversies in the 1970s and early 1980s (Savage-Rumbaugh et al., 1993), and there are studies of proto-language in a number of animals (e.g., Cheney & Seyfarth, 1990; Evans & Marler, 1997).

It is in this climate that evolutionary psychology has emerged. Indeed, it might be said that evolutionary psychology has actually helped create some of this climate. I have in mind especially Barkow, Cosmides, & Tooby's *The Adapted Mind* (1992), which not only presents the logic of the new discipline and a number of supportive studies from different scientific disciplines but also engages in a deliberate demolition job of what it calls "the Standard Social Science Model" (Cosmides & Tooby, 1992). That standard model, which, according to the authors, regards culture as preeminent and sees humans as in principle capable of learning anything, is said to underlie social science reasoning and be responsible for the wrongheadedness of much of anthropology and sociology.

The evolutionary psychologists have hit hard theoretically while collecting a number of existing "counter studies" to famous anthropological studies, showing how earlier cultural relativist anthropologists were mistaken. In this way they have prepared the terrain for the onslaught of their own paradigm, which presents a biologically grounded universal human mind with specific modules dedicated to solving specific types of problems. In the world of evolutionary psychology, cultural differences are played down in favor of a common humanity. The only difference allowed is the difference between the sexes, which is said to be based on a differently wired mind.

Not only did the evolutionary psychologists launch a massive campaign for their own perspective while kicking the enemy; it seems they also self-consciously set out to be as politically correct as possible. Well aware of the upheaval surrounding sociobiology—Cosmides and Tooby were both at Harvard at the time—they wanted to see to it that their message could not easily be misunderstood or misappropriated, and one way to do this was to proactively explain, in academic and popular fora, exactly what they meant and did not mean. Arguing for a universal human nature might sound like a politically good thing, but the proposed universal human nature was, after all, grounded in biology. And in the 1970s the critics had not let Wilson get away with his proposition of a genetically based human nature.

Recently, in their primer for evolutionary psychology, Cosmides and Tooby (2000) have taken care to point out why evolutionary psychology is different from sociobiology. They have made the situation rather difficult for political critics. Well aware of the attacks on sociobiology, they have carefully stated that they are interested in the evolved human mind, not genes, and in a universal human nature, not human differences. They do not employ population-genetic models and do not address genetic differences between populations. Neither do they discuss individual genetic differences. They explicitly distance themselves from human behavioral genetics (a psychological field that uses twin studies to calculate the relative contribu-tion of genetic and environmental factors to traits such as extroversion/introversion), which Wilson needed to include for his sociobiological ap-proach. Since they do not deal with genes, it is hard to construe evolution-ary psychologists as racists—the standard move in left-wing criticism of biological theories of human nature, much employed in the sociobiology controversy (see Segerstråle, 2000a, chap. 9). And because they are unin-terested in IQ differences, they cannot be connected to the repertory of stan-dard accusations against IQ research (see Segerstråle, 2000a, chaps. 12, 13, 14). In fact, they explicitly dismiss the idea of "general intelligence" (Cos-mides & Tooby, 2000).

In other words, Tooby and Cosmides have seemingly distanced them-selves from sociobiology because they are limiting themselves to the work-ings of the mind as it has evolved, but they have also done so for strategic reasons. Unlike Wilson, they are not interested in broader scenarios of gene-mind coevolution over time. Wilson, on his part, is unhappy with the at-tempt of evolutionary psychologists to act as if their approach was so radically different from sociobiology. According to him, they are one and the same. (Wilson is not getting recognition from evolutionary psychologists. Neither is Lorenz, the pioneer in seeing cognition as the product of an evolved, structured mind, and the one who launched the idea of learning as prepared [see Lorenz, 1977]). When it comes to emphasizing human universals, too, Wilson sees himself and Lumsden as the true pioneers. (In interview he referred to his and Lumsden's painstaking collection of supportive empirical studies in *Genes, Mind and Culture*).

10. The Resistance to Evolutionary Psychology

But in view of the trouble its proponents have taken not to fall into various political traps, why has evolutionary psychology not been received with open arms by the former critics of sociobiology? I can offer five reasons; there may be more.

First, there is the continuing fear of genetic determinism. The general climate has changed toward more acceptance of genetic explanation. There is great prevalence of "gene-talk" in the general culture. The gene, seen as the emblem of DNA, appears as a cultural icon (Nelkin & Lindee, 1995). At the same time there is little discussion of what exactly "the gene" is, or how it is actually expressed. In the early stages of the human genome project, leading figures presented the gene as a blueprint. Together with the DNA emblem, and the phrase "the selfish gene," the picture of the gene as immutable and deterministic may be hard to resist, especially as there are no compelling counter-icons (so far) emphasizing the importance of such things as development.

Worry about these developments has spread beyond the critics of sociobiology. According to a number of scientific critics, the computational model of the mind does not cover many important aspects of the mind and living systems, such as internal regulation, coordination, and feedback mechanisms. Among these critics are developmentally oriented biologists and psychologists (e.g., Bateson & Martin, 2000), developmental systems theorists (e.g., Oyama, 2000), researchers and theorists of cognitive processes (e.g., van Gelder & Port, 1995; Hutchins, 1996), and even a developmental cognitive neuroscientist (Johnson, 1997).

Second, although the idea of a universal human mind is arguably different from the universal human nature that caused Wilson so much trouble (because it involves neither behavioral genetics nor emphasis on individual variation), this universal mind is still presented as adaptive. This raised a red flag for people like Gould,[8] whose moral-cum-scientific agenda demanded anti-adaptationism. For him, the idea of a mind consisting of modules, each adapted for a specific task in the ancestral environment, appeared like a Panglossian anathema.

Moreover, the evolutionary psychologists' emphasis on design and "reverse engineering" is directly associated with Gould's arch enemy, Dawkins. Over the last two decades, it is largely Dawkins who has taken up Wilson's

mantle as the pro-sociobiological fighter, and Dawkins's main sparring partner in books and book reviews was the late Stephen J. Gould. The argument
is of a kind that is hard to resolve, because these evolutionists are systematically talking past each other. The issue is adaptation, in a broad sense.
Dawkins is interested in explaining the workings of evolution from a strictly
neo-Darwinist, selectionist perspective, using a "gene's-eye" perspective. He
is concentrating on explanation in terms of adaptation, and especially how
complex design can come about through the accumulation of small changes
over a long time (as is the case with the eye; see Dawkins, 1996), although
he recognizes that adaptation is not the only evolutionary force. Gould, on
the other hand, wanted to give a true, complex picture of the evolutionary
process, by accounting for the different evolutionary forces and levels of
selection that actually exist in nature. He paid particular attention to various types of constraints on adaptation and to forces operating at the macro-
evolutionary level (constraints and forces which Dawkins, incidentally,
recognizes). If Dawkins is a logician with an abstract model of evolution,
Gould was a "realist" with metaphysical yearnings. He felt sociobiologists
put too much emphasis on adaptation.

"Ultra-Darwinians" is the recent dismissive umbrella term used by
Gould and Niles Eldredge for those interested in adaptation and the evolution of design features. This label includes both sociobiologists and evolutionary psychologists. Meanwhile, according to these brothers-in-arms, it is
not the adaptationists, but rather the "pluralists" (Gould, 1997a, 1997b) or
"naturalists" (Eldredge, 1995), who have the correct insight into the real
workings of evolution.[9] But the sociobiologists and their friends have gone
on the counterattack. Their strategy has been to demonstrate that Gould
was factually wrong in his claims about adaptation (e.g., Dennett, 1995;
Maynard Smith, 1995; Alcock, 2000). To these exercises one might perhaps
say, with Lenin: "If the facts are against us, so much worse for the facts!"
Gould did not change his mind.

Third, there is the issue of sex differences—the hot potato of the sociobiology controversy. This is an issue that will not go away, because it is a cor-
nerstone of evolutionary psychological thinking. If anything, evolutionary
psychologists are reinforcing the idea of differences between the sexes with
such books as David Buss's *The Evolution of Desire* (1994). Meanwhile, the
biological grounding of sex differences—in the mind or elsewhere—is a sore
point for the liberal Left. And here there is a direct continuation with their
criticism of sociobiology: the fear that it will legitimize discriminatory social
policy and that people will begin using evolutionary psychological claims
about evolved female and male strategies as justifications for, say, promiscuous sexual practices, or even rape (cf. the upheaval about Thornhill &
Palmer's [2000] book, *A Natural History of Rape*). And as in the case of sociobiology, it does not help that evolutionary psychologists argue that only

when we know about our tendencies can we know how to counteract them (e.g., Buss, 2000). Feminists have been up in arms about such suggestions that women should avoid wearing short skirts.

Fourth, a theme that emerges again is the one about models and reality. Evolutionary psychologists have joined forces with cognitive neuroscience but are now being rebutted by affective neuroscientists, who argue that their modular model of the brain cannot hold. The reason is that it does not take into account the brain's anatomical structure or its evolutionary history. Why postulate modules in the neocortex? they say. Why not in the more ancient emotional brain that we share with other mammals? Why postulate massive modularity, and why not emphasize the processes of ontogeny? (See, for instance, Panksepp & Panksepp, 2000).

Interestingly, in the felt need to go to the anatomical level, at least one critic of sociobiology, Steven Rose (2000), has recently discovered ethology, which he now surprisingly invokes against evolutionary psychology! This is paradoxical, since the critics saw sociobiology as a direct continuation of the late 1960s ethological arguments about an innate human nature, which were at the time vehemently refuted by the Left.

Fifth, the metaphysical issue of free will and determinism will not go away. This was an important matter underlying the critics' opposition to sociobiology, and it is also underlying the critique of evolutionary psychology. Again, the critics' concern has to do with the worry that biological facts will be taken as legitimations for people's actions. I believe that this is an important reason that Gould, for instance, disliked evolutionary psychology, just as he disliked sociobiology. The critics of sociobiology seemed to believe in a "totally free" free will, not in any way influenced by genetic constraints. Because of culture—a totally separate realm—there were no constraints on our human potential or our social and cultural arrangements (see, for instance, Gould, 1976).

But what was the real issue behind this talk about genes and free will? Chorover (1979) formulated the concern of the critics when he argued that explanations that linked human behavior to evolution were in fact a biological version of the old idea of original sin. If behavior could be "explained away" as due to a type of sociobiological original sin, then individuals could not be held morally responsible for their actions and no guilt could be attributed. In other words, biological determinist explanations seemingly exonerated individuals; it was "all in the genes." Therefore, in order to sustain the idea of individual responsibility (and moral guilt!), free will had to be postulated. (Incidentally, the critics also disliked Skinner's behaviorism, because the idea of total conditioning was seen as another determinism taking away individual responsibility; see, e.g., Miller [1978]).

But there is irony in history. Toward the end of the millennium, as the climate changed from "environmentalism" (culturalism) toward better acceptance of "the gene," the worst may have happened from the point of view of the critics of sociobiology. Some believe that we may now be entering a new era of "genetic essentialism" (Nelkin & Lindee, 1995). That is, in the public's mind, genetics may become increasingly connected to questions of good and evil. According to Dorothy Nelkin and Susan Lindee, a whole new excuse may be developing: "It's not me, it's my genes," as a substitute for an earlier time's "the devil made me do it." In this worst-case scenario, people would be shamelessly referring to original sin of the sociobiological type— and get away with it! Little would be left of the notions of free will and individual responsibility that many critics of determinist ideas fought so hard for during the second part of the twentieth century.[10]

11. Reclaiming the Social Sciences

(The late) Dorothy Nelkin was a sociologist, and Susan Lindee is an anthropologist. And obviously, in order to understand what meaning scientific findings have for people and the real connection between facts and values, we need to know how people think and react. Social scientists are not only needed for helping understand meaning in everyday life, but also to help contextualize science itself. How a particular scientific claim is received has to do with many factors, including the particular academic climate at the time and the overall political situation. The meanings of biological arguments change over time.

Social scientists are indispensable, too, when it comes to providing critical interpretations of what to scientists may seem like a neutral fact, and for experimenting with various hypothetical futuristic scenarios. These kinds of exercises obviously should not be left to left-wing biologists, who may have their own particular agenda tagged on to their moral outrage. But in order to be effective mediators between scientists and the public, social scientists will need to understand the nature of scientific reasoning and possess basic knowledge in the relevant field (e.g., evolutionary biology).

I mention this against an impression of a mood of increasing scientism and natural science chauvinism after the so-called Science Wars in the mid-1990s. The Science Wars revolved around the (partly justified) charges that (parts of) the social sciences and humanities were turning increasingly "anti-science" (for an overview and analysis, see Segerstråle, 2000b). As a solution to a widely perceived Two Cultures problem, Wilson (1998) has suggested the establishment of universal "consilience" (unity of knowledge between the natural sciences, social sciences, and humanities), which would also manifest itself in education. Still, this unity of knowledge seems to be on the terms of the natural sciences and not take into account the special contributions that social scientists can make (on this, see Segerstråle, 2000a, chap. 18). The nature and value of social science may not be clear to natural scientists, and some may have the mistaken reductionist assumption that social science is not needed, because the solutions to the world's problems lie in the realm of natural science (though the events of September 11 should lay such preconceptions to rest). The various social sciences need to reassert themselves as respected partners in the academic enterprise. But for this, we need to get our act together.

It seems inevitable for the social sciences to have a serious reassessment of the ways in which they are both similar to and different from the natural sciences.[11] This is part of a very old discussion, but the current quest for integration of all the sciences has undoubtedly put pressure on the social sciences. So have the new developments in evolutionary biology. Some kind of response is needed, and traditional knee-jerk biophobia not acceptable any longer.[12] At the same time, an important aspect of the discussion ought to be renewed respect for different levels of explanation—the social, the psychological, the physiological, the genetic, and so on—and renewed respect for the particular insights and intuitions about the human condition offered by the humanities. These are all important for the understanding of complex reality; there is no reason to make the evolutionary level the primary explanatory one. Finally, one of the most powerful reasons for the difficulties in rapprochement between biology and the social sciences is the academic reward structure. Can something be done about that, so that researchers may get proper credit for interdisciplinary initiatives—which for social scientists may involve, among other things, learning to look at the world through the glasses of the purported "enemy"?

Notes

1. Hamilton's famous concept of "inclusive fitness," which explains how natural selection can favor altruism, was actually intended to extend to more than relatives (kin). The criterion was that the benefit of an altruist's behavior should fall on individuals who were likely to be altruistic, rather than on random members of the population. The typical case involved donor and beneficiary who were kin (and thus were likely to share genes "for" altruism), but Hamilton envisioned that the principle would also work if potential non-kin beneficiaries possessing altruistic genes had some easily identifiable phenotype. Dawkins later developed this criterion as "the green beard hypothesis."

2. Epigenetic rules are rules that govern the development (ontogeny) of a phenotype from an interaction between a genotype and its environment. Lumsden & Wilson (1981) suggested that epigenetic rules govern the development of mind.

3. Wilson developed this further in the chapter on religion in *On Human Nature* (1978).

4. According to Dennett (1995) what Gould calls "spandrels" should actually be called "pendentives." Terminology aside, it is Gould's argument that is important. Later Gould (Gould & Vrba, 1982) developed the related idea of "exaptation": evolution's subsequent use of a trait for a different purpose than it was originally designed for.

5. Lewontin has had an enormous influence on philosophers of biology (Callebaut, 1993).

6. An example is group selection, reintroduced by Sober & Wilson (1998). Group selection is very appealing to many people, exactly because of its seeming altruistic message. It makes it possible for people to pursue moral and scientific truth at the same time. Not surprisingly, in his review of Sober & Wilson's book (Lewontin, 1998) Lewontin seemed appreciative.

7. Steven Rose, "Britain's Lewontin," is the most blatant British exception, following a course very similar to the American critics of sociobiology.

8. Stephen J. Gould died on May 20, 2002.

9. Eldredge has chosen the term "naturalist" to denote someone with a concern for a true description of the way nature really works. I have used the term "realist" for this (as opposed to someone who is interested in abstract mechanisms or models). Eldredge's choice is confusing, because it is typically traditional naturalists (students of nature) who have later become sociobiologists (having adopted a neo-Darwinist explanatory framework of evolution as the change of gene frequencies in a population). "Naturalist" in the sense of "student of nature" can be usefully opposed to "experimentalist" (laboratory scientist). A clear opposition between these two types of scientists could be seen in the sociobiology controversy (see Segerstråle, 2000a, ch. 13).

10. I have in mind Jean-Paul Sartre and post–World War II existentialism, which postulated that humans have free choice, which means, for instance, that they can choose to disobey orders. This philosophy does not accept excuses or explanations based on biological, social, psychological, or other constraints.

11. But which of the natural sciences? While Wilson (1998 and earlier) sees physics as the model for biology (indeed, statistical population genetic formulae used by sociobiologists are similar to kinetic gas theories), someone like Ernst Mayr (e.g., 1997) emphasizes the difference between biology and physics.

12. The evolutionary paradigm is so far unpopular in the social sciences. Some reasons for this are social scientists' belief that their explanations must be socially grounded; a different timescale from evolutionary theory; ignorance of biological reasoning or outright biophobia; a critical and reformist ambition, which goes together with an "environmentalist" ambition; and the fact that an interest in biological explanation can be outright dangerous to your professional health (see the discussion of some

of these reasons and more in van den Berghe, 1990, and Segerstråle & Molnar, 1997).

Sociobiology, with its suggestion to cannibalize social science, certainly made itself unpopular as soon as it emerged. The reaction was especially strong in anthropology (e.g., Sahlins, 1976), but that did not prevent the emergence of evolutionary anthropology as a field (Chagnon & Irons, 1979; see Betzig, 1997, for a history and assessment). And already before the sociobiology controversy, there was the field of biosocial anthropology, established by Lionel Tiger and Robin Fox (1971 and later). The long-standing conflict between biological and cultural anthropologists has had more recent manifestations as well: Freeman's attack on Mead (1983, 1988), and the "response" by cultural anthropology to the vicious attack on Napoleon Chagnon's sociobiologically inspired Yanomamo research (e.g., Tierney, 2000; see current Web sites documenting the evolving conflict, including the American Anthropological Association's handling of the matter).

In political science there was an early interest in evolutionary ideas (e.g., Wiegele, 1979); later examples are Masters (1989) and Somit & Petersen (1997, 2005), who study, among other things, how evolutionary dominance hierarchies underlie political systems. However, this interest is limited to a minority of the profession. Sociology as a field has been among the most resistant, although a few sociologists (e.g., Collins, 1975, 1981; Giddens, 1984; Scheff, 1990) have used ethological and nonverbal theory in their theory-building efforts (following in the footsteps of sociologists such as G. H. Mead and Erving Goffman). One book trying to systematically connect classical sociological theory to evolutionary theory is Lopreato & Crippen (1999).

There are few books bringing an evolutionary perspective to bear on the social sciences as a whole. A recent effort is Barkow (1989), pioneering the approach of evolutionary psychology as a unifying perspective for the social sciences (for later examples, see Barkow, Cosmides, & Tooby, 1992). Segerstråle & Molnar (1997) strive to bring the social sciences and life sciences together around the interdisciplinary field of nonverbal communication under the motto "biology with a human face." Sanderson (2001) presents a synthesis of cultural materialist anthropology, classical sociological theory and neo-Darwinism from a conflict-theoretical perspective.

References

Alcock, J. (2000). *The Triumph of Sociobiology.* New York: Oxford University Press.
Allen, E., Beckwith, B., Beckwith, J., Chorover, S., Culver, D., Duncan, M., Gould, S., Hubbard, R., Inouye, H., Leeds, A., Lewontin, R. C., Mandansky, C., Miller, L. Pyeritz, R., Rosenthal, M., & Schreier, H. (1975). Letter. *New York Review of Books.* November 13, pp. 182, 184–186.

Alper, J., Beckwith, J., Chorover, S. L., Hunt, J., Judd, T., Lange, R. V., & Sternberg, P. (1976). The implications of sociobiology. *Science, 192,* 424–425.

Barkow, J. H. (1989). *Darwin, Sex and Status.* Toronto: University of Toronto Press.

Barkow, J. H., Cosmides, L., & Tooby, J. (1992). *The Adapted Mind: Evolutionary Psychology and the Generation of Culture.* New York: Oxford University Press.

Bateson, P., & Martin, P. (2000). *Design for a Life: How Behavior Develops.* London: Vintage Paperbacks.

Berghe, P. van den. (1980). Sociobiology: Several views. *Bioscience, 31,* 406.

Betzig, L. (Ed.). (1997). *Human Nature.* Oxford: Oxford University Press.

Bouchier, D. (1977). Radical ideologies and the sociology of knowledge. *Sociology, 11,* 29–46.

Buss, D. (1994). *The Evolution of Desire.* New York: Basic Books.

Buss, D. (2000). *The Dangerous Passion: Why Jealousy Is as Necessary as Love and Sex.* New York: Free Press.

Callebaut, W. (Ed.). (1993). *Taking the Naturalistic Turn; or, How Real Philosophy of Science Is Done.* Chicago: University of Chicago Press.

Chagnon, N. A., & W. Irons (Eds.). (1979). *Evolutionary Biology and Human Social Behavior: An Anthropological Perspective.* North Scituate, MA: Duxbury.

Cheney, D., & Seyfarth, R. (1990). *How Monkeys See the World.* Chicago: University of Chicago Press.

Chorover, S. (1979). *From Genesis to Genocide.* Cambridge, MA: MIT Press.

Collins, R. (1975). *Conflict Sociology.* New York: Academic Press.

Collins, R. (1981). On the micro-foundations of macro-sociology. *American Journal of Sociology, 86,* 984–1014.

Cosmides, L., & Tooby, J. (1992). The psychological foundations of culture. In J. H. Barkow, L. Cosmides, & J. Tooby (Eds.), *The Adapted Mind: Evolutionary Psychology and the Generation of Culture.* New York: Oxford University Press.

Cosmides, L., & Tooby, J. (2005). Evolutionary Psychology: A Primer. Retrieved February 10, 2005, from http://www.psych.ucsb.edu/research/cep/primer/html.

Davis, B. D. (1975). Social determinism and behavioral genetics. *Science, 26,* 189.

Davis, B. D. (1978). The moralistic fallacy. *Nature, 272,* 390.

Davis, B. D. (1986). *Storm over Biology: Essays on Science, Sentiment, and Public Policy.* Buffalo, NY: Prometheus Books.

Dawkins, R. (1982). *The Extended Phenotype: The Gene as Unit of Selection.* Oxford and San Francisco: Freeman.

Dennett, D. (1995). *Darwin's Dangerous Idea.* New York: Simon and Schuster.

De Waal, F. B. M. (1996). *Good Natured: The Origins of Right and Wrong in Humans and Other Animals.* Cambridge, MA: Harvard University Press.

De Waal, F. B. M. (Ed.). (2001). *Tree of Origin: What Primate Behavior Can Tell Us About Human Social Evolution.* Cambridge, MA: Harvard University Press.

Eldredge, N. (1995). *Reinventing Darwin: The Great Debate at the High Table of Evolutionary Theory.* New York: Wiley.

Eldredge, N., & Gould, S. J. (1972). Punctuated equilibria: An alternative to phyletic gradualism. In T. J. M. Schopf (Ed.), *Models in Paleobiology.* San Francisco: Freeman Cooper.

Evans, C., & Marler, P. (1997). Communication and signals of animals: Contributions of emotion and reference. In U. Segerstråle & P. Molnar (Eds.), *Nonverbal Communication: Where Nature Meets Culture* (pp. 151–170). Mahwah, NJ: Lawrence Erlbaum.

Freeman, D. (1983). *Margaret Mead and Samoa: The Making and Unmaking of an Anthropological Myth.* Cambridge, MA: Harvard University Press.

Freeman, D. (1988). *The Fateful Hoaxing of Margaret Mead: Historical Analysis of Her Samoan Research.* Boulder, CO: Westview.

Gelder, T. van, & Port, R. F. (Eds.). (1995). *Mind as Motion: Explorations in the Dynamics of Cognition.* Cambridge, MA: MIT Press.

Giddens, A. (1984). *The Constitution of Society: Outline of the Theory of Structuration.* Berkeley: University of California Press.

Gould, S. J. (1976). Biological potential vs. biological determinism. *Natural History 85.* Reprinted in A. L. Caplan, *The Sociobiology Debate* (pp. 343–351). New York: Harper & Row, 1978.

Gould, S. J. (1992). The confusion over evolution. *New York Review of Books,* Nov. 19, 47–54.

Gould, S. J. (1994). The evolution of life on the Earth. *Scientific American,* October, 85–91.

Gould, S. J. (1997a). Darwinian fundamentalism. *New York Review of Books,* June 12, pp. 34–37.

Gould, S. J. (1997b). Evolution: The pleasures of pluralism. *New York Review of Books,* June 26, pp. 47–52.

Gould, S. J., & Eldredge, N. (1977). Punctuated equilibria. *Paleobiology,* 3, 115–151.

Gould, S. J., & Lewontin, R. D. (1979). The Spandrels of San Marco and the Panglossian Paradigm: A critique of the Adaptationist Programme. *Proceedings of the Royal Society of London B, 205,* 581–598.

Gould, S. J., & Vrba, E. (1982). Exaptation: A missing term in the science of form. *Paleobiology, 8,* 4–15.

Hutchins, E. (1996). *Cognition in the Wild.* Cambridge, MA: MIT Press.

Huxley, T. H. (1898). *Evolution and Ethics and Other Essays.* New York: Appleton.

Jensen, A. R. (1969). How much can we boost IQ and scholastic achievement? *Harvard Educational Review, 39,* 1–123.

Johnson, M. (1997). *Developmental Cognitive Neuroscience: An Introduction.* Oxford: Blackwell.

Levins, R., & Lewontin, R. C. (1985). *The Dialectical Biologist.* Cambridge, MA: Harvard University Press.

Lewontin, R. C. (1972). The apportionment of human diversity. *Evolutionary Biology, 6,* 381–398.

Lewontin, R. C. (1975a). Interview. *Harvard Crimson,* December 3.

Lewontin, R. C. (1975b). Genetic aspects of intelligence. *Annual Review of Genetics, 9,* 387–405.

Lewontin, R. C. (1975c). Transcript of NOVA program, Public Television, WGBH Boston, #211. Transmission by PBS, February 2.

Lewontin, R. C. (1981a). Evolution/creation debate: A time for truth. *Bioscience, 31,* 559.

Lewontin, R. C. (1981b). On constraints and adaptation. *Behavioral and Brain Sciences, 4,* 244–245.

Lewontin, R. C. (1998). Survival of the nicest. Review of *Unto Others. New York Review of Books,* 22 Oct., 59–63.

Lewontin, R. C., Rose, S., & Kamin, L. (1984). *Not in Our Genes.* New York: Pantheon.

Lopreato, J., & Crippen, T. (1999). *Crisis in Sociology: The Need for Darwin.* New Brunswick, NJ: Transaction Publishers.

Lorenz, K. (1966). *On Aggression.* London: Methuen.

Lorenz, K. (1977). *Behind the Mirror: A Search for a Natural History of Human Knowledge* (R. Taylor, trans.). London: Methuen.

Lumsden, C. L., & Wilson, E. O. (1981). *Genes, Mind, and Culture: The Coevolutionary Process.* Cambridge, MA: Harvard University Press.

Masters, R. D. (1982). Is sociobiology reactionary? The political implications of inclusive-fitness theory. *Quarterly Review of Biology, 57,* 275–282.

Masters, R. D. (1989). *The Nature of Politics.* New Haven, CT: Yale University Press.

Maynard Smith, J. (1978). Optimization theory in evolution. *Annual Review of Ecology and Systematics, 9,* 31–56.

Maynard Smith, J. (1995). Review of D. Dennett, *Darwin's Dangerous Idea: Evolution and the Meanings of Life. New York Review of Books,* November 30, pp. 46–48.

Mayr, E. (1997). *This Is Biology.* Cambridge, MA: Harvard University Press.

Miller, L. G. (1978). Philosophy, dichotomies, and sociobiology. In A. Caplan (Ed.), *The Sociobiology Debate.* New York: Harper & Row, pp. 319–324.

Nelkin, D., & Lindee, M. S. (1995). *The DNA Mystique.* New York: Freeman.

Oyama, S. (2000). *The Ontogeny of Information: Developmental Systems and Evolution.* Durham, NC: Duke University Press.

Panksepp, J., & Panksepp, J. B. (2000). The seven sins of evolutionary psychology. *Evolution and Cognition, 6*(2), 109–131.

Queller, D. (1995). The spaniels of St. Marx and the Panglossian paradox: A critique of a rhetorical programme. *Quarterly Review of Biology, 70*(4), 485–489.

Rose, S. (2000). Escaping evolutionary psychology. In H. Rose & R. Rose (Eds.), *Alas, Poor Darwin: Arguments against Evolutionary Psychology* (pp. 247–265). London: Jonathan Cape.

Ruse, M., & Wilson, E. O. (1985). The evolution of ethics. *New Scientist*, 17 October, 50–53.

Sahlins, M. (1976). *The Use and Abuse of Biology*. Ann Arbor: University of Michigan Press.

Sanderson, S. (2001). *The Evolution of Human Sociality: A Darwinian Conflict Perspective*. London: Rowman and Littlefield.

Savage-Rumbaugh, S., Murphy, J., Seveik, R., Brakke, D., Williams, S., & Rumbaugh, D. (1993). *Language Comprehension in the Ape and Child*. Monographs of the Society for Research in Child Development, vol. 58. Chicago: University of Chicago Press.

Scheff, T. (1990). *Microsociology: Discourse, Emotion, and Social Structure*. Chicago: University of Chicago Press.

Segerstråle, U. (1986). Colleagues in conflict: An 'in vivo' analysis of the sociobiology controversy. *Biology and Philosophy, 1*(1), 53–87.

Segerstråle, U. (2000a). *Defenders of the Truth: The Battle for Science in the Sociobiology Debate and Beyond*. New York: Oxford University Press.

Segerstråle, U. (Ed.). (2000b). *Beyond the Science Wars: The Missing Discourse about Science and Society*. Albany: SUNY Press.

Segerstråle, U., & Molnar, P. (Eds.). (1997). *Nonverbal Communication: Where Nature Meets Culture*. Mahwah, NJ: Lawrence Erlbaum.

Sober, E., & Wilson, D. S. (1998). *Unto Others: The Evolution and Psychology of Unselfish Behavior*. Cambridge, MA: Harvard University Press.

Somit, A., & Peterson, S. A. (1997). *Darwinism, Dominance and Democracy: The Biological Basis of Authoritarianism*. Westport, CT: Praeger.

Somit, A., & Peterson, S. A. (2005). *The Failure of Democratic Nation Building: Ideology Meets Evolution*. New York: Palgrave Macmillan.

Thornhill, R., & Palmer, C. (2000). *A Natural History of Rape*. Cambridge, MA: MIT Press.

Tierney, P. (2000). *Darkness in Eldorado: How Scientists and Journalists Devastated the Amazon*. New York: W. W. Norton.

Tiger, L., & Fox, R. (1971). *The Imperial Animal*. New York: Holt, Rinehart, Winston.

Trivers, R. L. (1971). The evolution of reciprocal altruism. *Quarterly Review of Biology, 46*, 35–57.

Wiegele, T. (1979). *Biopolitics: Search for a More Humane Political Science*. Boulder, CO: Westview.

Wilson, E. O. (1975). *Sociobiology: The New Synthesis*. Cambridge, MA: Harvard University Press.

Wilson, E. O. (1977). Biology and the social sciences. *Daedalus 106*, 127–140.

Wilson, E. O. (1978). *On Human Nature*. New York: Bantam Books.

Wilson, E. O. (1980). Comparative social theory: The Tanner lecture on human values, University of Michigan (1979). In S. M. McMurrin

(Ed.), *The Tanner Lectures on Human Values* (pp. 48–73). Salt Lake City: University of Utah Press; Cambridge: Cambridge University Press.

Wilson, E. O. (1981). Interview with the author. Cambridge, MA.

Wilson, E. O. (1991). Sociobiology and the test of time. In M. H. Robinson & L. Tiger (Eds.), *Man and Beast Revisited*. Washington, DC: Smithsonian Institution Press.

Wilson, E. O. (1994). *Naturalist*. Washington, DC: Island Press.

Wilson, E. O. (1998). *Consilience: The Unity of Knowledge*. New York: Knopf.

5   Making Hay Out of Straw?
Real and Imagined Controversies
in Evolutionary Psychology

Robert Kurzban and
Martie G. Haselton

As evolutionary psychology has risen in popularity, it has attracted its share of detractors. Some critics have raised important issues that will ultimately require empirical testing to resolve. Others have attacked straw men: views inaccurately attributed to leading scholars in the field. In this chapter, we address both types of criticisms in an attempt to steer the debate in productive directions.

Straw Men

Genetic Determinism

The doctrine of genetic determinism holds that the behavior of organisms depends in no way on the environment; the organism's genes wholly determine the organism's behavior. In the realm of evolutionary psychology, this is often portrayed as the belief that human brains are "hard-wired," developing in particular ways independent of the environment in which they mature.

Do critics portray evolutionary psychology as genetically deterministic? Nelkin (2000) says, "Evolutionary principles imply genetic destiny. They deemphasize the influence of social circumstances" (p. 27). Herrnstein Smith (2000) echoes this remark, claiming that evolutionary psychologists "dismiss" cultural, historical, and individual variables (p. 167); she singles out Pinker's supposed claims of human sexuality's "definitive determination (in presumably all senses)" (p. 171) and immunity from social influences. Shakespeare and Erikson (2000) agree, suggesting that "[i]n these [evolutionary] approaches it is possession of a specific set of genes, or a particular configuration of a hard-wired brain, constituted via evolutionary mechanisms, which explains any given social phenomenon" (p. 231). Karmiloff-Smith (2000) also cautions that, in contrast to the evolutionary view, "behaviors are not simply triggered from genetically determined mechanisms" (p. 174), and later, that evolutionary psychologists should consider the developing organism's myriad interactions with the environment in contrast to "their one-sided approach" (p. 184).

More generally, critics equate biology with fixedness. H. Rose (2000) refers to "biological imperatives" and "biology-as-destiny" (p. 149), while Jencks (2000) talks about "built-in genetic program(s) . . . hard-wired into our brains by natural selection" (p. 34). Fausto-Sterling (2000) is skeptical about evolutionary psychology's "hard-wired view of the inflexibility of social arrangements" (p. 221).

Compare the positions attributed to evolutionary psychologists with the published views of evolutionary psychologists on this topic:

> Every feature of every phenotype is fully and equally codetermined by the interaction of the organism's genes . . . and its ontogenetic environments. (Tooby & Cosmides, 1992, p. 83)

> Every part of every organism emerges only via interactions among genes, gene products, and myriad environmental phenomena. (Symons, 1992, p. 140)

> Every part of human intelligence involves culture and learning. (Pinker, 1998, p. 33)

> It is a complete misconception to think that an adaptationist perspective denies or in the least minimizes the role of the environment in human development, psychology, behavior, or social life. (Tooby & Cosmides, 1992, p. 87)

Evolutionary psychologists do not merely acknowledge the undeniable influences of the environment—many of their research programs have focused on the specifics of how people respond contingently to its features. Belsky, Steinberg, and Draper (1991), for instance, proposed that one potentially important aspect of a maturing woman's environment is whether her father is present or absent. Their evolutionary model predicted that a father's absence would cause a woman to become sexually mature earlier and to be less restrictive in her sexual behavior. Drawing on this model, Ellis and colleagues demonstrated that father absence and family stress predicted early pubertal timing in girls (Ellis & Garber, 2000; Ellis et al., 1999). Other evolutionary psychologists have tested evolutionary hypotheses about contingent sexual strategies in men (Gangestad & Simpson, 2000).

In similar fashion, Sulloway (1996) suggested that differences among children's personalities within a family might reflect evolved strategies contingent on birth order. He predicted and found that early-born children, who have enjoyed a monopoly on parental attention, tended to be conservative and adhere to parental authority, while later-borns rebelled against the authority of dominant social institutions. Sulloway is one of many evolutionary psychologists whose theories of environmentally sensitive evolved strategies have driven empirical research programs (e.g., Hill & Hurtado, 1996; Hill, Thomson, Ross, & Low, 1997; Malamuth, 1998; Pedersen, 1991).

Cross-Societal Variation

Critics who assume either explicitly or implicitly that biological approaches imply behavioral fixity infer that societal variation presents a problem for evolutionary psychology. Two articles critical of Buss's (1989) evolutionary hypotheses about sex differences in mate preferences are illustrative. At issue was Buss's finding that, relative to women, men across 37 geographic regions spanning 6 continents and 5 islands placed a greater emphasis on physical attractiveness in a mate, whereas women placed a greater emphasis on ambition, status, and access to resources (Buss, 1989).

Based on social structural theory (Eagly, 1987) and related accounts, Eagly and Wood (1999) proposed that women's preferences for mates with access to resources might be driven cross-societally by institutions that varied in the extent to which women were permitted to acquire resources. To test this hypothesis, Eagly and Wood correlated measures of gender inequity with mate preferences measured by Buss (1989). Kasser and Sharma (1999) conducted a similar analysis using measures of gender disparity in educational access and reproductive rights.

In both studies, the authors found that these measures predicted the size of the sex differences in some of the mate preferences they investigated. By contrasting evolutionary and social structural hypotheses, the authors implied that patterned cross-societal variation predicted by the social structural accounts weakened evolutionary accounts of sex differences in mate preferences. Kasser and Sharma (1999) suggested that their findings were "counter to the strong evolutionary position that culture has a negligible effect on females' mate preferences." They further explained that "a more parsimonious explanation can be made without recourse to evolutionary mechanisms" (p. 376). In their title, "Evolved dispositions versus social roles," Eagly and Wood (1999) intimated that support for social roles hypotheses called into question evolutionary theorizing—which, by their rendering, entails "claims of invariance across cultures in sex-differentiated behavior" (p. 420).

These conclusions hinge critically on the idea that societal variability predictions flow from social structural accounts but not from evolutionary accounts. However, evolutionary psychologists contend that adaptations are structured to respond contingently to local social and ecological factors (see Cronk, this volume). For example, in 1989, evolutionist Bobbi Low proposed that natural selection might have shaped parental socialization of boys and girls to respond contingently to variation in (1) the prevalence of polygyny and (2) sex differences in resource control. This account successfully predicted that parents across societies would alter their child rearing practices to encourage female achievement and aggression as female control of resources increased (Low, 1989), a prediction similar to that advanced by Eagly & Wood (1999).

An additional example of this type of reasoning is Gangestad and Buss's (1993) evolutionary hypothesis regarding variation in preferences for physical attractiveness across different societies. Gangestad and Buss proposed that the emphasis men and women place on physical attractiveness in a mate might be partially explained by parasite prevalence. Over the course of human evolution, the number of parasites in the environment probably varied from place to place. Individuals' resistance to parasites would therefore be more important in some places than in others. Gangestad and Buss suggested that because physical attractiveness is in part a function of parasite resistance, mate preference mechanisms have evolved to place more weight on attractiveness as a mate selection criterion as parasite prevalence increases. Gangestad and Buss supported this prediction in an analysis of mate preferences across 37 geographical regions. They demonstrated a positive association between parasite prevalence and the emphasis individuals place on physical attractiveness within a society (Gangestad & Buss, 1993).

Many evolutionary psychologists endorse the view that there is a universal human nature. However, universal psychological mechanisms can and do generate variable behavior as a result of their design to respond adaptively to environmental circumstances (Barkow, 1989; Tooby & Cosmides, 1990). In fact, as Barkow (1989) has pointed out, given the broad range of environments humans were likely to have experienced over evolutionary history, a rigid and unresponsive psychology would constitute an exceptionally poor design.

In short, cross-societal variation itself does not present a problem for evolutionary psychology. The only way in which societal variability challenges evolutionary psychologists is the same way it challenges all social scientists: its likely causes are many and complex, making hypothesis formulation and testing a formidable (but not impossible) task.

Hyperadaptationism

Evolutionary psychology is often portrayed as overly adaptationist, endorsing the idea that all features of organisms are adaptations. This view is contrasted with the more "pluralistic" view, which Gould emphasized throughout his long and prolific career: that not all features of organisms are adaptations; and that there are also epiphenomenal by-products of other adaptations, and contingently historical artifacts that were adaptations in ancestral species but are no longer (e.g., Gould, 1997). Gould criticizes evolutionary psychologists for failing to recognize this, suggesting that the "internal error of adaptationism arises from a failure to recognize that even the strictest operation of pure natural selection builds organisms full of non-adaptive parts and behaviors" (p. 123). Gould is not the only one to make such claims. S. Rose (2000), for example, characterized the field this way: "Every feature of the phenotype, from the protein structures within its cells to its behavioral responses to environmental contingencies, must be considered as adaptations" (pp. 302–303).

It is very difficult to understand how critics come to attribute hyperadaptationism to evolutionary psychologists, as they endorse Gould's pluralism explicitly and frequently. Here are some representative examples:

> In addition to adaptations, the evolutionary process commonly produces two other outcomes visible in the designs of organisms: (1) concomitants or by-products of adaptations (recently nicknamed "spandrels"; Gould & Lewontin, 1979); and (2) random effects. (Tooby & Cosmides, 1992, p. 62)

> Organisms can be understood only as interactions among adaptations, by-products of adaptations, and noise. (Pinker, 1998, p. 174)

> The evolutionary process produces three products: naturally selected features (adaptations), by-products of naturally selected features, and a residue of noise. (Buss et al., 1998, p. 537)

Other evolutionary psychologists have made similar statements (see Dennett, 1995, p. 537; Daly and Wilson, 1988, p. 12). Not only do evolutionary psychologists acknowledge the existence of by-products and noise; they also explicitly test by-product hypotheses (e.g., Kurzban, Tooby, & Cosmides, 2001; Cosmides & Tooby, 1992). In addition, they acknowledge that adaptationist claims must be backed by evidence: "To show that an organism has cognitive procedures that are adaptations . . . one must also show that their design features are not more parsimoniously explained as by-products" (Cosmides & Tooby, 1992, p. 180).

Ironically, in the same volume of essays in which Gould and Rose's comments appear (Rose & Rose, 2000), Fausto-Sterling makes *exactly the reverse* criticism. She takes issue with Don Symons's (1979) speculation that the female orgasm might be a by-product rather than an adaptation (Fausto-Sterling, 2000, p. 211), existing only because of the male orgasm, with the design "carried over" to the other sex. Whichever view proves to be correct, Fausto-Sterling here seems guilty of precisely the sins of which evolutionary psychologists stand accused, while Symons is as pluralistic as Gould could ask.

Gould (2000) also questioned whether adaptation need be invoked for understanding why human males invest in their offspring. His explanation is this: "A man may feel love for a baby because the infant looks so darling and dependent and because a father sees a bit of himself in his progeny. This feeling need not arise as a specifically selected Darwinian adaptation" (p. 122).

Interestingly, in a very entertaining piece 20 years earlier, Gould (1979) showed how Disney's Mickey Mouse takes advantage of humans' preferences for neotenous features, changing over the course of his own evolution from his slightly shady start in "Steamboat Willie" to the modern, more neotenous Mickey Mouse. In Gould's own words: "When we see a living creature with babyish features, we feel an automatic surge of disarming tenderness. The adaptive value of this response can scarcely be questioned, for we must nurture our babies" (Gould, 1979, p. 33).

For Gould, the human preference for neoteny is adaptive (1979), yet not necessarily an adaptation (2000). And if not adaptation, the only alternative is a spandrel, or by-product. Gould's suggestion, then, is that parental love for babies is an accident, mere happenstance—a phenomenally improbable and obviously lucky state of affairs. If this claim were made of any other species, we doubt the idea would be entertained for a moment: is it possible that penguin dads care for penguin chicks *by accident*, rather than design?

In this chapter we are not attempting to elaborate evidence for parental investment adaptations in human males. Our point is simply that peoples' requirements differ in terms of how unlikely complex functional design must be before the case for adaptation is made. Stephen J. Gould (2000) is as skeptical as one could ask of a scientist, allowing for the possibility of unfathomably unlikely scenarios.

Controversies Surrounding the Application of Evolutionary Biology to Human Psychology

Steven Pinker (1998) used the example of an olive pitter to discuss the value of considering design. Imagine what critics of evolutionary approaches might say were someone to come across an olive pitter and speculate that it was good at pitting olives because it was designed to do so. Gould might claim

that this was an unfounded and possibly unfalsifiable "just so" story, emphasizing that there was no evidence of the history of the artifact, as nothing whatsoever was known about the factory in which it was produced.
Others would claim that a more "parsimonious" explanation would be that
it was good at pitting olives because it had a little plunger mechanism *here*,
a sharp point *there*, and so forth. Finally, as discussed above, they might claim
that it could very well be that the olive pitter is an incidental by-product,
the leftover material from a factory that makes, for example, sewing machines. This particular by-product, it would be argued, just happens to be
good at pitting olives.

These arguments—insufficient historical data, the sovereign status of
proximate explanations, and by-product hypotheses—are common criticisms of evolutionary psychology.

Gould asks, "How can we possibly obtain the key information that
would be required to show the validity of adaptive tales about the EEA? . . .
We do not even know the original environment of our ancestors" (p. 120).
Note that for Gould this information seems to be a *requirement* to show design. Benton (2000) is similarly concerned about the "fragmentary sources
of evidence available from the fossil record" (p. 262), and Fausto-Sterling
(2000) suggests that because we know so little about the ancestral past,
"evaluating competing hypotheses becomes very difficult" (p. 214). Gould
concludes that "the key strategy proposed by evolutionary psychologists for
identifying adaptation is untestable and therefore unscientific" (Gould,
2000, p. 120).

Evolutionary psychologists do indeed use what is believed to be true of
our species' evolutionary history to generate hypotheses. However, developing evidence of adaptation does not require precise knowledge of the history of selection because *evidence of adaptation in evolutionary psychology is
exactly the same as it is in evolutionary biology: evidence of special design.* A hypothesis about design should lead to testable predictions (for extended discussions of this issue, see Buss et al., 1998; Holcomb, 1998; Ketelaar & Ellis,
2000). The question is not whether we can know for certain what our ancestral past was like; the question is whether or not we can use what we do
know about ancestral environments to develop new hypotheses (Barkow,
1989). Consider that with each feature of the olive pitter the chef demonstrated, each exquisitely tuned to its function, an observer would become
increasingly convinced as to its purpose, knowing *nothing at all* about the
artifact's history.

Does a description of the mechanics of the olive pitter replace an explanation in terms of its design? S. Rose suggests that evolutionary psychologists
"insist on distal (in their slightly archaic language, 'ultimate') explanations
when proximate ones are so much more explanatory" (p. 3), and again later,
that "proximal mechanisms . . . are much more evidence-based as

determining levels of causation, should these be required, than evolutionary speculations" (p. 305; for similar claims, see H. Rose [2000], p. 146;
S. Rose [2000], p. 313).

Humans, like artifacts, have parts, and these parts have functions. It
seems reasonable to derive hypotheses about these functions from the
standpoint of design. We do not wish to suggest that alternative approaches for hypothesis development—reliance on observation, intuition,
or guesswork—are any less legitimate. However, providing a proximal explanation neither invalidates an ultimate explanation nor replaces it. This
is analogous to showing the mechanics by which an olive pitter pits and
claiming that it is therefore not designed to perform this function. Anything that is designed to accomplish a task must be instantiated physically
in the world. Whether a mechanism is an artifact or organic, and regardless of its function, it is possible to describe its operation in physical, proximate terms.

The claim that evolutionary psychologists "insist on distal" explanations
is mostly true, but misleading. It is misleading in that the implication is that
evolutionary psychologists insist on *only* distal explanations, to the exclusion
of proximate explanations. While most psychologists are content to think
only about proximate causation, evolutionary psychologists are interested in
multiple levels of analysis. We consider multilevel investigations a strength
in the field, not a flaw.

The Real Debate: Domain Specificity

There are areas of debate in which there are genuinely different points of
view. Some of these debates are between evolutionary psychologists and
those who endorse alternative non-evolutionary hypotheses (e.g., Buss,
Larsen, Westen, & Semmelroth, 1992; Harris, 2000), while other debates
take place within the field, among practitioners. Disagreements can take
place on logical grounds (e.g., Pinker, 1998, vs. Fodor, 2000), differing
interpretations of existing data (e.g., Buss & Duntley, 2000, vs. Daly &
Wilson, 1988), or, the largest category, as-yet-unknown answers to questions that will ultimately be decided empirically.

The single most critical arena of legitimate debate in evolutionary psychology is the extent to which the human mind is "modular" or "domain
specific." These terms are used differently by different authors, but very generally, modularity refers to the extent to which the mind consists of a large
number of very functionally specific and relatively isolated information-
processing devices as opposed to a smaller number of more general systems. Another way to put this is to ask how many mental "organs" there

are, and the extent to which the organs themselves are composed of specialized subsystems.

Most evolutionary psychologists favor some variation of the view that the mind is likely to possesses many functionally distinct mental organs, with some anchoring each pole of a continuum from extreme (Sperber, 1994) to modest (Mithin, 1996) modularity. This debate ranges across disciplines, discussed by philosophers, neuroscientists, psychologists, and anthropologists. Recently, Pinker's (1998) *How the Mind Works*, which defended a modular view, was challenged by Fodor's (2000) cleverly titled *The Mind Doesn't Work That Way*.

The critical point is that challenges to domain-specific hypotheses in the form of hypotheses about more general mechanisms are thoroughly legitimate. In fact, these challenges are welcome alternatives to arguments centering on the false dichotomies of the past: biological versus cultural, innate versus learned, genetic versus environmental. Any given psychological mechanism can be more or less domain specific, but all mechanisms must result from an interaction of genes and environment. As discussed above, it is on this latter point that all reasonable parties agree, despite protestations of the critics to the contrary.

Challenges to domain-specific hypotheses have spawned productive debates. The question of whether face recognition is performed by a mechanism specialized for this task is one example, and here progress has been made, with experimental and neuropsychological evidence accumulating in favor of the domain-specific view (Kanwisher, 2000). Certainly the debate surrounding the question of the specificity of language learning has been a fruitful one (Pinker, 1994), as has the controversy surrounding specificity in the mechanisms underpinning children's acquisition of knowledge in the areas of biology, folk psychology, and physics (Hirschfeld & Gelman, 1994).

Nowhere is this debate more vivid than in discussions of culture. Ideas, norms, and rules that differ between societies are all acquired by some kind of learning mechanism. In the case of religion, for example, Boyer (2001) has shown that the religious ideas observed across societies share certain important properties. He argues that because domain-specific mechanisms generate religious ideas out of an alphabet of possible components, certain ideas—such as a deity that exists only on Wednesdays—either do not arise or do not get widely transmitted. In contrast, ideas about entities that violate intuitive ontologies—such as artifacts with humanlike qualities—continuously appear in religious traditions. Other researchers have similarly addressed transmission of cultural ideas, postulating various degrees of specificity (e.g., Barkow, 1989; Boyd & Richerson, 1985).

Conclusion

In summary, debates should move past mischaracterizations and toward a discussion of genuine issues of contention. In order for fruitful debates to occur, all parties will need to agree that evolutionary psychologists argue the following:

1. The environment is extremely important to any organism's development.
2. Organisms have parts that are not adaptations, but by-products or noise.
3. Hypotheses that do not yield new insights are not useful.
4. There are multiple levels of explanation for any given phenomenon.
5. Claims for adaptation require support, usually in the form of evidence of special design.

There is no guarantee, of course, that any particular piece of evolutionary psychology will conform to these ideals. However, we are optimistic that debates that transcend the common misattributions and move to an earnest discussion of core issues of contention will result in far greater understanding of the human mind and behavior.

We thank Jerry Barkow, Clark Barrett, and April Bleske for helpful comments on earlier drafts of this chapter.

References

Barkow, J. J. (1989). *Darwin, sex, and status: Biological approaches to mind and culture.* Toronto: University of Toronto Press.

Belsky, J., Steinberg, L., & Draper, P. (1991). Childhood experience, interpersonal development, and reproductive strategy: An evolutionary theory of socialization. *Child Development, 4,* 647–670.

Benton, T. (2000). Social causes and natural relations. In H. Rose & S. Rose (Eds.), *Alas, poor Darwin: Arguments against evolutionary psychology* (pp. 249–270). New York: Harmony Books.

Boyd, R., & Richerson, P. J. (1985). *Culture and the evolutionary process.* Chicago: University of Chicago Press.

Boyer, P. (2001). *Religion explained: The evolutionary origins of religious thought.* New York: Basic Books.

Buss, D. (1989). Sex differences in human mate preferences: Evolutionary hypotheses tested in 37 cultures. *Behavioral and Brain Sciences, 12,* 1–49.

Buss, D. M., & Duntley, J. D. (2000). *The killers among us: A co-evolutionary theory of homicide.* Paper presented to the Annual Meeting of the Human Behavior and Evolution Society, Amherst, MA, June 8.

Buss, D. M., Haselton, M. G., Shackelford, T. K., Bleske, A. L., & Wakefield, J. C. (1998). Adaptations, exaptation, and spandrels. *American Psychologist, 53,* 533–548.

Buss, D. M., Larsen, R. J., Westen, D., & Semmelroth, J. (1992). Sex differences in jealousy: Evolution, physiology, and psychology. *Psychological Science, 4,* 251–255.

Cosmides, L., & Tooby, J. (1992). Cognitive adaptations for social exchange. In J. H. Barkow, L. Cosmides, & J. Tooby (Eds.), *The adapted mind: Evolutionary psychology and the generation of culture* (pp. 163–228). New York: Oxford University Press.

Daly, M., & Wilson, M. (1988). *Homicide.* New York: Aldine de Gruyter.

Dennett, D. C. (1995). *Darwin's dangerous idea: Evolution and the meanings of life.* New York: Simon & Schuster.

Eagly, A. H. (1987). *Sex differences in social behavior: A social-role interpretation.* Hillsdale, NJ: Lawrence Erlbaum.

Eagly, A. H., & Wood, W. (1999). The origins of sex differences in human behavior: Evolved disposition versus social roles. *American Psychologist, 54,* 408–423.

Ellis, B. J., & Garber, J. (2000). Psychosocial antecedents of variation in girls' pubertal timing: Maternal depression, stepfather presence, and marital and family stress. *Child Development, 71,* 485–501.

Ellis, B. J., McFadyen-Ketchum, S., Dodge, K. A., Pettit, G. S., & Bates, J. E. (1999). Quality of early family relationships and individual differences in the timing of pubertal maturation in girls: A longitudinal test of an evolutionary model. *Journal of Personality and Social Psychology, 77,* 387–401.

Fausto-Sterling, A. (2000). Beyond difference: Feminism and evolutionary psychology. In H. Rose & S. Rose (Eds.), *Alas, poor Darwin: Arguments against evolutionary psychology* (pp. 209–247). New York: Harmony Books.

Fodor, J. (2000). *The mind doesn't work that way: The scope and limits of computational psychology.* Cambridge, MA: MIT Press.

Gangestad, S. W., & Buss, D. M. (1993). Pathogen prevalence and human mate preferences. *Ethology and Sociobiology, 14,* 89–96.

Gangestad, S. W., & Simpson, J. A. (2000). The evolution of human mating: Trade-offs and strategic pluralism. *Behavioral and Brain Sciences, 23,* 573–644.

Gould, S. J. (1979). Mickey Mouse meets Konrad Lorenz. *Natural History, 88,* 30–36.

Gould, S. J. (1997). Evolution: The pleasures of pluralism. *New York Review of Books,* June 26.

Gould, S. J. (2000). More things in heaven and earth. In H. Rose & S. Rose (Eds.), *Alas, poor Darwin: Arguments against evolutionary psychology* (pp. 101–126). New York: Harmony Books.

Gould, S. J., & Lewontin, R. (1979). The spandrels of San Marco and the Panglossian program: A critique of the adaptationist program. *Proceedings of the Royal Society of London, 250,* 281–288.

Harris, C. R. (2000). Psychophysiological responses to imagined infidelity: The specific innate modular view of jealousy reconsidered. *Journal of Personality and Social Psychology, 78,* 1082–1091.

Herrnstein Smith, B. (2000). Sewing up the mind: The claims of evolutionary psychology. In H. Rose & S. Rose (Eds.), *Alas, poor Darwin: Arguments against evolutionary psychology* (pp. 155–172). New York: Harmony Books.

Hill, E. M., Thomson Ross, L., & Low, B. S. (1997). The role of future unpredictability in human risk-taking. *Human Nature, 8,* 287–325.

Hill, K., & Hurtado, A. M. (1996). *Ache life history: The ecology and demography of a foraging people.* New York: Aldine de Gruyter.

Hirschfeld, L. A., & Gelman, S. A. (1994). *Mapping the mind: Domain specificity in cognition and culture.* New York: Cambridge University Press.

Holcomb, H. R., III. (1998). Testing evolutionary hypotheses. In C. Crawford & D. R. Krebs (Eds.), *Handbook of evolutionary psychology: Ideas, issues, and applications* (pp. 303–334). Mahwah, NJ: Lawrence Erlbaum.

Jencks, C. (2000). EP, phone home. In H. Rose & S. Rose (Eds.), *Alas, poor Darwin: Arguments against evolutionary psychology* (pp. 33–54). New York: Harmony Books.

Kanwisher, N. (2000). Domain specificity in face perception. *Nature Neuroscience, 3,* 759–763.

Karmiloff-Smith, A. (2000). Why babies' brains are not Swiss army knives. In H. Rose & S. Rose (Eds.), *Alas, poor Darwin: Arguments against evolutionary psychology* (pp. 173–187). New York: Harmony Books.

Kasser, T., & Sharma, Y. S. (1999). Reproductive freedom, educational equality, and females' preference for resource-acquisition characteristics in mates. *Psychological Science, 10,* 374–377.

Ketelaar, T., & Ellis, B. J. (2000). Are evolutionary explanations unfalsifiable? Evolutionary psychology and the Lakatosian philosophy of science. *Psychological Inquiry, 11,* 1–21.

Kurzban, R., Tooby, J., & Cosmides, L. (2001). Can race be erased? Coalitional computation and social categorization. *Proceedings of the National Academy of Sciences, 98,* 15387–15392.

Low, B. S. (1989). Cross-cultural patterns in the training of children: An evolutionary perspective. *Journal of Comparative Psychology, 103,* 311–319.

Malamuth, N. M. (1998). An evolutionary-based model integrating research on the characteristics of sexually coercive men. In J. Adair, K. Dion, & D. Belanger (Eds.), *Advances in psychological science, vol. 1: Social, personal, and cultural aspects* (pp. 151–184). Hove, UK: Psychology Press.

Mithin, S. (1996). *The prehistory of the mind: The cognitive origins of art, religion, and science.* London: Thames and Hudson.

Nelkin, D. (2000). Less selfish than sacred? Genes and the religious impulse in evolutionary psychology. In H. Rose & S. Rose (Eds.), *Alas, poor Darwin: Arguments against evolutionary psychology* (pp. 17–32). New York: Harmony Books.

Pedersen, F. A. (1991). Secular trends in human sex ratios: Their influence on individual and family behavior. *Human Nature, 2*, 271–291.

Pinker, S. (1994). *The language instinct.* New York: HarperCollins.

Pinker, S. (1998). *How the mind works.* New York: W. W. Norton.

Rose, H. (2000). Colonizing the social sciences? In H. Rose & S. Rose (Eds.), *Alas, poor Darwin: Arguments against evolutionary psychology* (pp. 127–153). New York: Harmony Books.

Rose, H., & Rose, S. (Eds.). (2000). *Alas, poor Darwin: Arguments against evolutionary psychology.* New York: Harmony Books.

Rose, S. (2000). Escaping evolutionary psychology. In H. Rose & S. Rose (Eds.), *Alas, poor Darwin: Arguments against evolutionary psychology* (pp. 299–320). New York: Harmony Books.

Shakespeare, T., & Erikson, M. (2000). Different strokes: Beyond biological determinism and social constructionism. In H. Rose & S. Rose (Eds.), *Alas, poor Darwin: Arguments against evolutionary psychology* (pp. 229–247). New York: Harmony Books.

Sperber, D. (1994). The modularity of thought and the epidemiology of representations. In L. H. Hirschfeld & S. A. Gelman (Eds.), *Mapping the mind: Domain specificity in cognition and culture* (pp. 39–67). New York: Cambridge University Press.

Sulloway, F. J. (1996). *Born to rebel: Birth order, family dynamics, and creative lives.* New York: Pantheon Books.

Symons, D. (1979). *The evolution of human sexuality.* New York: Oxford University Press.

Symons, D. (1992). On the use and misuse of Darwinism in the study of human behavior. In J. H. Barkow, L. Cosmides, & J. Tooby (Eds.), *The adapted mind: Evolutionary psychology and the generation of culture* (pp. 137–159). New York: Oxford University Press.

Tooby, J., & Cosmides, L. (1990). The past explains the present: Emotional adaptations and the structure of ancestral environments. *Ethology and Sociobiology, 11*, 375–424.

Tooby, J., & Cosmides, L. (1992). The psychological foundations of culture. In J. H. Barkow, L. Cosmides, & J. Tooby (Eds.), *The adapted mind: Evolutionary psychology and the generation of culture* (pp. 19–136). New York: Oxford University Press.

PART III

Human and Nonhuman Primates

While all evolutionists share a basic Darwinian framework, there are various schools of thought as to how that framework is to be applied to human beings. Historically, at least, behavioral ecologists and evolutionary psychologists have often diverged sharply (Barkow, 1984, 1990; Symons, 1989). The emphasis for evolutionary psychology is on the evolved *psychology*, the disposition or mechanism underlying actual behavior. The human behavioral ecologists have often focused on whether patterns of observed social behavior in actual human societies could be a means by which individuals enhanced their genetic fitness, and/or whether the behavior was in accordance with evolutionary theory. A vertically integrated perspective strengthens the behavioral ecology approach: We need to know both the extent to which a pattern of social behavior is enhancing fitness, and the underlying evolved psychological mechanisms that enabled individuals to generate this pattern (Barkow, 1989; Borgerhoff Mulder et al., 1997, p. 272; Richerson, Thornhill, & Voland, 1997). The great strength of behavioral ecology has always been its use of ethnographic and other naturalistic data and its focus on a wide variety of human societies. In recent years the boundaries among the various schools of evolutionary thought have become somewhat blurred, and Cronk's chapter reflects this praiseworthy tendency toward overlap. He begins by discussing work that one might consider "classical" behavioral ecology, but he soon goes on to include authors (such as Buss and Daly & Wilson) who are deeply concerned with the psychological level. Cronk also emphasizes the "feminist sensibility" of much evolutionary research, a point that complements Campbell's discussion (this volume) of feminism and evolutionary psychology.

Cronk's own work among the Mukogodo illustrates the differences between a behavioral ecology approach and an evolutionary psychology one. He finds that, just as theory predicts, Mukogodo parents favor their daughters rather than their sons during times of scarce resources, because under these conditions the reproductive prospects of the daughters are better than those of the sons. An evolutionary psychologist would use much the same theory but would focus on the presumed evolved mechanism that somehow determines gender privileging in response to changes in perceived resource availability. The two approaches complement one another: more than that, each is incomplete without the other.

Cronk's discussion of the relationship between culturally defined and biologically defined success is a good example of vertical integration—the two types of success are generally closely associated, and thus highly compatible with evolutionary psychology theories of prestige and self-esteem (e.g., Barkow, 1975, 1980).

Where Cronk is essentially teaching us how Darwinian theory can give insight into ethnography, that is, the study of cultural practices, primatologists Rodseth and Novak are showing us how to study social structure. Social scientists have long assumed that, given human uniqueness, it is unnecessary to study nonhuman primate sociology in any great detail. Rodseth and Novak demonstrate rather dramatically that, as it turns out, the uniqueness of our human sociology becomes apparent only through study of the social organization of our relatives! Evolutionary psychologists have had much to say about human mate selection and about sexual jealousy, but the clear implication of Rodseth and Novak's work is that it is our capacity for bonding and our tolerance of members of the same sex that distinguishes us from the other primates, and perhaps has made the development of large-scale society possible. Other primates organize either in terms of same-sex bonds but very weak male-female bonds; or else they have strong male-female bonds and weak same-sex bonds. But human societies typically have both strong same-sex bonds and strong male-female bonds. Human (but not nonhuman primate) males "seem to be able to maintain a relatively stable sexual bond in combination with a stable and extended network of male-male bonds." Similarly, only human females have enduring bonds with males while at the same time having stable and extended same-sex networks.

Rodseth and Novak's apparent theoretical breakthrough begs for challenge from students of world ethnography, but I am confident that it will ultimately be accepted as a major constraint and enabler on the varieties of social organization that can develop in human societies. Its implication for psychologists is that research on human same-sex/cross-sex bonding capacity, and on how this ability relates to the development of sociality in children, is needed. For social scientists, the question raised by the Rodseth/Novak finding is dual: what factors lead individuals and societies to favor one type of bond rather than the other? Rodseth and Novak's insights need to be integrated across the human sciences.

For primate females (including our ancestors) to be able to sustain enduring bonds with one another, there must have been reduced competition among them for food (as among bonobos). Rodseth and Novak speculate that this reduction of female-female competition came about not because male hunters were providing meat but because of the cooking of tubers. (Their early date for the use of fire, however, is controversial.)

References

Barkow, J. H. (1975). Strategies for self-esteem and prestige in Maradi, Niger Republic. In T. R. Williams (Ed.), *Psychological Anthropology* (pp. 373–388). The Hague and Paris: Mouton.

Barkow, J. H. (1980). Prestige and self-esteem: A biosocial interpretation. In D. R. Omark, F. F. Strayer, & D. G. Freedman (Eds.), *Dominance Relations: An Ethological View of Human Conflict and Social Interaction* (pp. 319–332). New York: Garland.

Barkow, J. H. (1984). The distance between genes and culture. *Journal of Anthropological Research, 37,* 367–379.

Barkow, J. H. (1989). *Darwin, Sex, and Status: Biological Approaches to Mind and Culture.* Toronto: University of Toronto Press.

Barkow, J. H. (1990). Beyond the DP/DSS controversy. *Ethology and Sociobiology, 11,* 341–351.

Borgerhoff Mulder, M., Richerson, P. J., Thornhill, N. W., & Voland, E. (1997). The place of behavioral ecological anthropology in evolutionary social science. In P. Weingart, S. D. Mitchell, P. J. Richerson, & S. Maasen (Eds.), *Human by Nature: Between Biology and the Social Sciences* (pp. 253–281). Mahwah, NJ: Lawrence Erlbaum.

Symons, D. (1989). A critique of Darwinian anthropology. *Ethology and Sociobiology, 10,* 131–144.

6   Behavioral Ecology and the Social Sciences

Lee Cronk

The Development of Human Behavioral Ecology

Behavioral ecologists use evolutionary biological theory to study the behavior of living organisms. Behavioral ecology's theoretical roots are much the same as those of evolutionary psychology. Specifically, both fields began to take shape in the 1960s and 1970s following a series of theoretical breakthroughs chiefly by W. D. Hamilton, George C. Williams, and Robert Trivers on the evolutionary biological bases of behavior. Hamilton (1964) pointed out that because related individuals share some of the same genes by virtue of the fact that they have common ancestors, selection may sometimes favor genes that lead their bearers to do things that harm their own reproductive interests if in so doing they substantially increase the reproductive success of relatives. This became the centerpiece of what is sometimes called "selfish gene theory" (Dawkins, 1976), the idea that we can gain great insight into behavior by focusing on the differential reproduction not of groups or individuals, but of genes. Williams (1966) contributed a key argument for why selection is likely in most circumstances to act most strongly through the differential survival and reproduction of individual organisms and the genes they carry rather than through groups of organisms. In a series of seminal articles in the early 1970s, Trivers (Trivers, 1971, 1972, 1974; Trivers & Hare, 1976; Trivers & Willard, 1973) extended selfish gene thinking to topics such as reciprocity, parental behavior, and sexual selection.

This flurry of theoretical progress rapidly transformed the study of animal behavior and led some animal behaviorists, most notably Richard D. Alexander (1974, 1979) at the University of Michigan and Edward O. Wilson at Harvard University (1975, 1978), to try to apply the new paradigm to the study of human behavior. At roughly the same time, some anthropologists were excited by the accomplishments in animal behavior studies and began to use ideas from that field to reanalyze existing data on human behavior, society, and culture, and to design new studies to test specific predictions derived from evolutionary theory. This began with cross-cultural studies, including John Hartung's analysis of wealth inheritance (1976) and Mildred Dickemann's work on female infanticide (1979a, 1979b) and purdah (1981). These were quickly followed by fieldwork-based studies on such topics as foraging patterns (e.g., Smith & Winterhalder, 1981; Hawkes, Hill, & O'Connell, 1982), parenting (e.g., Chagnon, Flinn, & Melancon, 1979), mating (e.g., Irons, 1979) and social behavior (e.g., Chagnon, 1979; Chagnon & Bugos, 1979; and Hames, 1979), and the rate of production of such studies increased dramatically during the 1980s (see Borgerhoff Mulder, 1991; Cronk, 1991a; and Smith, 1991a, 1991b for reviews).

As is the case with many new fields, it has taken time for a consensus to develop on what to call this approach. In the 1970s, many followed E. O. Wilson's lead and called it "sociobiology," while a few used anthropologist Lionel Tiger's older label "biosociology," instead. These neologisms reflected a felt need to distinguish the new approach based on the ideas of Hamilton, Williams, and Trivers from such earlier approaches as cultural ecology, human ecology, and ecological anthropology (see Orlove, 1980 for a review). When Wilson's application of evolutionary theory to human behavior attracted a great deal of criticism (e.g., Sahlins, 1976; Lewontin, Rose, & Kamin, 1984; Kitcher, 1985), "sociobiology" became less popular as a label, even though the approach itself was flourishing. Various other labels have been tried by both proponents and opponents of the new paradigm, including "socioecology," "evolutionary ecology," "Darwinian ecological anthropology," "evolution and behavior studies," and "ethology." Most of the differences among these labels are cosmetic, but to some extent they do reflect slight differences between various groups of researchers in theoretical or substantive foci. In the 1980s and 1990s the label "behavioral ecology" came to be used more often than any other, so that is the one chosen for use in this chapter.

The Method of Human Behavioral Ecology

Human behavioral ecologists share not only a distinct body of theory, but also a general method for deciding what questions are interesting to ask and how best to answer them. Human behavioral ecology's modus operandi can be demonstrated by looking at a study conducted by Monique Borgerhoff Mulder of the University of California at Davis of the marriage system of the Kipsigis, a farming and herding people in western Kenya. She was interested in how people make choices about who to marry and why, in particular, some women and their parents choose husbands and sons-in-law who already have one or more wives. Borgerhoff Mulder was led to this problem not only by her familiarity with the Kipsigis but also by existing behavioral ecological theories of mating systems and mate choice. A common mating system among both humans and nonhumans is polygyny, in which one male mates with several females. One type of polygyny identified by behavioral ecologists occurs when males defend important resources such as nesting sites and food-bearing territories in order to mate with the females who need those resources. This is called *resource defense polygyny* (see Emlen & Oring, 1977). A question raised by resource defense polygyny is why a female would mate with an already mated male if an unmated male, who would provide the female with access to all of the resources he has monopolized, is also available. In order to explain such behavior, ornithologist Gordon Orians (1969) proposed that if the quantity or quantity of the resources monopolized by the males varies a great deal from one male to another, then sometimes a female might gain access to more or better resources if she mates with a male who is already mated, even though she will be forced to share the resources with at least one other breeding female, rather than by mating with a solitary male who has few or poor resources. This *polygyny threshold* model has been successfully applied to a variety of bird species (e.g., the indigo bunting: Carey & Nolan, 1975, 1979).

Among the Kipsigis, women typically move in with their husbands at marriage. Husbands own land and livestock, and they can have more than one wife at a time. Borgerhoff Mulder wondered whether women and their families selected husbands with an eye toward their control of resources, chiefly land, taking into account the fact that if a woman marries an already-married man, she will have to share his land with his earlier wives. The data support this prediction: Kipsigis women have a statistically significant tendency to choose men according to the amount of land they offered the woman to farm, regardless of the number of cowives they would have as a result (Borgerhoff Mulder, 1990).

Borgerhoff Mulder's test of Orians's polygyny threshold model among the Kipsigis demonstrates one common technique of human behavioral ecologists: Study the behavior of nonhuman behavioral ecologists and use their models in the study of our own species. Human behavioral ecologists also share with nonhuman behavioral ecologists both a reliance on quantitative observational techniques (e.g., Borgerhoff Mulder & Caro, 1985) and an emphasis on empirical tests of falsifiable hypotheses derived from their understanding of evolutionary biological theory. However, even though

human behavioral ecologists have great admiration for the elegance and re-
finement that is now routine in nonhuman behavioral ecology, they also
heed the advice of evolutionary theorist Alan Grafen that "a good field-
worker is nobody's poodle" (1987, p. 221). Rather than limiting themselves to things that have already been studied among other species,
human behavioral ecologists often use evolutionary thinking to shed light
on a wide variety of human behaviors that have no clear parallels among
nonhumans. For example, Borgerhoff Mulder (1988) herself has conducted what may be the best single study of intrasocietal variations in
bridewealth payments, using them as a window onto the mate preferences
of Kipsigis men.

As behavioral and social scientists, human behavioral ecologists also
must consider a variety of methodological and epistemological issues that
nonhuman behavioral ecologists do not worry about at all. One such issue
is the dichotomy that runs throughout the social sciences between methodological collectivism and methodological individualism. Human behavioral
ecologists are methodological individualists, meaning that they analyze social phenomena as a product of the actions of individuals. An interest in the
individual has deep roots in anthropology, going back at least to the work of
Bronislaw Malinowski (1939) and running through such British anthropologists as Raymond Firth (1936) and such Americans as Melville Herskovits
(1940). Inspired in part by the work of such sociologists as George Homans
(1967), methodological individualism experienced a brief fluorescence in
anthropology in the 1960s thanks to such political anthropologists as F. G.
Bailey (1969) and Fredrik Barth (1965) and such economic anthropologists
as Harold Schneider (1974). Another strain of methological individualism
has influenced anthropology through psychological anthropology. This tradition of methodological individualism contrasts with a Durkheimian tradition of methodological collectivism in the social sciences that gives primacy
to forces external to the individual such as society, culture, and power.
Methodological individualism does not deny that social pressures, cultural
traits, and power relationships influence individual behavior, but it considers explanations of individual behavior that rely upon such concepts to be
begging the question. If all social and cultural phenomena arise fundamentally from the actions of individuals, then explanations of individual behavior that refer to collective phenomena are, by necessity, incomplete and, by
extension, unsatisfying. On the other hand, some human behavioral ecologists are interested in the collective phenomenon of culture and do appreciate that social and cultural phenomena can have emergent properties that
cannot be entirely predicted from a knowledge of the behaviors of the individuals involved (Cronk, 1988, 1995, 1999, pp. 50–51). Reconciliation of
these two approaches may be found in a vertically integrated approach, such
as that advocated by Barkow (1989; see also Winterhalder & Smith, 1992

for more on behavioral ecology's methodological, epistemological, and metatheoretical foundations).

Human Behavioral Ecology and Social Problems

Although the research agendas of most human behavioral ecologists have been driven primarily by theoretical concerns, many of their findings are highly relevant to the normative concerns that have traditionally motivated much research in the social and behavioral sciences. Here I will briefly discuss behavioral ecological research on three topics of enormous practical concern: the status of women, child abuse and neglect, and social competition.

Human Behavioral Ecology and the Treatment of Women

Evolutionary approaches to human behavior have encountered considerable resistance in some quarters of the behavioral and social sciences. Much of that resistance has come from scholars of gender, who argue that an emphasis on the biology of sex obscures the ways in which gender identities and relations between genders are socially and culturally constructed (e.g., Bem, 1993). However, a rapidly growing body of research has demonstrated that an evolutionary perspective can provide great insights into issues as central to gender studies as the status and treatment of women. The degree to which the intellectual tide has turned may be indicated by the popularity of Helen Fisher's (1999) recent argument that evolution has endowed women with many natural advantages compared to men. Many human behavioral ecologists now share Patricia Adair Gowaty's belief that, in addition to shedding light on the condition of women around the world and in prehistory, evolutionary biology also "suggests strategies for women to use in our efforts to gain, regain, and maintain autonomy" (Gowaty, 1992, p. 239). Toward this end, behavioral ecologists have examined such issues as male violence toward women (e.g., Smuts, 1992), women's marital strategies (e.g., Borgerhoff Mulder, 1992; Strassmann, 1997, 2000), the origins of patriarchy (e.g., Smuts, 1995, Hrdy, 1997; see also Hrdy, 1981), and the forced separation of women and men through such mechanisms as claustration and veiling (e.g., Dickemann, 1979a, 1979b, 1981; see Buss & Malamuth, 1996, and Gowaty, 1992 for overviews).

Beverly Strassmann's analysis of menstrual huts among the Dogon of Mali exemplifies how behavioral ecology can shed light on the treatment of women (Strassmann, 1992, 1996). Seclusion of menstruating women in special structures is a common practice recorded in a large number of societies from around the world, including the Kalasha of Pakistan (Parkes, 1990), the Slave Athabaskans of Canada (Spencer et al., 1977, p. 110), and the Saramaka of Suriname (Price, 1993). These and other practices surrounding menstruation have received a lot of attention from cultural anthropologists, particularly feminist ones (e.g., Buckley & Gottlieb, 1988), reflecting the cultural significance given to menstruation in many societies. Strassmann spent two years among the Dogon conducting a detailed study of their economic and reproductive patterns, including their use of menstrual huts.

Although ovulation itself in humans is not accompanied by the sorts of swellings and other outward signs common in other species, menstrual huts and other menstrual taboos have the effect of advertising women's reproductive status. Strassmann suggests that such public information about the timing of a woman's monthly cycle may make it difficult for women to obfuscate the timing of the onset of pregnancy, which may be useful to men if, as evolutionary theory would predict, they are concerned about impregnating their wives and about being cuckolded. Such information might be especially important in a group like the Dogon, where women spend most of their reproductive years not cycling owing either to pregnancy or postpartum amenorrhea. During the 29 months of Strassmann's study, women aged 20 through 34 years spent 29% of the time pregnant, 56% of the time in postpartum amenorrhea, and only 15% of the time cycling. Thus, while a woman in an economically developed society with widespread birth control and low fertility might cycle nearly every month during a typical 30-year reproductive career (i.e., from menarche to menopause), women in societies like the Dogon may ovulate relatively few times during their entire lives.

Based on this line of reasoning, Strassmann suggests that menstrual taboos among the Dogon are anticuckoldry tactics. A variety of types of data support this interpretation. Dogon men themselves report that they are greatly concerned with cuckoldry, and they told Strassmann that they think that the seclusion of menstruating women does help husbands and patrilineages to avoid cuckoldry. Furthermore, visits to the huts are not fully voluntary on the part of the wives; rather, wives are obligated to visit the huts in order not to ritually contaminate the men's religious altars, and Dogon women actually prefer, ceteris paribus, to marry men who have converted to Islam or Christianity because then they will not need to visit the huts.

Given that women would prefer not to visit the huts and that such visits may help to constrain their sexual behavior, it is reasonable to suppose that they may try to mislead others about their reproductive status by visiting the huts when they are not really menstruating and by not visiting the huts when they are. Strassmann studied the honesty of women's hut visits by comparing the pattern of their visits with the hormonal patterns found in their urine, which she collected periodically from a sample of 93 women over a period of 10 weeks. The pattern of menstrual periods indicated by the hormonal assays matches very closely the pattern of visits to the menstrual huts, indicating that cheating in menstrual hut visits is rare. This matches the view of Dogon women themselves, who report that cheating is very uncommon. All of these findings support Strassmann's hypothesis that Dogon menstrual taboos are part of a system developed and imposed by Dogon men to control the sexual lives of Dogon women.

Human Behavioral Ecological Research on Child Abuse and Neglect

The central precept of human behavioral ecology is that human beings are organisms designed by natural selection. Because natural selection is driven by differential reproduction, a straightforward expectation is that humans and other organisms should behave in ways that help their offspring to survive and reproduce. The fact that both human and nonhuman parents are known sometimes to neglect, abuse, and even kill their own offspring is an obvious challenge to this perspective, and a great deal of human behavioral ecological research has been done on these topics as a result (e.g., Gelles & Lancaster, 1987; Hausfater & Hrdy, 1984). The findings may help efforts to help identify children at risk for abuse and neglect and develop social reforms that might help reduce their risk.

Behavioral ecologists often pose questions about adaptive design in terms of the costs and benefits of a behavior to an organism's inclusive fitness (Hamilton, 1964). The phrase "inclusive fitness" refers to the number of copies of its genes an organism is able to get into the next generation. Thinking about the genetic costs and benefits of particular behaviors often helps to clarify why they occur. For example, it would indeed be a contradiction to evolutionary theory if it were routine and widespread for parents to kill their biological offspring. But homicide of one's own biological children is, in most societies, rather rare. In American and Canadian societies, for example, psychologists Martin Daly and Margo Wilson of McMaster University have shown that a child is much more likely to be abused or killed by an unrelated adult living in the same home (often, though not always, a stepfather or a friend of the child's mother) than by a biological parent (Daly & Wilson, 1988). Although the legal penalties for the abuse or murder of a child are so severe that this can in no way be seen as adaptive, evolutionary theory does help to shed light on the pattern. On the one hand, it makes sense that humans would have been designed by natural selection to be highly tolerant of and solicitous toward their own offspring. On the other hand, because in the past there would have been a weaker selection pressure (if any) in favor of being tolerant of the demands and annoyances of unrelated infants, some people may find it particularly difficult to control their rage when they are unrelated to the child provoking it.

Elsewhere, however, it is clear that parents do sometimes neglect, abuse, and even abandon their children (see Hrdy, 1999 for many examples). Often, one sex of offspring is more likely to be neglected, abused, or even killed than the other. Female infanticide is the most common pattern (see Dickemann, 1979b for an evolutionary analysis), but male-biased infanticide has also been reported (e.g., among the Ayoreo of Bolivia by Bugos & McCarthy, 1984). Much of my own research has focused on a pattern of daughter favoritism among the Mukogodo of Kenya, an impoverished and low-status group of Maasai-speaking pastoralists (Cronk, 1989, 1991b, 2000). Although there is absolutely no evidence that the Mukogodo abuse their children or have ever practiced infanticide, I have documented in a variety of ways a broad tendency on the part of Mukogodo parents to favor their daughters over their sons. For example, Mukogodo mothers and other caregivers tend to hold infant girls more often than infant boys and to remain closer to them when not holding them. In addition, girls are nursed longer and more frequently and are more likely to be taken for medical care than boys. The results of this favoritism include better growth performance by Mukogodo girls than boys (measured as height-for-age, weight-for-age, and weight-for-height). Survivorship among young girls is so much better than among boys that the sex ratio of children ages 0–4 years is 67 boys to every 100 girls.

A number of explanations for this daughter favoritism are possible. For example, it might be that Mukogodo parents favor their daughters because of the bridewealth payments, usually consisting of several head of cattle and some sheep and goats, that they attract. However, there is no correlation between how many daughters a man has married off and either his herd size, the number of wives that he himself is subsequently able to marry, or the number of wives that his sons are subsequently able to marry. Furthermore, although all of the groups surrounding the Mukogodo also demand bridewealth payments, they show no signs of daughter favoritism. A better explanation is that the Mukogodo are responding to the relatively good prospects of their daughters compared to their sons. Mukogodo women virtually all get married, often to wealthy men from neighboring ethnic groups. Mukogodo men, on the other hand, often have a hard time accumulating the necessary bridewealth and frequently must delay marriage until middle age or forgo marriage entirely because of their general poverty and low ethnic status.

The Mukogodo pattern of daughter favoritism fits predictions made by evolutionary biologist Robert Trivers and mathematician Dan Willard (1973). They noted that if the reproductive prospects of male and female offspring differ in a way that is predictable from the parents' condition during the time of investment, natural selection would favor parents who invest more heavily in that sex with the better reproductive prospects. Because in many species the variance in reproductive success is greater for males than for females, the conditions faced by an individual during development will typically have a greater impact on the reproductive success of males than females. The net result is often that males reared when conditions are good will outreproduce their sisters, while females reared when conditions are bad will outreproduce their brothers. The Mukogodo appear to be in the latter situation: Due to their poverty and low status, girls' prospects are much better than boys', and it makes sense for Mukogodo parents to favor their daughters. Although this pattern of daughter favoritism increases Mukogodo parents' numbers of grandchildren, this is not simply a demonstration of the common folk wisdom that people like to have many grandchildren. In two surveys of Mukogodo women's reproductive goals and preferences, I have found that they express a bias in favor of sons, not daughters, and Mukogodo parents appear to be entirely unaware of the daughter favoritism in their behavior. Mukogodo daughter favoritism seems to be not a conscious strategy for enhancing one's number of grandoffspring but, rather, a deeply rooted evolved predisposition shared by a wide variety of species that is triggered by specific environmental circumstances. This demonstrates the value of an evolutionary approach in identifying circumstances that lead to patterns of child neglect of which even the parents themselves may not be aware.

Status Striving and Social Competition

One way that a new theoretical approach can make a contribution is by revealing previously undetected patterns in well-known data. Human behavioral ecology has had this kind of effect on our understanding of status striving and social competition across human societies. In the social sciences generally and cultural anthropology specifically, emphasis is placed on the tremendous variability in culture and behavior across societies. In the area of social competition, it is easy to see that this traditional approach makes a real contribution in that the determinants of status and rank do indeed vary widely across human societies. In some, wealth is the key, while in others, personality characteristics, hunting skills, success in warfare, or ability to keep the peace are more important. The conclusion of most social scientists is that this variability is evidence of how human motivations are social constructions rather than biological endowments. What behavioral ecologists see when they examine these same data, on the other hand, is a certain constant: Everywhere we look, status and rank are important to many people, and they routinely compete for status and prestige in ways that are locally appropriate and acceptable.

In the 1970s, anthropologist and behavioral ecologist William Irons suggested that the widespread tendency for people across cultures to consider high status an important goal, combined with the diversity of ways in which people attempt to accomplish this goal, might help link the new approach with existing traditions of cross-cultural research in anthropology. Specifically, he proposed a simple hypothesis: "In most human societies cultural success consists in accomplishing those things which make biological success (that is, high inclusive fitness) probable" (Irons, 1979, p. 258). If this is true, then we ought to be able to detect a correlation between the success of individuals in achieving success as it is defined in their own societies and in achieving reproductive success or, more broadly, inclusive fitness. It should be noted that this hypothesis is in no way contingent on anyone being aware of the connection between cultural and reproductive success. If culture is serving to guide people to behave in ways that in their particular local circumstances enhance reproduction, it should do so even if people are unaware not only of the goal of reproduction but even of how biological reproduction works.

One of the first tests of this hypothesis was Irons's own study of Yomut Turkmen pastoralists of northern Iran. He found that wealth correlated well with men's lifetime reproductive success (Irons, 1976, 1979). Similarly, Monique Borgerhoff Mulder (1987) found the same correlation among Kipsigis agropastoralists in western Kenya, as did I among Mukogodo pastoralists in north central Kenya (Cronk, 1991c). In all of these cases, the circumstances are somewhat similar: local definitions of male status and definitions of success are mainly determined by wealth, livestock are a large part of what constitutes wealth, substantial bridewealth must be paid by grooms to their in-laws in order to marry, and polygyny is allowed. Given these conditions, it may not seem surprising that men's wealth would correlate with both their numbers of wives and their reproductive success. But the situation is not as obvious as it might seem at first glance. If the local definitions of "success" were arbitrary cultural constructions and nothing more, then it would be surprising indeed to find so many societies in which success is defined largely in terms of wealth accumulation. The fact that wealth is a major determinant of status and prestige in so many societies in so many different parts of the world suggests that local definitions of success may be designed for a purpose rather than arbitrary.

But what about societies in which wealth is either not accumulated at all or not the sole or even a major correlate of status or prestige? In some societies, for instance, certain personality traits might be more important than wealth accumulation. The editor of this volume, Jerome Barkow, conducted an early test of this idea among two culturally distinct groups of Hausa-speakers of Nigeria, Muslim Hausa and non-Muslim Maguzawa (Barkow, 1977). Among both groups of Hausa-speakers, as among the Yomut, Kipsigis, and Mukogodo, wealth correlates with male reproductive success. But Barkow asked the interesting question of whether an individual's conformity with the personality characteristics most valued in his community might also influence his reproductive success. Among Muslim Hausa, emotional inhibition and restraint is valued. It is considered best always to appear to be a friendly and cheerful regardless of one's inner emotional state. The Maguzawa, in contrast, do not appear to place much value on emotional inhibition, and are much more likely to display their emotions openly. Interestingly, among the Muslim Hausa there is a correlation among men between emotional inhibition and reproductive success, but no such correlation among the Maguzawa. In other societies, a variety of other locally valued characteristics correlate with reproductive success, including political status (Betzig, 1986; Chagnon, 1979), hunting skills (Kaplan & Hill, 1985), involvement in violence (Chagnon, 1988), and peace-keeping (Moore, 1990). The pattern emerging seems to provide strong support for Irons's hypothesis in natural fertility societies (i.e., those without access to modern contraceptives): achievement of success as it is locally defined is a good predictor both of an individual's status and of his reproductive success, regardless of the details of the local environment, economy, or social system. This suggests that the highly variable definitions of high status across human societies may indeed be cultural constructions, but not randomly variable ones. Rather, local opinions about what constitutes success may be the outcomes of ongoing negotiations among fundamentally similar actors in highly variable environmental, political, social, and historical situations.

Human Behavioral Ecology and Evolutionary Psychology

Guided by their shared body of theory and method, human behavioral ecologists have done a large amount of high-quality empirical work over the past 20 to 30 years in many different societies on a wide variety of topics. Virtually every area of traditional concern in the social sciences, including marriage, kinship, economics, and politics, has been touched by the behavioral ecological approach (for reviews, see Borgerhoff Mulder, 1991; Cronk, 1991a; and Smith, 1991a, 1991b). Human behavioral ecology has matured enough over the past 20 years or so that many practitioners now feel that it is ready to expand both empirically to cover new topics and theoretically to incorporate new concepts. One promising and rapidly developing area is the conjunction between human behavioral ecology and evolutionary psychology.

Although they share a foundation in evolutionary theory, behavioral ecology and evolutionary psychology differ in a variety of ways. For example, behavioral ecologists and evolutionary psychologists tend to conceive of the "environment" in different ways. While evolutionary psychologists pay attention to the immediate environment experienced by an individual over the course of his or her lifetime, behavioral ecologists conceive of the environment in a much broader sense as a general ecological, social, economic, and political context experienced by people in a particular society. Thus while an evolutionary psychologist might focus on how behavior is influenced differently by the environments experienced by the firstborn child in a family and the lastborn child in a family (e.g., Sulloway, 1996), a behavioral ecologist is more likely to focus on how foraging behavior is influenced differently by the savannah environment of Hadza hunter-gatherers in Tanzania and the arid environment of !Kung hunter-gatherers in Botswana and Namibia (e.g., Blurton Jones, Hawkes, & Draper, 1994).

Another difference between behavioral ecologists and evolutionary psychologists is on the issue of the psychological mechanisms that lie between an organism's history of natural selection and the more immediate issue of how its behavior is generated by its mind and brain. Critics of human behavioral ecology have seen the lack of detailed attention to psychological mechanisms as one of the field's main shortcomings (e.g., Vayda, 1995). The behavioristic style of human behavioral ecology is demonstrated by a now classic study of foraging among the Ache of Paraguay by Kristen Hawkes, Kim Hill, and James F. O'Connell (1982). By collecting detailed information about how long Ache men and women spent foraging, which species they chose to pursue, how long it took to pursue and process them, and how many calories they received as a result of their time and effort, Hawkes and her colleagues were able to show that Ache foraging behavior is "optimal"— that is, it fits the predictions of a set of essentially microeconomic models developed by animal behaviorists. In short, Ache foragers choose the correct set of species to pursue, including such animals as deer and peccaries along with a variety of plant foods, insects, and honey, if their goal is to obtain the most calories possible in the least amount of time possible. A logical next step would be to examine the psychological mechanisms that lead Ache and others to forage optimally. An idea about how this might proceed was suggested by one of Hawkes et al.'s Ache informants, who mentioned that monkeys are not a favorite food because they have little fat. Such rules of thumb and folk wisdom point to the possibility of using Herbert Simon's notion of bounded rationality to fill in the gap between optimization models and actual behavior (Simon, 1992).

Bounded rationality is increasingly popular among researchers in fields ranging from animal behavior and psychology to economics and political science who have previously relied upon rational choice and optimization models. Simon suggested that because of time constraints and the limits of the brain's computing power, it is usually not possible for decision makers to calculate optimal strategies. Rather, they may use heuristics or rules of thumb to make a quick decision based on only a small subset of the information potentially available. In some situations, it is clear that some heuristic must be in use or a behavior could not occur as quickly as it routinely does. For example, when a ball is hit in cricket or baseball, a fielder is expected to try to intercept it. One way to do this would be to calculate where the ball will land using a set of differential equations using information about the curvature of the ball's flight path and its acceleration. Clearly, most fielders do no such thing. Rather, there is evidence that they use a couple of simple heuristics. One, the linear-trajectory hypothesis, holds that a fielder should adjust his speed and direction so that the apparent trajectory of the ball seems straight from his point of view (McBeath, Shaffer, & Kaiser, 1995). When the ball is hit directly at the fielder, the zero-acceleration hypothesis predicts that he will run so as to keep the apparent speed of the ball constant (McLeod & Dienes, 1993).

Animals also face the need to make quick decisions, and to do so with much less computational power than humans have at their disposal. Rüdiger Wehner (Wehner, Michel, & Antonsen, 1996; see also Wehner, 1997) has shown that *Cataglyphis* ants of the Sahara Desert accomplish difficult navigational tasks not by developing a detailed and information-rich mental map of their surroundings but rather by using a set of simple rules, including a system for keeping track of the angle of the sun in the sky. This computational machinery allows the ant to wander in search of food as much as 200 meters from its home and then to return home on a very straight and direct path.

Ball-catching fielders and navigating ants face a strikingly similar problem: how to navigate across a plane while lacking either the time or the computational power to calculate the optimal route. But even in situations where time and computational power are abundant, the simple heuristics predicted by bounded rationality may be used in place of complex calculations of optimality. For example, German psychologist Gerd Gigerenzer and his colleagues have demonstrated the power of the very simple heuristic of familiarity or recognizability in the selection of stocks. During a recent bull market, they were able to beat the market index by about 13% simply by investing in a set of companies that were most familiar to German pedestrians (Gigerenzer, Todd, & the ABC Research Group, 1999). Human behavioral ecologists might make use of bounded rationality to shed light on such decisions as how foragers select foods to eat. A study of foraging that combines human behavioral ecology, cognitive anthropology, evolutionary psychology—and perhaps a dash of the study of the evolution of the sense of taste (e.g., Hladek & Simmen, 1996)—would seem to be the logical next step.

Conclusion

A new field may develop best by setting aside potential problems and doggedly pursuing its particular research agenda in order to find out how far it can go in explaining a particular set of phenomena. Both evolutionary psychology and human behavioral ecology have done that, and each has amply demonstrated the fundamental merit of its approach. Evolutionary psychology has demonstrated that a great deal of light can be shed on the brain and mind through the application of the concept of adaptation. More specifically, evolutionary psychologists have made a strong case that the human mind is particularly adept at certain tasks, such as monitoring compliance with social rules, learning language, and selecting mates, that are likely to have been especially important in human evolution. Human behavioral ecology has shown that the tremendous variations in human behavior across societies largely reflect adaptive responses to variable environments, conceived of as including not only physical elements but also a people's social, political, and economic situation and their history. More specifically, human behavioral ecology has shown that human behavior largely conforms to the predictions of models derived from evolutionary theory, particularly in areas crucial to an individual's inclusive fitness, such as food choice and acquisition, social behavior, mate choice and acquisition, parental behavior, and social behavior.

Having accomplished these things, both fields should now be ready to enter a more experimental phase. For human behavioral ecology, this would include dealing with topics usually set aside, such as culture and psychological mechanisms. For evolutionary psychology, it might include an increased interest in cross-cultural studies. Happily, these are complementary goals, and the future relationship between human behavioral ecology and evolutionary psychology is sure to be even richer and more mutually beneficial than in the past.

I would like to thank Jerome Barkow, William Irons, Beth Leech, John Patton, Beverly Strassmann, and Larry Sugiyama for their helpful comments on earlier drafts of this chapter and Thomas Seeley for a key reference. I retain responsibility for any errors or shortcomings.

References

Alexander, Richard D. (1974). The evolution of social behavior. *Annual Review of Ecology and Systematics, 5,* 325–383.

Alexander, Richard D. (1979). *Darwinism and Human Affairs.* Seattle: University of Washington Press.

Bailey, F. G. (1969). *Stratagems and Spoils: A Social Anthropology of Politics.* Oxford: Basil Blackwell.

Barkow, Jerome H. (1977). Conformity to ethos and reproductive success in two Hausa communities: An empirical evaluation. *Ethos, 5,* 409–425.

Barkow, Jerome H. (1989). *Darwin, Sex, and Status.* Toronto: University of Toronto Press.

Barth, Fredrik. (1965). *Political Leadership among Swat Pathans.* London: Athlone.

Bem, Sandra L. (1993). *The Lenses of Gender: Transforming the Debate on Sexual Equality.* New Haven, CT: Yale University Press.

Betzig, Laura. (1986). *Despotism and Differential Reproduction: A Darwinian View of History.* Hawthorne, NY: Aldine de Gruyter.

Blurton Jones, Nicholas, Kristen Hawkes, & Patricia Draper. (1994). Differences between Hadza and !Kung children's work: Affluence or practical reason? In Ernest S. Burch Jr. & Linda J. Ellanna (Eds.), *Key Issues in Hunter-Gatherer Research* (pp. 189–215). Oxford: Berg.

Borgerhoff Mulder, Monique. (1987). On cultural and reproductive success. *American Anthropologist, 89,* 617–634.

Borgerhoff Mulder, Monique. (1988). Kipsigis bridewealth payments. In L. Betzig, M. Borgerhoff Mulder, & Paul Turke (Eds.), *Human Reproductive Behaviour: A Darwinian Perspective.* Cambridge: Cambridge University Press.

Borgerhoff Mulder, Monique. (1990). Kipsigis women's preferences for wealthy men: Evidence for female choice in mammals? *Behavioral Ecology and Sociobiology, 27,* 255–264.

Borgerhoff Mulder, Monique. (1991). Human behavioral ecology. In J. R. Krebs & N. B. Davies (Eds.), *Behavioral Ecology: An Evolutionary Approach,* 3rd ed. (pp. 69–98). Oxford: Blackwell Scientific.

Borgerhoff Mulder, Monique. (1992). Women's strategies in polygynous marriage: Kipsigis, Datoga, and other East African cases. *Human Nature, 3*(1), 45–70.

Borgerhoff Mulder, Monique, & T. Caro. (1985). The use of quantitative observational techniques in anthropology. *Current Anthropology, 25,* 323–335.

Buckley, Thomas, & Alma Gottlieb (Eds.). (1988). *Blood Magic: The Anthropology of Menstruation.* Berkeley: University of California Press.

Bugos, Paul E., Jr., & Lorraine M. McCarthy. (1984). Ayoreo infanticide: A case study. In Glenn Hausfater & Sarah Blaffer Hrdy (Eds.), *Infanticide: Comparative and Evolutionary Perspectives* (pp. 503–520). Hawthorne, NY: Aldine.

Buss, David M., & Neil M. Malamuth (Eds.). (1996). *Sex, Power, and Conflict: Evolutionary and Feminist Perspectives.* New York: Oxford University Press.

Carey, M., & V. Nolan Jr. (1975). Polygyny in indigo buntings: A hypothesis tested. *Science, 190,* 1296–1297.

Carey, M., & V. Nolan Jr. (1979). Population dynamics of indigo buntings and the evolution of avian polygyny. *Evolution, 33,* 1180–1192.

Chagnon, Napoleon A. (1979). Mate competition, favoring close kin, and village fissioning among the Yanomamö Indians. In Napoleon A. Chagnon & William Irons (Eds.), *Evolutionary Biology and Human Social Behavior: An Anthropological Perspective* (pp. 86–132). North Scituate, MA: Duxbury.

Chagnon, Napoleon A. (1988). Life histories, blood revenge, and warfare in a tribal population. *Science, 238,* 985–992.

Chagnon, Napoleon A., & Paul E. Bugos Jr. (1979). Kin selection and conflict: An analysis of a Yanomamö ax fight. In N. A. Chagnon & W. Irons (Eds.), *Evolutionary Biology and Human Social Behavior: An Anthropological Perspective.* North Scituate, MA: Duxbury.

Chagnon, Napoleon A., Mark V. Flinn, & Thomas F. Melancon. (1979). Sex-ratio variation among the Yanomamo Indians. In N. A. Chagnon & W. Irons (Eds.), *Evolutionary Biology and Human Social Behavior: An Anthropological Perspective* (pp. 290–320). North Scituate, MA: Duxbury.

Cronk, Lee. (1988). Spontaneous order analysis and anthropology. *Cultural Dynamics, 1*(3), 282–308.

Cronk, Lee. (1989). Low socioeconomic status and female-biased parental investment: The Mukogodo example. *American Anthropologist, 91*(2), 414–429.

Cronk, Lee. (1991a). Human behavioral ecology. *Annual Review of Anthropology, 20,* 25–53.

Cronk, Lee. (1991b). Preferential parental investment in daughters over sons. *Human Nature, 2*(4), 387–417.

Cronk, Lee. (1991c). Wealth, status, and reproductive success among the Mukogodo of Kenya. *American Anthropologist, 93,* 345–360.

Cronk, Lee. (1995). Is there a role for culture in human behavioral ecology? *Evolution and Human Behavior, 16*(3), 181–205.

Cronk, Lee. (1999). *That Complex Whole: Culture and the Evolution of Human Behavior.* Boulder, CO: Westview.

Cronk, Lee. (2000). Female-biased parental investment and growth performance among Mukogodo children. In L. Cronk, N. Chagnon, & W. Irons (Eds.), *Adaptation and Human Behavior: An Anthropological Perspective* (pp. 197–215). Hawthorne, NY: Aldine de Gruyter.

Daly, Martin, & Margo Wilson. (1988). *Homicide.* New York: Aldine de Gruyter.

Dawkins, Richard. (1976). *The Selfish Gene.* Oxford: Oxford University Press.

Dickemann, Mildred. (1979a). Female infanticide, reproductive strategies, and social stratification: A preliminary model. In Napoleon A. Chagnon & William Irons (Eds.), *Evolutionary Biology and Human Social Behavior: An Anthropological Perspective* (pp. 321–367). North Scituate, MA: Duxbury.

Dickemann, Mildred. (1979b). The ecology of mating systems in hypergynous dowry societies. *Social Science Information, 18,* 163–195.

Dickemann, Mildred. (1981). Paternal confidence and dowry competition: A biocultural analysis of purdah. In R. D. Alexander & D. Tinkle

(Eds.), *Natural Selection and Social Behavior: Recent Research and New Theory* (pp. 417–438). New York: Chiron.

Emlen, S. T., & L. W. Oring. (1977). Ecology, sexual selection and the evolution of mating systems. *Science, 197,* 215–223.

Firth, Raymond. (1936). *We, the Tikopia.* London: Allen and Unwin.

Fisher, Helen. (1999). *First Sex: The Natural Talents of Women and How They Are Changing the World.* New York: Random House.

Gelles, Richard J., & Jane B. Lancaster. (1987). *Child Abuse and Neglect: Biosocial Dimensions.* Hawthorne, NY: Aldine de Gruyter.

Gigerenzer, Gerd, Peter M. Todd, & the ABC Research Group. (1999). *Simple Heuristics That Make Us Smart.* New York: Oxford University Press.

Gowaty, Patricia Adair. (1992). Evolutionary biology and feminism. *Human Nature, 3*(3), 217–249.

Grafen, Alan. (1987). Measuring sexual selection: Why bother? In J. W. Bradbury & M. B. Andersson (Eds.), *Sexual Selection: Testing the Alternatives* (pp. 221–233). New York: Wiley.

Hames, Raymond B. (1979). Relatedness and interaction among the Ye'wana: A preliminary analysis. In Napoleon A. Chagnon and William Irons (Eds.), *Evolutionary Biology and Human Social Behavior: An Anthropological Perspective* (pp. 238–249). North Scituate, MA: Duxbury.

Hamilton, W. D. (1964). The evolution of social behavior. *Journal of Theoretical Biology, 7,* 1–52.

Hartung, John. (1976). On natural selection and the inheritance of wealth. *Current Anthropology, 17,* 607–622.

Hausfater, Glenn, & Sarah Blaffer Hrdy (Eds.). (1984). *Infanticide: Comparative and Evolutionary Perspectives.* Hawthorne, NY: Aldine.

Hawkes, Kristen, Kim Hill, & James O'Connell. (1982). Why hunters gather: Optimal foraging and the Aché of eastern Paraguay. *American Ethnologist, 9,* 379–398.

Herskovits, Melville. (1940). *The Economic Life of Primitive Peoples.* New York: Knopf.

Hladek, Claude Marcel, & Bruno Simmen. (1996). Taste perception and feeding behavior in nonhuman primates and human populations. *Evolutionary Anthropology, 5*(2), 58–71.

Homans, George. (1967). *The Nature of Social Science.* New York: Harcourt, Brace.

Hrdy, Sarah Blaffer. (1981). *The Woman That Never Evolved.* Cambridge, MA: Harvard University Press.

Hrdy, Sarah Blaffer. (1997). Raising Darwin's consciousness: Female sexuality and the prehominid origins of patriarchy. *Human Nature, 8*(1), 1–49.

Hrdy, Sarah Blaffer. (1999). *Mother Nature: A History of Mothers, Infants, and Natural Selection.* New York: Pantheon.

Irons, William. (1976). Emic and reproductive success. Paper presented at the 75th annual meeting of the American Anthropological Association, Washington, DC.

Irons, William. (1979). Cultural and biological success. In N. A. Chagnon & W. Irons (Eds.), *Evolutionary Biology and Human Social Behavior:*

An Anthropological Perspective (pp. 257–272). North Scituate, MA: Duxbury.

Kaplan, Hillard S., & Kim Hill. (1985). Hunting ability and reproductive success among Ache foragers: Preliminary results. *Current Anthropology 26*, 131–133.

Kitcher, Philip. (1985). *Vaulting Ambition: Sociobiology and the Quest for Human Nature.* Cambridge, MA: MIT Press.

Lewontin, Richard, Steven Rose, & Leon Kamin. (1984). *Not in Our Genes: Biology, Ideology and Human Nature.* New York: Pantheon.

Malinowski, Bronislaw. (1939). The group and the individual in functional analysis. *American Journal of Sociology, 44*, 938–964.

McBeath, M. K., D. M. Shaffer, & M. K. Kaiser. (1995). How baseball outfielders determine where to run to catch fly balls. *Science, 268*, 569–573.

McLeod, P., & Z. Dienes. (1993). Running to catch the ball. *Nature, 362*, 23.

Moore, John H. (1990). The reproductive success of Cheyenne war chiefs: A contrary case to Chagnon's Yanomamö. *Current Anthropology, 31*(3), 322–330.

Orians, Gordon. (1969). On the evolution of mating systems in birds and mammals. *American Naturalist, 103*, 589–603.

Orlove, Benjamin S. (1980). Ecological anthropology. *Annual Review of Anthropology, 9*, 235–273.

Parkes, Peter. (1990). *Kalasha: Rites of Spring.* Film and videotape. Manchester, UK: Granada.

Price, Sally. (1993). *Co-Wives and Calabashes* (2nd ed.). Ann Arbor: University of Michigan Press.

Sahlins, Marshall. (1976). *The Use and Abuse of Biology.* Ann Arbor: University of Michigan Press.

Schneider, Harold. (1974). *Economic Man.* New York: Free Press.

Simon, Herbert. (1992). *Economics, Bounded Rationality, and the Cognitive Revolution.* Hants, UK: Edward Elgar.

Smith, Eric Alden. (1991a). Human behavioral ecology: I. *Evolutionary Anthropology, 1*(1), 20–25.

Smith, Eric Alden. (1991b). Human behavioral ecology: II. *Evolutionary Anthropology, 1*(2), 50–55.

Smith, Eric Alden, & Bruce Winterhalder (Eds.). (1981). *Hunter-Gatherer Foraging Strategies.* Chicago: University of Chicago Press.

Smuts, Barbara. (1992). Male aggression against women: An evolutionary perspective. *Human Nature, 3*(1), 1–44.

Smuts, Barbara. (1995). The evolutionary origins of patriarchy. *Human Nature, 6*(1), 1–32.

Spencer, Robert F., & J. D. Jennings. (1977). *The Native Americans* (2nd ed.). New York: Harper and Row.

Strassmann, B. I. (1992). The function of menstrual taboos among the Dogon: Defense against cuckoldry? *Human Nature, 3*, 89–131.

Strassmann, B. I. (1996). Menstrual hut visits by Dogon women: A hormonal test distinguishes deceit from honest signaling. *Behavioral Ecology, 7*, 304–315.

Strassmann, B. I. (1997). Polygyny as a risk factor for child mortality among the Dogon. *Current Anthropology, 38,* 688–695.

Strassmann, B. I. (2000). Polygyny, family structure, and child mortality: A prospective study among the Dogon of Mali. In L. Cronk, N. Chagnon, & W. Irons (Eds.), *Adaptation and Human Behavior: An Anthropological Perspective.* New York: Aldine de Gruyter.

Sulloway, Frank J. (1996). *Born to Rebel: Birth Order, Family Dynamics, and Creative Lives.* New York: Pantheon.

Trivers, Robert. (1971). The evolution of reciprocal altruism. *Quarterly Review of Biology, 46,* 35–57.

Trivers, Robert. (1972). Parental investment and sexual selection. In B. Campbell (Ed.), *Sexual Selection and the Descent of Man* (pp. 136–179). Hawthorne, NY: Aldine de Gruyter.

Trivers, Robert. (1974). Parent-offspring conflict. *American Zoologist, 14,* 249–264.

Trivers, Robert, & Hope Hare. (1976). Haplodiploidy and the evolution of social insects. *Science, 191,* 249–263.

Trivers, Robert, & Dan E. Willard. (1973). Natural selection of parental ability to vary the sex ratio of offspring. *Science, 179,* 90–92.

Vayda, Andrew P. (1995). Failures of explanation in Darwinian ecological anthropology, parts I and II. *Philosophy of the Social Sciences, 25,* 219–249 and 360–375.

Wehner, Rüdiger. (1997). Sensory systems and behaviour. In John R. Krebs & Nicholas B. Davies (Eds.), *Behavioural Ecology: An Evolutionary Approach,* 4th ed. (pp. 19–41). Oxford: Blackwell Science.

Wehner, Rüdiger., B. Michel, & P. Antonsen. (1996). Visual navigation in insects: Coupling of egocentric and geocentric information. *Journal of Experimental Biology, 199,* 129–140.

Williams, George C. (1966). *Adaptation and Natural Selection.* Princeton, NJ: Princeton University Press.

Wilson, Edward O. (1975). *Sociobiology: The New Synthesis.* Cambridge, MA: Harvard University Press.

Wilson, Edward O. (1978). *On Human Nature.* Cambridge, MA: Harvard University Press.

Winterhalder, Bruce, & Eric Alden Smith. (1992). Evolutionary ecology and the social sciences. In Eric Alden Smith & Bruce Winterhalder (Eds.), *Evolutionary Ecology and Human Behavior* (pp. 3–23). Hawthorne, NY: Aldine de Gruyter.

7 The Impact of Primatology on the Study of Human Society

Lars Rodseth and
Shannon A. Novak

Primatology is on the front lines of an epic struggle to unite the study of human beings with the study of other living things (Wilson, 1998; Gould, 2003). Social scientists have held a variety of positions in this struggle, but many of them maintain the view that "a fundamental difference of kind—not of degree—separates man from all other animals" (L. A. White, 1949, p. 30). In particular, the capacity to organize social life on the basis of symbolic communication is often seen as a cultural Rubicon that humans alone have crossed. As a result, the findings of primate research are argued to be irrelevant to the study of human culture and society.

Here we contend that the cultural Rubicon, though real enough, should not by itself impede the comparative analysis of human and nonhuman behavior. The vast cognitive and cultural differences between humans and other primates are temporarily omitted from our analysis, not because we see these differences as unimportant, but because they are ordinarily so prominent that they tend to obstruct our view of distinctive *behavioral* patterns that deserve consideration in their own right. The study of behavioral complexity, we argue, deserves a place in social analysis *alongside* the study of cultural messages and rules (Hinde, 1987; Paul, 1987; Barkow, 1989; Cronk, 1999). Such an approach, while recognizing the critical role of language and other forms of symbolic communication in any complete account of a human group, also allows for the possibility of behavioral patterning that is not represented in the group's own symbolic understandings. And because patterning of this kind is not unique to *Homo sapiens*, the same kinds of data can be collected and the same theoretical problems can be addressed in the study of other species. A good many animals, as Alfred Kroeber (1952, p. 118) noted, live in "cultureless societies." The addition of culture obviously complicates the analysis of social relationships, but it does not eliminate the common "design space" within which human and other animal societies can be compared (cf. Dennett, 1995, pp. 143–144).

Along with the complexities of language and cultural symbolism comes the unprecedented diversity of human social arrangements. In fact, based on ethnographic comparison alone, we may be left with the impression that human social variation is virtually unlimited and that nothing (or nothing very interesting) is characteristic of human societies as a set. With the benefit of comparison across *species*, however, it can be shown that human societies form not just a scatter but a distinctive *cluster* within a wider range of social possibilities (Rodseth et al., 1991; Rodseth & Wrangham, 2004).

To sharpen the focus in the present context, human societies are compared in particular with those of orangutans, gorillas, common chimpanzees, and bonobos, the four living apes (or *hominoids*) with whom we share a common ancestor less than 15 million years ago. After surveying the recent history of ideas about human society, we summarize how human patterns of transfer between groups, affiliations between females, and competition between foraging parties seem to diverge from the comparable patterns observed in our closest evolutionary relatives. In the concluding section, we return to the role of culture in human behavior and argue the case for an integrated science of human and other primate societies.

Taking Aim at a Political Animal

Human societies have been subject to scientific investigation for at least 150 years (Stocking, 1987). Monkey and ape societies, by contrast, have been studied for less than half that time (Haraway, 1989). In fact, "virtually nothing systematic was known about the natural behavior of a single monkey or ape until Clarence Ray Carpenter began his study of the howler monkeys of Panama in 1931" (DeVore, 1965, p. vii). The promising start by Carpenter (1934, 1935, 1940) was interrupted by the Second World War. Twenty years went by before a wave of classic field studies (DeVore, 1962; Goodall, 1963; Jay, 1963) signaled the beginning of the "Prolific Period" of primate research (Ribnick, 1982). Behavioral primatology, in this light, is a late-twentieth-century development, rather like cognitive science or molecular genetics. Yet unlike these other fields, primatology is a decidedly "low-tech" enterprise, relying mainly on naturalistic observation rather than experimental manipulation or laboratory engineering. In this sense it has much in common with ethnographic fieldwork, the study of a particular human group by an intimate observer who seeks to describe and understand the patterning of everyday life.

Until an "ethnographic record" of nonhuman primates had been compiled, it was difficult to draw systematic comparisons between monkey, ape, and human social behavior. This left unanswered many basic anthropological questions. If the human being is a political animal, as Aristotle argued, is this true of any other primate? How do the differences between men and women compare to sex differences in baboons or chimpanzees? Is the family a uniquely human grouping, or does it exist in other species as well? Such questions are among the most profound that can be asked, yet only in recent decades has there been any reasonable hope of answering them.

In fact, for most of the twentieth century, anthropologists might write with some authority about human *universals* (Brown, 1991), but could only speculate about human *uniqueness* in comparison with other primates. By the end of the century, the situation had been transformed. Four decades of intensive field research had demonstrated that chimpanzees in particular share with humans a number of key social patterns (Goodall, 1986; Wrangham & Peterson, 1996; Pusey, 2001). In other ways, however, humans had come to appear all the more unusual, even alongside their closest living relatives. Now it is possible to go beyond the ancient oppositions between "man" and "beast" and to draw much more rigorous and refined comparisons between human and nonhuman societies.

The Band-and-Bond Model

In taking on this task, we might first consider how human sociality has traditionally been understood among social scientists and philosophers. What is the fundamental form of the human group? Most observers have tended to assume what we call a "band-and-bond" model of human society. The band or other local group, according to this model, is an aggregation of households, each of which is based on a conjugal bond.

Foreshadowed in the writings of Aristotle (1981, pp. 57–58), the band-and-bond model was first developed in anthropology by A. R. Radcliffe-Brown (1930, 1931, p. 435) and Ralph Linton (1936, p. 209). In surveying the social organization of hunter-gatherers around the world, Julian Steward (1936, 1955) helped to establish an image of the foraging band as a patrilineal unit composed of several conjugal families. Variations on this theme appeared in writings of Murdock (1949), White (1949), Lévi-Strauss (1956), Sahlins (1959), and Service (1962), among many others.

The general trend in these analyses was to emphasize that some elements of human society, such as the family, might be continuous with those of nonhuman primate societies, but other elements, such as interfamily or intergroup alliance, were uniquely human. Thus Leslie A. White (1949, p. 316), for example, held that "unless some way had been found to establish strong and enduring social ties between families, social evolution could have gone no farther on the human level than among the anthropoids." Similarly, Lévi-Strauss (1956, pp. 277–278) argued that "what makes man really different from the animal is that in mankind, a family could not exist if there were no society: i.e., a plurality of families ready to acknowledge that there are other links than consanguineous ones, and that the natural process of filiation can only be carried on through the social process of affinity." Natural or "blood" relations, in other words, must be supplemented by marital alliances and other bonds between families for a truly human society to emerge. Despite the evident variety in their schemes, most anthropologists seemed to concur with Aristotle that the household *(oikos)* is "established according to nature for the satisfaction of daily needs," while the village or other community *(kome)* is "the first association of a number of houses for the satisfaction of something *more* than daily needs" (1981, pp. 57–58).

Does Hunting Make Us Human?

All of this theorizing about human social organization was based on precious little knowledge of what makes people different from other primates. In the 1950s, however, biological anthropologists began to reconceptualize their enterprise, shifting away from static typologies of anatomical patterns and toward the analysis of evolutionary processes within living populations. The movement's leader was Sherwood Washburn, who argued that adaptive context and way of life were fundamental to an understanding of biological traits. In the case of humans, hunting was seen as the hallmark of the animal's adaptation, as reflected in morphological characteristics such as bipedalism and expanded cranial capacity (Washburn & Avis, 1958). The growing influence of Washburn's views led in 1966 to a landmark conference titled "Man the Hunter" (on the historical significance of this meeting, see Kuper, 1994, pp. 68–69; Stanford, 1999, pp. 37–39). Here biological and sociocultural anthropologists were brought together to discuss and integrate their findings about hunter-gatherer populations, both in the ethnographic record and in the course of human evolution. When the conference proceedings were published two years later (Lee & DeVore, 1968), both the foraging band and the conjugal bond were cast in a rather different light.

First, the band was reconceptualized as an extremely flexible community, with no consistent preference for patrilocal residence or for patrilineal kinship (Murdock, 1968, pp. 19–20). This image replaced Steward's "neat formulation" with what seems at first a "confusing and disorderly picture" (Lee & DeVore, 1968, p. 9): "Brothers may be united or divided, marriage may take place within or outside the local group, and local groups may vary in numbers from one week to the next." The new concept of the band was based on mounting ethnographic evidence from studies of Kalahari Bushmen (Lee, 1968), Mbuti Pygmies (Turnbull, 1968), and Hadza (Woodburn, 1968), among other foraging peoples. Over time, however, one case in particular—the !Kung San of the Kalahari (e.g., Marshall, 1976; Lee, 1979)—came increasingly to exemplify hunter-gatherers in general. The !Kung followed an extremely variable residence pattern, with a married couple living near the parents of either the husband or the wife depending on circumstances or personal choice. The assumption that any one ethnographic example could be seen as representative of most hunter-gatherers would eventually fall into serious doubt (Ember, 1978; Kent, 1996, pp. 3–4), but in the meantime the !Kung case by itself seemed to discredit Steward's model of the patrilocal, patrilineal band.

If the band was now seen as a much more fluid and disordered grouping, there remained within the band the universal and predictable unit of the nuclear family. The second revision emerging from the 1966 conference was a specific account of the evolution of the family—the so-called hunting hypothesis. The hunting way of life, according to this hypothesis, had transformed primate *mating* into human *marriage*. In a sense, the emphasis on hunting was "deeply ironic," as Stanford (1999, p. 37) notes, because most of the conference participants came away convinced that "the importance of meat in the diets of foraging people had been exaggerated." At the same time, the single most influential idea to emerge from "Man the Hunter" was presented in this passage by Washburn and Lancaster (1968, p. 301):

> When males hunt and females gather, the results are shared and given to the young, and the habitual sharing between a male, a female, and their offspring becomes the basis for the human family. According to this view, the human family is the result of the reciprocity of hunting, the addition of a male to the mother-plus-young social group of the monkeys and apes.

Drawing on recent field research, Washburn and Lancaster suggested that primate society always contains a mother-young grouping, but *not* a family in the sense of a sexually bonded pair (1968, p. 301). This contrasts with the earlier arguments of Linton (1936, p. 209) and Murdock (1949, p. 79), for example, who assumed a continuity between the human nuclear family and some "germinal" social unit among nonhuman primates. In a footnote, Washburn and Lancaster (1968, p. 302 n. 5) conceded that the monogamous pair found in gibbons resembles the human nuclear family, but went on to argue that "the gibbon group is based on a different biology from that of the human family and has none of its reciprocal economic functions."

What was uniquely human about the family, then, was not merely a stable sexual bond but an economic alliance based on the male provisioning of females and young through hunting.

Debuting on the heels of bestsellers such as *The Territorial Imperative* (Ardrey, 1966) and *The Naked Ape* (Morris, 1967), the hunting hypothesis was easily blended with the popular ethology and sociobiology of the day (Tiger & Fox, 1971; Ardrey, 1976). At the same time, the emphasis on male provisioning as the driving force of human social evolution provoked a backlash among feminist anthropologists, who answered the hunting hypothesis with their own "gathering hypothesis" (Linton, 1971; Tanner & Zihlman, 1976; Zihlman, 1978). In light of the evidence that some "hunters" relied more on plant resources than on game animals (Lee, 1968), these feminists argued that the productive activities of women had been systematically neglected or ignored in models of human evolution. Gathering rather than hunting was argued to be the key human adaptation leading to technological innovation and increasing brain size. In some versions of the gathering hypothesis, women were seen as largely self-sufficient producers, and the sexual division of labor that Washburn and Lancaster had cast as the hallmark of the family was all but eliminated from the story of human origins (Fedigan, 1986, p. 34).

Yet the idea that marriage is a fundamentally economic institution was hardly touched by this critique, and an emphasis on "the cooperation of man and wife" (Radcliffe-Brown, 1931, p. 435) soon resurged in several new accounts of human evolution. One response, then, to the gathering hypothesis was "to superimpose the new model on the older hunting scheme, and to emphasize a mixed economy in which early hominid men and women were mutually interdependent" (Fedigan, 1986, p. 35). In the influential scenario presented by Isaac (1978, 1980), for example, males and females were argued to range widely in pursuit of different kinds of food, then to rendezvous at a home base where their products could be shared (see also Isaac & Crader, 1981). In another prominent account (Lovejoy, 1981), vegetation rather than meat is assumed to have been the crucial element in the early hominid diet, yet the family still depended on male provisioning because childrearing females were relatively sedentary, while males could range much farther in search of food.

From the Hunting Hypothesis to the Primate Paradigm

Variations on the hunting hypothesis dominated anthropological discussion about human social organization for about twenty years, from the mid-1960s to the mid-1980s. Over the same period, the "ethnographic record" of monkey and ape societies accumulated rapidly. As the new findings were

incorporated into the framework of evolutionary theory, behavioral primatology was reaching a point of synthesis (Wrangham, 1979, 1980; Hrdy,
1981; Hinde, 1983; Hausfater & Hrdy, 1984). Its coming of age is conveniently marked by the publication of Jane Goodall's *Chimpanzees of Gombe*
(1986), the product of a quarter century of research at the same field site
and an instant classic of hominoid ethnography. During the following
decade, in a steady stream of publications, the primate data were synthesized and brought to bear on the central problems of human social evolution (Ghiglieri, 1987, 1989; Maryanski, 1987, 1992, 1996; Wrangham,
1987a, 1987b; Foley, 1989, 1992; Foley & Lee, 1989, 1996; Knauft, 1991;
Manson & Wrangham, 1991; Rodseth et al., 1991; Boehm, 1992, 1993,
1999; Smuts, 1992, 1995; Di Fore & Rendall, 1994; Wrangham & Peterson,
1996).

While the new arguments were in many ways extremely innovative,
they tended to reaffirm band-and-bond as the basic pattern of human social
organization. In fact, the image of the band tended to draw back from the
fluid and disorderly picture presented by Lee and DeVore (1968, p. 9) and
to be revised again in the direction of Steward's patrilocal model. This
change came as a result of two key developments. First, there was a reaction
to the overemphasis on the !Kung as a representation of foragers in general.
When a more diverse sample of hunter-gatherers was considered, the prevailing residence pattern was argued to be patrilocality after all (Ember,
1978). In some well-known cases, such as the Mbuti and other Pygmies, earlier characterizations of the kinship system as bilateral and of residence as
bilocal were shown to be inaccurate. Thus, while these African foragers
do not have "a strong patrilineal ideology . . . they do tend to practice
patrilocal residence where related men hunt together" (Hewlett, 1996,
pp. 232–233). Second and more important, the new primatological field
data suggested that female dispersal was characteristic of the African apes,
those nonhuman primates most closely related to the hominid line. This
contrasted sharply with the pattern of male dispersal and female bonding
prevailing among Old World monkeys (Wrangham, 1980; van Schaik,
1989). Chimpanzees societies in particular were now known to be social
networks or communities formed around a core of related males who remained in their natal territories throughout their lives. The obvious par-
allel between this pattern and the widespread pattern of patrilocal
residence among humans was drawn initially by Wrangham (1987a)
and Gighlieri (1987) and was quickly established as a basic tenet of
subsequent analyses (e.g., Foley & Lee, 1989, 1996; Smuts, 1992, 1995;
Maryanski, 1996). In a recent statement of this principle, Foley (1999,
p. 380) writes that "it is large, male kin-bonded groups with dispersing females that provide the thread of historical continuity to hominid socioecological evolution."

With this, the patrilocal band was reestablished in anthropological theory as the most prominent model of the foraging group. Behind this image, however, the rather "confusing and disorderly picture" first adumbrated by Lee and DeVore (1968, p. 9) has hardly disappeared. Some anthropologists remain convinced that "social organization and residence tend to be shifting, open, and flexible among nonintensive foragers" (Knauft, 1991, p. 406). Many others are uneasy about reducing the social patterns of all hunting and gathering populations to any one model. Foraging societies in the ethnographic record are simply not uniform enough to project the patrilocal model back into the Pleistocene (Hrdy, 1999, p. 102):

> It is . . . certain that unlike other Great Apes, women must have lived in families and relied on other group members to help provision children who took unusually long to become independent. But beyond these points, relatively little about these early social environments is certain. We cannot know . . . what kind of families women lived in (whose "in-laws," for example, they lived nearest to). . . . Men's ability to control where women in their group went and what they did would have varied a great deal, depending on who else was there to back the women up. Who else was there would depend on local subsistence patterns and history, for apart from a universal tendency for primate females to avoid mating with close kin, women exhibit no clear and consistent predispositions either to leave or to remain near kin.

Just how well the patrilocal model fits the ethnographic evidence is a question to which we will return.

As for the origin of the family, the scenario proposed by Washburn and Lancaster (1968) is by no means out of contention in recent debates (e.g., Stanford, 1999; Kaplan et al., 2000, p. 173), though it is on the defensive against a range of new arguments (e.g., Wrangham et al., 1999; Hawkes et al., 2000). The mechanism of male provisioning still plays a pivotal role in many recent accounts, even when the authors do not explicitly endorse the hunting hypothesis (e.g., Foley & Lee, 1996, p. 63; Foley, 1999, p. 381, emphasis added):

> If male kin bonding is the continuity element in social evolution, male-female relationships and the nature of parental care are the novelties. *Higher quality resources which can be shared* and weaning foods are the key resource structures that are likely to have changed mating and parenting strategies within the group, and led to the cognitive shifts underlying close relationships between the sexes, in association with delayed life history strategies and high levels of parental care.

The clear implication is that hominid males came to specialize in producing meat or some other shareable food that they could exchange with particular adult females, giving rise to "close relationships between the sexes." A similar scenario is envisioned by Stanford (1999, pp. 212–216), though he emphasizes the use of meat by males as a manipulative social tool and use of sex by females as an incentive for men to hunt.

All advocates of the hunting hypothesis agree on at least one point, that the human pair bond is founded not on sexuality per se but on a division of labor between the sexes, including some degree of male provisioning of females. Yet the only kind of provisioning considered in this context is the production of game animals in exchange for mating opportunities or gathered foods. What *other* kinds of goods or services might be provided by males and might be the basis of the family received little attention until the early 1980s, when the human pair bond was reconsidered in the wider context of animal mating systems. Monogamy in gibbons and other primates had been passed over by Washburn and Lancaster (1968) as irrelevant to the human case precisely because the gibbon group was thought to be lacking in any of the family's "reciprocal economic functions." Twenty years later, primatologists began to suggest a range of such functions to explain the evolution of stable relationships between the sexes (e.g., Wrangham, 1979; Rutberg, 1983; van Schaik & van Hooff, 1983). These arguments drew attention to "various possible services provided by the male which substantially raise the female's (and hence the male's own) reproductive output" (van Schaik & Dunbar, 1990, p. 33). In this light, a gibbon male and female might rely on each other not for goods, as a husband and wife are assumed to do, but for certain critical *services*.

One recurring element in these explanations is male protection of females from various outside threats or competitors. Thus males are argued to protect mothers from infanticide, to reduce predation risk, and to help defend an exclusive territory or other resource (van Schaik & Dunbar, 1990, pp. 40–48; van Schaik, 1996). The male, in effect, acts on behalf of his female partner as a "hired gun" (Wrangham, 1979; Wrangham & Peterson, 1996, p. 151) or "bodyguard" (Mesnick, 1997). Gorillas provide an especially vivid example of this pattern in that they form polygynous one-male groups, apparently on the basis of the female's attraction to a particular male as a protector from outside male coercion (Watts, 1989).

Application of this reasoning to human social evolution soon resulted in several important new scenarios for the origin of the human pair bond (e.g., van Schaik & Dunbar, 1990, pp. 55–56; Smuts, 1992, 1995; Mesnick, 1997, pp. 236–243; Wrangham et al., 1999; Blurton Jones et al., 2000). These scenarios vary in the precise threat faced by females and against which males are seen as defending. Infanticide, sexual harassment, theft of valued resources, and general coercion by outside males have all been singled out as the crucial risk to females. Taken together, however, these "bodyguard" explanations form a distinct cluster in opposition to the hunting hypothesis and other forms of what have been called "male-provisioning" hypotheses (Wrangham et al., 1999).

In short, if the chimpanzee community provided a model for new thinking about the human band, the other African ape—the gorilla—helped stimulate new thinking about the evolution of the human pair bond. Even as male bonding and female dispersal were seen as patterns shared by humans and chimpanzees, relatively stable sexual bonds based on male protection were seen as patterns shared by humans and gorillas. The ironic result, then, was to confirm the combination of band and pair bond as the hallmark of human social organization, even if each of these social units taken by itself was now seen as analogous to a unit in one of the African apes.

The Human Place in Great Ape Space

The band-and-bond model has proven to be an extremely resilient way of describing human social organization. The model's limitations, however, become apparent when we attempt to make systematic comparisons between humans and nonhuman animals. Specifically, the band and the sexual pair bond are not strictly comparable because the first is a kind of social grouping, while the second is a kind of social relationship. Because cross-specific comparison is facilitated by analysis on a relationship-by-relationship basis (Hinde, 1983, 1987), the concept of the band must be analyzed into its component parts. A band is a dense network of social relationships. Even if we consider only adult relationships, these can be formed between males, between females, or between a male and a female, yet the concept of the band tells us nothing specific about the patterning of these relationships. As humans, our tendency is to take for granted that local groups consist of multiple males and multiple females, all of whom consistently form relationships on both a same-sex and opposite-sex basis. The peculiar nature of this kind of social organization becomes apparent only when the constituent relationships of the human band are compared with their counterparts in nonhuman primate societies.

Building on earlier analyses (Foley & Lee, 1989, 1996; Rodseth et al., 1991; Rodseth & Novak, 2000), we attempt here to generate a set of "species-neutral" categories for cross-specific comparison. Perhaps the simplest way to do this is to construct a matrix in which same-sex relationships are plotted against opposite-sex relationships (Figures 7.1 and 7.2). Because both of these kinds of relationships are found in human and nonhuman primates, we arrive at a common "design space" within which to make

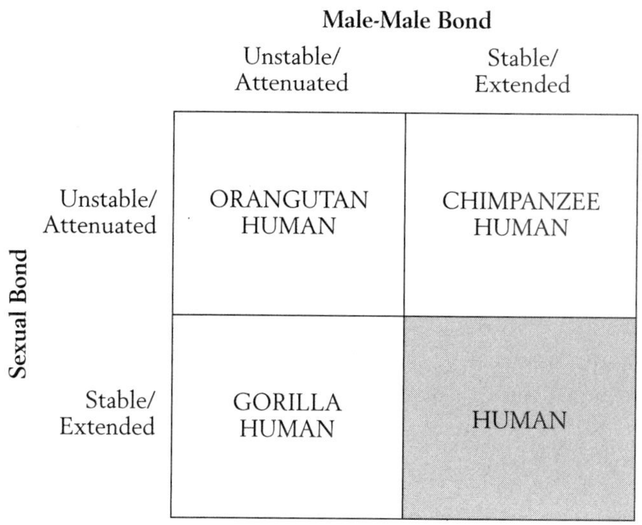

Male-Male Bond

	Unstable/ Attenuated	Stable/ Extended
Unstable/ Attenuated	ORANGUTAN HUMAN	CHIMPANZEE HUMAN
Stable/ Extended	GORILLA HUMAN	HUMAN

Sexual Bond

Figure 7.1. *Four male social spheres*

cross-specific comparisons. At the same time, this approach allows us to explore the ways in which a sexual relationship such as the human pair bond can be combined with a variety of other kinds of relationships, whether or not this gives rise to the kind of dense social network exemplified by the human band. In fact, as Figures 7.1 and 7.2 demonstrate, a variety of

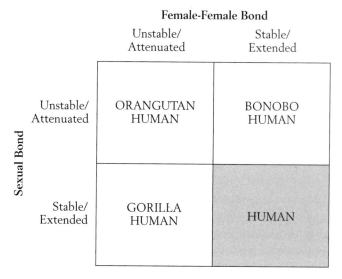

Female-Female Bond

	Unstable/ Attenuated	Stable/ Extended
Unstable/ Attenuated	ORANGUTAN HUMAN	BONOBO HUMAN
Stable/ Extended	GORILLA HUMAN	HUMAN

Sexual Bond

Figure 7.2. *Four female social spheres*

primate social systems in addition to the human band are generated by different combinations of the same underlying relationships.

To streamline our presentation, we have made a number of simplifying assumptions. First, all relationships have been assigned a binary value, either stable/extended or unstable/attenuated. This is obviously an artificial characterization, but it allows the broad patterns of relationships to be more easily grasped and compared. Second, only relationships among adults are considered; parent-child and other relationships involving juveniles are left out of the analysis. Third, all opposite-sex relationships are for our purposes considered to be sexual relationships, while same-sex relationships are considered to be nonsexual—homosexuality, in other words, is left out of the analysis. These assumptions are especially unrealistic, of course, but they allow us to capture broad patterns that would otherwise be obscured. Fourth, and perhaps most important, what we have called "relationships" are to be understood in a very specific way. A "relationship" involves some degree of *advantage* to the participants, who gain more by coordinating their action than they would by acting alone (Wrangham, 1982, p. 270; see also van Schaik, 1989). *This is not to be confused with friendly affiliation or even spatial proximity.* Merely exchanging pleasantries, even on a routine basis, does not make a relationship in our sense. Female gorillas often live in close proximity and remain tolerant of each other over long periods, yet do not form relationships. Ongoing interaction is not even necessary to a relationship. Taking turns cooking or watching each other's children implies a mutualistic relationship, even if little or no interaction goes on between the partners. Furthermore, as should be obvious from these examples, relationships do not necessarily involve residential proximity. Those who live together may or may not be in relationships, and those in relationships may or may not live together.

Figure 7.1 represents the social space defined by sexual bonds in combination with male-male bonds. This allows us to classify the typical situations faced by human males and their counterparts among the four great apes. What is immediately apparent about this matrix is the way in which the nonhuman cases are confined to only one or two cells while the human patterns are distributed across all four. Elsewhere we have described variation in the social modes of men and discussed examples of the patterns found in each of the four cells (Rodseth & Novak, 2000). For present purposes, our classification is intended to capture patterns that are *regularly* found in human societies, even if these patterns are not typical or dominant in those societies. Thus, what we call "satellites"—males whose sexual and same-sex relationships are unstable or attenuated—are common in many human populations, even if they always remain in the minority. One of the cells in Figure 7.1, furthermore, is occupied by humans only. Human males are apparently capable of *combining* relationships in a way that no great ape does. Specifically, only humans seem to be able to maintain a relatively stable sexual bond in combination with a stable and extended network of male-male bonds.

Turning to Figure 7.2, a similar pattern is observed. Again, each of the great ape patterns is distributed in a much more limited way than the human pattern. The female apes, in fact, are consistently confined to one of the situations represented by one cell of the matrix. Significantly, however, human females seldom if ever follow the relatively solitary pattern that is typical of both orangutan and chimpanzee females. The solitary existence led by both female and male orangutans is well known (Rodman & Mitani, 1987; van Schaik & van Hooff, 1996). Female chimpanzees, while sharing a community range, spend as much as two-thirds of their time alone with infants (Wrangham & Smuts, 1980) and interact more with males in their group than with females (Wrangham, Clark, & Isabirye-Basuta 1992). Among humans, however, females are always found in social groups and almost universally form alliances with other adults in those groups. This is in sharp contrast to the human male pattern, suggesting a gendered asymmetry in human sociality (Rodseth & Novak, 2000, p. 349).

At the same time, human females, like human males, are unique among living hominoids in maintaining a sexual bond *along with* stable and extended same-sex bonds. Human sociality is doubly remarkable, then, insofar as adults of both sexes are capable of forming enduring bonds with both same-sex and opposite-sex partners. This is the ultimate configuration of relationships undergirding the band and other forms of the human community.

The Human Divergence From Three Hominoid Trends

Perhaps the most important implication of the above exercise is that human sociality *transcends* that of any other living hominoid. This is true, it should be noted, not merely in the sense that humans have language or other unique cognitive capacities upon which human sociality depends. It is also true in the more surprising sense that humans are regularly found in social combinations that we might *expect* to find in other primates but in fact do not. At the same time, each of the great apes seems to shed light on some *dimension* of human sociality. Common chimpanzees, for example, might have a great deal to tell us about human male-male relationships, while the case of gorillas might help to clarify the ultimate causes of the human pair bond. Yet because human groups range over such a vast area of "social space," an analogy with the social system of any one primate is unlikely to do justice to the human pattern.

Common chimpanzees in particular provide a tempting model for comparison with small-scale human societies, whether in prehistory or in the ethnographic record. The realization that the chimpanzee community, unlike most primate societies, is based on male kinship bonds and that males cooperate to attack members of neighboring communities has prompted comparisons with human band and tribal organization (e.g., Manson & Wrangham, 1991; Wrangham & Peterson, 1996). Yet these human-chimpanzee parallels make the social and ecological *differences* between the two species all the more intriguing. One such difference—the lack of exclusive sexual alliances or pair bonds in chimpanzees—is well known (Goodall, 1965, p. 451; Fox, 1975). Yet three other, perhaps equally important, differences have not received the attention they deserve. First, in all study populations, chimpanzees are consistently male philopatric, while human patterns of postmarital residence are far more variable. Second, chimpanzee females are much less gregarious than women and seldom form stable alliances with other females in the way that women often do. Third, competition for food resources is apparently less intense among women in a foraging band than among the females in a chimpanzee community—an ecological difference that might account for the above differences in social behavior. Let us consider these three points in more detail.

The Not-So-Patrilocal Band

All the apes, including chimpanzees, follow a pattern of female dispersal at sexual maturity. This sets the apes apart from most of the Old World monkeys, in which the prevailing patterns are male dispersal and female bonding (Wrangham, 1980). In light of this fact, human patterns of postmarital residence have been seen as consistent with the dispersal patterns of apes in general or with chimpanzees in particular (e.g., Ghiglieri, 1987; Foley & Lee, 1989). Thus Wrangham (1987a, p. 61) describes human societies as "substantially more similar to the African apes in their tendency for female exogamy than they are to Old World Monkeys, which show clear patterns of female endogamy in many species." Similarly, Smuts (1995, p. 13) argues that

> modern humans show the typical great ape pattern of female dispersal away from kin (although there are important exceptions). This pattern of female dispersal is particularly significant when it is remembered that the opposite pattern holds in many other primates and mammals in general.

The "important exceptions" are not elaborated by Smuts, but Barnard (1983, p. 197), Knauft (1991), and others maintain that small-scale foraging societies have extremely flexible residence patterns and cannot be characterized as predominantly patrilocal.

Nevertheless, "the frequency with which patrilocal residence is reported ethnographically and the fact the female chimpanzees (unlike the females of most primate species) tend to leave their natal groups have together stimulated arguments about the continuity of female dispersal in all descendants of our common ancestor" (Hawkes, O'Connell, & Blurton Jones, 1997, p. 561). Wrangham (1987a, 1987b) was perhaps the first to use the social organization of African hominoids, including humans, to reconstruct the social organization of their common ancestor. Following Wrangham, a number of authors have proceeded from the assumption that this common ancestor was most likely to have followed a pattern of female dispersal and male philopatry. Foley (1999, p. 381) explicitly suggests that this pattern has been fixed throughout the evolutionary history of the entire hominid lineage:

> A switch to dispersing males would have been individually lethal and likely to make such groups highly vulnerable. As such, male kin bonding may represent something of an irreversible strategy in social evolution, unless there is a complete loss of sociality or communities become so large that sex-specific dispersal/residence patterns become unnecessary.

The portrait of social organization that emerges from these analyses is surprisingly inflexible and static over long stretches of hominid evolution. Yet it must be remembered that the original reconstruction of the common ancestral pattern was based in part on a controversial characterization of the contemporary human pattern. Before we conclude that female dispersal or male kin bonding is "an irreversible strategy" in human social evolution, we should be sure that contemporary humans have not reversed the strategy already.

Human residence patterns, as O'Connell, Hawkes, and Blurton Jones (1999, p. 477) rightly note, are not only extremely variable but "evidently sensitive to local ecological conditions, especially as they affect female subsistence." Even granting, then, the predominance of patrilocal residence in the ethnographic record (Rodseth et al., 1991, p. 230), the question persists of whether humans in general can be characterized as female dispersing and male philopatric (e.g., Knauft, 1991, pp. 405–406; Davis & Daly, 1997, p. 408; Hawkes, O'Connell, & Blurton Jones 1997, pp. 561–562). In the case of chimpanzees, no such question arises in the first place for the simple reason that chimpanzee dispersal patterns are invariant—all known chimpanzee populations, despite significant variations in other aspects of their social organization, follow a pattern of male philopatry. In fact, there is no confirmed case of an adult male chimpanzee transferring to another community (cf. Goodall, 1986, pp. 86–87).

Against this standard, the cross-cultural pattern of human male philopatry is quite inconsistent (Alvarez, 2004; Marlowe, 2004). Even if we accept that nearly 70% of societies in the ethnographic record can be classified as patrilocal (Murdock, 1967; Levinson & Malone, 1980, pp. 99–101), this leaves over 30% of the variation to be accounted for. Moreover, such classification is made at the level of the population as a whole; individual variation in residence patterns is inevitably collapsed to derive a dominant pattern. Within many "patrilocal" societies, there may be numerous examples of individual men marrying out of their natal groups, and this by itself sets off the human pattern sharply from that of chimpanzees.

In this case, then, primate comparison turns out to be a double-edged sword. On the one hand, Wrangham (1987a, p. 61) was indeed correct to argue that human societies are "substantially more similar to the African apes in their tendency for female exogamy *than they are to Old World Monkeys*" (emphasis added). On the other, once we adopt Wrangham's perspective and reconceptualize humans as descendants of female-dispersing African hominoids, we are struck at once by the anomaly that humans represent against this background. Now the question becomes not so much why humans like other apes tend to be female-dispersing, but why humans have evolved such flexibility in their residence patterns to allow for rates of male dispersal and female philopatry that are unprecedented among the apes.

Men Are From Gombe, Women Are From Wamba

Closely related to the issue of sex-biased dispersal is that of sex differences in social relationships. At the same time, these two issues must be kept carefully distinct inasmuch as common residence does not always imply social bonding, while unrelated individuals from different natal groups may closely associate or even form stable alliances. In fact, in the case of humans, patterns of residence, gregariousness, and social bonding are largely independent of each other (Rodseth et al., 1991, p. 240).

Inferring social relationships from residence patterns has been a convenient strategy, not just within primatology but within social and cultural anthropology as well (e.g., Murdock, 1949, p. 202). Yet nowhere are the pitfalls of this approach more evident than in the context of the chimpanzee-human comparison. Let us grant for the moment the validity of the analogy between chimpanzee male philopatry and human patrilocality. What does not follow from this is that chimpanzees and humans exhibit analogous sex differences in gregariousness and bonding. To demonstrate this, let us compare closely the social relationships among females in the two species.

Chimpanzee females are "often less gregarious than males, spending more time alone, meeting fewer different individuals per day, and traveling in smaller parties" (Wrangham, 2000, p. 248; see also Goodall, 1986). There is significant variation across chimpanzee populations, with bonding between females quite rare in the East African sites of Gombe, Mahale, and Kibale but much more common in the West African sites of Bossou (Sugiyama, 1988; Sakura, 1994) and Taï (Boesch, 1991, 1996). Without infants, furthermore, adult females are as gregarious as adult males, suggesting that asociality is a result not of gender but of motherhood (Wrangham, 2000). Yet the relatively solitary existence of female chimpanzees and their lack of social alliances are consistent with their pattern of dispersal from their natal groups—females, in other words, "migrate at least partly to reduce feeding competition" (Sterck, Watts, & van Schaik, 1997, p. 294), and this same competition precludes them "from forming the cohesive groups necessary for the maintenance of female kin bonds" (Strier, 1999, p. 301). Patterns of residence, gregariousness, and kinship, then, tend to coincide in common chimpanzees.

When we turn to humans, however, the situation is quite different. Even when they transfer to unrelated groups, women everywhere tend to be far more gregarious than female chimpanzees. Because human mothers with infants usually have access to food and company at a home base, they are not forced to forage in a relatively solitary manner as chimpanzee mothers are (see below). Moreover, even unrelated women in the most extreme patriarchal societies regularly form close and enduring friendships (e.g., Abu-Lughod, 1986). How often such friendships are genuine alliances for purposes of competition against others is difficult to demonstrate empirically, but there is some ethnographic evidence to suggest that this is the case (e.g., Kyakas & Wiessner, 1992). Women's sociality, then, would seem to resemble neither the semisolitary pattern of female chimpanzees nor the pattern of association without bonding seen in female gorillas (Rodseth et al., 1991, p. 231).

Stable bonds between females *regardless* of residence pattern seem to be characteristic of only one great ape—the bonobo. Sometimes called "pygmy chimpanzees," bonobos are distinguished from common chimps by their somewhat smaller heads and less robust bodies. As closely related species of the same genus *(Pan)*, the two chimpanzees are similar in many ways, yet they inhabit distinct geographic ranges and apparently form quite different kinds of societies. While common chimps are found in both East and West Africa, bonobos live only in Central Africa to the south of the Congo (or Zaire) River (Wrangham & Peterson, 1996, p. 222). Here, in the mid-1970s, Takayoshi Kano took up residence in the village of Wamba and began the first systematic study of bonobos in the wild (Kano, 1992; see also F. J. White, 1992, 1996; de Waal, 1997).

What Kano and his associates discovered about bonobos would change the way primatologists think about the social behavior of all the hominoids, including humans. Like common chimpanzees, bonobos consistently follow a pattern of female dispersal. Yet among bonobos, an immigrant female is soon incorporated into the resident female network by way of elaborate homosexual relationships. All the females in this network cooperate to defend against threats by resident males. The communitywide scale and cohesiveness of female bonds in bonobos makes them distinct from the individually differentiated and situational bonds typically found among women (but see the Igbo case discussed by van Allen, 1997). Bonobos and humans, in forming stable female alliances at all, are clearly running against the general hominoid trend, a fact that has not always been recognized in comparative primate sociology.

In fact, women's bonding patterns, like their patterns of dispersal and residence, have often been equated with the respective patterns of common chimpanzees (e.g., Foley & Lee, 1989, p. 905; cf. Rodseth et al., 1991, p. 229, n. 4). But the view that women, like female chimpanzees, exhibit "weak" bonds and only "limited cooperation" (Ghiglieri, 1987, p. 343, 1989, p. 373) is difficult to sustain unless these words are given very special definitions. And definitions are indeed at issue in any attempt to characterize women's (or men's) relationships precisely. Consider the fine distinction drawn by Wrangham (1987a, p. 62) between "friendships" and "alliances":

> Human females have relationships which may include strikingly friendly aspects, but they rarely involve physical aggression or systematic alliance relationships in which women form predictable alliances against other women (Irons, 1983). This is not to say they are unknown. In some societies such relationships can be very important. Competition between matrilineal clans over women's rights to land, for example, provides a parallel to the behavior seen in Old World monkeys (e.g., among the Hopi, who are also matrilocal . . .). In most societies, however, long-term female relationships involve friendships rather than competitive alliances.

Friendships, according to this interpretation, do not qualify as competitive alliances unless they (1) involve physical aggression or (2) are more systematic and predictable than women's relationships usually are, according to most ethnographic accounts. What is striking about this distinction is the way it reflects the constraints of primatological method more than our own intuitions about (human) friendships. A primatologist must have an operationalized definition of "alliance" based on observable, nonlinguistic behavior; under these circumstances, cooperation in physical aggression and predictability of mutual support are excellent criteria for establishing that an alliance exists between two individuals. Imagine a primate, however, in which most aggression is not physical but verbal and for whom most competition is not an open struggle but a surreptitious campaign to denigrate or socially isolate one's rivals. Now the behavioral criteria that were useful in identifying alliances in other primates are of much less help.

Let us grant that women's relationships usually involve less physical aggression than do men's. Let us grant further that women in most societies "do not form coalitions *for purposes of violence against their own sex* in the way that men do everywhere" (Rodseth et al., 1991, p. 231). It does not follow that women's relationships are merely friendships rather than competitive alliances. A growing literature testifies to the elaborate nature of women's political lives, even in societies in which public politics and "foreign policy" are dominated by men (e.g., Schuster & DeVore, 1983; Burbank, 1994). If women usually fight verbally and often through an intermediary (Schuster & Hartz-Karp, 1986; Björkqvist, Österman, & Kaukiainen 1992; Lagerspetz & Björkqvist, 1992), this is nonetheless a form of fighting, and a form in which alliances between women may be highly systematic, predictable, and crucial to the outcome of the conflict. There is a striking contrast between this pattern of bonding and the social (or *a*social) patterns of other female hominoids—with the possible exception of bonobos.

In light of this argument, we propose a revision of the "Relationships among Females" chart originally presented by Wrangham (1987a, p. 59) and reproduced here as Table 7.1. In our revised version (Table 7.2), bonding is defined as the formation of stable competitive coalitions, whether or not the competition involves physical aggression. Humans and bonobos, according to this definition, are both female-bonded species, even with female dispersal. The capacity of women and female bonobos to maintain alliances with unrelated females is a unique pattern among hominoids and an extremely unusual one among primates in general. This pattern deserves as much attention as the patterns of collective violence that seem to be shared by men and male chimpanzees (Wrangham & Peterson, 1996).

Table 7.1 Relationships Among Females

	Breed in Natal Group	Frequency of Forming Alliances With Females
Gorilla	Rarely	Rare
Bonobo	Rarely?	Unknown
Chimpanzee	Rarely	Rare
Human	Rarely	Rare
Common Ancestor	Rarely	Rare

Note: Reproduced from Wrangham (1987). "Common Ancestor" refers to the fossil hominoid from which the living apes and humans are descended.

Table 7.2 Relationships Among Females

	Breed in Natal Group	Frequency of Forming Alliances With Females
Gorilla	Rarely	Rare
Bonobo	Rarely?	Common*
Chimpanzee	Rarely	Rare
Human	Variable*	Common*
Common Ancestor	Rarely	Rare?*

Note: An asterisk (*) denotes a change from Wrangham (1987). "Common Ancestor" refers to the fossil hominoid from which the living apes and humans are descended.

Unscrambling the Competition

Without the case of bonobos, we might be forced to conclude that female sociality in all the apes is extremely attenuated, making women appear all the more anomalous. Yet recent research has confirmed that bonobo females are strikingly gregarious and form elaborate, enduring bonds among themselves (Kano, 1992; White, 1992, 1996; de Waal, 1997). Why bonobos should be so unlike common chimpanzees in this way is a question of special interest to students of human behavior insofar as the same mechanism allowing enhanced female sociality in bonobos might be at work in the case of humans. In other words, if we knew the conditions that permit bonobos, unlike chimpanzees, to maintain such elaborate female-female relationships, this might provide a clue as to how and why human social evolution has taken a similar path.

A solution to the chimpanzee-bonobo problem is suggested by Wrangham's "scramble-competition hypothesis" (Wrangham et al., 1996; Wrangham, 2000). This hypothesis proposes that food resources distributed in very small and dispersed patches force individuals to spread apart during feeding, thus reducing group size. In two of the great apes—orangutans and common chimpanzees—competition for ripe fruit is apparently so intense that females, especially mothers with infants, associate very little. In gorillas, by contrast, such competition does not drive females apart. When fruits are scarce, gorillas shift to a lower-quality but more evenly distributed food resource, so-called terrestrial herbacious vegetation (THV). The relative lack of feeding competition allows gorilla females to affiliate closely (though they bond to the breeding male in their group rather than to each other). Like gorillas, bonobos are able to rely on THV as a substantial part of their diet (Malenky et al., 1994; Malenky & Wrangham, 1994); this has been argued to promote the more cohesive groups (Wrangham et al., 1996) and greater female gregariousness (Wrangham, 2000) observed in bonobos as opposed to common chimpanzees.

If humans, as argued in this chapter, are comparable to bonobos in forming elaborate and enduring female relationships, one reason for this is immediately suggested by Wrangham's solution to the chimpanzee-bonobo problem: scramble competition among foraging women, as among female bonobos, must be less intense than it is among female chimpanzees. In turning to humans, however, Wrangham (2000, p. 258) uses the scramble competition hypothesis to argue for precisely the opposite conclusion:

> I have not found data on whether [human] males are more gregarious than mothers, but it is clear that, as in other infant-carrying primates, the travel costs of motherhood are substantial (Blurton Jones, Hawkes, & O'Connell, 1989). The comparison suggests that intense scramble competition may have constrained the potential for female bonding in human foragers, as in chimpanzees.

To judge from this argument, one might expect women—especially mothers with infants—to forage alone or in very small groups, as do female chimpanzees. On the contrary, however, the available evidence suggests that women seldom forage alone and often do so in rather large groups (Kaplan et al., 2000, p. 175), averaging perhaps three to six among the !Kung, for example, and from four to eight among the Hadza (P. Wiessner and K. Hawkes, personal communications). Such gregariousness is probably attributable in part to the risk of harassment from outside males. Yet if scramble competition were as great in humans as in common chimpanzees, mothers in such large groups would be unable to acquire enough food.

The question then becomes: what conditions would reduce scramble competition among humans in comparison with chimpanzees so as to permit the level of gregariousness and social bonding observed among women? The likely answer would seem to involve a food resource, analogous to THV among gorillas and bonobos, that would serve as a fallback food, a reliable staple found in larger patches than are ripe fruits and most other high-quality resources. What this food resource might be is now a matter of some debate. Adherents of the hunting hypothesis might argue that men in effect create an artificial "patch" by sharing game with women and children (cf. Kaplan et al., 2000, pp. 174–175). Yet the success rates of hunters, according to an alternative argument, are too low to provide a reliable food supply of the kind we are seeking (Hawkes, 1990, 1993; O'Connell, Hawkes, & Blurton Jones 1999).

In this light, Hawkes and others have suggested that tubers and other underground storage organs (USOs) may have been the critical resource added to hominid diets. Wrangham has also seen USOs as important in hominid diets, but for different reasons: roots are what allowed early hominids to migrate out of the forests and into the savanna woodlands (Wrangham &

Peterson, 1996, chap. 3). Eaten raw, however, USOs would have served at best as an important *supplement* to hominid diets, according to Wrangham et al. (1999). What transformed roots from a supplement to a staple in human diets was cooking, which Wrangham et al. (1999) estimate was being practiced by early *Homo* by 1.9 million years ago. Cooking, in effect, would create the artificial "patch" at the home base that would allow more cohesive groups to be sustained, despite fission-fusion foraging during the day. By the same reasoning, cooking might have served as the mechanism by which gregariousness and social bonding were promoted among hominid females.

Whatever the precise mechanism, if scramble competition were reduced, another important change in hominid social behavior would tend to follow: a shift away from the ancestral, chimpanzee-like pattern of consistent male philopatry and toward a mixed pattern of patrilocal, matrilocal, and bilocal residence. Such a shift would reflect the increasing benefits under some circumstances of women remaining together in their natal groups—what Hawkes, O'Connell, and Blurton Jones (1997, p. 561) call "the advantages of proximity for matrilineally related females." Noting that female chimpanzees do sometimes stay with their mothers, Hawkes et al. predict that as the benefits of cooperation between mothers and daughters increase, "patterns of female sociability and sex-biased dispersal [would] be altered as a consequence" (1997, pp. 561–562). Reliance on deep underground tubers, for example, or other resources that young juveniles cannot exploit on their own might favor the evolution of female philopatry, especially if grandmothers can carry infants or otherwise provide assistance to mothers (Hawkes, O'Connell, & Blurton Jones, 1987, 1997; Hawkes et al., 2000). Whether or not the "grandmother hypothesis" is correct in detail, what is important for present purposes is the serious challenge it poses to the now widely held view that human social organization is based on male kinship bonding through patrilocal residence (O'Connell, Hawkes, & Blurton Jones 1999, p. 477).

Summing Up the Human Pattern

If human social organization is a conglomeration of patterns found in other primates, it remains a *selective* conglomeration, a unique fusion of traits found especially in our closest phylogenetic relatives, the African apes. It would be tempting at this point to suggest that human social organization is but a recombination of three African ape patterns: a gorilla-like sexual bond, a chimpanzee-like bond among males, and a bonobo-like bond among females. Such a suggestion would, in effect, reaffirm the band-and-bond model that has been so enduring in twentieth-century anthropology, with this important proviso: The human band, *even if patrilocal,* is never merely a male kinship network to which females are attached through sexual bonds. This proviso runs counter to the tendency in some recent evolutionary analyses to reduce human social organization to the formula of "male bonds + sexual bonds = the local community" (e.g., Ghiglieri, 1987, p. 343, 1989, p. 373; Foley & Lee, 1989, 1996; Maryanski, 1996, p. 83). Any adequate characterization of human social organization must recognize that women's sociality is more elaborate than any other female hominoid's, with the possible exception of bonobos, and that the band or other local community is always a "high-density network" (Maryanski, 1996, pp. 76–78) constituted by multiple overlapping alliances between women as well as between men and between sexual partners.

The traditional band-and-bond model was a convenient first approximation of "the unusual human social system in which pair-bonds are embedded within multi-male, multi-female communities" (Wrangham et al., 1999, p. 567). This nesting of pair bonds within communities is enough by itself to make human societies quite odd among most other animal groupings (Rodseth et al., 1991, p. 235). Yet the nesting of social units in human societies usually goes beyond this two-level hierarchy, with descent groups, sodalities, religious cults, and other groupings uniting members of different families within the same community. Relationships between communities, furthermore, are uniquely elaborated in human societies. And all of this is true despite the fact that human traveling parties are not stable herds or troops but quite variable subgroups that usually break up and recombine many times over during daylight hours. When such "fission-fusion" parties are found in other primates, such as chimpanzees and spider monkeys, the social network is always quite low in density, to use Maryanski's (1996) terms, while in humans the same kind of subgroups are found within a very dense network. Beyond the question, then, of how humans maintain pair bonds within communities is the more formidable one of how humans maintain such dense networks that combine multilevel social organization with fission-fusion parties (Rodseth & Novak, 2000, p. 338).

The answer is likely to involve what was factored out of our analysis at the start: language and other uniquely human cognitive abilities that tend to uncouple social relationships from spatial proximity (Rodseth et al., 1991, pp. 239–240). The human community is a primate society, to be sure, and involves a medley of the simpler themes played by African apes in particular. Yet this "music" is especially strange not because of its component themes but because of the way it plays in people's minds even when others are not around. Human society is, no doubt, what many social scientists have always claimed it to be: a moral order based in part on cultural rules and understandings that are only occasionally reflected in social behavior "on the ground." Does this mean that the proper object of social scientific investigation is the moral order "behind" the behavior? And if monkeys and apes lack such a moral order, does this obviate any comparison between human and other primate societies? By way of conclusion, let us return to the topic of culture and consider the special challenges it poses to a comparative primate sociology.

The Primatologist's Magic

Behavioral primatology and sociocultural anthropology are anchored in the same field method—the intimate observation and description of daily life in a local setting. At the same time, however, an ethnographer is not limited to the naturalistic study of *behavior*, and can always *ask* her subjects what they do and why—an option that is unavailable to the student of monkey or ape society. The powerful emphasis in anthropology on reported rather than directly observed behavior has tended to sharpen the contrast between ethnographic and primatological description. Most sociocultural anthropologists would undoubtedly agree with Clifford Geertz that a naturalistic account of behavior alone is inappropriate to the study of meaningful human activity. "I-am-a-camera, 'phenomenalistic' observation," as Geertz (1973, pp. 6–7) called it, is incapable of discriminating between an involuntary twitch and a conspiratorial wink.

The recent anthropological emphasis on symbolic as opposed to behavioral analysis owes much to the "culturology" of Leslie White (1949, p. 22), who argued that the capacity to use symbols "transformed our anthropoid ancestors into men and made them human" (see also Geertz, 1973, p. 68). As a result, according to White (1949, pp. 34–35), "the nonsymbolic behavior of Homo sapiens is the behavior of man the animal; the symbolic behavior is that of man the human being." Although our nonsymbolic behaviors—our "yawns, stretches, coughs, scratches"—may be compared with those of other animals, our symbolic behaviors are uniquely human, in White's view, and cannot be so compared. A half century after White pronounced that the symbol alone "made mankind human," many sociocultural anthropologists still hold some version of this view (e.g., Sahlins, 1999, p. 400). There is a "key dimension," as Eric Wolf put it, "that distinguishes human adaptations (and human troubles) from those of other animals—the ability to generate regular forms of behavior by manipulating signs that allow people to imagine the worlds they thus create" (1999, p. 288).

Yet Wolf's own emphasis on the *manipulation* of signs suggests that the worlds people imagine should not be taken for the worlds they actually create. Much of the "symbolic behavior" with which sociocultural anthropology has been especially concerned is actually a distorted reconstruction of such behavior on the part of either the anthropologist or the "natives" themselves. Even if people everywhere tend to explain their behavior in terms of social conventions or ideals, the patterning of that behavior cannot be predicted on the basis of cultural rules alone (Firth, 1964, p. 35; Barth, 1966). This lack of fit between the "rules of the game" and the way the game is actually played has been a central problem of social and cultural theory in the late twentieth century (e.g., Bourdieu, 1977; Giddens, 1979; Dirks, Eley, & Ortner 1994). As a result, sociocultural anthropologists are increasingly concerned with *comparing* cultural rules and observed practices, in part to understand how such rules are created in the first place (e.g., Sahlins, 1981; Barth, 1987). Why people believe what they do about their social lives is still a question of immense anthropological interest. Why they *do* what they do, however, is a separate issue that can be investigated only on the basis of a careful record of actual behavior.

Thus, even if all human action involves the use of symbols and can only be fully explicated in its local cultural context, much can be learned from "I-am-a-camera, 'phenomenalistic' observation." Such observation is perhaps the only way to capture the subtle and shifting patterning of relationships between individuals of various age, sex, and kinship categories. Some individuals form most of their relationships with members of their own sex, others with members of the opposite sex; some do so with kin, others with non-kin. The patterning of these relationships, quite apart from the meanings attached to them by the participants, is an important measure of human social complexity and hardly a trivial matter to capture ethnographically.

To "possess real scientific aims," to live and work "right among the natives," and to cross-check observations through multiple modes of data collection and analysis—these were the techniques that Bronislaw Malinowski described as the "ethnographer's magic" (1922, p. 6). Yet a similar magic is employed by the field primatologist seeking to understand the behavioral complexity of baboons or chimpanzees. As the ethnographic record of nonhuman primates continues to expand, it will come to rival that of humans. What to do with such an immensely valuable record is a question that now looms, not only for primatologists but for social scientists everywhere.

We would like to thank Jerome Barkow, James O'Connell, and Richard W. Wrangham for their thoughtful comments on early drafts of this chapter.

References

Abu-Lughod, L. (1986). *Veiled Sentiments.* Berkeley: University of California Press.

Allen, J. van. (1997). "Sitting on a man": Colonialism and the lost political institutions of Igbo women. In R. R. Grinker & C. B. Steiner (Eds.), *Perspectives on Africa* (pp. 536–549). Cambridge, MA: Blackwell.

Alvarez, H. (2004). Residence groups among hunter-gatherers: A view of the claims and evidence for patrilocal bands. In B. Chapais & C. M. Berman (Eds.), *Kinship and Behavior in Primates*. New York: Oxford University Press.

Ardrey, R. (1966). *The Territorial Imperative*. New York: Dell.

Ardrey, R. (1976). *The Hunting Hypothesis*. New York: Atheneum.

Aristotle. (1981). *The Politics* (T. A. Sinclair, Trans.). London: Penguin.

Barkow, J. H. (1989). *Darwin, Sex, and Status: Biological Approaches to Mind and Culture*. Toronto: University of Toronto Press.

Barnard, A. (1983). Contemporary hunter-gatherers: Current theoretical issues in ecology and social organization. *Annual Review of Anthropology, 12,* 193–214.

Barth, F. (1966). *Models of Social Organization*. Royal Anthropological Institute Occasional Paper 23. London: Royal Anthropological Institute of Great Britain and Ireland.

Barth, F. (1987). *Cosmologies in the Making: A Generative Approach to Cultural Variation in Inner New Guinea*. Cambridge: Cambridge University Press.

Björkqvist, K., K. Österman, & A. Kaukiainen. (1992). Indirect aggression: Conceptions and misconceptions. In K. Björkqvist & P. Niemelä (Eds.), *Of Mice and Women: Aspects of Female Aggression* (pp. 51–64). San Diego: Academic Press.

Blurton Jones, N., K. Hawkes, & J. F. O'Connell. (1989). Studying costs of children in two foraging societies: Implications for schedules of reproduction. In V. Standon & R. Foley (Eds.), *Comparative Socioecology of Mammals and Man* (pp. 365–390). London: Blackwell.

Blurton Jones, N., F. W. Marlowe, K. Hawkes, & J. F. O'Connell. (2000). Paternal investment and hunter-gatherer divorce rates. In L. Cronk, N. Chagnon, & W. Irons (Eds.), *Adaptation and Human Behavior: An Anthropological Perspective* (pp. 69–90). New York: Aldine.

Boehm, C. (1992). Segmentary "warfare" and the management of conflict: Comparison of East African chimpanzees and patrilineal-patrilocal humans. In A. H. Harcourt & F. B. M. de Waal (Eds.), *Coalitions and Alliances in Humans and Other Animals* (pp. 137–173). Oxford: Oxford University Press.

Boehm, C. (1993). Egalitarian society and reverse dominance hierarchy. *Current Anthropology, 34,* 227–254.

Boehm, C. (1999). *Hierarchy in the Forest: The Evolution of Egalitarian Behavior*. Cambridge, MA: Harvard University Press.

Boesch, C. (1991). The effects of leopard predation on grouping patterns in forest chimpanzees. *Behaviour, 117,* 220–241.

Boesch, C. (1996). Social grouping in Taï chimpanzees. In W. C. McGrew, L. F. Marchant, & T. Nishida (Eds.), *Great Ape Societies* (pp. 101–113). Cambridge: Cambridge University Press.

Bourdieu, P. (1977). *Outline of a Theory of Practice*. Cambridge: Cambridge University Press.

Brown, D. E. (1991). *Human Universals*. New York: McGraw-Hill.

Burbank, V. K. (1994). *Fighting Women: Anger and Aggression in Aboriginal Australia*. Berkeley: University of California Press.

Carpenter, C. R. (1934). A field study of the behavior and social relations of howling monkeys. *Comparative Psychology Monographs, 10*, 1–168.

Carpenter, C. R. (1935). Behavior of red spider monkeys in Panama. *Journal of Mammalogy, 16*, 171–180.

Carpenter, C. R. (1940). A field study in Siam of the behavior and social relations of the gibbon, *Hylobates lar. Comparative Psychology Monographs, 16*, 1–212.

Cronk, L. (1999). *That Complex Whole: Culture and the Evolution of Human Behavior*. Boulder, CO: Westview.

Davis, J. N., & M. Daly. (1997). Evolutionary theory and the human family. *Quarterly Review of Biology, 72*(4), 407–435.

Dennett, D. C. (1995). *Darwin's Dangerous Idea: Evolution and the Meanings of Life*. New York: Simon and Schuster.

DeVore, I. (1962). *The Social Behavior and Organization of Baboon Troops*. PhD diss., University of Chicago.

DeVore, I. (1965). Preface to *Primate Behavior: Field Studies of Monkeys and Apes* (pp. vii–x). New York: Holt, Rinehart and Winston.

Di Fore, A., & D. Rendall. (1994). Evolution of social organization: A reappraisal for primates by using phylogenetic methods. *Proceedings of the National Academy of Sciences, USA, 91*, 9941–9945.

Dirks, N. B., G. Eley, & S. B. Ortner (Eds.). (1994). *Culture/Power/History: A Reader in Contemporary Social Theory*. Princeton, NJ: Princeton University Press.

Ember, C. R. (1978). Myths about hunter-gatherers. *Ethnology, 17*, 439–448.

Fedigan, L. M. (1986). The changing role of women in models of human evolution. *Annual Review of Anthropology, 15*, 25–66.

Firth, R. (1964). *Essays on Social Organization and Values*. London School of Economics Monographs on Social Anthropology, no. 28. London: Athlone Press.

Foley, R. A. (1989). The evolution of hominid social behaviour. In V. Standen & R. A. Foley (Eds.), *Comparative Socioecology* (pp. 473–494). Oxford: Blackwell Scientific.

Foley, R. A. (1992). Evolutionary ecology of fossil hominids. In E. A. Smith & B. Winterhalds (Eds.), *Evolutionary Ecology and Human Behavior* (pp. 131–164). Chicago: Aldine de Gruyter.

Foley, R. A. (1999). Hominid behavioural evolution: Missing links in comparative primate socioecology. In P. C. Lee (Ed.), *Comparative Primate Socioecology* (pp. 363–386). Cambridge: Cambridge University Press.

Foley, R., & P. Lee. (1989). Finite social space, evolutionary pathways and reconstructing hominid behavior. *Science, 243*, 901–906.

Foley, R., & P. Lee. (1996). Finite social space and the evolution of human social behaviour. In J. Steele & S. Shennan (Eds.), *The Archaeology of*

Human Ancestry: Power, Sex and Tradition (pp. 47–66). London: Routledge.

Fox, R. (1975). Primate kin and human kinship. In R. Fox (Ed.), *Biosocial Anthropology* (pp. 9–35). New York: Wiley.

Geertz, C. (1973). *The Interpretation of Cultures*. New York: Basic Books.

Ghiglieri, M. P. (1987). Sociobiology of the great apes and the hominid ancestor. *Journal of Human Evolution, 16*, 319–357.

Ghiglieri, M. P. (1989). Hominoid sociobiology and hominid social evolution. In P. G. Heltne & L. A. Marquardt (Eds.), *Understanding Chimpanzees* (pp. 370–379). Cambridge, MA: Harvard University Press.

Giddens, A. (1979). *Central Problems in Social Theory: Action, Structure and Contradiction in Social Analysis*. Cambridge: Cambridge University Press.

Goodall, J. (1963). Feeding behavior of wild chimpanzees: A preliminary report. In *The Primates: Proceedings of the Symposium Held on 12th–14th April 1962*. Zoological Society of London *Symposia, 10*, 39–47.

Goodall, J. (1965). Chimpanzees of the Gombe Stream Reserve. In I. DeVore (Ed.), *Primate Behavior: Field Studies of Monkeys and Apes* (pp. 425–473). New York: Holt, Rinehart and Winston.

Goodall, J. (1986). *The Chimpanzees of Gombe: Patterns of Behavior*. Cambridge, MA: Harvard University Press.

Gould, S. J. (2003). *The Hedgehog, the Fox, and the Magister's Pox: Mending the Gap between Science and the Humanities*. New York: Three Rivers Press.

Haraway, D. (1989). *Primate Visions: Gender, Race, and Nature in the World of Modern Science*. New York: Routledge.

Hausfater, G., & S. B. Hrdy (Eds.). (1984). *Infanticide: Comparative and Evolutionary Perspectives*. Hawthorne, NY: Aldine de Gruyter.

Hawkes, K. (1990). Why do men hunt? Some benefits for risky strategies. In E. Cashdan (Ed.), *Risk and Uncertainty in Tribal and Peasant Economies* (pp. 145–166). Boulder, CO: Westview.

Hawkes, K. (1993). Why hunter-gatherers work: An ancient version of the problem of public goods. *Current Anthropology, 34*, 341–361.

Hawkes, K., J. F. O'Connell, & N. G. Blurton Jones. (1987). Hardworking Hadza grandmothers. In V. Standen & R. Foley (Eds.), *Comparative Socioecology of Mammals and Man* (pp. 341–366). London: Blackwell.

Hawkes, K., J. F. O'Connell, & N. G. Blurton Jones. (1997). Hadza women's time allocation, offspring provisioning, and the evolution of long postmenopausal life spans. *Current Anthropology, 38*, 551–577.

Hawkes, K., J. F. O'Connell, N. G. Blurton Jones, H. Alvarez, & E. L. Charnov. (2000). The grandmother hypothesis and human evolution. In L. Cronk, N. Chagnon, & W. Irons (Eds.), *Adaptation and Human Behavior: An Anthropological Perspective* (pp. 237–258). New York: Aldine.

Hewlett, B. (1996). Cultural diversity among African Pygmies. In S. Kent (Ed.), *Cultural Diversity among Twentieth-Century Foragers: An African Perspective* (pp. 215–244). Cambridge: Cambridge University Press.

Hinde, R. A. (1987). *Individuals, Relationships and Culture*. Cambridge: Cambridge University Press.

Hinde, R. A. (Ed.). (1983). *Primate Social Relationships*. Oxford: Blackwell.

Hrdy, S. B. (1981). *The Woman That Never Evolved*. Cambridge, MA: Harvard University Press.

Hrdy, S. B. (1999). *Mother Nature: Maternal Instincts and How They Shape the Human Species*. New York: Ballantine Books.

Irons, W. (1983). Human female reproductive strategies. In S. K. Wasser (Ed.), *Social Behavior of Female Vertebrates* (pp. 169–213). New York: Academic Press.

Isaac, G. L. (1978). The food sharing behavior of protohuman hominids. *Scientific American 238*(4), 90–108.

Isaac, G. L. (1980). Casting the net wide: A review of archeological evidence for early hominid land-use and ecological relations. In L. K. Konigsson (Ed.), *Current Arguments on Early Man* (pp. 226–251). Oxford: Pergamon.

Isaac, G. L., & D. C. Crader. (1981). To what extent were early hominids carnivorous? An archaeological perspective. In R. S. Harding & G. Teleki (Eds.), *Omnivorous Primates: Gathering and Hunting in Human Evolution* (pp. 37–103). New York: Columbia University Press.

Jay, P. C. (1963). *The Ecology and Social Behavior of the Indian Langur Monkey*. PhD diss., University of Chicago.

Kano, T. (1992). *The Last Ape: Pygmy Chimpanzee Behavior and Ecology*. Palo Alto, CA: Stanford University Press.

Kaplan, H., K. Hill, J. Lancaster, & A. M. Hurtado. (2000). A theory of human life history evolution: Diet, intelligence, and longevity. *Evolutionary Anthropology, 9*, 156–185.

Kent, S. (Ed.). (1996). *Cultural Diversity among Twentieth-Century Foragers: An African Perspective*. Cambridge: Cambridge University Press.

Knauft, B. M. (1991). Violence and sociality in human evolution. *Current Anthropology, 32*, 391–428.

Kroeber, A. L. (1952). *The Nature of Culture*. Chicago: University of Chicago Press.

Kuper, A. (1994). *The Chosen Primate: Human Nature and Cultural Diversity*. Cambridge, MA: Harvard University Press.

Kyakas, A., & P. Wiessner. (1992). *From Inside the Women's House: Enga Women's Lives and Traditions*. Buranda, Australia: Robert Brown & Associates.

Lagerspetz, K. M. J., & K. Björkqvist. (1992). Indirect aggression in girls and boys. In L. R. Huesmann (Ed.), *Aggressive Behavior: Current Perspectives* (pp. 131–150). New York: Plenum.

Lee, R. B. (1968). What hunters do for a living, or, how to make out on scarce resources. In R. B. Lee & I. DeVore (Eds.), *Man the Hunter* (pp. 30–48). Cambridge, MA: Harvard University Press.

Lee, R. B. (1979). *The !Kung San: Men, Women, and Work in a Foraging Society*. Cambridge: Cambridge University Press.

Lee, R. B., & I. DeVore (Eds.). (1968). *Man the Hunter*. Chicago: Aldine.

Levinson, D., & M. J. Malone. (1980). *Toward Explaining Human Culture: A Critical Review of the Findings of Worldwide Cross-Cultural Research.* New Haven, CT: HRAF Press.

Lévi-Strauss, C. (1956). The family. In H. L. Shapiro (Ed.), *Man, Culture, and Society* (pp. 261–285). New York: Oxford University Press.

Linton, R. (1936). *The Study of Man.* New York: D. Appleton-Century.

Linton, S. (1971). Woman the gatherer: Male bias in anthropology. In S. E. Jacobs (Ed.), *Women in Perspective: A Guide for Cross-Cultural Studies* (pp. 9–21). Urbana: University of Illinois Press.

Lovejoy, C. O. (1981). The origin of man. *Science, 211,* 341–350.

Malenky, R. K., S. Kuroda, E. O. Vineberg, & R. W. Wrangham. (1994). The significance of terrestrial herbaceous foods for Bonobos, Chimpanzees, and Gorillas. In R. W. Wrangham, W. C. McGrew, F. B. M. de Waal, & P. G. Heltne (Eds.), *Chimpanzee Cultures* (pp. 59–75). Cambridge, MA: Harvard University Press.

Malenky, R. K., & R. W. Wrangham. (1994). A quantitative comparison of terrestrial herbaceous food consumption by *Pan paniscus* in the Lomako Forest, Zaïre, and *Pan troglodytes* in the Kibale Forest, Uganda. *American Journal of Primatology, 32,* 1–12.

Malinowski, B. (1922). *Argonauts of the Western Pacific.* New York: Dutton.

Manson, J. H., & R. W. Wrangham. (1991). Intergroup aggression in chimpanzees and humans. *Current Anthropology, 32,* 369–390.

Marlowe, F. W. (2004). Marital residence among foragers. *Current Anthropology, 45,* 277–284.

Marshall, L. (1976). *The !Kung of Nyae Nyae.* Cambridge, MA: Harvard University Press.

Maryanski, A. R. (1987). African ape social structure: Is there strength in weak ties? *Social Networks, 9,* 191–215.

Maryanski, A. R. (1992). The last ancestor: An ecological network model on the origins of human sociality. *Advances in Human Ecology, 1,* 1–32.

Maryanski, A. R. (1996). African ape social networks: A blueprint for reconstructing early hominid social structure. In J. Steele & S. Shennan (Eds.), *The Archaeology of Human Ancestry: Power, Sex and Tradition* (pp. 67–90). London: Routledge.

Mesnick, S. L. (1997). Sexual alliances: Evidence and evolutionary implications. In P. A. Gowaty (Ed.), *Feminism and Evolutionary Biology: Boundaries, Intersections, and Frontiers* (pp. 207–260). New York: International Thomson.

Morris, D. (1967). *The Naked Ape.* New York: Dell.

Murdock, G. P. (1949). *Social Structure.* New York: Free Press.

Murdock, G. P. (1967). *Ethnographic Atlas.* Pittsburgh: University of Pittsburgh Press.

Murdock, G. P. (1968). The current status of the world's hunting and gathering peoples. In R. B. Lee & I. DeVore (Eds.), *Man the Hunter* (pp. 13–20). Cambridge, MA: Harvard University Press.

O'Connell, J. F., K. Hawkes, & N. G. Blurton Jones. (1999). Grandmothering and the evolution of *Homo erectus*. *Journal of Human Evolution, 36*, 461–485.

Paul, R. A. (1987). The individual and society in biological and cultural anthropology. *Cultural Anthropology, 2*, 80–93.

Pusey, A. E. (2001). Of genes and apes: Chimpanzee social organization and reproduction. In F. de Waal (Ed.), *Tree of Origin: What Primate Behavior Can Tell Us about Human Social Evolution*. Cambridge, MA: Harvard University Press.

Radcliffe-Brown, A. R. (1930). The social organization of Australian tribes. Part I. *Oceania, 1*, 34–63.

Radcliffe-Brown, A. R. (1931). The social organization of Australian tribes. Part III. *Oceania, 1*, 426–456.

Ribnick, R. (1982). A short history of primate field studies: Old World monkeys and apes. In F. Spencer (Ed.), *A History of American Physical Anthropology 1930–1980* (pp. 49–73). New York: Academic Press.

Rodman, P., & J. Mitani. (1987). Orangutans: Sexual dimorphism in a solitary species. In B. B. Smuts, D. L. Cheney, R. M. Seyfarth, R. W. Wrangham, & T. T. Struhsaker (Eds.), *Primate Societies* (pp. 146–154). Chicago: University of Chicago Press.

Rodseth, L., & S. A. Novak. (2000). The social modes of men: Toward an ecological model of human male relationships. *Human Nature, 11*, 335–366.

Rodseth, L., & R. W. Wrangham. (2004). Human kinship: A continuation of politics by other means? In B. Chapais & C. M. Berman (Eds.), *Kinship and Behavior in Primates*. New York: Oxford University Press.

Rodseth, L., R. W. Wrangham, A. M. Harrigan, & B. B. Smuts. (1991). The human community as a primate society. *Current Anthropology, 32*(3), 221–254.

Rutberg, A. T. (1983). The evolution of monogamy in primates. *Journal of Theoretical Biology, 104*, 93–112.

Sahlins, M. D. (1959). The social life of monkeys, apes and primitive men. In M. H. Fried (Ed.), *Readings in Anthropology*, vol. 2 (pp. 186–199). New York: Crowell.

Sahlins, M. D. (1981). *Historical Metaphors and Mythical Realities*. Ann Arbor: University of Michigan Press.

Sahlins, M. D. (1999). Two or three things that I know about culture. *Journal of the Royal Anthropological Institute* (n.s.), 5, 399–421.

Sakura, O. (1994). Factors affecting party size and composition of *chimpanzees (Pan troglodytes verus)* at Bossou, Guinea. *International Journal of Primatology, 15*, 167–183.

Schaik, C. P. van. (1989). The ecology of social relationships amongst female primates. In V. Standen & G. R. A. Foley (Eds.), *Comparative Socioecology, the Behavioral Ecology of Humans and Other Mammals* (pp. 195–218). Oxford: Blackwell Scientific.

Schaik, C. P. van. (1996). Social evolution in primates: The role of ecological factors and male behaviour. *Proceedings of the British Academy,*
88, 9–31.

Schaik, C. P. van, & R. I. M. Dunbar. (1990). The evolution of monogamy
in large primates: A new hypothesis and some crucial tests. *Behaviour,*
115, 30–62.

Schaik, C. P. van, & J. A. R. A. M. van Hooff. (1983). On the ultimate
causes of primate social systems. *Behaviour, 85,* 91–117.

Schaik, C. P. van, & J. A. R. A. M. van Hooff. (1996). Toward an understanding of the orangutan's social system. In W. C. McGrew, L. F.
Marchant, & T. Nishida (Eds.), *Great Ape Societies* (pp. 3–15). Cambridge: Cambridge University Press.

Schuster, I., & I. DeVore. (1983). Women's aggression: An African case
study. *Aggressive Behavior, 9,* 319–331.

Schuster, I., & Hartz-Karp, J. (1986). Kinder, kueche, kibbutz: Women's
aggression and status quo maintenance in a small scale community.
Anthropological Quarterly, 59, 191–199.

Service, E. R. (1962). *Primitive Social Organization: An Evolutionary Perspective.* New York: Random House.

Smuts, B. B. (1992). Male aggression against women: An evolutionary perspective. *Human Nature, 3,* 1–44.

Smuts, B. B. (1995). The evolutionary origins of patriarchy. *Human Nature, 6,* 1–32.

Stanford, C. B. (1999). *The Hunting Apes: Meat Eating and the Origins of
Human Behavior.* Princeton, NJ: Princeton University Press.

Sterck, E. H. M., D. P. Watts, & C. P. van Schaik. (1997). The evolution of
female social relationships in nonhuman primates. *Behavioural Ecology
and Sociobiology, 41,* 291–309.

Steward, J. H. (1936). The economic and social basis of primitive bands.
In R. H. Lowie (Ed.), *Essays on Anthropology in Honor of Alfred Louis
Kroeber* (pp. 311–350). Berkeley: University of California Press.

Steward, J. H. (1955). *Theory of Culture Change: The Methodology of Mul-
tilinear Evolution.* Urbana: University of Illinois Press.

Stocking, G. W., Jr. (1987). *Victorian Anthropology.* New York: Free Press.

Strier, K. B. (1999). Why is female kin bonding so rare? Comparative sociality of neotropical primates. In P. C. Lee (Ed.), *Comparative Primate Socioecology* (pp. 300–319). Cambridge: Cambridge University
Press.

Sugiyama, Y. (1988). Grooming interactions among adult chimpanzees at
Bossou, Guinea, with special reference to social structure. *International Journal of Primatology, 9,* 393–407.

Tanner, N. M., & A. L. Zihlman. (1976). Women in evolution, part I: Innovation and selection in human origins. *Signs, 1,* 585–608.

Tiger, L., & R. Fox. (1971). *The Imperial Animal.* New York: Dell.

Turnbull, C. M. (1968). The importance of flux in two hunting societies.
In R. B. Lee & I. DeVore (Eds.), *Man the Hunter* (pp. 132–137). Cambridge, MA: Harvard University Press.

de Waal, F. (1997). *Bonobo: The Forgotten Ape*. Berkeley: University of California Press.

Washburn, S. L., & V. Avis. (1958). Evolution of human behavior. In A. Roe & G. G. Simpson (Eds.), *Behavior and Evolution* (pp. 421–436). New Haven, CT: Yale University Press.

Washburn, S. L., & C. S. Lancaster. (1968). The evolution of hunting. In R. B. Lee & I. DeVore (Eds.), *Man the Hunter* (pp. 293–303). Cambridge, MA: Harvard University Press.

Watts, D. P. (1989). Infanticide in mountain gorillas: New cases and a reconsideration of the evidence. *Ethology, 81*, 1–18.

White, F. J. (1992). Pygmy chimpanzee social organization: Variation with party size and between study sites. *American Journal of Primatology, 26*, 203–214.

White, F. J. (1996). Comparative socio-ecology of *Pan paniscus*. In W. C. McGrew, L. F. Marchant, & T. Nishida (Eds.), *Great Ape Societies* (pp. 29–41). Cambridge: Cambridge University Press.

White, L. A. (1949). *The Science of Culture*. New York: Grove Press.

Wilson, E. O. (1998). *Consilience: The Unity of Knowledge*. New York: Vintage.

Wolf, Eric R. (1999). *Envisioning Power: Ideologies of Dominance and Crisis*. Berkeley: University of California Press.

Woodburn, J. (1968). Stability and flexibility in Hadza residential groupings. In R. B. Lee & I. DeVore (Eds.), *Man the Hunter* (pp. 103–110). Cambridge, MA: Harvard University Press.

Wrangham, R. W. (1979). On the evolution of ape social systems. *Social Science Information, 18*, 335–368.

Wrangham, R. W. (1980). An ecological model of female-bonded primate groups. *Behaviour, 75*, 262–300.

Wrangham, R. W. (1982). Mutualism, kinship, and social evolution. In King's College Sociobiology Group (Ed.), *Current Problems in Sociobiology* (pp. 269–289). Cambridge: Cambridge University Press.

Wrangham, R. W. (1987a). The significance of African apes for reconstructing human social evolution. In W. G. Kinzey (Ed.), *Primate Models of Hominid Evolution* (pp. 51–71). Albany, NY: SUNY Press.

Wrangham, R. W. (1987b). Evolution of social structure. In B. B. Smuts, D. L. Cheney, R. M. Seyfarth, R. W. Wrangham, & T. T. Struhsaker (Eds.), *Primate Societies* (pp. 282–296). Chicago: University of Chicago Press.

Wrangham, R. W. (2000). Why are male chimpanzees more gregarious than mothers? A scramble competition hypothesis. In P. M. Kappeler (Ed.), *Primate Males: Causes and Consequences of Variation in Group Composition* (pp. 248–258). Cambridge: Cambridge University Press.

Wrangham, R. W., & D. Peterson. (1996). *Demonic Males: Apes and the Origins of Human Violence*. Boston: Houghton Mifflin.

Wrangham, R. W., & B. B. Smuts. (1980). Sex differences in the behavioral ecology of chimpanzees in the Gombe National Park, Tanzania. *Journal of Reproductive Fertility Supplement, 28*, 13–31.

Wrangham, R. W., C. A. Chapman, A. P. Clark-Arcadi, & G. Isabirye Ba-
suta. (1996). Social ecology of Kanyawara chimpanzees: Implications
for understanding the costs of great ape groups. In W. C. McGrew,
L. F. Marchant, & T. Nishida (Eds.), *Great Ape Societies* (pp. 45–57).
Cambridge: Cambridge University Press.

Wrangham, R. W., A. P. Clark, & G. Isabirye-Basuta. (1992). Female social
relationships and social organization of Kibale Forest chimpanzees. In
T. Nishida, W. C. McGrew, P. Marler, M. Pickford, & F. B. M. de Waal
(Eds.), *Topics in Primatology, Vol. 1: Human Origins* (pp. 81–98).
Tokyo: University of Tokyo Press.

Wrangham, R. W., J. H. Jones, G. Laden, D. Pilbeam, & N. Conklin-Brit-
tain. (1999). The raw and the stolen: Cooking and the ecology of
human origins. *Current Anthropology, 40,* 567–594.

Zihlman, A. L. (1978). Women in evolution, part II: Subsistence and social organization among early hominids. *Signs, 4,* 4–20.

PART IV

Sociology and Criminology

Walsh is one of those bringing the evolution revolution to criminology (see Ellis & Walsh, 2000). His chapter will be seen by some as the most controversial in this volume, for he forthrightly argues that criminal behavior, like all human behavior, is rooted in our evolutionary history and psychology and not simply a production of environment acting on clay. Our very dependence on reciprocity and fairness—reciprocal altruism—makes inevitable strategies for cheating and therefore counterstrategies to guard against being cheated, and our social emotions are involved in both sets of strategies. Our capacity for rage, jealousy, intimidation, violence and the threat of violence, and much other behavior of extreme moral reprehensibility evolved because, in some times and places, they were tactics that furthered the ends of adaptation. This does not make them acceptable today: neither in the court of law nor (one hopes) the court of public opinion does pleading Darwin constitute a legitimate defense. Sibling rivalry is no doubt an evolved behavioral tendency reflecting competition over limited parental resources (Trivers, 1974), but any parent who fails to discourage it needs a visit from the Children's Aid Society. Darwin does not exonerate (as was discussed in the Introduction). Walsh takes pains to make clear that he is not excusing crime but demystifying it the better to control and limit it. Of course, he gives the environment pride-of-place, as all good Darwinians must. Biological theories that slight environment are as incomplete as environmental theories that ignore our biology.

"Today, the evolutionary study of human culture is a divided field," writes sociologist Bernd Baldus. Divided it certainly is but unified as well, for the numerous competing approaches overlap sufficiently to permit at least the hope and perhaps the expectation of eventual synthesis. Baldus begins with the ideas of the late Donald T. Campbell, who argued that a blind-variation/selective-retention model underlies evolution (and many other processes). We have a source of variants, and selection among them is blind to their eventual impact on adaptation. While genetic mutation is one source of variants, for Baldus our minds are another. Baldus posits a process of internal selection of these (wide-ranging) variants, a process which he terms "lived adaptation" and which he equates with *agency*. The latter is a familiar concept in the social sciences and is usually contrasted with *structure*. Where structure connotes determinism, agency connotes the role of undetermined human volition and implies contingency. Evolutionary psychologists, using a different framework and discourse, generally see decision making as the outcome of complex processes involving the interplay of evolved mechanisms and the use of surprisingly simple decision rules, a "bounded rationality" (see Gigerenzer & Selten, 2003). Baldus uses "agency" as a way to underscore contingency and "internal selection" by "mind" as a source of variation rivaling that of mutation, an emphasis he ascribes to Charles Darwin![1] An evolutionist might translate Baldus's position as being nothing but a focus on behavioral plasticity, in which case it is uncontroversial. After all, the argument that behavioral plasticity within a given environment plays an important role in natural selection can be traced back to Baldwin (1896) and is known as the "Baldwin effect." Baldus's arguments also appear to overlap with much more recent work, especially that of the evolutionary psychologist/social scientist Satoshi Kanazawa, whose thesis is that our "general intelligence" is a specialized module for dealing with novelty and creativity (Kanazawa, 2004). Baldus sees his novelty-generating mechanism as somehow less controlled by genes, less bound by algorithms than the various other mechanisms proposed by evolutionary psychologists, though he accepts that both his novelty-generator and the more standard evolved mechanisms (modules) of evolutionary psychology are equally products of biological evolution. It is doubtful that there are evolutionary psychologists who would disagree with his conclusion that "an evolutionary sociology is therefore a probabilistic, non-deterministic science." Baldus and evolutionary psychologists would also agree that some things are much more probable than are others (e.g., gossip and language used as social grooming, as opposed to widespread vows of silence).

In an ideal world, Baldus's view of a Darwinian sociology and the behavioral ecology described by Cronk (this volume) would be combined and reconciled. Cronk emphasizes adaptation to environment and Baldus contingency: reconciliation would probably be along the lines of Baldus's Campbellian blind variants meeting Campbellian retention criteria set by the environment. But the purpose of this collection is not to resolve disputes but to invite engagement, and Baldus is a sociologist who is clearly engaged with Darwinian thought. In particular, his addition of agency to the set of concepts evolutionists must consider is a valuable contribution. Social scientists should think of evolutionary psychologists as seeking to unpack the black box of "agency" (and the related concept from which it apparently derives, "free will").

Note

1. Baldus's position in part can be situated in the long-lasting, ongoing debate among evolutionists about contingency. Contingency was a major theme of the late Stephen Jay Gould (1989), for example, a stance heavily criticized by the more mainstream evolutionary thinking of Simon Conway Morris (1998).

References

Baldwin, J. M. (1896). A new factor in evolution. *American Naturalist, 30,* 441–451.

Ellis, L., & Walsh, A. (2000). *Criminology: A Global Perspective.* New York: Allyn & Bacon.

Gigerenzer, G., & Selten, R. (Eds.). (2003). *Bounded Rationality: The Adaptive Toolbox.* Cambridge, MA: MIT Press.

Gould, S. J. (1989). *Wonderful Life: The Burgess Shale and the Nature of History.* New York: W. W. Norton.

Kanazawa, S. (2004). General intelligence as a domain-specific adaptation. *Psychological Review, 111*(2), 512–523.

Morris, S. C. (1998). *The Crucible of Creation: The Burgess Shale and the Rise of Animals.* New York: Oxford University Press.

Trivers, R. L. (1974). Parent-offspring conflict. *American Zoologist, 14,* 249–264.

8 Evolutionary Psychology and Criminal Behavior

Anthony Walsh

Introduction

In 1977, renowned criminologist C. Ray Jeffery wrote that criminology should have dropped the major sociological theories of crime "twenty years ago" (now 40-plus years ago) in favor of more biologically informed theories if it hoped to remain a viable discipline (1977, p. 284). Given the remarkable advances in the biological sciences made during the latter half of the twentieth century, it was clear even then that Jeffery had a point. I want to make the same point in modified fashion. I modify it because although recent biosocial studies provide considerable support for the role of biological factors in antisocial behavior, they also continue to provide strong support for the role of the environment (Lyons et al., 1995; Kendler, 1995; O'Connor et al., 1998; Plomin, 1995; Walsh, 2002).

Sociological theories of crime should be considered incomplete rather than incorrect, and rather than dropping theories I believe still have something to offer, I suggest that they can be improved and extended by integrating relevant biosocial concepts. I hope to convince the reader that what has been called *vertical integration* (conceptual consistency across the social/behavioral and natural sciences [Barkow, 1989; Cosmides, Tooby, & Barkow, 1992; Wilson, 1998]) is vital for the furtherance of criminological theory. Because this essay is addressed to fellow criminologists and other social scientists, I feel that an understanding of the importance of vertical integration in criminological theory will be best achieved by not straying too far afield. I thus organize my discussion around traditional criminology issues, beginning with a discussion of the basic questions of rule-making and rule-breaking from the perspective of evolutionary psychology. I then look at specific types of crimes from this perspective, followed by a discussion of evolutionary theories of criminal behavior.

Sociology, criminology's parent discipline, has long suffered from "biophobia," an affliction that some fear could lead to its demise as a respectable scientific discipline (Ellis, 1977, 1996; Rossi, 1984; Udry, 1995; Van den Berghe, 1990; Walsh, 1995a, 2002). Sociologists still cling to the slogan provided by Emile Durkheim: "The determining cause of a social fact should be sought among the social facts preceding it" (1982, p. 134). Although Durkheim probably meant this to be a boundary axiom defining the purview of sociology, sociologists came to think of it as "a true statement about the nature of the world instead of a set of deliberate blinders to help them to focus their attention" (Udry, 1995, p. 1267). Since Durkheim, most sociologists have come to consider nonsocial causes of human behavior as inconsequential. Sociology has not been content to simply cultivate its own garden; it has gone out of its way to attack and discredit explanations of human conduct proffered by other disciplines, particularly by biology (Degler, 1991; Wright & Miller, 1998).[1]

Sociologists may well inquire why they should be concerned with other levels of analysis. After all, their domain of interest lies in examining the causes of human behavior rooted in the organization and functioning of social groups, not in individual factors. They may correctly note that when people come together in groups they often behave differently from when they are alone, creating a sui generis reality. While it is true that the whole is greater than the sum of its parts, what we theorize about emergent properties of the whole must be consistent with what is known about the parts, which invariably help us to better understand the whole. Lower-level explanations of human behavior often absorb the explanatory efficiency of broad social categorizations such as race, gender, age, and class, and add incremental validity to them (see Lubinski & Humphries [1997] and Walsh [1997] for a number of illustrations of this).

Criminology is perhaps the subdiscipline of sociology that has been most hostile to biology. Each new criminology textbook reminds us how wrong Lombroso was, the absurdity of phrenology, and other such early attempts to "biologize" criminology. The discussion of "biological criminology" usually ends there because authors of these books seriously misunderstand what modern biocriminology is all about (Wright & Miller, 1998). The results of a recent survey showed that few criminologists have taken any biology beyond a required introductory course, and sociopolitical ideology largely determines their allegiance to a particular theory (Walsh & Ellis, 1999). Few appear to realize that biology has advanced light-years from the time when Gall was feeling cranial bumps, and today's biology cannot be countered with ad hominem arguments and straw men. As Sandra Scarr has pointed out, the only way for behavioral scientists to allay their fears of biology and its place in social science is to learn some (1993, p. 1350).

The Importance of the Environment in Biosocial Approaches to Criminal Behavior

I assure my more traditional criminological colleagues of two very important things: (1) that they have nothing to fear from the incorporation of biological factors into criminology, and (2) that biosocial approaches take environmental factors very seriously, and even tell us things about those factors that we would not otherwise be aware of.

There is one mistaken notion that I must discuss—the mistake of conflating the distinction between the terms "biological" and "genetic." Biological variability in such things as hormonal levels is probably just as likely to be accounted for by environmental factors as by genetic factors. Evolutionary approaches are fundamentally environmental in that they describe how environments, through natural selection, have shaped the behavior of organisms as they strategically adapt to their environments, and how environmental inputs are needed for the emergence of behavior (Cartwright, 2000). Similarly, behavior geneticists realize that genetic influences on behavior cannot be understood without understanding the complementary influence of the environment (Plomin, 1995), neuroscientists recognize that many neural connections develop epigenetically according to experience (Smith, 1993), and endocrinologists are aware that psychosocial phenomenon are powerful sources of hormonal activation (Hrdy, 1999). We hope that traditional criminologists will eventually become as open to the role of biological factors in explaining behavior as biologists are to the role of the environment.

There is no single biosocial approach to the study of human behavior any more than there is a single environmental approach. David Buss (1990) identifies three general biosocial approaches to the study of human behavior: evolutionary, behavior genetic, and physiological. Although they employ different theories and methods, work with different units of analysis, and invoke different levels of causation, they are not the contradictory stew we find when we survey the plethora of strictly environmental theories in sociology. Besides having in common the tremendous potential to illuminate human nature, biosocial approaches are vertically integrated; i.e., their principles are conceptually consistent across all three levels of analysis. Although I concentrate on evolutionary psychology, all biosocial approaches are so "environment-friendly" that I am tempted to call them "biologically-informed environmental approaches." Evolutionary psychology will not (and cannot) cannibalize the social sciences. We will always need the social sciences, Barkow (1992, p. 635) assures us, but he also reminds us that "psychology underlies culture and society, and biological evolution underlies psychology." That is all I am asking criminologists to accept.

The Evolution of Antisocial and Criminal Behavior

Few social scientists balk at the notion that human anatomy and physiology are products of evolution. We observe some aspect of complex morphology and infer that it was selected over alternate designs because it best served some particular function that proved useful in assisting the proliferation of its owners' genes. Although there is no other scientifically viable explanation for the origin of *basic* behavioral design, most social scientists probably dismiss the idea of human behavioral patterns as products of the same natural process. If we accept the notion that evolution shaped our minds and our behavior, we have to accept that many of our less admirable traits such as deception, cheating, and violence owe their present existence to the fact that they were useful to the reproductive success (the total number of an organism's descendants, and thus its genes) of our distant ancestors, as were more positive traits such as altruism, nurturance, and love.

We do not, of course, display evolved patterns of behavior in order to maximize genetic fitness: "Evolutionary psychology is not a theory of motivation. . . . Fitness consequences are invoked not as goals in themselves, but rather to explain why certain goals have come to control behavior at all, and why they are calibrated in one particular way rather than another" (Daly & Wilson, 1988a, p. 7). Parents nurture and love their children, for example, not because a subconscious genetic voice tells them that if they do they will have greater genetic representation in future generations. They do so because ancestral parents who loved and nurtured their children saw more of them grow to reproductive age and pass on those traits. Parents who did not love and nurture their children compromised the viability of their offspring, and thus the probability of pushing their genes into the future.

Cooperation Creates a Niche for Cheating

How can criminal behavior, including such heterogeneous acts as murder, theft, rape, and assault, be conceived of as an evolved adaptation when it is clearly maladaptive in modern environments? First, because a behavior is currently maladaptive does not mean that mechanisms underlying it are not evolved adaptations (designed by natural selection to solve some environmental problem). Our modern environments are so different in many respects from the environments our species evolved in that traits and behaviors selected for their adaptive value then may not be adaptive at all today. Conversely, traits and behaviors that appear to be adaptive today may not have a history of natural selection (Barkow, 1984; Daly, 1996; Mealey, 1995). An adaptation is a current feature with a past; a feature that is currently adaptive may or may not have a future. Second, the specifics of criminal behavior (or of any other social behavior for that matter) are not themselves adaptations: "Genes do not code themselves for jimmying a lock or stealing a car. . . . The genome does not waste precious DNA encoding the specifics" (Rowe, 1996, p. 285).

Criminal behavior of any kind is behavior that exploits and deceives others in a variety of ways for selfish ends. Deception and selfishness can clearly be seen to provide advantages in the form of reproductive success across a wide variety of animal species (Alcock, 1998; Ellis, 1998; Ellis & Walsh, 1997). It is this general tendency to seek one's own interests, sometimes at the expense of others, that is the adaptation, not any specific behavior. Although people differ in their readiness to exploit and deceive, under the right conditions we all probably will. Most evolutionary psychologists view criminal behavior (cheating) as a "conditional" strategy, the preparedness for which is ubiquitous in the human species (Figueredo, 1995; Lykken, 1995).

Most of us rarely seek to blatantly exploit and deceive others in criminal ways. *Homo sapiens* is a highly social and cooperative species. As Allman (1994, p. 147) puts it: "If evolutionary psychology predicts anything 'innate' about people it is that their minds are exquisitely crafted by evolution to form cooperative relationships built on trust and kindness." It is the case in all social species that much more can be accomplished for the well-being and survival of their members if all follow the norm of cooperation rather than any alternative. However, it is commonly accepted that individual organisms do not behave "for the good of the group," although it may often appear as if they do (but see Wilson & Sober [1994] for a defense of the group selection hypothesis). Individuals have been adapted to strive to maximize their own fitness (or, perhaps more correctly, to execute adaptations), and happily this can most often be best achieved by adhering to the rules of cooperation and altruism—by "being nice."

Cooperative and altruistic behavior is observed in all social species, but unless directed at close genetic kin, it tends to be contingent on reciprocal behavior on the part of the recipient (Machalek, 1996). Altruism can thus be viewed as behavior ultimately designed to serve the purposes of the altruist; it is discriminative and tends to cease when the individuals to whom it is directed do not reciprocate. Again, this does not imply a whispering gene urging us to be nice in order to maximize our fitness. We cooperate and act altruistically (and tend to feel good when we do) because our distant ancestors who behaved this way enjoyed greater reproductive success than those who did not, thus passing on the genes for the brain structures and neurotransmitters that presumably underlie the trait (Barkow, 1997).

Social living is characterized by conflict; i.e., by competition over scarce resources such as food, status, and mates, as well as by cooperation and reciprocal altruism. Because both cooperation and conflict occur among groups of reciprocal altruists (genetically unrelated individuals who give with the expectation of receiving the equivalent in return), it creates an obvious niche for cheats (Alexander, 1987; Mealey, 1995; Trivers, 1991). Cheats are individuals in a population of cooperators who signal their own cooperation but then fail to reciprocate after receiving benefits from others. If there are no deterrents against cheating, it is in an individual's fitness interests to obtain resources and assistance from others under the assumption of reciprocity and then to default, thus gaining resources at zero cost. Biologists have studied such behavior (termed "social parasitism") among a variety of non-human animal species (Alcock, 1998; Wilson, 1975), and its ubiquity implies that it has had positive fitness consequences (Machalek, 1996). Antisocial and criminal behavior may be viewed as extreme forms of cheating, or defaulting on the rules of reciprocity in the human species (Lykken, 1995; Machalek & Cohen, 1991). But cheating behavior comes at the cost of the likely refusal of others to assist the cheater in the future. Thus, before deciding to default, the individual must weigh the costs and benefits of cooperating versus defaulting. This has been nicely illustrated in the famous Prisoners' Dilemma game outlined below.

Suppose two criminal accomplices—Bill and Frank—are being held in jail for an alleged crime. They have both sworn that each would never "rat" on the other. The evidence against both is weak, prompting the prosecutor to approach each man separately and offer him a deal. If Bill testifies against Frank, Bill will be released and Frank will get 10 years, and vice versa. If both testify, both will be convicted and receive a reduced 5-year sentence because of their cooperation with the prosecutor. If neither testifies—that is, if they cooperate with each other as they had sworn to do—both will be convicted of a minor crime carrying a sentence of only 1 year in prison. The dilemma is that Bill and Frank are being held in separate cells so that they cannot communicate with one another and cement their agreement not to default on their promise. Under these circumstances, Bill's best strategy is to testify regardless of what Frank does because it will either get him released (if Frank does not testify) or 5 years (if he does). Both outcomes are better than the 10 years he will receive if he remains true to his promise but Frank does not. The same holds true for Frank. Knowing that "honor among thieves" is a fallacy, each testifies against the other and receives a sentence of 5 years. The paradox is that although the payoff for cheating when the other actor does not is high, if both cheat they are both worse off than if they had cooperated with one another.

The Prisoners' Dilemma, while illustrating that mutual cooperation produces the best payoff, also illustrates how "rational" it is to cheat in circumstances of limited interaction and communication. With frequent interaction and communication, which is the normal situation for social species, cheating becomes a far less rational strategy. Cheats can prosper only in a population of "suckers" (unconditional altruists). Suckers would soon be driven to extinction by cheats, leaving only cheats to interact with other cheats. A population of pure cheats is not likely to thrive either, and selection for cooperation is likely to occur rapidly (Machalek, 1996). "Pure" suckers and "pure" cheats" are thus unlikely to exist in large numbers, if at all, in any social species. The vast majority of human beings are "grudgers" who can be suckered now and again because they abide by the norms of mutual trust and cooperation, but they will not offer resources in the future to those who sucker them (Raine, 1993). In the real world, cheaters interact with populations of "grudgers" in a repeated game of Prisoners' Dilemma in which players adjust their strategies according to their experience with other players in the past, and each player reaps in the future what he or she has sown in the past (Machalek, 1996).

How do cheats manage to continue to follow their strategy given how grudgers respond to them when they are unmasked? In computer simulations of interactions between populations of cheats, suckers, and grudgers, cheats are always driven to extinction, as evolutionary theory would predict (Raine, 1993; Allman, 1994). The problem with such simulations is that players are constrained to operate within the same environment in which their reputations quickly become known. In the real world, cheats can move from location to location meeting and cheating a series of grudgers who are susceptible to one-time deception. This is exactly what we observe among the more psychopathic criminals. They move from place to place, job to job, and relationship to relationship, leaving a trail of misery behind them before their reputation catches up to them (Hare, 1993; Lykken, 1995). In modern societies, cheats are much more likely to prosper in large cities than in small traditional communities, where the threat of exposure and retaliation is great (Ellis & Walsh, 1997; Machalek & Cohen, 1991; Mealey, 1995).

In common with Emile Durkheim (1982), evolutionary psychologists view crime as normal, albeit regrettable behavior engaged in by normal individuals engaged in normal social processes (Cohen & Machalek, 1994). If criminal behavior is in fact normal, it follows that the potential for it must be in us all and that it must have conferred some evolutionary advantage on our distant ancestors. Thus, there is nothing in evolutionary psychology that posits that criminals possess a defective genome, or that they represent some sort of evolutionary atavism à la Cesare Lombroso. The universality, and hence the normalcy, of the antisocial impulse may be gauged by noting that when the carrying capacity of the cheater niche grows, more and more individuals will adopt the cheater strategy. The 300% increase in crime noted in Hungary after the demise of communism (Gonczol, 1993), as well as roughly similar figures reported in Russia (Dashkov, 1992), reflect social, political, and economic phenomena that provide an expanded niche for exploitation. The momentous change from a state-controlled economy to a market economy experienced to varying degrees in these nations resulted in anomic social deregulation. Social deregulation may serve as a "releaser" of criminal behavior at various levels as it interacts with varying individual thresholds for antisocial behavior. Individuals at the bottom of the social status heap who perceive themselves as unable to secure resources legitimately may thus view criminal behavior as an adaptive response to their predicament. As Wright (1994, p. 244) points out, this is the sort of environmentalism supported by most sociologists, not the genetic determinism that evolutionary psychology is so often falsely accused of supporting.

The Social Emotions and Detecting Cheats

In order to be successful grudgers in enduring reciprocal relationships, mechanisms for detecting cheats had to evolve. The mechanisms posited by a number of theorists (Griffiths, 1990; Mealey, 1995; Nesse, 1990) are the social emotions (so called because they partly depend on socialization for their existence, as opposed to the primary emotions, such as fear and anger). Emotions are involuntary and invasive "limbic system overrides" shaped by natural selection that serve to adjust our behavior in social situations (Barkow, 1989, p. 121). Mutual cooperation evokes a deepened sense of friendship, a sense of pride, and a heightened sense of obligation and gratitude that enhances future cooperation. Mutual cheats feel rejected and angry, and when one party cooperates and the other cheats, the cooperator feels angry and betrayed, and the cheater feels anxiety and guilt (Nesse, 1990). Because we find the emotions accompanying mutual cooperation rewarding and those accompanying defection punishing, the more intensely we feel the emotions the less likely we are to cheat. Conversely, the less we feel them the more likely we are to prefer the immediate fruits of cheating over concerns of reputation and its effects on future interactions. Emotions keep our temptations in check, then, by "overriding" rational calculations of immediate gain.

Emotions have evolved as integral parts of our social intelligence that serve to provide clues about the kinds of relationships (cooperative vs. uncooperative) that we are likely to have with others. Perhaps because we experience them, we are able to detect them in others. Body language, facial expressions, the "way" things are said, all provide a basis for judging the re-liability and intentions of others. The social emotions "cause positive and negative feelings that act as reinforcers or punishers, molding our behavior in a way that is not economically rational for the short term but profitable and adaptive in situations where encounters are frequent and reputation is important" (Mealey, 1995, p. 525).

A number of theorists have viewed the tension between grudgers (rec-iprocal altruists) and cheats as having provided the basis for the human sense of justice (Beckstrom, 1993; Walsh, 2000a; Walsh & Hemmens, 2000; Wilson, 1998). Victims of cheaters feel angry and hurt due to being treated unfairly, and confusion and frustration due to losing the expectation of pre-dictability ("I scratched your back, but you didn't scratch mine!"). These evolved emotions amount to what some people might call "moral outrage," without which there would be no motivation to react against those who vi-olate the norms of reciprocity and we might all have become conscienceless psychopaths (Daly & Wilson, 1988a). Negative feelings like these are as-suaged by punishing violators because punishment signals the restoration of fairness and predictability (cheaters may be less likely to cheat in the future, and potential cheaters will be deterred). Nonhuman animal studies have shown that dominant animals (and sometimes coalitions of nondominant animals) punish the behavior of conspecifics ("retaliatory aggression") that reduce their fitness by cheating, stealing, or parasiting (reviewed in Clutton-Brock & Parker, 1995).

It has even been suggested that cheating has been essential to the evolution of reciprocal altruism (a mechanism so central to a social life dominated by interacting nonrelated individuals) precisely because it has strengthened the social emotions that demand justice and punishment. By helping to extinguish the negative emotions associated with victimization, punishment reinforces our sense of the justness of moral norms (Boyd & Richerson, 1992; Machalek, 1996; Machalek & Cohen, 1991; Walsh, 2000a). Criminologists will recognize the affinity of this line of thinking with Durkheim's thoughts on the normality of crime and the function of pun-ishment in maintaining social norms.

Violent Crime and Status

A range of violent acts, including infanticide, siblicide, lethal male fights, forced copulation, xenophobia, and rudimentary warfare, has been docu-mented for a wide range of nonhuman species from insects to chimpanzees (Alcock, 1998; Pater, 1990; Wrangham & Peterson, 1996). The ubiquity of such acts across species, and across human cultures and historical periods, strongly implies that such violent behaviors have served important evolu-tionary purposes.

It is a central tenet of evolutionary theory that the human brain evolved in the context of overwhelming concerns for resource and mate acquisition. When food, territory, and mates are plentiful, pursuing them violently is an unnecessary waste of energy involving the risk of serious injury or death. When resources become scarce, however, acquiring them any way one can may become worth the risk (Barkow, 1989). Among our ancestral males, those who were most successful in acquiring resources gained rank and status and, thereby, access to a disproportionate number of females. As Daly and Wilson (1988a, p. 132) have remarked: "*Homo sapiens* is very clearly a creature for whom differential social status has consistently been associated with variations in reproductive success." Today status is not necessarily associated with aggression and violence (typically, quite the opposite today in most modern societies), but it almost certainly was more so in our ancestral environments (Chagnon, 1996; Wrangham & Peterson, 1998). As the species moved from a nomadic lifestyle to civilization, it was typically the most successful warriors that became a nation's aristocracy (Baumeister, Smart, & Boden, 1996). Because females prefer males with rank and status, genes inclining males to aggressively pursue their interests (which sometimes meant becoming violent) enjoyed greater representation in subsequent generations. From the evolutionary point of view, violence is something human males (as well as males in numerous other species) are designed by nature to do. Wherever we look in the world, males are far more likely than females to be both the victims and the perpetrators of all kinds of violent acts (Badcock, 2000; Barak, 1998; Campbell, 1999).

Homicide and Assault

Gratuitous violence within the in-group was probably rare in hominid ancestral environments. Natural selection has not favored violent competition for access to females as a dominant strategy in long-lived species. Males in long-lived species have time to move up status hierarchies and acquire mates relatively peacefully rather than risk their lives in desperate mating battles early in their lives (Alcock, 1998). The selection for size and strength among males resulting in males who are much larger (up to 100% or more in some species) reflects a polygynous mating history in which dominance is established by physical battles among males.

Early hominids (*Australopithecus anemensis* and *afarensis*) were also 50% to 100% larger than females (Geary, 2000). The low degree of sexual dimorphism among modern *Homo sapiens* (males are only about 10% larger than females, on average) indicates an evolutionary shift from violent male competition for mates to a more monogamous mating system and an increase in paternal investment (Plavcan & van Schaik, 1997). However, there is evidence in the archeological literature indicating that homicide was much more common in evolutionary environments than it is today (Edgerton, 1992). In cultures where polygyny and low paternal investment still exist, we find homicide rates greatly exceeding those of any modern society. The Agta have a rate of 326 per 100,000, and the Yanomamo one of 166 per 100,000 (Ellis & Walsh, 2000, p. 71). Chagnon (1996) also presents data showing that homicide rates in many of today's pre-state societies are many times greater than in any modern industrial society. Indeed, because the Yanomamo practice polygyny, homicide translates directly into reproductive success; males who have killed the most in intervillage warfare (and are thus the most respected) have about three times as many wives and children than those who have killed least or not at all (Chagnon, 1988).

Whatever our evolutionary history of violence may have been, any inclination to act one way or another is necessarily channeled by the brain, a modular system designed by natural selection to generate behavior appropriate to the situations we find ourselves in. It bears repeating that because the brain was designed to solve adaptive problems by evoking adaptive behavior, this does not mean that similar behavior promotes fitness in environments so vastly different from the hunter-gatherer environments in which our species evolved its most uniquely human characteristics (Tooby & Cosmides, 1990, 1992). Indeed, today extreme violence against sexual rivals or against sexual partners is likely to reduce reproductive success by resulting in long prison sentences for perpetrators (Kanazawa & Still, 2000).

Because high status has contributed to human reproductive success, and because a capacity for controlled aggression has contributed to attaining it, selection for aggression, which sometimes means violent aggression, is an evolutionary given (Daly & Wilson, 1988a). Although killing rival suitors and rival claimants to resources and territory doubtless conferred a reproductive advantage on the killers, evolutionary psychologists do not claim that there is an evolved mechanism dedicated to homicide. Behaviors that were adaptive, however, such as male sexual propriety, jealousy, aggressive resource acquisition, and status striving, would have occasionally manifested themselves in homicide. Thus, although there are genes governing neurophysiological processes that facilitate violence, their expression is facultative. Competition between modern human males is rarely in the form of brute physical combat; rather, it is for culturally prescribed ways of achieving power, wealth, esteem, and status, the acquisition of which draws females to the most successful competitors (Barkow, 1989). Within human and nonhuman primate groups with established dominance hierarchies, social rules restrain the emergence of widespread violent conflict (Bernard, 1990; Raleigh et al., 1991).

Violent confrontations among humans over issues ultimately related to reproductive success are typically observed (as many traditional criminological theories point out) in the most disadvantaged environments lacking firmly established dominance hierarchies and in which social restraints have largely dissolved. These environments have been termed "honor subcultures," in which taking matters into one's own hands is seen as the only way to obtain the all-important "juice" (respect) on the street (Mazur & Booth, 1998). In such subcultures, status is viewed as a zero-sum game in which gaining status requires taking it from somebody else (Anderson, 1999). Both official statistics and victimization survey data consistently show that violent behavior is highly concentrated among the uneducated, unmarried, unpropertied, and unemployed young males in our society who have little to lose and often much to gain from it (Barak, 1998; Walsh, 2002). These are the human analogs of the "cheater" males in other species, following their conditional cheater strategies. Assaults and homicides among this group are typically the result of seemingly trivial altercations over matters of honor, respect, and reputation in the context of a culture where the violent defense of such intangibles is a major route to status (Bernard, 1990). Such actions tell others, "You can't push *me* around!" (c.f. Fessler, this volume). Moreover, such assaults and homicides tend to take place in front of an audience composed of friends of the killer and the victim, thus squeezing the maximum amount of "juice" from the incident (Anderson, 1999; Baumeister, Smart, & Boden, 1996; Wilson & Daly, 1985).

Because status has positive fitness consequences for males, males are calibrated to seek it. Precisely how it will be pursued will depend on the cultural context. The cost-benefit ratio of violent behavior engaged in by culturally disadvantaged males for some of the most trivial reasons, while seeming to defy rational choice assumptions, is quite understandable when viewed by the light of evolutionary theory. From an evolutionary perspective, the more young males come to devalue the future, the more risks they are willing to take to obtain their share of street respect, which in turn provides them with enhanced mating opportunities. Enhancing mating opportunities is not typically their conscious motivation, of course. The male brain has been calibrated to seek respect in their social groups because respect led to increased fitness in evolutionary environments. Again, this does not mean that such behavior is necessarily adaptive in modern environments; neither does it mean that these young males are consciously thinking of reproductive success, or even of sexual opportunities. Our psychological mechanisms were crafted to solve the problems faced in quite different environments than the inner cities of the modern world.

It should be pointed out that killing related to issues of status and honor was not unique to disadvantaged males in previous times. Daly and Wilson point out that killing has been "a decided social asset in many, perhaps most, prestate societies" (1988a, p. 129). They further point out that dueling, many times over trivial matters of "honor," was ubiquitous among the aristocracy of Europe and the American South until fairly recently in history. These duels were often tied to trivial threats to self-esteem and were instrumental in enhancing the duelists' honor and reputation, thus providing a public validation of their self-worth (Baumeister, Smart, & Boden, 1996).

Experiments with a variety of nonhuman primates have shown that serotonin-based mechanisms underlie the dominance hierarchies that are of such concern among males (Zuckerman, 1990). Artificially augmenting serotonin activity in male vervet monkeys typically results in their attaining high dominance status in the troop (Raleigh et al., 1991). In drug-free naturalistic settings, the highest-ranking males in a hierarchy typically have the highest levels of serotonin (which, among other things, promotes confidence and self-esteem), and the lowest-ranking generally have the lowest levels. In established dominance hierarchies, low-ranking males typically defer without much fuss to higher-ranking males over access to females and other resources. When the hierarchy is disrupted or is in flux, which it frequently is, these same lower-level males may become the most aggressive in the competition for resources (the similarity with the various "social disorganization" models in traditional criminology is obvious here). Those rising to positions of status in the new dominance hierarchy tend to be those who most aggressively seek it, which involves, above all, successfully forming alliances with other high-status males and females (Raleigh et al., 1991; Wrangham & Peterson, 1996). Serotonin levels of newly successful males rise to levels commensurate with their new status (Brammer, Raleigh, & McGuire, 1994).

The same kinds of relationships between serotonin levels and self-esteem, status, impulsivity, and violence are consistently found among human males (Raine, 1993; Virkkunen & Linnoila, 1990; Virkkunen, Goldman, & Linnoila, 1996). As indicated above, rising to a dominant position in a hierarchy is not simply, or even primarily, a matter of individual combativeness among primates. As Raleigh and his colleagues (1991) point out, confident and ambitious individuals in primate troops form alliances, coalitions, and "gangs," just as aspiring human leaders do, to help them to achieve their aim. Given the reciprocal relationship between social status and body chemistry, it may well be that serotonergic mechanisms have been naturally selected to equip us for the social statuses we find ourselves in within well-ordered groups, and also to equip those with little to lose with the necessary mechanisms to attempt to elevate their status by taking risks when social restraints are weak (Brammer, Raleigh, & McGuire, 1994; Weisfeld, 1999; Wright, 1994).

Testosterone, which also fluctuates in response to environmental demands, is another proximate mechanism forged by natural selection to help us cope with situations that call for aggressive responses. Various studies have shown African American males to have higher levels of testosterone than white males (Ellis & Nyborg, 1992; Rose et al., 1986). Although evidence indicates that the heritability of plasma testosterone is about 0.60 (Harris, Vernon, & Boomsma, 1998), higher testosterone levels among black males may reflect the greater status challenges black males face in their "honor subcultures" rather than differences in "true" testosterone base rates (Mazur & Booth, 1998; Walsh, 1991). Significantly, no black/white differences in testosterone levels are found among prepubescent males, older males, males who have attended college, and males raised outside honor subcultures (Mazur & Booth, 1998). Significant black/white differences in testosterone are thus apparently not found when black males not participating in honor subcultures are compared with their white peers.

Some researchers suggest that testosterone is more directly linked to dominance behavior than to aggressiveness per se (Bernhardt, 1997; Mazur & Booth, 1998). Of course, aggressiveness of some sort is almost required in order to achieve dominance, although it is seldom expressed violently in modern state societies where formal and informal rules constrain it. Displays of self-esteem and self-assurance that signal the ability (if not necessarily the willingness) to invest in offspring has replaced dominance based on fighting ability in many primate species, where alliance building and subtle displays of fighting ability rather than brute force sustain dominance rankings (Barkow, 1989). Violent attempts to gain status tend to be expressed most readily among nonhuman primates when alliances and coalitions break down and alpha males can no longer get away with mere bluster.

It may be that elevated testosterone is most likely to result in violence when it is present in conjunction with low serotonin (Bernhardt, 1997). Administering testosterone to nondominant rats increases dominance behavior, and administering serotonin reverses the process and returns the rats to nondominant status. Bernhardt postulates that individuals with high base rates of testosterone are more inclined than those with lower base levels to engage in dominance-seeking behaviors. The more dominance-seeking behavior a person engages in, the greater the likelihood of that person experiencing a frustrating event as he interacts with others seeking the same thing. If such a person also has a low level of serotonin, he will likely interpret frustration more aversively and impulsively, which increases the likelihood of responding too aggressively to frustration. Natural selection has provided us with the necessary neurohormonal mechanisms that allow us to respond to challenges to our reproductive efforts (either directly or indirectly) in ways dictated by the environments we find ourselves in. All of this points to the futility of attempting to explain criminal behavior exclusively in either biological or environmental terms, and to the importance of an evolutionary frame of reference.

Rape

The behavior of all animals is ultimately about reproductive success, and forced copulation is the cheater act that can have the most direct reproductive consequences. Many evolutionary theorists posit that males in some primate species, including humans, possess a genetically invariant predisposition toward forced copulation, although they argue about whether the disposition is an adaptation per se or a by-product of other adaptations that promote sexual assault (see Thornhill & Thornhill, 1992, and commentaries). Indeed, the coauthors of a recent book on the evolutionary origins of rape (Thornhill & Palmer, 2000) admit that they differ on this point. Although neither viewpoint avers that every man is equally likely to engage in sexual assault, even under the same environmental conditions, both contend that all men share the propensity because they all share the same evolutionary history. Ancestral males who were most inclined to pursue multiple sexual opportunities, forcefully or otherwise, would have enjoyed greater reproductive success than males who did not, thus leaving modern males with a genetic legacy inclining them to do the same.

It must be made clear from the onset that forced copulation is just one possible male reproductive strategy that may be followed simultaneously with others. The vast majority of copulations in any species are not forced, and when a copulation is forced, it tends to be a tactic of last resort pursued only after other tactics have failed (Ellis, 1991; Thornhill & Palmer, 2000; Wrangham & Peterson, 1996). Sexual assault is a high-risk behavior most likely to be committed by males lacking the status or power to acquire their desired number of copulations by consent. In other words, predatory rape is an alternative conditional strategy that is most likely to occur among low-status young males living in environments with high rates of other forms of violence (Figueredo & McCloskey, 1993; Kanazawa & Still, 2000).

The key to understanding rape behavior in evolutionary theory is the tremendous disparity in parental investment between males and females. The only necessary male investment in reproducing their genes is the time spent copulating. The path to increasing their reproductive success is thus to seek copulation with multiple partners, and males have an evolved propensity to do so. Female parental investment is enormous, and copulating with multiple partners cannot generally enhance female reproductive success. Although there are some ecological niches in which this is not true, the best overall fitness strategy for females was, and is, to secure male parental investment in exchange for exclusive sexual access. Promiscuity would be maladaptive because few males would invest resources in offspring that are not likely to be theirs (Barkow, 1989; Buss, 1994; Wright, 1994).[2]

Because our ancestral females faced this problem, modern women share an evolved tendency to resist casual copulation, or at least to be much more discriminating about it than modern males in most circumstances (Buss, 1994; Weisfeld, 1999). Thus, two conflicting reproductive strategies have evolved: the careful and discriminating female strategy, and the reckless and indiscriminate male strategy. Rape was and is sometimes the result of this disparity. Males in ancestral environments who were most inclined to pursue copulation opportunities with multiple partners, which may have occasionally included forced copulation, probably enjoyed greater fitness than those who did not, thus passing on these inclinations to their male offspring (Smuts, 1992; Thornhill & Thornhill, 1992).

We can accept without question that forced copulation increases fitness among nonhuman animals, but may find it distasteful to apply similar reasoning to humans. If we claim that rape (or any other violent behavior) is a product of natural selection, aren't we justifying it and implying that it is morally acceptable? No, we are not; and to claim that we are is to commit the *naturalistic fallacy*, the confusion of *is* with *ought*. Nature simply is, what ought to be is a moral judgment, and to say that forced copulation is natural mammalian behavior no more constitutes moral approval than to claim that we approve of disease and death because we call these unwelcome events natural also. Rape in a modern context is a maladaptive consequence of a mating strategy that may have been adaptive in the environments in which our species evolved; it is a morally reprehensible crime that requires strong preventative legal sanctions. Calling something "natural" does not dignify it or place it beyond the power of culture to modify, as manifestly it is not.

Similarly, the assertion that evolutionary theory cannot explain the rape of males, children, and postmenopausal women, or sexual assaults that do not include vaginal intercourse because such acts do not enhance reproductive success (e.g., Grauerholz & Koralewski, 1991) also misunderstands evolutionary logic. I will say it again: It is axiomatic in evolutionary theory that organisms are not adapted to directly seek ultimate goals; they are adapted to directly seek proximate goals (in this case, sexual pleasure) that themselves blindly serve ultimate goals (Symons, 1992). Nonreproductive sex is no more an adaptation per se than is the nurturing of pets; both are examples of the nonadaptive diffusion of general tendencies that *are* adaptive (Lykken, 1995). Evolution is a mindless algorithmic process. Indeed, we often consciously attempt to thwart maximizing our fitness via the use of contraception as we continue to seek and enjoy the mechanism that promotes it (Barkow, 1989). It is for this reason that Tooby and Cosmides (1992, p. 54) refer to organisms as "adaptation executors" rather than "fitness maximizers."[3]

There are many individual differences separating males who do and who do not rape, which requires an examination that goes beyond specieswide tendencies. Lee Ellis's (1991) "synthesized" theory of rape attempts to do this by integrating propositions from evolutionary psychology, behavior genetics, and operant psychology. Ellis's basic thesis is that rape *behavior* is learned via reinforcement principles (being "pushy" yields increasing levels of sexual satisfaction, thus reinforcing "pushiness"), but the *motivation* behind rape behavior is unlearned. According to Ellis, the motivation behind rape behavior is the male sex drive coupled with the drive to possess and control. Because of neurohormonal factors, these evolved drives are stronger in some males than in others, and the stronger the drives, the more easily males will learn the kinds of behavior that may lead to rape. These same neurohormonal factors also tend to result in lessened sensitivity to painful consequences—both their own and their victims'.

The evidence offered by biosocial theories of rape make it difficult to maintain the position that rape is nonsexual, that it is motivated by hatred of females or by attempts to maintain male social and economic privilege, or that it is a product of differential gender socialization, as various social learning theorists (Brownmiller, 1975; Gilmartin, 1994) have maintained. Rape is obviously a violent and despicable act, but from an evolutionary perspective, violence is usually a tactic used to achieve an end, not an end in itself.

Domestic Violence

Evidence from many cultures around the world indicates that the single most important cause of domestic violence (including homicide) is male jealousy and suspicion of infidelity (Burgess & Draper, 1989; Daly & Wilson, 1988a; Lepowsky, 1994). Males can only infer their paternity, while females are always certain of their maternity. This fact has been responsible for the almost universal double standard in adultery laws (punishing wives' adultery more severely than husbands' adultery) prior to the present time in modern state cultures (Daly & Wilson, 1988a). Male paternal uncertainty alone would lead us to predict that males will become more emotionally aroused than females by their partner's infidelity, either real or imagined. This has been confirmed by laboratory findings indicating that males in bonded relationships are more jealous (as measured by EEG readings and self-reports) than females when told to imagine their mates engaging in sexual intercourse with someone else. Females in bonded relationships were more jealous when imagining their mates falling in love with another female (Buss et al., 1992). Although both sexes became jealous when imagining both scenarios, significantly, males were more emotionally upset by actions carrying the threat of cuckoldry, and females by actions threatening the loss of resources.

Males in several nonhuman animal species acting as if they claim proprietary rights over females have been observed attacking females showing sexual interest in other males (Smuts, 1993; Ellis & Walsh, 1997). From an evolutionary point of view, it is significant that nonhuman primates are particularly likely to be assaulted when they are ovulating and stray too far away from the male who has claim to them (reviewed in Smuts, 1992). Given the strong evidence of violence against females designed to control their sexual behavior in other species, particularly in primates, we can assume with some confidence that similar behavior among humans has the same ultimate goal. With relatively rare exceptions, domestic violence worldwide is overwhelmingly directed at females by males (Arias, Samois, & O'Leary, 1987; Harrison & Esqueda, 1999).

Assaults against spouses or lovers are primarily driven by male fitness-promoting mechanisms such as sexual proprietariness, jealousy, and suspicion of infidelity. To the extent that males invest resources in females and their offspring, assaultive tendencies aimed (consciously or subconsciously) at maintaining a mate's fidelity will have been favored by natural selection (Buss, 1994; Smuts, 1992, 1993). On average, males who were least tolerant of threats of cuckoldry, real or imagined, would have left the most offspring. We can be sure that males who were indifferent to the adaptive problem of paternal certainty are not our ancestors. This intolerance does not mean that males have a dedicated mechanism for domestic abuse; it means they have evolved mechanisms such as jealousy and possessiveness and that sometimes these mechanisms prompt some men to batter women in whom they have invested resources when they perceive threats of infidelity.

There is little doubt that men everywhere tend to hold proprietary views of their wives and lovers (Allman, 1994; Smuts, 1992). If male violence against spouses and lovers is a mechanism that evolved largely to prevent real or imagined infidelity, it should be most common in environments where the threat of infidelity (and hence cuckoldry) is most real. Such environments would be those where marriages are precarious, where moral restrictions on pre- and extramarital sexual relationships are weakest, and where out-of-wedlock birth rates are highest (Burgess & Draper, 1989). These are precisely the same environments in which intrasex assault and homicide (often directly or indirectly over women) are most common (Centerwell, 1995; Greenberg & Schneider, 1994). Domestic violence assaults are not only more prevalent in such environments; they also tend to occur more frequently and to be more injurious (Clarke, 1998; Mann, 1995; Rasche, 1995).

Although by no means limited to the lower classes, domestic violence is most often committed by "competitively disadvantaged (CD) males" (Burgess & Draper, 1989; Figueredo & McClosky, 1993). CD males have low mate value because they have less to offer in terms of resources or prospects of acquiring them, which, ceteris paribus, should make their mates less desirous of maintaining the relationship with them, and thus more likely to seek other partners. Lacking alternative means of controlling their part- ners' behavior (i.e., of assuring sexual fidelity), CD males may turn to vio- lently coercive tactics to intimidate them (Figueredo & McClosky, 1993). Despite male efforts to control sexual access to "their" women, DNA data indicate that between 1% and 30% (depending on the culture or subculture) of children are sired by someone other than the putative father (Birkenhead & Moller, 1992; Brock & Shrimpton, 1991). Evolutionary psychologists con- sider efforts to control the sexual behavior of females in whom they have in- vested resources to be "normal" or "natural" under the circumstances, which evokes anger from feminists and other social scientists. But, as is the case with other violent behaviors discussed here, evolutionary psychologists join their colleagues in condemning domestic violence as morally reprehensible behavior deserving of punishment. In other words, behavior should be judged by its consequences, not by its origins (thou shalt not commit the nat- uralistic fallacy; nor shalt thou shoot the messenger).

Child Abuse and Infanticide

An evolutionary explanation for child abuse/neglect and infanticide is almost a contradiction in terms; after all, evolution by natural selection is all about preserving our genetic material. Evolutionary psychologists do not suggest that these behaviors are adaptations any more than they suggest that homi- cide, rape, or spousal battery are adaptations. Infanticide may have some positive fitness consequences under the conditions outlined below, but as Symons points out, it is not infanticide per se that is an adaptation, but "rather the general mechanisms of emotion [parental solicitude] and cogni- tion [cost-benefit calculations within a stressful context] that are the adaptations, regardless of infanticide's effect on reproductive success" (1987, p. 140). Abuse and neglect, especially of one's own offspring, can- not be considered adaptive either. Nevertheless, our understanding of these egregiously criminal acts can be enhanced by taking advantage of the theo- retical insights provided by evolutionary theory.

Because intimate contact generates both cooperation and conflict, the risk of homicide rises with the amount of time people spend in intimate con- tact with one another (known stranger murders in the United States have been fairly constant at only about 13% over the last two decades [Adler, Mueller, & Laufer, 1998, p. 234]). Despite this generalization, the killing of genetic kin, who tend to spend a great deal of time together in intimate con- tact, is the rarest form of homicide. Unfortunately, because researchers tend to lump genetic and nongenetic "relatives" together in homicide statistics, we get a greatly exaggerated picture of the dangers of fatal victimization by genetic relatives. Citing studies from Canada, Denmark, the United States, India, and thirteenth-century England, Daly and Wilson (1988a) find that nongenetic cohabitants are approximately 11 times more likely to be murdered by the person living with them than are genetic cohabitants. It has been found in a number of studies in which the victim/offender relationship was known that the perpetrator was a blood relative only in 2% to 6% of the homicides of cohabitants (reviewed in Raine, 1993).

Evolutionary theory correctly predicts empirical findings that show that close genetic relatives are extremely unlikely to kill one another. However, there are environmental conditions under which the killing of infant offspring may have enhanced the killers' *inclusive fitness* (personal fitness plus the increased fitness of close genetic relatives) in ancestral environments. The killing of offspring may increase inclusive fitness in several ways. When our ancestral mothers had too many mouths to feed with available resources, lacked a mate, or had children who were unlikely to be able to contribute to the family well-being because of chronic illness or deformity, a "triage" strategy may have been the best one available. Such a strategy increases the probability of the survival of the most reproductively viable of their offspring, while a strategy of trying to nurture each offspring equally may have resulted in the survival of none. Studies have found that the probability of abuse, neglect, and infanticide among nonhuman animals increases when the food supply is low, when the litter size is large, when an infant has low reproductive viability, and, in biparental species, when the female lacks the assistance of a mate (Allman, 1994; Ellis & Walsh, 1997). These are precisely the conditions under which we find most human incidences of infanticide and abuse and neglect: that is, under conditions of poverty, within large families, in single-parent families, and against children who are physically or mentally handicapped (Daly & Wilson, 1988a; Gelles, 1991; Ellis & Walsh, 1997). Legalities and politics aside, these are often the very same conditions that lead women to seek an abortion, which from an evolutionary point of view may be considered the functional equivalent of infanticide.

A good proportion of infanticidal behavior is either performed or instigated by males who are genetically unrelated to the victim. In many nonhuman animal species, especially in nonhuman primate species, a new male claiming a female commences to kill any offspring sired by the female's previous mate (reviewed in Van Hooff, 1990). Killing infants puts an end to breastfeeding, which prompts the female's return to estrus and provides an opportunity for the new male to produce his own offspring (Hrdy, 1999). Needless to say, these infanticidal animals make no conscious connection between their behavior and their genetic fitness. Evolutionary logic simply avers that ancestral males who behaved that way were more reproductively successful than those who did not. In a number of pre-state cultures, human males acquiring wives with dependent children may also kill any children from a previous relationship (Daly & Wilson, 1988a). Although this increases the genetic fitness of the killers at the expense of the fitness of the fathers of the victims, males in these societies are no more aware of this fact than are nonhuman primates. According to evolutionary psychology, the mental mechanism behind much male-initiated infanticide is probably: "Don't waste precious resources on children for whom I have no warm feelings."

Children in state societies are at greater risk for maltreatment, including homicide, when not raised by both biological parents. Although the vast majority of stepparents do not maltreat or kill their stepchildren, the risk of maltreatment of all kinds is greatly elevated in stepfamilies. In one study of child abuse cases in Canada, Daly and Wilson (1985) found that stepchildren between birth and 4 years old were 25 times more likely than children residing with both biological parents to be abused. This fell to 9 times more likely in the 11- to 15-year-old age category. It gets even worse for fatal abuse, where again we find the risk to be greater the younger the child is. Although the killing of children by parents (either biological or step) is an extremely rare occurrence, a child living with a stepparent (typically a stepfather or live-in boyfriend) is approximately 100 times more likely to be fatally abused than a child living with both biological parents (Daly & Wilson, 1988b, 1996). In Darwinian terms, stepparenting is a fitness reducer and is a chore reluctantly undertaken as a condition for gaining access to the child's mother's reproductive potential.

Stepparenting also significantly increases the risk of *sexual* abuse of stepchildren, with stepfathers being at least five times more likely to sexually abuse their daughters than are biological fathers (Finkelhor, 1984; Glaser & Frosh, 1993). Stepfathers or live-in boyfriends may find their stepdaughters to be every bit as sexually attractive and desirable as females who are complete strangers—that is, the incest avoidance mechanism has not been triggered. The close physical proximity of opposite-sexed individuals early in life appears to be the evolved mechanism that triggers the incest avoidance mechanism that dulls sexual attraction between them, genetically related or not (Thornhill & Thornhill, 1987; van den Berghe, 1987).

The earlier in a child's life the stepparenting, begins the less likely there will be any sexual attraction between parent and child. Evolutionists argue that stepparents and live-ins represent an elevated risk for physical and sexual abuse, or even murder, an argument that is well supported empirically (Glaser & Frosh, 1993; Ellis & Walsh, 1997; Daly & Wilson, 1988a, 1988b). The stepparent-stepchild relationship is more tenuous than the biological parent-child relationship because it does not rest on the firm basis of early bonding, and therefore on the mutual trust, nurturance, and solicitude that such a relationship engenders. In decrying the ever decreasing number of children who live with both biological parents, Robert Wright

(1994, p. 104) remarks: "Whenever marital institutions—in either kind of society [monogamous or polygynous]—are allowed to dissolve, so that divorce and unwed motherhood are rampant, and many children no longer live with both natural parents, there will ensue a massive waste of the most precious evolutionary resource: love."[4]

Needless to say, the vast majority of stepparents do not neglect, abuse, or kill their stepchildren, and many genuinely love and nurture them. Cartwright (2000) considers this a puzzle to explain in selectionist terms, but we may view it as another example of the nonadaptive diffusion of general tendencies that are adaptive.

Specific Evolutionary Theories of Crime

I have thus far explored the logic of evolutionary theory as it pertains to criminal and antisocial behavior in general. I now briefly explore specific evolutionary theories of criminal and antisocial behavior: *cheater theory, conditional adaptation theory, alternative adaptation theory*, and the *"staying alive" hypothesis*. All four theories focus on reproductive strategies (apportioning mating effort versus parenting effort) and the tactics that flow from them as their foundation. It is emphasized that psychological processes were selected to foster reproductive success, not criminality. However, the processes or tactics (lying, deception, self-centeredness, aggression) that serve to facilitate certain reproductive strategies are also conducive to criminal activity. The "staying alive" hypothesis is specific to female criminality.

Cheater Theory

Cheater theory rests ultimately on the broad asymmetry between the reproductive strategies of males and females. There is much more variability in male reproductive success, with some males leaving no offspring, and others fathering large numbers. This is particularly so in polygynous species and polygynous human cultures, and possibly so in human evolutionary environments. Females have a much lower potential reproductive ceiling than males, although almost all females will probably reproduce. The major factor in female reproductive success has been to secure and hold on to the assistance of a mate to raise her offspring. Given lower variation but greater reproductive certainty, females have evolved a mating strategy inclining them to be choosier about whom they will mate with than males are (Badcock, 2000; Cartwright, 2000; Buss, 1994; Wright, 1994).

Male reproductive success is potentially greater the more females a male can have sex with, and males have an evolved desire for multiple partners.

Males can respond to the more reticent female strategy in one of two ways: They can comply with female preferences and help a single female raise their offspring, or they can either trick or force a female to have sex and then move on to the next female. These two strategies have been called Cad vs. Dad (Cashdan, 1993). Just as almost all males have committed some form of delinquent act during adolescence (Moffitt, 1993), almost all heterosexual males have probably used cheater tactics (falsely proclaiming love and fidelity and the use of some form of coercion) to obtain sex in their youth. The vast majority of males, however, will eventually settle down and help a female to raise their young, just as the vast majority will desist from antisocial behavior. This "dad" strategy is facilitated by the social emotions, particularly love (Fisher, 1998; Walsh, 1995b). The "cad" strategy, however, is likely to be followed by males who are deficient in the social emotions, such as chronic criminals and psychopaths, well after adolescence (Ellis & Walsh, 1997; Lykken, 1995). The basic point of cheater theory is that criminal activity is facilitated by the same traits that make for the successful pursuit of a cheater sexual strategy.

It is important to stress that cheater theory does not postulate that criminal behavior reflects a defective genome; rather, it reflects a normal, albeit morally regrettable, alternative adaptive strategy. That is, it has been suggested that a small subset of individuals exist for whom cheating is an obligatory rather than a conditional strategy. The continued presence of chronic cheats among us indicates that we have a less than perfect ability to detect and punish them. As previously indicated, because humans are trustworthy cooperators they are vulnerable to cheats.

According to a number of theorists, a coevolutionary "arms race" similar to the coevolution of predator and prey has molded the sensibilities of cooperators and chronic cheats alike. Just as cooperators have undergone evolutionary tuning of their senses for detecting cheats, cheats have evolved mechanisms that serve to hide their true intentions (Cartwright, 2000; Mealey, 1995; Trivers, 1991). The posited mechanism aiding cheats is a muting of the neurohormonal mechanisms that regulate the social emotions so that cheats have little real understanding of what it is like to feel guilt, shame, anxiety, and sympathy. Selection for self-deception (think of some of the defense mechanisms in psychoanalytic theory) would even better enable the cheater to pursue his interests without detection (Alexander, 1987; Dugatkin, 1992; Nesse & Lloyd, 1992). Because chronic cheats operate "below the emotional poverty line" (Hare, 1993, p. 134), they do not reveal clues that would allow others to judge their intentions. Lacking an emotional basis for self-regulation, chronic cheats make social decisions exclusively on the basis of rational cost-benefit calculations (Mealey, 1995; Trivers, 1991).

According to Mealey (1995), the traits conducive to cheating are normally distributed in the population, but there is a small but stable percentage of individuals at one extreme of the distribution for whom cheating is an obligate strategy. These individuals are the few "primary sociopaths," or psychopaths (3% to 4% of males, and less than 1% of females [Mealey, 1995]), who appear to exist in every society. An obligate cheater strategy is likely to evolve alongside the more typical environmentally-dependent strategy when its fitness gains are *frequency-dependent*. Frequency-dependent selection occurs when an alternative mating strategy enjoys high reproductive success when few practice it, but low success when it becomes more common. Frequency-dependent strategies eventually result in organisms that are genotypically, not just phenotypically, different.

The greatly fluctuating levels of reproductive success attending a frequency-dependent strategy, combined with the evolution of counter-pressures against cheating in the population as a whole, assures that obligate cheaters are rare in any population (Moore & Rose, 1995; Lykken, 1995). In other words, when there are few cheats in a population each cheat enjoys numerous opportunities to exploit its unwary members, but when many follow a cheater strategy, not only are there fewer "suckers" per cheat, there is a greater awareness of the strategy in the population and thus a lowered probability of its success. Further, cheaters come more and more in contact with each other, usually resulting in a net loss to both (Dugatkin, 1992; Machalek, 1995).

Although there is abundance of evidence that psychopaths have a greatly diminished capacity to experience the social emotions (Hare, 1993, 1996; Lykken, 1995; Patrick, 1994), the proposition that there is a distinct behavioral type in human populations for which deception and exploitation is an obligate rather than a conditional strategy is probably the most difficult evolutionary proposition for criminologists to accept. Many evolutionary scholars disagree with it, but others do not (see commentaries following Mealey's [1995] article). However, obligate and conditional cheater reproductive strategies, each with its own distinct genetic basis, do exist in numerous animal species (Alcock, 1998), and there is some evidence that psychopathy constitutes a discrete taxonomic class (a categorical rather than continuous variable) *phenotypically* (Harris, Rice, & Quinsey, 1994; Skilling, Quinsey, & Craig, 2001). This evidence, of course, does not mark psychopaths as distinct from nonpsychopaths *genotypically*. Absent the kinds of genetic experiments relevant to this issue conducted with nonhuman animals, we may never know with certainty whether there is a distinct genetically based human cheater morph.

The vast majority of criminals are not psychopaths, and the cheater strategy they employ is probably conditional rather than obligate. As mentioned earlier, conditional strategies (for which the entire population is monomorphic) are evolutionarily more advantageous because of the flexibility they offer. In a variety of nonhuman animal species, cheater strategists (variably labeled as "sneakers," "mimics," "floaters," and "satellites") are typically males who are reproductively disadvantaged in some way (Alcock, 1998). As is also the case among humans, the most disadvantaged male animals are the young who have not yet established themselves in the social hierarchy, have limited resources, and cannot contend physically with older and more powerful conspecifics. Although not the most profitable way of acquiring copulations, the cheater strategy is marginally adaptive because it does provide more reproductive opportunities than would be the case if disadvantaged males simply waited for their situation to improve, which may never happen. Because a conditional cheater strategy has some fitness consequences, genes governing the neurohormonal mechanisms that allow us to respond to environmental conditions by changing our behavior (cooperator to cheater, and vice versa) have survived in us all. In a very real sense, then, the antisocial impulse is universal but is constrained by rules which most of us profit from following most of the time.

Conditional Adaptation Theory (CAT)

As the name suggests, CAT proposes that people adopt different reproductive strategies conditionally—that is, according to the environmental conditions they find themselves in, rather than genetic reasons. Draper and Harpending (1982) suggested that a uniform reproductive strategy would not be evolutionarily viable for every individual since environmental circumstances often vary drastically. They further postulated that early childhood is a sensitive period in which an individual's future reproductive strategy is calibrated, primarily by father absence. Blain and Barkow (1985) further suggested that this calibration would include physiological processes that affect the timing of the individual's puberty; father absence would accelerate the onset of puberty and sexual activity. Blain and Barkow's prediction has been supported by a number of studies (reviewed by Rossi, 1997). Although father absence was initially considered the primary stressor, later work has tended toward more general childhood attachment processes: "By the age of five to seven years children have usually developed mental images or 'internal working models' of social-emotional relationships based on the quality of their attachments" (Chisholm, 1993, p. 6).

According to the theory, children unconsciously monitor their environments and will tend to adopt an unrestricted (promiscuous) sexual strategy if they perceive that interpersonal relationships are ephemeral and unreliable (as indexed by such things as parental divorce, witnessing others engaging in short-term relationships, and lack of attachment to parents/caregivers). Individuals who learned the opposite (experiencing stable pair bonding and secure parental attachment) will tend to adopt a more restricted strategy. In other words, their early home environment represents a prototype for children, providing them with a set of expectations regarding interpersonal relationships that set them on two distinct reproductive pathways and provide them with the neurophysiological traits that facilitate them. Needless to say, neither strategy is consciously chosen; rather, both flow from subconscious expectations based on early experiences of the stability/instability and quality of interpersonal relationships.

Unlike the cheater theory, which emphasizes male reproductive strategies only, CAT includes features that allow for predictions about the involvement of women in antisocial behavior as well as men. Thus, in addition to the "Cad vs. Dad" dichotomy to describe male mating strategies, CAT includes the "whore vs. Madonna" dichotomy that defines female mating strategies (Fisher, 1992, p. 94). According to CAT, if a female has come to view men as primarily "cads," she will not expect long-term parental investment and will emphasize her sexuality to procure short-term investment from a variety of males, as Hrdy (1999, see endnote 3) indicates. If she views them primarily as "dads," she will emphasize chastity and fidelity, thereby maximizing the probability of securing long-term parental investment. A number of studies have shown that a low level of parental attachment results in a pattern of unrestrictive sexuality in adulthood, as well as transient pair-bonding, as indexed by high levels of divorce (Belsky, 1997; Walsh, 1995b, 1999).

Although CAT stresses the facultative expressions of alternative reproductive strategies, some of its proponents concede that children may vary in their susceptibility to environmental influences for genetic reasons (Hrdy, 1999; Walsh, 1999). It has also been noted that the variables related to restrictive/unrestrictive sexual behavior, such as warmth/nurturance, impulsivity/constraint, altruism/egoism, and empathy/insensitivity, are highly heritable (MacDonald, 1997). Children receive a suite of genes as well as an environment from their parents that may bias them in the direction of one reproductive strategy rather than another. In other words, genetic differences may also in part be responsible for the different reproductive strategies, and the negative and ephemeral relationships observed among the sexually unrestricted may be a consequence of their strategy rather than a cause.

Harpending and Draper (1988) provide anthropological evidence supportive of CAT. They contrasted the behavior of two cultures inhabiting drastically different ecological environments: the !Kung bushmen, who inhabit the inhospitable Kalahari Desert in South Africa; and the Mundurucu, who inhabit the resource-rich Amazon basin. Because conditions are harsh in the Kalahari, life is precarious, cooperative behavior is imperative, and parenting effort is favored over mating effort. The Mundurucu's rich ecology, on the other hand, frees males to fight, raid other groups, and engage in competition for females. Under these conditions, mating effort is favored over parenting effort. What is most interesting from a criminological perspective is that cultures emphasizing mating effort exhibit behaviors that would be considered antisocial in Western societies, such as low-level parental care, aggressiveness, "protest masculinity," and transient bonding (Harpending & Draper, 1988; Ember & Ember, 1998). These behaviors, however, are adaptive in such cultures, and may well be adaptive in certain subcultures of modern industrial societies also.

A further example from a prestate society of conditional adaptation is that of the Ache, a group of South American Indians. Intertribal warfare and intratribal status-driven club fights among the Ache result in high male mortality and, therefore, great shortages of available mates for females. A fatherless Ache child has about a 50% chance of surviving childhood, compared with about 86% for children with fathers. Under conditions of severe male shortage, it is adaptive for females unlikely secure a permanent mate to advertise her sexuality rather than her fidelity and copulate with a number of males, thereby gaining some resources from each male, or even convincing one of them that the child is his. Such behavior increases the probability that her child will survive to adolescence, and by doing so she increases the probability that her genes will be represented in subsequent generations (Hill & Hurtado, 1996).

Alternative Adaptation Theory (AAT)

AAT differs from CAT in that it proposes that humans are arrayed along a continuum regarding where they have a tendency to focus their reproductive efforts, but largely for genetic rather than environmental reasons (Rowe, 1996). At one extreme is mating effort and at the other is parenting effort. Rowe (1996, p. 270) states that "crime can be identified with the behaviors that tend to promote mating effort and noncrime with those that tend to promote parenting effort." The best demographic predictors of where reproductive effort is focused are gender and age, which are also the best demographic predictors of criminal and other antisocial behaviors. Mid-adolescence to early adulthood is a period of intense male reproductive effort, replete with competitiveness, risk-taking, and violence aimed ultimately at securing more mating opportunities than the next male (Mazur & Booth, 1998; Weisfeld, 1999). As Martin Daly (1996, p. 193) put it: "There are many reasons to think that we've been designed [by natural selection] to be maximally competitive and conflictual in young adulthood."

In general, males and the young emphasize mating effort and females and older persons emphasize parenting effort. In terms of individual traits, the suite of traits useful for focusing on mating effort, such as deceitfulness, impulsiveness, sensation-seeking, and hedonism, are also useful in pursuing criminal activity. Conversely, traits useful for focusing resources on parenting effort, such as empathy, conscientiousness, and altruism, are also useful for prosocial activity. The great majority of males for whom cheating is a conditional strategy will shift their strategy toward parenting effort as they mature, but a small number of males will pursue a cheater strategy across the lifecourse. In this respect Rowe agrees with Mealey (1995) that a small number of individuals exist for whom cheating is a genetically obligate strategy due to frequency-dependent selection.

A third predictor of a person's reproductive strategy according to AAT (but not considered a factor in other evolutionary theories of crime) is intelligence, with those of relatively high intelligence generally opting for parenting effort and those of relatively low intelligence generally opting for mating effort. It is not assumed that low intelligence is intrinsically antisocial (or high intelligence intrinsically prosocial, for that matter), only that it makes the procurement of resources needed to advertise parental effort to prospective females problematic. Low intelligence also makes it difficult to learn and appreciate the moral norms of society. Thus, a strategy emphasizing mating effort is similar to criminal behavior in that direct and immediate methods are used to procure resources illegitimately; little thought is given to the consequences either to the self or to the victim (Gottfredson & Hirschi, 1990). Conversely, parenting effort is embedded in a prosocial lifestyle in which resource procurement relies on the patient and intelligent accumulation of social and occupational skills that are attractive to females. Thus, reproductive strategies mirror antisocial/prosocial behavior in terms of emphases on immediate versus delayed gratification.

AAT makes the same predictions as CAT regarding early onset of sexual behavior and number of sexual partners, but would explain the relationship by indicating that both criminal activity and a high level of mating effort is sustained by the same suite of traits that are moderately to highly heritable. Also unlike CAT, Rowe (1996, p. 290) places little emphasis on childhood experiences, pointing out that behavior genetic studies consistently show that the rearing environment stressed by CAT has little or no lasting influence on an individual's personality or intelligence. The relationship between childhood experiences and the adoption of a particular reproductive strategy could be the result of the genes children share with the parent(s) providing those experiences rather than of the experiences per se.

The "Staying Alive" Hypothesis: Women and Crime

The major concern of feminist criminology has long been to explain the universal fact that women are far less likely than men to involve themselves in criminal activity (Price & Sokoloff, 1995, p. 3). Whenever and wherever records have been kept, it has been found that males commit the over-whelming proportion of criminal offenses, and the more serious and violent the offense, the more males dominate in its commission (Campbell, 1999). This fact is not in dispute, although explanations of it are. The traditional sociological view of gender differences in crime and other forms of deviant behavior is that they are products of differential socialization: that men are socialized to be aggressive, ambitious, and dominant, women to be nurtur-ing and passive; and that women will be as antisocial and criminal as men with female emancipation. The majority of studies relating to this issue, however, actually support the *opposite* of the emancipation hypothesis: that is, as the trend toward gender equality has increased, females have tended to commit fewer rather than more crimes relative to males (Ellis & Walsh, 2000, p. 388).

Other efforts to account for gender differences aver that the greater supervision of females versus males account for the gender gap (Mears, Ploeger, & Warr, 1998). However, controlling for supervision level results in the same large gap in male/female offending (Gottfredson & Hirschi, 1990, p. 148), and a meta-analysis of 172 studies found a nonsignificant ten-dency for boys to be *more* strictly supervised than girls (Lytton & Romney, 1991). As Dianna Fishbein (1992, p. 100) summed up the issue: "Cross-cultural studies do not support the prominent role of structural and cultural influences of gender-specific crime rates as the type and extent of male ver-sus female crime remains consistent across cultures."

The primary evolutionary account of why females are much less prone to criminal and other forms of antisocial behavior is provided by Anne Campbell's (1999) "staying alive" hypothesis. Campbell's argument has to do with evolved sex differences in basic biology relevant to parental invest-ment and status striving. Because a female's obligatory parental investment is greater than a male's, and because of the greater dependence of the infant on the mother, a mother's presence is more critical to offspring survival (and hence to the mother's reproductive success) than is a father's. Given that a female's survival is more critical to her reproductive success (in terms of maximizing the probability that her offspring will survive) than a male's sur-vival is to his, Campbell argues that females have evolved a propensity to avoid engaging in behaviors that pose survival risks, which includes many forms of criminal and antisocial behavior. The practice of keeping nursing children in close proximity in ancestral environments posed an elevated risk of personal injury to both mother and child if the mother placed herself in risky situations (Beckerman, 1999).

The evolved proximate mechanism Campbell proposes is a greater propensity for females to experience many different situations as fearful. She surveys evidence showing that there are no sex differences in fearfulness across a number of contexts *unless* a situation contains a significant risk of physical injury. Fear of injury accounts for the greater tendency of females to avoid or remove themselves from potentially violent situations and to employ indirect and low-risk strategies in competition and dispute resolution relative to males. Simply put, ancestral females who were most fearful of situations containing a high risk of physical injury or death were more likely to survive. The survival of these females, in turn, increased the probability of the survival of their offspring, thus passing on the genes underlying the fear response to potentially dangerous situations.

This greater female concern for personal survival also has implications for sex differences in status seeking. Recall that males exhibit greater variance in reproductive success than females but less parental certainty, and thus have more to gain and less to lose than females by engaging in intrasexual competition for mating opportunities. Striving for status and dominance can be a risky business, and because attaining status is less consequential for females than for males, there has been less evolutionary pressure for the selection of mechanisms useful in that endeavor for females. Males' reproductive success may often rest on involving themselves in risky situations, so high fear levels would have handicapped them in this endeavor.

Campbell points out that although females do engage in intrasexual competition for mates, it is rarely in the form of violence and aggression in any primate species. Most of it is decidedly low key, low risk, and chronic, as opposed to male competition, which is high key, high risk, and acute. The female assets most pertinent to reproductive success are youth and beauty, which one either has or does not. Male assets are the resources females desire for their reproductive success, and unlike youth and beauty, these assets can be achieved in competition with other males. Males are willing to incur high risks to achieve the status and dominance that bring them resources and thus access to more females.

Campbell also notes that when females engage in crime they almost always do so for instrumental reasons, and the crimes themselves rarely involve risk of physical injury. Both robbery and larceny/theft involve expropriating resources from others, but females constitute about 43% of arrests for larceny/theft and only about 7% of arrests for robbery, a crime carrying a relatively high risk for personal injury. There is no mention in the literature that female robbers crave the additional payoffs of dominance that male robbers do, or seek reputations as "hardasses" (Katz, 1988). High-status, dominant, and aggressive females are not particularly desirable as mates, and certainly a woman with a reputation as a "hardass" would be most unattractive. Campbell (1999, p. 210) notes that while women do aggress and do steal, "they rarely do both at the same time because the equation of resources and status reflects a particularly masculine logic."

It is important to realize that sex differences in aggression, dominance seeking, and sexual promiscuity are related to parental investment, rather than sex (gender) per se. It is the level of parental investment and its twin process, sexual selection, that exert pressure for the selection of the neuro-hormonal mechanisms that underlie these behaviors. Parental investment is not greater for females in every species, however. In a number of bird and fish species males contribute greater parental investment (e.g., incubating the eggs and feeding the young), and in these species it is the female who takes the risks, who is promiscuous and the aggressor in courtship, and who engages in intrasexual competition for mates (Betzig, 1999). Males and females in these species thus assume characteristics that are the opposite of those of males and females in species in which the females assume all or most of the burden of parenting. This sex-role reversal provides support for Campbell's thesis and underlines the usefulness of cross-species comparisons.

The Evidence for Evolutionary Theories of Crime

All three theories we have discussed make essentially the same predictions regarding the correlates of criminal behavior. The major predictions have to do with sexual behavior; the stability of pair bonds; and child care, supervision, and attachment. Table 8.1 presents 539 studies reviewed by Ellis and Walsh (2000) pertaining to these issues. These studies include official and self-report data of a variety of criminal and antisocial behaviors derived from a number of different countries. Note that 481 studies were supportive of the predictions made by evolutionary theories of crime, 51 were null, and only 7 were nonsupportive. Null and nonsupportive studies were exclusively self-report studies of relatively minor offenses.

Of course, a number of non-evolutionary theories would also predict many of the same relationships. These theories would typically invoke supraindividual factors such as social class, discrimination, status frustration, or "subculture of violence" as explanations. Although these factors provide part of the picture, they are descriptors rather than explanations, phenomena that themselves require explanation. As with many phenomena in the social and behavioral sciences, they are generic terms for a number of functionally integrated biological and psychological structures and processes that we call evolved adaptations. The explanatory shortcomings of non-evolutionary criminological theories vis-à-vis these correlates of crime are briefly addressed below.

- Non-evolutionary theories cannot account for why men everywhere and always commit far more criminal and antisocial acts than females. The socialization argument implies that there could be cultures in which male and female crime rates were equal, or even where female rates were higher. No such culture has ever been identified. Evolutionary theories are fully compatible with proximate-level biosocial

Table 8.1 Studies of the Relationship Between Criminal, Delinquent, and Other Antisocial Behavior and Concepts From Evolutionary Theories of Crime*

Being married			Out-of-wedlock births			Intactness of parental marriage bond			Parent/child attachment		
Sup.	n.s.	Nonsup.	Sup.	n.s.	Nonsup.	Sup.	n.s.	Nonsup.	Sup.	n.s.	Nonsup.
14	4	1	8	0	0	198	39	2	48	5	2

Parental competency, supervision, & discipline			Parental abuse			Number of sex partners			Age of onset of sexual behavior		
Sup.	n.s.	Nonsup.	Sup.	n.s.	Nonsup.	Sup.	n.s.	Nonsup.	Sup.	n.s.	Nonsup.
72	0	2	59	2	0	51	1	0	31	0	0

Note: *Sup. = Number of supportive studies; n.s. = number of nonsignificant studies; Nonsup. = number of nonsupportive studies. From Ellis & Walsh, *Criminology: A Global Perspective* (2000).

theories that emphasize neurohormonal differences between the sexes that incline far more males to greater antisocial behavior than females. Evolutionary theory adds to these explanations by offering plausible explanations for why these differences exist in the first place—in other words, what reproductive functions did (and do) they serve?

- Non-evolutionary theories cannot specify why males find it so important to control women by behavior (rape, battering) identical with that observed in other animal species under the same general conditions. Nor can they explain why competitively disadvantaged males more readily turn to violence in attempts to accomplish this than do their higher-status counterparts. The fact that these same behaviors occur in a variety of other species makes it extremely difficult to maintain that they are the result of differential socialization or of hatred of women, or why the great majority of victims of rape are primarily of reproductive age despite the greater vulnerability of younger and older females (Thornhill & Palmer, 2000).

- Non-evolutionary theories cannot account for the age curve in crime; the age peak in delinquency remains "unexplained by any known set of sociological variables" (Shavit & Rattner, 1988, p. 1457). Gottfredson and Hirschi (1990, p. 139) also contend that the age effect is basically inexplicable since it is an invariant phenomenon across time and space. Evolutionary psychology does not view it as inexplicable. Rather, it views delinquency to be an adaptive response to temporary environmental contingencies. Delinquents are behaving similarly to young males in other primate species in that they are temporarily following a conditional cheater strategy, and the majority will desist when opportunities arise to gain status and other valued resources legitimately. As is the case with other primate species, mid-adolescence and early adulthood is a period of intense competition among males, replete with risk-taking and some degree of violence aimed ultimately at securing more mating opportunities than the next male. As Daly (1996, p. 193) pointed out above, males have been designed by evolution to be at their most competitive during adolescence and young adulthood. The proximate mechanisms that facilitate this competition may also facilitate criminal and antisocial behavior in some environments (Walsh, 2000b).

Conclusion

Evolutionary psychology agrees with mainstream sociology that we humans are social beings who desire to follow social rules, but it does not romanticize us as inherently good beings who commit bad acts only when forced into them by evil social institutions. We are nepotistic reciprocal altruists who know that we can realize our self-interests more often by cooperating

258 SOCIOLOGY AND CRIMINOLOGY

(following rules) than by not cooperating. The apparent paradox of social beings committing antisocial acts is resolved when we realize that our very desire to cooperate generates deviance by providing opportunities for non-cooperators. In common with many criminological theories, evolutionary psychologists aver that the individuals most likely to commit antisocial acts are those who are disadvantaged in the competition for wealth, power, and status, the evolutionary precursors of reproductive success. The addition of evolutionary explanatory concepts to such theories would not only enrich and broaden their repertoire of concepts; it would ground them in the one existing theory that has the potential to add unity and coherence across all disciplines that study the behavior of living things.

I have noted throughout this essay that evolutionary psychologists not only *do not* discount the role of the environment in explaining human behavior; but, rather, that they emphasize its tremendous importance. Without the environment, remarked David Lykken (1995, p. 85), "your genome would have created nothing more than a damp spot on the carpet." Nature and nurture are so inextricably linked that one is unimaginable without the other (except in terms of "wet spots" on the one hand and lifeless "moonscapes" on the other). Evolutionary psychology points to the kinds of environments in which we should expect the kinds of behaviors that trouble us most to emerge, and it is the only extant metatheory that is capable of uniting, integrating, and making sense of the disparate data on human behavior which come to us from so many theories from so many disciplines.

The value of evolutionary theory to criminology is not limited to providing a metatheory or introducing new theories. It can be fruitfully applied to traditional theories, thereby expanding and enhancing them. Criminologists will have recognized many concepts in this volume that cohere with their favored theories of crime and criminality, particularly theories that focus on status striving (anomie/strain theory), disorganized and disrupted environments (social disorganization theory), the family and attachment (social control theory), and peer influence during adolescence (differential association theory). Evolutionary and other biosocial (behavior genetic and neurohormonal) concepts are applied to a range of traditional criminological theories in Walsh (2002).

Jerome Barkow asks us to "imagine evolutionary biology and population genetics as one island continent, and the social-behavioral sciences as another. Now is the time for ending false dichotomies and for emphasizing continuities. Now is the time to position the social-behavioral sciences in their proper place as a seamless continuation of biology" (1989, p. 18). To become vertically integrated in the way envisioned does not mean that criminologists need to become expert evolutionary psychologists, behavior geneticists, endocrinologists, or neuroscientists in order to study crime and criminality. They must at least be students of those sciences, however, if they are to develop theories that maintain vertical consistency with them. If they do not they will become irrelevant, as Alice Rossi (1984) warned biologically ignorant sex-role researchers in her 1983 presidential address to the American Sociological Association. In this "decade of the brain" and in the age of the Human Genome and Human Genetic Diversity Projects, biological data relevant to understanding criminal behavior are pouring in at a remarkable rate. Criminologists have an unprecedented opportunity to join other scientists in interdisciplinary analyses of criminal behavior with these data. If criminologists pass up this opportunity, we can be sure that the torch will be passed to other disciplines—the study of criminality is too important to remain mired in premodern science.

Notes

1. It should be noted that Durkheim was careful to distinguish between social facts and biological and psychological facts and between crime and criminality: "From the fact that crime is a phenomenon of normal sociology, it does not follow that the criminal is an individual normally constituted from the biological and psychological points of view" (1982, p. 106).

2. Sarah Blaffer Hrdy (1999) indicates that a woman's reproductive success depends not on the number of copulations she experiences but on keeping such offspring as she does produce alive to reach reproductive age themselves. Hrdy avers that it may benefit the fitness of a mateless female with offspring to set up "networks of well-disposed men to help protect and provision her offspring" (1999, p. 246) in exchange for sexual favors. This strategy is most likely to be followed in environments of male scarcity due to high rates of adult male mortality and mate desertion. She cites a number of pre-state cultures in which this female fitness strategy is common, but she also indicates that it is "the emotional calculus behind the decisions that inner-city mothers make every day" (1999, p. 251).

3. An excellent illustration of why the phrase "adaptation executors" is preferable to "fitness maximizers," at least when describing modern humans, is Perusse's (1992) data on fertility and social class in modern industrial societies. In modern societies, fertility rates tend to decline with increased social status, thus reversing the age-old positive correlation between social status and reproductive success. High-status males, utilizing evolutionarily novel contraceptive technology, are obviously not striving to maximize their fitness. However, Perusse found that they are executing adaptations in that they enjoy more copulations (or *number of potential conceptions*, to use Perusse's terminology) with more partners than lower-status males, particularly as they grow older and acquire more resources. In a precontraceptive society these men would have been fitness maximizers; now they are simply adaptation executors.

4. Some readers will view this as a moral rather than scientific statement. There are obviously many cases in which divorce is more beneficial to

both mother and children than is remaining in an abusive marriage. However, we should not confuse variation with central tendency. The consequences of not being reared in a two-parent family *range* from positive to negative, but the *central tendency* is negative. A number of meta-analyses of the impact of divorce on children have found many negative consequences *overall*, and no positive consequences *overall* (Amato & Keith, 1991a, 1991b).

However, we must be careful about attributing correlations between divorce and the behavior and attitudes of the children of divorce to divorce per se, given the fairly robust findings that the heritability of divorce is around .50 (Jockin, McGue, & Lykken, 1996; McGue & Lykken, 1992). People with heritable traits (insensitivity, aggressiveness, impulsiveness, etc.) that increase the likelihood of unfavorable outcomes in other areas of their lives bring those traits with them to their marriages, which make them difficult to live with. This obviously does not mean that all, or even the majority, of divorced people possess these traits. Marriage is a mix of two people which produces a "third personality" that is not necessarily predictable from the personalities each brings to it.

References

Adler, F., Mueller, G., & Laufer, W. (1998). *Criminology* (3rd ed.). Boston: McGraw-Hill.

Alcock, J. (1998). *Animal behavior: An evolutionary approach* (6th ed.). Sunderland, MA: Sinauer Associates.

Alexander, R. (1987). *The biology of moral systems.* New York: Aldine de Gruyter.

Allman, W. (1994). *The stone age present.* New York: Simon & Schuster.

Amato, P., & Keith, P. (1991a). Parental divorce and adult well-being: A meta-analysis. *Journal of Marriage and the Family, 53*, 43–58.

Amato, P., & Keith, P. (1991b). Parental divorce and the well-being of children: A meta-analysis. *Psychological Bulletin, 110*, 26–46.

Anderson, E. (1999). *Code of the street: Decency, violence, and the moral life of the inner city.* New York: W. W. Norton.

Arias, I., Samois, M., & O'Leary, K. (1987). Prevalence and correlates of physical aggression during courtship. *Journal of Interpersonal Violence, 2*, 82–90.

Badcock, C. (2000). *Evolutionary psychology: A critical introduction.* Cambridge, England: Polity Press.

Barak, G. (1998). *Integrating criminologies.* Boston: Allyn & Bacon.

Barkow, J. (1984). The distance between genes and culture. *Journal of Anthropological Research, 37*, 367–379.

Barkow, J. (1989). *Darwin, sex and status: Biological approaches to mind and culture.* Toronto: University of Toronto Press.

Barkow, J. (1992). Beneath new culture is an old psychology: Gossip and social stratification. In J. Barkow, L. Cosmides, & J. Tooby (Eds.), *The adapted mind: Evolutionary psychology and the generation of culture* (pp. 627–637). New York: Oxford University Press.

Barkow, J. (1997). Happiness in evolutionary perspective. In N. Segal, G. Weisfeld, & C. Weisfeld (Eds.), *Uniting psychology and biology* (pp. 397–418). Washington, DC: American Psychological Association.

Baumeister, R., Smart, L., & Boden, J. (1996). Relation of threatened egotism to violence and aggression: The dark side of self-esteem. *Psychological Review, 103*, 5–33.

Beckerman, S. (1999). Violence, sex, and the good mother. *Behavioral and Brain Sciences, 22*, 215–216.

Beckstrom, J. (1993). *Darwinism applied: Evolutionary paths to social goals.* Westport, CT: Praeger.

Belsky, J. (1997). Attachment, mating, and parenting. *Human Nature, 8*, 361–381.

Berghe, P. van den. (1987). Incest taboos and avoidance: Some African applications. In C. Crawford, M. Smith, & D. Krebs (Eds.), *Sociobiology and psychology: Ideas, issues, and applications* (pp. 353–371). Hillsdale, NJ: Lawrence Erlbaum.

Berghe, P. van den. (1990). Why most sociologists don't (and won't) think evolutionarily. *Sociological Forum, 5*, 173–185.

Bernard, T. (1990). Angry aggression among the truly disadvantaged. *Criminology, 28*, 73–96.

Bernhardt, P. (1997). Influences of serotonin and testosterone in aggression and dominance: Convergence with social psychology. *Current Directions in Psychological Science, 6*, 44–48.

Betzig, L. (1999). When women win. *Behavioral and Brain Sciences, 22*, 217.

Birkenhead, T., & Moller, A. (1992). Faithless females seek better genes. *New Scientist*, July, 34–38.

Blain, J., & Barkow, J. H. (1988). Father involvement, reproductive strategies, and the sensitive period. In Kevin MacDonald (Ed.), *Sociobiology and Human Development* (pp. 373–396). New York: Garland.

Boyd, R., & Richerson, P. (1992). Punishment allows the evolution of cooperation (or anything else) in sizable groups. *Ethology & Sociobiology, 13*, 171–195.

Brammer, G., Raleigh, M., & McGuire, M. (1994). Neurotransmitters and social status. In L. Ellis (Ed.), *Social stratification and socioeconomic inequality*, Vol. 2: *Reproductive and interpersonal aspects of dominance and status* (pp. 75–91). Westport, CT: Praeger.

Brock, D., & Shrimpton, A. (1991). Nonpaternity and prenatal genetic screening. *Lancet, 388*, 1151–1153.

Brownmiller, S. (1975). *Against our will: Men, women, and rape.* New York: Simon & Schuster.

Burgess, R., & Draper, P. (1989). The explanation of family violence: The role of biological, behavioral, and cultural selection. In L. Ohlin & M. Tonry (Eds.), *Family violence.* Chicago: University of Chicago Press.

Buss, D. (1990). Toward a biologically-informed psychology of personality. *Journal of Personality, 58*, 1–16.

Buss, D. (1994). *The evolution of desire.* New York: Basic Books.

Buss, D., Larsen, R., Westen, D., & Semmelroth, J. (1992). Sex differences in jealousy: Evolution, physiology, and psychology. *Psychological Science, 3,* 251–255.

Campbell, A. (1999). Staying alive: Evolution, culture, and women's intrasexual aggression. *Behavioral and Brian Sciences, 22,* 203–214.

Cartwight, J. (2000). *Evolution and human behavior.* Cambridge, MA: MIT Press.

Cashdan, E. (1993). Attracting mates: Effects of paternal investment on mate attraction strategies. *Ethology and Sociobiology, 14,* 1–23.

Centerwell, B. (1995). Race, socioeconomic status, and domestic homicide. *Journal of the American Medical Association, 273,* 1755–1758.

Chagnon, N. (1988). Life histories, blood revenge, and warfare in a tribal population. *Science, 239,* 985–992.

Chagnon, N. (1996). Chronic problems in understanding tribal violence and warfare. In G. Bock & J. Goode (Eds.), *Genetics of criminal and antisocial behavior* (pp. 202–236). Chichester, UK: Wiley.

Chisholm, J. (1993). Death, hope, and sex: Life history theory and the development of reproductive strategies. *Current Anthropology, 34,* 1–34.

Clarke, J. (1998). *The lineaments of wrath: Race, violent crime, and American culture.* New Brunswick, NJ: Transaction.

Clutton-Brock, T., & Parker, G. (1995). Punishment in animal societies. *Nature, 373,* 209–216.

Cohen, L., & Machalek, R. (1994). The normalcy of crime: From Durkheim to evolutionary ecology. *Rationality and Society, 6,* 286–308.

Cosmides, L., Tooby, J., & Barkow, J. (1992). Introduction: Evolutionary psychology and conceptual integration. In J. Barkow, L. Cosmides, & J. Tooby (Eds.), *The adapted mind: Evolutionary psychology and the generation of culture* (pp. 3–15). New York: Oxford University Press.

Daly, M. (1996). Evolutionary adaptationism: Another biological approach to criminal and antisocial behavior. In G. Bock & J. Goode (Eds.), *Genetics of criminal and antisocial behavior* (pp. 183–195). Chichester, UK: Wiley.

Daly, M., & Wilson, M. (1985). Child abuse and other risks of not living with both parents. *Ethology & Sociobiology, 6,* 197–210.

Daly, M., & Wilson, M. (1988a). *Homicide.* New York: Aldine de Gruyter.

Daly, M., & Wilson, M. (1988b). Evolutionary social psychology and family homicide. *Science, 242,* 519–524.

Daly, M., & Wilson, M. (1996). Violence against stepchildren. *Current Directions in Psychological Science, 5,* 77–81.

Dashkov, G. (1992). Quantitative and qualitative changes in crime in the USSR. *British Journal of Criminology, 32,* 160–165.

Degler, C. (1991). *In search of human nature: The decline and revival of Darwinism in American social thought.* New York: Oxford University Press.

Draper, P., & Harpending, H. (1982). Father absence and reproductive strategies: An evolutionary perspective. *Journal of Anthropological Research, 38,* 255–273.

Dugatkin, L. (1992). The evolution of the "con artist." *Ethology and Socio-biology, 13,* 3–18.

Durkheim, E. (1982). *Rules of sociological method.* New York: Free Press.

Edgerton, R. (1992*). Sick societies: Challenging the myth of primitive harmony.* New York: Free Press.

Ellis, L. (1977). The decline and fall of sociology: 1975–2000. *American Sociologist, 12,* 56–66.

Ellis, L. (1991). A synthesized (biosocial) theory of rape. *Journal of Consulting and Clinical Psychology, 59,* 631–642.

Ellis, L. (1996). A discipline in peril: Sociology's future hinges on curing its biophobia. *American Sociologist, 27,* 21–41.

Ellis, L. (1998). Neo-Darwinian theories of violent criminality and antisocial behavior: Photographic evidence from nonhuman animals and a review of the literature. *Aggression and Violent Behavior, 3,* 61–110.

Ellis, L., & Nyborg, H. (1992). Racial/ethnic variation in male testosterone levels: A probable contributor to group differences in health. *Steroids, 57,* 72–75.

Ellis, L., & Walsh, A. (1997). Gene-based evolutionary theories in criminology. *Criminology, 35,* 229–276.

Ellis, L., & Walsh, A. (2000). *Criminology: A global perspective.* Boston: Allyn & Bacon.

Ember, M., & Ember, C. (1998). Facts of violence. *Anthropology Newsletter,* October, 14–15.

Figueredo, A. (1995). The epigenesis of sociopathy. *Behavioral and Brain Sciences, 18,* 556–557.

Figueredo, A., & McClosky, L. (1993). Sex, money, and paternity: The evolutionary psychology of domestic violence. *Ethology and Sociobiology, 14,* 353–379.

Finkelhor, D. (1984). *Child sexual abuse: New theory and research.* New York: Free Press.

Fishbein, D. (1992). The psychobiology of female aggression. *Criminal Justice and Behavior, 19,* 9–126.

Fisher, H. (1992). *Anatomy of love: The natural history of monogamy, adultery, and divorce.* New York: W. W. Norton.

Fisher, H. (1998). Lust, attraction, and attachment in mammalian reproduction. *Human Nature, 9,* 23–52.

Geary, D. (2000). Evolution and proximate expression of human paternal investment. *Psychological Bulletin, 126,* 55–77.

Gelles, R. (1991). Physical violence, child abuse, and child homicide: A continuum of violence or distinct behaviors? *Human Nature, 2,* 59–72.

Gilmartin, P. (1994). *Rape, incest, and child sexual abuse: Consequences and recovery.* New York: Garland.

Glaser, D., & Frosh, S. (1993). *Child sex abuse.* Toronto: University of Toronto Press.

Gonczol, K. (1993). Anxiety over crime. *Hungarian Quarterly, 129,* 87–99.

Gottfredson, M., & Hirschi, T. (1990). *A general theory of crime.* Stanford: Stanford University Press.

Grauerholz, E., & Koralewski, M. (1991). What is known and not known about sexual coercion. In E. Grauerholz & M. Koralewski (Eds.), *Sexual coercion: A sourcebook on its nature, causes, and prevention* (pp. 187–198). Lexington, MA: Lexington.

Greenberg, M., & Schneider, D. (1994). Violence in American cities: Young black males is the answer, but what is the question? *Social Science and Medicine, 39,* 179–187.

Griffiths, P. (1990). Modularity and the psychoevolutionary theory of emotion. *Biology and Philosophy, 5,* 175–196.

Hare, R. (1993). *Without conscience: The disturbing world of the psychopaths among us.* New York: Pocket Books.

Hare, R. (1996). Psychopathy: A clinical construct whose time has come. *Criminal Justice and Behavior, 23,* 25–54.

Harpending, H., & Draper, P. (1988). Antisocial behavior and the other side of cultural evolution. In T. Moffitt & S. Mednick (Eds.), *Biological contributions to crime causation* (pp. 293–307). Dordrecht: Martinus Nyhoff.

Harris, G., Rice, M., & Quinsey, V. (1994). Psychopathy as a taxon: Evidence that psychopaths are a discrete class. *Journal of Consulting and Clinical Psychology, 62,* 387–397.

Harris, J., Vernon, P., & Boomsma, D. (1998). The heritability of testosterone: A study of Dutch adolescent twins and their parents. *Behavior Genetics, 28,* 165–171.

Harrison, L., & Esqueda, C. (1999). Myths and stereotypes of actors involved in domestic violence: Implications for domestic violence culpability attributions. *Aggression and Violent Behavior, 4,* 129–138.

Hill, K., & Hurtado, A. (1996). *Ache life history.* New York: Aldine de Gruyter.

Hooff, J. Van. (1990). Intergroup competition in animals and man. In J. Van der Dennen & V. Falger (Eds.), *Sociobiology and conflict: Evolutionary perspectives on competition, cooperation, violence and warfare* (pp. 23–54). London: Chapman and Hall.

Hrdy, S. (1999). *Mother nature: A history of mothers, infants, and natural selection.* New York: Pantheon.

Jeffrey, C. R. (1977). Criminology—Whither or wither? *Criminology, 15,* 283–286.

Jockin, V., McGue, V., & Lykken, D. (1996). Personality and divorce: A genetic analysis. *Journal of Personality and Social Psychology, 71,* 288–299.

Kanazawa, S., & Still, M. (2000). Why men commit crimes (and why they desist). *Sociological Theory, 18,* 434–447.

Katz, J. (1988). *Seductions of crime: Moral and sensual attractions in doing evil.* New York: Basic Books.

Kendler, K. (1995). Genetic epidemiology in psychiatry: Taking both genes and environment seriously. *Archives of General Psychiatry, 52,* 895–899.

Lepowsky, M. (1994). Women, men, and aggression in egalitarian societies. *Sex Roles, 30,* 199–211.

Lubinski, D., & Humphrys, L. (1997). Incorporating intelligence into epidemiology and the social sciences. *Intelligence, 24,* 159–201.

Lykken, D. (1995). *The antisocial personalities*. Hillsdale, NJ: Lawrence Erlbaum.

Lyons, M., True, W., Eusen, S., Goldberg, J., Meyer, J., Faraone, S., Eaves, L., & Tsuang, M. (1995). Differential heritability of adult and juvenile antisocial traits. *Archives of General Psychiatry, 53*, 906–915.

Lytton, H., & Romney, D. (1991). Parents' differential socialization of boys and girls: A meta-analysis. *Psychological Bulletin, 109*, 267–296.

MacDonald, K. (1997). Life history theory and human reproductive behavior: Environmental/contextual influences and heritable variation. *Human Nature, 8*, 327–359.

Machalek, R. (1995). Basic dimensions and forms of social exploitation: A comparative analysis. *Advances in Human Ecology, 4*, 35–68.

Machalek, R. (1996). The evolution of social exploitation. *Advances in Human Ecology, 5*, 1–32.

Machalek, R., & Cohen, L. (1991). The nature of crime: Is cheating necessary for cooperation? *Human Nature, 2*, 215–233.

Mann, C. (1995). Women of color and the criminal justice system. In B. Price & N. Sokoloff (Eds.), *The criminal justice system and women: Offenders, victims, and workers* (pp. 118–119). New York: McGraw-Hill.

Mazur, A., & Booth, A. (1998). Testosterone and dominance in men. *Behavioral and Brain Sciences, 21*, 353–397.

McGue, M., & Lykken, D. (1992). Genetic influence on the risk of divorce. *Psychological Science, 3*, 368–373.

Mealey, L. (1995). The sociobiology of sociopathy: An integrated evolutionary model. *Behavioral and Brain Sciences, 18*, 523–559.

Mears, D., Ploeger, M., & Warr, M. (1998). Explaining the gender gap in delinquency: Peer influence and moral evaluations of behavior. *Journal of Research in Crime and Delinquency, 35*, 251–266.

Moffitt, T. (1993). Adolescent-limited and life-course persistent antisocial behavior: A developmental taxonomy. *Psychological Review, 100*, 674–701.

Moore, C., & Rose, M. (1995). Adaptive and nonadaptive explanations of sociopathy. *Behavior and Brain Sciences, 18*, 566–567.

Nesse, R. (1990). Evolutionary explanations of emotions. *Human Nature, 1*, 261–289.

Nesse, R., & Lloyd, A. (1992). The evolution of psychodynamic mechanisms. In J. Barkow, L. Cosmides, & J. Tooby (Eds.), *The adapted mind: Evolutionary psychology and the generation of culture* (pp. 601–620). New York: Oxford University Press.

O'Connor, T., Deater-Deckard, K., Fulker, D., Rutter, M., & Plomin, R. (1998). Genotype-environment correlations in early childhood and adolescence: Antisocial behavioral problems and coercive parenting. *Developmental Psychology, 34*, 370–381.

Pater, P. (1990). The study of conflict. In J. Van der Dennen & V. Falger (Eds.), *Sociobiology and conflict: Evolutionary perspectives on competition, cooperation, violence and warfare* (pp. 1–19). London: Chapman and Hall.

Patrick, C. (1994). Emotions and psychopathy: Startling new insights. *Psychophysiology, 31*, 319–330.

Perusse, D. (1992). Culture and reproductive success in industrial societies: Testing the relationship at the proximate and ultimate levels. *Behavioral and Brain Sciences, 16*, 267–283.

Plavcan, J., & Schaik, C. van. (1997). Intrasexual competition and body weight dimorphism in anthropoid primates. *American Journal of Physical Anthropology, 103*, 37–68.

Plomin, R. (1995). Genetics and children's experiences in the family. *Journal of Child Psychology and Psychiatry, 36*, 33–68.

Price, B., & Sokoloff, N. (1995). Theories and facts about women offenders. In B. Price & N. Sokoloff (Eds.), *The criminal justice system and women: Offenders, victims, and workers* (pp. 1–10). New York: McGraw-Hill.

Raine, A. (1993). *The psychopathology of crime: Criminal behavior as a clinical disorder*. San Diego: Academic Press.

Raleigh, M., McGuire, M., Brammer, G., Pollock, D., & Yuwiler, A. (1991). Serotonergic mechanisms promote dominance acquisition in adult vervet monkeys. *Brain Research, 559*, 181–190.

Rasche, C. (1995). Minority women and domestic violence: The unique dilemmas of battered women of color. In B. Price & N. Sokoloff (Eds.), *The criminal justice system and women: Offenders, victims, and workers* (pp. 246–261). New York: McGraw-Hill.

Rose, R., Bernstein, L., Judd, H., Hannish, R., Pike, M., & Henderson, B. (1986). Serum testosterone levels in healthy young black and white men. *Journal of the National Cancer Institute, 76*, 45–48.

Rossi, A. (1984). Gender and parenthood: American Sociological Association, 1983 presidential address. *American Sociological Review, 49*, 1–19.

Rossi, A. (1997). The impact of family structure and social change on adolescent sexual behavior. *Children and Youth Services Review, 19*, 369–400.

Rowe, D. (1996). An adaptive strategy theory of crime and delinquency. In J. Hawkins (Ed.), *Delinquency and crime: Current theories* (pp. 268–314). Cambridge: Cambridge University Press.

Scarr, S. (1993). Biological and cultural diversity: The legacy of Darwin for development. *Child Development, 64*, 1333–1353.

Shavit, Y., & Rattner, A. (1988). Age, crime, and the early lifecourse. *American Journal of Sociology, 93*, 1457–1470.

Skilling, T., Quinsey, V., & Craig, W. (2001). Evidence of a taxon underlying serious antisocial behavior in boys. *Criminal Justice and Behavior, 28*, 450–470.

Smith, D. (1993). Brain, environment, heredity, and personality. *Psychological Reports, 72*, 3–13.

Smuts, B. (1992). Male aggression against women: An evolutionary perspective. *Human Nature, 3*, 1–44.

Smuts, B. (1993). Male aggression and sexual coercion of females in nonhuman primates and other mammals: Evidence and theoretical implications. *Advances in the Study of Behavior, 22*, 1–63.

Symons, D. (1987). If we're all Darwinians, what's the fuss about? In C. Crawfors, M. Smith, & D. Krebs (Eds.), *Sociobiology and psychology: Ideas, issues, and applications* (pp. 121–146). Hillsdale, NJ: Lawrence Erlbaum.

Symons, D. (1992). The use and misuse of Darwinism in the study of human behavior. In J. Barkow, L. Cosmides, & J. Tooby (Eds.), *The adapted mind: Evolutionary psychology and the generation of culture* (pp. 137–159). New York: Oxford University Press.

Thornhill, N., & Thornhill, R. (1987). Evolutionary theory and rules of mating and marriage pertaining to relatives. In C. Crawford, M. Smith, & D. Krebs (Eds.), *Sociobiology and psychology: Ideas, issues, and applications* (pp. 373–400). Hillsdale, NJ: Lawrence Erlbaum.

Thornhill, R., & Palmer, C. (2000). *A natural history of rape*. Cambridge, MA: MIT Press.

Thornhill, R., & Thornhill, N. (1992). The evolutionary psychology of men's coercive sexuality. *Behavioral and Brain Sciences, 15*, 363–421.

Tooby, J., & Cosmides, L. (1990) On the universality of human nature and the uniqueness of the individual: The role of genetics and adaptation. *Journal of Personality, 58*, 17–67.

Tooby, J., & Cosmides, L. (1992). The psychological foundations of culture. In J. Barkow, L. Cosmides, & J. Tooby (Eds.), *The adapted mind: Evolutionary psychology and the generation of culture* (pp. 19–136). New York: Oxford University Press.

Trivers, R. (1991). Deceit and self-deception: The relationship between communication and consciousness. In M. Robinson & L. Tiger (Eds.), *Man and beast revisited* (pp. 175–191). Washington, DC: Smithsonian Institution Press.

Udry, J. (1995). Sociology and biology: What biology do sociologists need to know? *Social Forces, 73*, 1267–1278.

Virkkunen, M., Goldman, D., & Linnoila, M. (1996). Serotonin in alcoholic violent offenders. In G. Bock & J. Goode (Eds.), *Genetics of criminal and antisocial behavior*. Chichester, UK: Wiley.

Virkkunen, M., & Linnoila, M. (1990). Serotonin in early onset, male alcoholics with violent behavior. *Annals of Medicine, 22*, 327–331.

Walsh, A. (1991). *Intellectual imbalance, love deprivation, and violent delinquency: A biosocial perspective*. Springfield, IL: Charles C. Thomas.

Walsh, A. (1995a). *Biosociology: An emerging paradigm*. New York: Praeger.

Walsh, A. (1995b). Parental attachment, drug use, and facultative sexual strategies. *Social Biology, 42*, 95–107.

Walsh, A. (1997). Methodological individualism and vertical integration in the social sciences. *Behavior and Philosophy, 25*, 121–136.

Walsh, A. (1999). Life history theory and female readers of pornography. *Personality and Individual Differences, 27*, 779–787.

Walsh, A. (2000a). Evolutionary psychology and the origins of justice. *Justice Quarterly, 17*, 841–864.

Walsh, A. (2000b). Behavior genetics and anomie/strain theory. *Criminology, 38*, 1075–1107.

Walsh, A. (2002). *Biosocial criminology: Introduction and integration.* Cincinnati: Anderson.

Walsh, A., & Ellis, L. (1999). Political ideology and American criminologists' explanations for criminal behavior. *Criminologist, 24,* 1–17.

Walsh, A., & Hemmens, C. (2000). *From law to order: The theory and practice of law and justice.* Lanham, MD: American Correctional Association.

Weisfeld, G. (1999). *Evolutionary principles of human adolescence.* New York: Basic Books.

Wilson, D., & Sober, E. (1994). Reintroducing group selection to the human behavioral sciences. *Behavioral and Brain Sciences, 17,* 585–608.

Wilson, E. O. (1975). *Sociobiology: The new synthesis.* Cambridge, MA: Harvard University Press.

Wilson, E. O. (1998). *Consilience: The unity of knowledge.* New York: Knopf.

Wilson, M., & Daly, M. (1985). Competitiveness, risk taking, and violence: The young male syndrome. *Ethology and Sociobiology, 6,* 59–73.

Wrangham, R., & Peterson, D. (1996). *Demonic males: Apes and the origins of human violence.* Boston: Houghton Mifflin.

Wright, R. (1994). *The moral animal: Evolutionary psychology and everyday life.* New York: Pantheon Books.

Wright, R. A., & Miller, J. (1998). Taboo until today? The coverage of biological arguments in criminology textbooks, 1961 to 1970 and 1987 to 1996. *Journal of Criminal Justice, 26,* 1–19.

Zuckerman, M. (1990). The psychophysiology of sensation-seeking. *Journal of Personality, 58,* 314–345.

9 Evolution, Agency, and Sociology

Bernd Baldus

Almost from the day it was published in 1859, Darwin's *The Origin of Species* was drawn into the politics of a turbulent century. Darwin, aware of the social implications of his theory, had limited his consideration of human cultural evolution to the single remark that "much light will be thrown (by the theory of natural selection) on the origin of man and his history" (Darwin, 1958, p. 449). But this did not prevent his theory from quickly becoming embroiled in the political debates of the day.

Darwin's theory of evolution arrived in a society whose "respectable classes" were torn between euphoria over technical, scientific, and economic progress on one hand, and profound fears of social conflict on the other. The *Origin of Species* was published in the same year as Dickens's *Tale of Two Cities*, a book that captivated large audiences with its chilling image of revolutionary women knitting while counting out the number of prisoners climbing the scaffold on their way to the guillotine. To many readers it must have appeared as if they were knitting the shroud of civilized society. The revolutionary terror, personally experienced by Comte de Saint-Simon (one of the founders of sociology) and subsequently embellished by literary license, cast a long shadow over the nineteenth century. Fears that it could happen again were reinforced by repeated and widespread economic crises and social conflict in industrializing countries.

Early social scientists and evolutionists phrased these concerns as a more intellectual paradox. On one hand, the new market-based society had fought and overcome the old feudal order by demanding more individual freedom and greater equality. But these very demands seemed to generate centrifugal forces which, depending on one's political leanings, promised further radical social and political change or presaged social disintegration and chaos. The origins of social order, not the origin of species, was the mystery of mysteries that topped the agenda of nineteenth-century social science.

Darwin's theory was quickly drawn into these debates. To English radicals, evolution suggested that individuals and entire classes could rise from humble origins to better things, a view supported by those on the Darwinian Left such as Alfred Russel Wallace and Thomas Henry Huxley. Darwin's cousin Galton found in the *Origin* the basis for the heredity of human abilities and the potential of a eugenic "science of breeding the best," an idea that appealed to the Left because it seemed to oppose aristocratic privilege, and to the Right because it seemed to confirm it. To social Darwinists the theory of natural selection justified the position of the middle and upper classes in the new industrial social structure.

Hitched to these agendas, Darwin's theory was soon transformed beyond recognition. For Darwin, differential fitness led to differential reproductive success which produced much diversity but no hierarchy; any attempt to order its results would be "hopeless; who will decide whether a cuttle-fish be higher than a bee" (Darwin, 1958, p. 331). Social Darwinists, on the other hand, were interested in inequality in the here and now. For them "fitness" was a matter of desirable or detrimental character traits which explained wealth and poverty. Darwin had described a process of descent with modification which could be traced back to ancestral events but could not be reduced to an ultimate cause or essence and therefore followed no predictable path. By contrast, early sociologists were very much interested in ultimate causes and progressive advancement. Their "evolutionary" models of society drew not on Darwin but on the physiological functions of bodily organs and the development of the embryo into a fully grown organism. Darwin's evolution included a large measure of chance, imperfection, and lack of direction. Nineteenth-century sociologists, however, were looking for "scientific" clarity, determinism, and laws. Marx saw in Darwin's theory "a natural-scientific basis for the class struggle in history," Herbert Spencer the law of progressive differentiation and functional specialization, Ernst Haeckel proof of the nationalist destiny of the "master race."

By the end of the nineteenth century, evolutionism was anything but a unified body of thought. Numerous and often contradictory "evolutionary" theories had emerged that differed significantly from Darwin's ideas. The resulting confusion marked the beginning of a long, uneasy, and sometimes hostile relationship between sociology and evolutionary theory. Today, sociologists may quietly concede *some* links between biology and social behavior. They may even admit that some of what we do, from prenatal smoking to the global destruction of environments, bears risks for our reproductive success and our long-term survival as a species (Beck, 1992). The majority of sociologists, however, look upon evolutionary theory with a mixture of ignorance and professional disdain.[1]

Two problems have proven particularly intractable for an evolutionary study of human culture. One is the presence in social systems of numerous adaptively redundant, suboptimal, or even dysfunctional traits which, by no stretch of the biological imagination, can be explained in terms of their past or present contribution to human reproductive fitness. The second is the problem of agency. The process of natural selection, at least as it is understood in most contemporary biology, seems to be a purely external force not under the control of the individual organism. By contrast, human culture appears to be the product of intentional, purposive choice by individual actors.

Darwin and the Evolution of Culture

Both the problem of "useless traits" and of the role of individual agency in evolution and evolutionary design had been very much on Darwin's mind. In the *Origin of Species* he sketched a process in which variations, appearing blindly (i.e., not caused by their eventual adaptive utility), were used by individual organisms interacting with their environment. Those variations that proved advantageous in the competition for limited resources increased the organism's "fitness," the chances of leaving offspring which inherited the favorable variation and benefited in the same way. The cumulative effect of this natural selection of favored variations was their long-term increase in a population and the eventual emergence of a new species.

Selection involved individual organisms in two very different roles. In one, *inheritance*, they were passive carriers of traits: they inherited variations, the raw material of natural selection, and passed favored variations on to future generations. Between these two processes lay a second, equally important role: the *active internal adaptation of organisms during their lifetime*. Here variations that arose unconnected to adaptive needs were tried out in the organism's actual ecological life context to find out how they could be put to use. Inherited variations that were not used, and thus did not change the relationship between organism and environment, remained without selective consequence. Often the environment alone selected what was "useful"; no active involvement by the organism was necessary. But there were also many cases where the adaptive utility of a variation did not reveal itself automatically. The potential value of an inherited variation had to be discovered through trial and error and retained through day-to-day use and "habit" in order to result eventually in increased reproductive success. Organisms were active agents in this process; they "seized on the many and widely diversified places in the polity of nature" and "partook of the advantages which they inherited" (Darwin, 1958, pp. 112, 117). This activity required mental faculties.

Much of the *Origin* was devoted to examining the effects of natural selection on the physical characteristics of animals and humans. But from the start Darwin was convinced that evolution also led from animal feelings and cognition to human culture. As early as 1838 he had promised himself "never [to] allow that because there is a chasm between man . . . and animals that man has different origin" (cited in Moore, 1985, p. 453). His early notebooks contained many observations of animal behavior which suggested emotions and intelligence. Animals could feel happy and sad; could be playful or suspicious; could display terror and courage, magnanimity and revenge; and had powers of reasoning and imagination. The evolutionary explanation of mind, agency, and morality was "the citadel itself," and Darwin became increasingly bent on conquering it.

The first obstacle on the way was the problem of useless traits. Darwin, a keen observer of nature, marveled at the often exquisite fit between traits and environment. But he also noted the many barely serviceable "imperfections" and the "useless traits" of no recognizable adaptive value. Rudimentary or vestigial organs were extremely common in nature. In mammals, tailbone structures in tailless species, useless digits in the wings of birds, useless wings in flightless birds, or fetal teeth in toothless whales all bore evidence to the fact that the products of natural selection were anything but perfect. Most of these nonfunctional traits could be accounted for as remnants of organs rendered useless by changes in the environment, as structures too small or too well hidden to be obliterated by the economy of natural selection or, in the example of the functional sutures in the skulls of mammals and the nonfunctional ones in the skulls of birds, as modifications of ancestral anatomical forms.

That left a sufficient number of traits whose existence Darwin could not explain by their adaptive value, including the peacock's tail, cited in *The Descent of Man* as a prime example of a nonadaptive trait. A particularly disturbing problem was partially formed components of complex organs, still under construction by natural selection. Here the argument frequently raised by Darwin's critics was that it was easy to show the adaptive utility of fully formed features such as feathers or eyes, but much more difficult to demonstrate how natural selection could have preserved only partially formed and functionally useless organ parts. This criticism, driven home by the publication of Mivart's *On the Genesis of Species* in 1871, gave Darwin "a cold shudder." The sixth edition of the *Origin* addressed these objections. It offered numerous examples of the gradual evolution of body parts and showed that the same organs could serve different functions and that incipient wings could provide an adaptive advantage before being fully formed. But Darwin knew that this was not the complete answer: in the same edition he also emphasized that selection by the blind forces of nature was not the only process involved in evolutionary design:

> As my conclusions have lately been much misrepresented, and it has been stated that I attribute the modification of species exclusively to natural selection, I may be permitted to remark that in the first edition of this work, and subsequently, I placed in a most conspicuous position—namely at the close of the Introduction—the following words. "I am convinced that natural selection has been the main, but not the exclusive, means of modification." This has been to no avail. Great is the power of steady misrepresentation. (Darwin, 1958, p. 395)

Darwin saw the connection between, on the one hand, nonadaptive traits and incomplete organs, and, on the other, the problem of evolutionary design—the process that assembled spontaneous variations into complex physiological forms. Both had to be produced by the same forces. This was particularly evident in the sphere of human behavior. Darwin's encounter with Fuegian natives during his voyage on the *Beagle* had taught him that the extraordinary latitude and flexibility of human culture went far beyond what could be interpreted as adaptations to a hostile environment. The three Fuegians whom Captain Fitzroy returned to their homeland after their "civilizing" stay in England had in a short time acquired many of the habits of English society and abandoned them just as quickly once they returned. This proved to Darwin the cultural continuity between "savages" and London society, but also the plasticity of culture, which included many ephemeral, useless, or even maladaptive traits. He gave this topic much prominence in the *Descent of Man*. Traits such as the relative lack of body hair, racial differences, or musical ability among humans could not contribute to survival and reproductive success and could therefore not be a product of natural selection. Others, such as cooperation, altruism, and moral faculties, while clearly advantageous, were complex, deliberately assembled social constructions:

> It might have been an immense advantage to man to have sprung from some comparatively weak creature. The slight corporeal strength of man, his little speed, his want of natural weapons, etc., are more than counterbalanced, firstly by his intellectual powers, through which he has, whilst still remaining in a barbarous state, formed for himself weapons, tools, etc., and secondly by his social qualities which lead him to give aid to his fellow-men and to receive it in return. (Darwin, 1981, pp. 156, 157)

Darwin addressed the evolution of human culture in two late works. Here he argued that traces of many human intellectual and moral faculties could be found in animals, and that a single formative process—evolution—could explain both. *The Expression of the Emotions in Man and Animals* (1872) focused on how humans expressed feelings such as anger, happiness, or surprise and showed their link to similar facial or bodily expressions in animals. The second book, *The Descent of Man* (1871), also argued for the continuity of cultural evolution in animals and human beings but concentrated specifically on aesthetic and moral traits that had no direct adaptive advantage.

To explain their presence, Darwin developed a theory of sexual selection. Traits such as the elaborate coloration used in courtship displays exceeded what was required for survival. Darwin argued that their selection was governed by internal standards of beauty and taste that led females to mate with males who displayed the preferred characteristics. In sexual selection nature acted no longer as the arbiter of survival, but as a source of options for choices the organism made. Sexual selection was not Lamarckian: tastes and preferences did not *cause* the appearance of preferred characteristics. And it was still external in that the characteristics of one sexual partner were selected by the other. The theoretical significance of sexual selection lay in giving the active choice by organisms a prominent and explicit selective role in evolution.

This idea had a direct bearing on three important aspects of evolution. First, it required only a small step to locate the process of internal selection entirely inside the evolving organism, whose preferences determined how its inherited traits were used and retained. Second, such internal selection added a source of variability to mutation and environmental change: internal evaluation greatly increased the possible adaptive uses of mutations and environmental change, and the likelihood of suboptimal but nonlethal error while these uses were tried out during the organism's lifetime. Third, and perhaps most important, internal selection suggested a solution to the thorny problem of evolutionary design. Selection, whether external or sexual, could account for the differential survival of discrete traits. But neither could fully explain how these traits were assembled into complex organic or cultural designs. The question of who or what could replace William Paley's "divine watchmaker" in accounting for the intricate complexity of structure and function in nature posed for Darwin "perhaps [the] greatest difficulty to [the] whole theory" of evolution. Even his friends had problems with the idea that "the law of the higglety-pigglety," guided only by external selection, could fashion complex organic forms from undirected variations supplied by nature.

The answer to this question lay in the similarity between sexual selection and the artificial selection which Darwin had described in the first chapter of the *Origin*. Here the breeder assembled desired traits from accidental variations supplied by nature, either by keeping only the "best" animals or by pursuing a detailed image of a preferred breed. The breeder's intent added a crucial third element—direction—to the variations that provided the material with which evolution worked, and to the competition for resources that fueled the dynamics of selection. Darwin (1981, p. 398) noted that sexual selection closely resembled artificial breeding. Internal preferences in animals could therefore have the same generative, design-producing effects in evolution as the breeder's preconceived ideas of desirable traits. Selection now took place *inside* a mentally active, purposive organism. Its preferences determined which of the variations supplied by nature would be used, and in what manner. Internal selection could therefore be crucial in assembling variations in a particular direction (Darwin, 1965, p. 40; Smith, 1978, p. 261).

Darwin never doubted that this process differed from that described by Jean-Baptiste Lamarck. Variations occurred in all directions. They were not caused by the needs or desires of organisms. Apart from basic laws of growth and structural constraint, nature offered no inherent source of evolutionary direction. But the exploration and use of randomly provided variations by organisms could lead to the assemblage of such variations into complex functional designs. Darwin's interest was therefore increasingly drawn to the activity of organisms while they were alive.

Natural selection now took a range of different forms. On one end stood the purely external selection where, for example, in a variable species those individuals whose coloration stood out more clearly against their favorite resting background became easier prey. Here, environmental forces alone preserved those whose color concealed them better. The species under selection made no contribution to this process; it acted as it always had. On the other end stood a process of natural selection where organisms explored the potential of mutations provided by nature, or new uses of existing traits: flycatchers hovered like kestrels in one spot or dove into the water like kingfishers; birds that were normally seed-eaters killed small birds in the manner of a shrike, and black bears swam "for hours with widely open mouth, thus catching, almost like a whale, insects in the water" (Darwin, 1958, p. 107). Here internal selection set the stage; differential inheritance to future generations followed in its wake:

> To take as an illustration the case of the larger titmouse, this bird often holds the seeds of the yew between its feet on a branch, and hammers with its beak till it gets at the kernel. Now what special difficulty would there be in natural selection preserving all the slight individual variations in the shape of the beak, which were better and better adapted to break open the seeds, until a beak was formed as well constructed for this purpose as that of the nuthatch, at the same time that habit, or compulsion, or spontaneous variations of taste, led the bird to become more and more a seed eater? In this case the beak is supposed to be

slowly modified by natural selection, subsequently to, but in accordance with slowly changing habits or taste. (Darwin, 1958, p. 250)

Darwin concluded the *Descent* with a statement that clearly established a role for the mind in assembling the products of evolution and in guiding its course:

> He who admits the principle of sexual selection will be led to the re-markable conclusion that the cerebral system not only regulates most of the existing functions of the body, but has indirectly influenced the pro-gressive development of various bodily structures and of certain mental qualities. Courage, pugnacity, perseverance, strength and size of body, weapons of all kinds, musical organs, both vocal and instrumental, bright colors, stripes and marks, and ornamental appendages, have all been indirectly gained by one sex or the other, through the influence of love and jealousy, through the appreciation of the beautiful in sound, color or form, and through the exertion of a choice; and these powers of the mind manifestly depend on the development of the cerebral sys-tem. (Darwin, 1981, part 2, p. 402)

The Transformation of Darwin's Theory

The publication of the *Descent* touched a raw nerve. The suggestion that evolution produced much that was imperfect, mediocre and even useless; that evolutionary history was subject to spontaneous change and therefore followed no predictable path; and—most important—that the mind had an active, direction-giving role in evolution did not sit well with nineteenth-century science.

Three powerful intellectual currents worked against Darwin's theory. One was the religious legacy of human beings as the pinnacle of creation, a position that even Darwin's secular contemporaries were reluctant to aban-don. Wallace, the codiscoverer of natural selection, was one of the first to uncouple human culture from evolution. Cultural evolution obeyed differ-ent forces; "intellectual and moral faculties . . . must have another origin . . . in the unseen universe of the Spirit" (Wallace cited in Gruber, 1981, p. 31). Most sociologists, including Marx, followed suit. Darwinian evolution came to an end with the beginning of human history. Human culture was a fun-damentally different matter, initiated by a "moral flash" which bestowed the gift of rational thought on humanity, much like the invisible spark from the hand of God in the Sistine Chapel infused Adam with a soul.

The second obstacle was political: a deeply rooted fear of the destruc-tive potential of unrestrained human agency. The overriding ideological problem of the time was to rein in "exaggerated" notions of freedom and equality unleashed by industrialization and make them compatible with the new bourgeois social order. Mivart complained that the *Descent* violated convictions held by "the majority of cultivated minds" and would unsettle "our half-educated classes." Without constraints there would be no right or wrong, no obedience and no order. No man could be "a free moral agent"; consciousness had to be kept in check by "an absolute and immutable rule *legitimately* claiming obedience" (Mivart cited in Desmond & Moore, 1991, p. 583). Most nineteenth-century social scientists agreed and opted for a strangely schizophrenic view of social actors. On the one hand, they paid lip service to human freedom and agency, especially freedom of choice and contract in the new industrial markets, and linked them to the promise of social progress. At the same time they tied human action to universal "social laws" that confirmed the necessity of order and saw social change as the sequential advancement of human societies along a linear and predictable path. Even Marx, that quintessential advocate of revolution, did not trust human agency alone to accomplish the task of political change; he felt more comfortable invoking a mechanism of material forces which assured that the process went in the right direction. A theory of human cultural evolution which suggested that absolutely anything was possible was, by the ideological standards of the nineteenth century, decidedly not politically correct.

Finally, there was a growing fascination with the natural sciences, especially the methodological attraction of objective measurement of biological and social facts, and the promise of finding lawlike cause-effect relationships that would eventually explain the workings of the entire complex social mechanism. Comte had this in mind in his vision of a positivist "social physics" (later renamed sociology) as the queen of all sciences. Among biologists, the rediscovery of Mendel's laws at the turn of the century encouraged similar hopes that evolutionary theory would become an experimental science. Social science and biology began to ignore irregular and nonmeasurable events, including cognitive processes.

By 1900, Darwin's work on agency and voluntaristic forces in evolution had been purged from social sciences and biology. Social scientists opted for an ambiguous mind-nature dualism that affirmed the uniqueness and superiority of the human mind but allowed it to operate only within the strict confines of external functional imperatives or behavioral laws. Durkheim settled sociology with the injunction that the causes of a social fact should be sought only in other social facts, not in the sphere of individual motives and action. In psychology, behaviorism reduced cognition to reactions of subjects to external stimuli of pleasure and pain that could be completely controlled in the laboratory. Concepts such as freedom, self, and agency merely expressed our ignorance of social behavior and would disappear as our knowledge expanded.

Autonomous man serves to explain only the things we are not yet able to explain in other ways. His existence depends upon our ignorance, and he naturally loses status as we come to know more about behaviour. The task of a scientific analysis is to explain how the behaviour of a person as a physical system is related to the conditions under which the human species evolved and the conditions under which the individual lives. (Skinner, 1971, p. 12)

Internal, unmeasurable events were of no interest. Human behavior was assumed to be controlled by causal mechanisms, stimulus-response sequences, or rational choice, which reduced the complexity of social behavior to simple cost-benefit calculations. Intentions and goals were either standardized or explicitly ignored. So was the vast body of nonrational human action. Sociological positivism, behaviorism, neoclassical economics and neo-Darwinist biology all saw individuals as agents of external forces with little or no control over their fate.

Instead of Darwin, sociologists placed their faith in the Second Coming of a sociological Newton. Social and natural systems were seen as fully determined mechanisms that could be reduced to their smallest components. Like the cogs, levers, and cranks of a machine, they functioned together in linear, deterministic causal relationships. Effects were proportional to their causes: Small causes produced small effects, and large causes large effects. Other things being equal, the same effects always followed the same causes. Social processes were therefore reversible, repeatable, and predictable.

The complexity and unpredictability of human behavior was dismissed as an apparent rather than a generic property of culture. The irregularities and redundancies that cropped up so disturbingly often in real life were hidden behind constants, concealed in statistical error terms, or set aside as "unexplained variance." Functional and rational choice theories dismissed irrational or dysfunctional social behavior as residual "anomie" or looked for its "latent" functions. Durkheim's argument that crime in fact strengthened the feeling of righteousness among upright citizens and therefore reinforced social solidarity was only the first of many "just so" stories of sociological functionalism. Redundant or dysfunctional traits were seen as temporary irritants that would disappear with further research or could be accepted as unimportant "fuzzy edges" of otherwise "successful explanatory models" of a fundamentally orderly social world (Collins, 1989, p. 128).

The rejection of Darwin produced a paradoxical result. With positivism emerging as its major paradigm, sociology became a predominantly empirical science that compiled masses of data of the social world. These data showed culture to be probabilistic rather than deterministic. Their structure was taxonomic and historical: cultural traits could be grouped by common characteristics and traced to ancestral events, but not to ultimate causes or forces. Human choices were as often as not irrational, their outcomes far from optimal, and their consequences far from predicted. The course of history resembled more a random walk than a fixed progressive path. In short, the social reality reflected in sociologists' data had the telltale properties of an evolutionary process.[2]

Sociological theory could make no sense of these facts. The inability to discover the hoped-for laws of behavior became "a source of embarrassment and confusion to quantitative sociologists" (Turner, 1987, p. 15). Contemporary sociology is drowning in a sea of data for which it has no coherent theoretical explanation, and faces unprecedented doubts regarding its basic premises (Baldus, 1990; Bernard, 1993; Bryant, 1992; Collins, 1986; Turner & Turner, 1990; Quadagno & Knapp, 1992). It foundered on the same obstacles that had already preoccupied Darwin. The complexity and unpredictability of human culture defied the search for social laws, and the role of human agency became mired in seemingly interminable structure-agency debates that forever reshuffled the conceptual deck one way or the other and produced commonplace observations such as Anthony Giddens's (1984) observation that the "duality of structure" both constrains and enables social action, or Pierre Bourdieu's (1977, 1992) assertion that human action is both "structured" and "structuring."

Post-Darwinian biology fell under the spell of the same forces. Neo-Darwinism disconnected Darwin's views on the adaptive activity of organisms during their lifetime from the rest of his theory. It focused instead on the external sphere of variation and inheritance. The discovery of heritable units of genetic information shifted biological interest from individual organisms to genes and, with the emergence of the New Synthesis in the 1930s, to populations. *The Descent of Man* was dismissed as "a strange book" (Ruse, 1979, p. 247). Darwin's interest in the role of cognition in evolution was treated as a lapse into a never fully abandoned Lamarckism (Richards, 1987, p. 195). Numerous critics of sexual selection denounced the idea that animals could make choices, and tried to prove that apparently redundant characteristics such as the peacock's tail were really adaptive after all (Cronin, 1991). Biology rejected internal mental operations such as consciousness, awareness, or intent as anthropomorphic. They became a virtual taboo in neo-Darwinist theory (Griffin, 1984, p. 22).

The most obvious casualty of this transformation was Darwin's interest in the role of mind and agency in evolution. Organisms became epiphenomena of genes, controlled by exogenous forces. They no longer had any independent role to play and were reduced to machines made of meat, compelled by a few innate drives or needs (such as hunger, sex, and fear) to engage in an unceasing search for adaptively optimal uses of given faculties in given environments. A strict economy of external culling eliminated all suboptimal or redundant traits. Brains now appeared as fitness-maximizing special-purpose organs, like hands or kidneys, neural computers composed of combinatorial algorithms for accurate adaptive reasoning about plants and animals, objects and people (Pinker, 1997) or of a large number of domain-specific modules, each producing preprogrammed adaptive responses and goals (Barkow, 1989, p. 131; Tooby & Cosmides, 1989; Barkow, Cosmides, & Tooby, 1992) which coordinated organisms' behavior with information about their environment. Alternatively, they—and the bodies attached to them—functioned as meme-machines (Blackmore, 1999) that replicated and propagated standardized components of culture such as memes or culture-gens.

Though they remained cognizant of the problem of redundant cultural traits, modular and memetic theories were forced to see agency, self, and consciousness as residual or exceptional by-products of genetic selection. Modular theories of the brain viewed them as fitness-enhancing deceptions that disguised deeper biological drives (Barkow, 1989, p. 98). For memeticists, self and consciousness were illusions constructed by memes to increase their chances of social acceptance. Culture was entirely dissociated from its carriers; it came into existence simply because it was advantageous to itself (Dawkins, 1976, p. 214). Dennett (1991) suggested that agency and consciousness did not exist. We only had to explain why people thought they did. In reality brains were in a constant state of cognitive pandemonium, with different contents competing for "cerebral celebrity," giving the appearance of intentional and goal-directed thought. None of these approaches left much room for an independent, generative, design-producing role of the brain: "There is no deliberation, no planning, no 'mind,' nothing incorporating ends or goals to direct the selection. It is achieved through nothing more forward-looking than pressures of the environment" (Cronin, 1991, p. 19). Evolutionary design became a simple additive process: "6 percent (vision) is better than 5, 7 percent better than 6, and so on up the gradual, continuous series" (Dawkins, 1986, p. 81). Neo-Darwinist biology focused mainly on the adaptive improvement of already given designs in controlled environments, effectively sidestepping the question how they had been assembled in the first place.

Whether, as in the case of theories of the modular brain, human culture was seen as an extension of evolutionary processes, or, as in the case of memetics, as an analog to the process of natural selection, cultural traits ultimately had to be explained in terms of their fitness or reproductive effects, or at least in terms of the "truth" or "utility" of memes, ideas, or thought products. Any such effort quickly confronted the fact that "we do a great deal that doesn't make much biological sense" (Barash, 1979, p. 226). Error, maladaptive behavior, suboptimal technologies, and dysfunctional cultural traits abounded in human societies. The "survival of the mediocre" (Hallpike, 1986), not the survival of the optimal, was the hallmark of cultural selection. While beliefs, values, and goals often profoundly influenced human culture, they could not be compared or ordered in terms of an abstract calculus of utility or progress.

Having reduced Darwin's theory of evolution by half to a process of genetic variation and external selection, and faced with an extraordinary complex and "biologically frivolous" (Pinker, 1997, p. 531) human culture, evolutionary analyses of human behavior had to resort to expedients. Nonadaptive traits were interpreted as "perverted" or "hypersocial" expressions of hidden adaptive interests (Barkow, 1989), as "runaway" or inflationary processes (Boyd & Richerson, 1985) that exaggerated adaptive traits, or as "cultural inertia" that preserved originally adaptive but now neutral or harmful cultural characteristics (Alexander, 1979, p. 77; Cavalli-Sforza & Feldman, 1981). Numerous "runaway" or "work-around" explanations were proposed for the human brain. Wilson (1978) suggested that their rapid growth resulted from a positive feedback loop where growing brains allowed for greater cultural capacity, which in turn selected for even larger brains. Alternatively, brains were the product of adaptive pressures for social intelligence (Humphrey, 1976), for the need for social deception and manipulation (Whiten and Byrne's [1997] "Macchiavellian intelligence"), or for greater strategic intelligence needed in endemic tribal warfare (Alexander, 1989). Still others saw the brain evolving from a runaway sexual selection where mating favored a rapidly expanding range of cultural artifacts (Miller, 2000). Such notions were hard to reconcile with known principles of evolution and raised the danger that the "entire enterprise of interpreting culture as enlarged inclusive-fitness-optimizing strategies must fall" (Barkow, 1989, p. 283).

The basic dilemma facing all these efforts was that as long as specific cultural traits were related to their reproductive success or to the human capacity to "estimate subconsciously or consciously the probable fitness effects of employing alternative behaviour patterns" (Wrangham, 1980, p. 174), the flexibility and directedness of human culture could not be treated as a characteristic in its own right, but only as an exception to, or side effect of, genetic selection. The dilemma was essentially similar to that of sociological functionalism: to the extent that lasting social institutions are considered "functional," it becomes difficult to consider change and creativity as anything other than deviance or anomie. Even authors such as Campbell, Boyd and Richerson, or Miller, who make considerable efforts to account for the autonomy of cultural evolution, are hampered by the fact that they try to continue to see this autonomy through the lens of the genetic inheritance paradigm. Campbell's internal vicarious selectors ultimately "represent" past adaptation through natural selection and are merely its mental reflection in the form of adaptive instincts or behavioral predispositions (Campbell, 1974, p. 146). Miller acknowledges the "frivolity" of culture and the human

capacity "for the rapid, unpredictable generation of highly variable alternatives" (Miller, 2000, p. 405). He then uses a fitness- and sexual selection–
based explanation where human creativity as a specific trait evolves initially
as an adaptive strategy of randomizing behavior to confuse predators and
avoid capture (Miller, 2000, p. 392). This leads to the runaway reengineer-
ing of the brain "to randomly activate and recombine ideas" (Miller, 2000,
p. 405), which is enhanced by sexual selection because the production of
novelty is a desirable source of entertainment and a valued indicator of youth
and general fitness. Boyd and Richerson's "dual inheritance model" assumes
that culture is not only shaped by genes but can exert its own selective pressure on them, with the result that cultural norms may be imposed on human
genes (Boyd & Richerson, 1985). But these cultural "decisions" are either
symbolic markers which protect local ecological adaptations against im-
ported cultural traits from other populations who have adapted to different
ecological niches (Boyd & Richerson, 2000, p. 14), or they are reduced to
simplified psychological processes such as the calculation of costs and benefits, conformity with the most common behavior variants, or the imitation
of "successful" people. Ultimately here, too, human choice merely represents "efficient proximal vicarious selectors" (Boyd & Richerson, 2000, p. 10)
that anticipate maladaptive problems and solve them before they occur.
They are thus essentially surrogates for natural selection and will be replaced
by the latter if they do not work. Boyd and Richerson (2000, p. 27) clearly
recognize that the central problem of an evolutionary analysis of culture is
"to know how strong is the effect of natural selection on cultural variation
relative to forces that derive from human agency." But by continuing to employ fitness as the key to unlocking the puzzle of cultural variability, in-
ventiveness, and design, they are unable to understand the full role of
agency in evolution.

Today, the evolutionary study of human culture is a divided field. Most
biologists will concede some autonomy of culture from reproductive success. Actual explanations range from strong adaptationist programs, which
continue to look for fitness-enhancing elements in all cultural traits, to
weaker programs, which maintain that only core codes, universals, or the
deep structure of the brain are the result of fitness-related selection and that
these are surrounded by more flexible subprograms and -codes (Lopreato,
1984; Barkow, 1989; Lumsden & Wilson, 1981; Wilson, 1998), or which
rely on a variety of extension mechanisms such as culture stretch and runaway processes.

Not a few authors have concluded that cultural selection is partly or entirely the result of non-evolutionary Lamarckian processes controlled by "a
system of poorly understood internal drives and rewards that direct the activity and choices of the individual . . . towards maximizing self satisfaction"
(Cavalli-Sforza & Feldman, 1981, p. 363). Memeticists such as Blackmore

(2000) argued that an entirely new and unique dual replication process, one genetic, one memetic, emerged with the evolution of human beings. Even Gould, not usually keen to be seen in this company, suggested that "cultural evolution can proceed so quickly because it operates, as biological evolution does not, in the Lamarckian mode—by the inheritance of acquired characteristics" (Gould, 1981, p. 325). The high rate of innovation, the variety of adaptively redundant cultural traits, and the role of human agency in combining them into cultural patterns could not be explained. Darwin's "citadel" remained unconquered.

Evolution, Redundancy, and Agency

An alien observer of our culture would no doubt be struck by two characteristics. On one hand it would be quickly evident that we share not only physical but also behavioral and cultural species characteristics. When we laugh or cry, perceive colors and proportions and tonal harmony, fall in love and raise children, learn languages, age, and die, our behavior, while variable, varies around an identifiable mean and is universally understood, regardless of where and when we live. A good part of what we do *has* its roots in our genes. Modern evolutionary psychology, including research on the brain, has made great strides in identifying the cultural reflections of these roots, and in unravelling the neural processes through which they work. Our culture, like our body, bears the stamp of our evolutionary past.

But our visitor would also find that we are extraordinarily inventive and inquisitive, that we write symphonies, watch soap operas and build space stations, frequently change our minds, and do marvelously well in making the best of uncertain environments. As a result, new human behaviors constantly emerge; our culture is prone to unpredictable change and is capable of exquisite design, numbing mediocrity, and irrational destructiveness.

In order to understand how genetic determination and human agency coexist, we must return to Darwin's balance between the active internal adaptation of organisms during their life course, and the registration of its results on the genetic ledger. The inheritance of adaptive characteristics is only half the story of evolution. Without trial-and-error exploration, the potential adaptive uses of many variations will remain undiscovered and therefore unselected. Without differential inheritance of those that are used no evolution can take place. Organisms must first find those uses of the traits they inherit, and of the environments they encounter, which allow them to solve the problem of living before they can pass their traits on to future generations. This search takes place while they are alive. When internal and inherited selection are considered together, *evolution appears as an active, choice-making process that leaves a genetic trace.*

Genetic and internal adaptation are interrelated but distinct processes. Both are essential elements of evolution. Genetic change works through mutation, reproduction, and inheritance, and replicates by copying strands of DNA. It changes gene frequencies across life spans and is therefore relatively slow. Organisms are passive recipients of these changes. Internal selection changes behavior frequencies during the life span. It is fast and replicates through learning, observation, imitation, and symbolic communication. Organisms are active participants in this process. Genetic and internal selection interact: the first provides blind phenotypic resources; the second explores their possible uses and channels their differential inheritance.

Given these differences, one process cannot be taken as a template for the other. Confounding the two has led the evolutionary study of human culture into a frustrating and largely fruitless search for cultural analogs or extensions of genes, mutations, chemical information codes, and biological fitness. *What unites genetic and internal selection is not their identity but a more fundamental underlying principle: all evolution produces blind variety—genetic, behavioral, and cognitive—in response to unpredictable and contingent environments, and from this variety it selects workable and eventually heritable solutions.*

Internal selection, the lived, experimental half of evolution, has four distinct characteristics: the high plasticity of trials and selectors, the fallibility of internal selection, the dual retention of its results, and the generative role of the mind.

1. In genetic selection *plasticity and variation* are reflected in Darwin's "excess reproduction" and more specifically in blind (i.e., non-Lamarckian) genetic variation. In the internal adaptation during the organism's lifetime variation occurs as blind behavior- or thought-trials that explore inherited abilities and physical and social environments for their use to the organism. "Blind" does not mean that variation must be truly random or chaotic. The causes of both genetic and behavioral variation may be well known, and their frequency may be quite predictable. Nor does it mean that they are unguided: their direction is determined by the composition of the genotype, and, in the case of thought or behavior trials during internal adaptation, by existing information and by the perceived needs, preferences, or purposes of organisms. The real reason for the production of blind variety lies in the fact that social and natural environments are to a substantial degree contingent, unknown, and unpredictable. *The production of blind variety is the best possible response to such environmental uncertainty because it increases the probability that a workable "fit" is found between variation and unknown environment.* Conversely, the more uncertain environments are, the more likely it is that dedicated and fixed responses will have lethal consequences. Evolution can therefore be expected to favor plasticity, whether genetic or cultural, in all contingent environments, especially in highly complex and unpredictable social contexts.

Plasticity is evident both in exploratory behavior- and thought-trials and in the internal evaluation of their results. The apparent paradox here is that internal selection increases internally generated variation in order to reduce the complexity of its external world. From the point of view of the living, adapting organism, any genetic change caused by mutation blends with the sum total of its physical, behavioral, and cognitive/mental endowment. On the other side, natural or social environments appear as opportunities and risks. Their unpredictability may be inherent—the result of nonlinear change—or perceived—the result of incomplete information. Trial-and-error exploration employs both ability and environment as resources which, from the organism's vantage point, are usually indistinguishable. Campbell's great contribution to the understanding of internal selection was to recognize that the probing and exploring of environments is made more efficient by the evolution of visual scanning that stands in for physical locomotion, of communication and language that permit the transmission of "virtual" representations of actual states or environments, and of memory and thought trials that store these representations for unrestricted recall and operate on them. These vicarious modes of exploration replace the more costly direct interaction with environments and lead to major adaptive gains in the speed, economy, and precision of trial-and-error exploration (Campbell, 1970, 1974).

High plasticity also characterizes the internal standards for the evaluation of the results, and the retention in habit or memory of those that work. Luhmann (1995, 1997) is one of the few sociologists who recognized that the emergence of social systems and their culture involves the selective reduction of complexity through the generation of *Sinn* or meaning. Utility is not a fixed, built-in property of traits or environments but a function of the preferences and actions of the individual. It is a frequent error in evolutionary analyses unfamiliar with the empirical complexity of social behavior to assume that "for any given environmental situation, there is often one best thing to do" (Miller, 2000, p. 393). In reality, abilities and environments always offer more opportunities than the organisms can use. The adaptive potential of an object or an environment is not inherent but problematic; it is constructed by the organism during its lifetime. For the living organism, the same environmental condition can have multiple, changing, and overlapping uses. From this vantage point the idea, as Hull (1990) puts it, is as much a myth as the gene. Neither are carriers of fixed, intrinsic codes of information. Their meaning is determined by the organism. The lesson of game theory is that many social dilemmas offer no finite or optimal solution. Their benefits and costs depend on short- or long-term horizons, or on the value placed on self-interest or the collective good. Because they face different options of often uncertain value, behavior trials and internal selection always contain valuational components. Their accuracy—that is, the correspondence between perceived and actual features of environments—can therefore not serve as a measure of adaptive fitness. Culture does not differ "from genes in that people are passive recipients of their genes but active agents with respect to culture" (Boyd & Richerson, 2000, p. 2). The reduction of complexity by making "sense" from the multiple potential uses of inherited abilities and the multiple opportunities offered by environments is the crucial contribution of internal selection to the process of evolution.

Evolution thus favors the increased flexibility of trials and of internal selectors. The more complex the trials, the more options to choose from, and the more complex the preferences, the more potential uses can be extracted from traits or environments. Internal criteria for evaluation and choice begin with the simple feedback processes typical of the bonding of enzymes and proteins, evolve into hard-wired instincts, and eventually into the highly flexible human goals, which make it possible to surround environments with a wide variety of meanings and goals in order to extract from them as much utility as possible. Here, the process is supported by the evolution of internal vicarious selectors: freely imagined desires, wants, objectives, and interests that can be tried out in imagined, memorized, or real environments (Campbell, 1974). Both the evolution of virtual representations of environments in vision, symbolic communication, and memory and the evolution of virtual goals and objectives precedes the emergence of human beings. Behavioral innovation and the social transmission of new habits are common in many animal species, especially those that live in complex social environments. While our access to mental states of animals is severely limited, we know that even the most extraordinary biological change, whether it is flight or human consciousness, must have its evolutionary antecedents.

2. All trial-and-error exploration and internal selection must be *fallible:* it must allow for experimentation with nonlethal consequences. Organisms must be able to be wrong and to learn from mistakes if they are to make choices that allow them to live and reproduce. Living is always more than surviving; internal adaptation is always richer and more complex than genetic adaptation. Redundancy is therefore the inevitable by-product of all trial and error. Suboptimal, nonadaptive, or even maladaptive behavior is the normal feature of all internal selection. If behavior is not sufficiently maladaptive to affect reproductive success, its biological basis will be retained by genetic selection. Selection, whether internal or genetic, is a sufficing process, not an optimizing process.

3. Redundant by-products of internal selection do not disappear. Internal adaptation leads to *dual retention:* the selection of usable fits between trials, environments, and internal selectors is accompanied by the retention of a pool of useless trials and obsolete selections. Once again it is Luhmann who recognized that the reduction of complexity involves both the selection of preferred meaning and the production of unused options that are not lost

but retained as a source of future alternatives (Luhmann, 1995, 1997). This culture pool, just like those parts of the gene pool that are not expressed in the phenotype, serves as a continuing insurance against an unpredictable future.

4. Inherited and lived adaptation favor two very different functions of the brain. The first leads to the modular, special-purpose brain, whose dedicated and genetically relatively invariant elements adapt human beings to characteristics of their environment that are relatively stable. The modular brain contains the tried-and-true record of past adaptation. It encourages the correspondences between specific perceptions and behaviors, on one hand, and fairly constant aspects of our environment. Its prescriptions can become obsolete or run out of control. Our body's craving for fat, salt, or sugar served us well when they were in short supply but has become maladaptive in a culture of cheap and abundant fast food. Our natural physiological response to periodic fear-induced stress becomes debilitating in modern work environments where anxiety is low-key but chronic and release is blocked by work schedules and rules of conduct.

By contrast, internal adaptation and selection require a *generative brain*, the highly flexible brain of creative variation and choice. This brain is a general-purpose, random-access, variety-producing, and variety-assembling organ. It makes it possible to imagine outcomes of actions that have not yet taken place, to anticipate the response or motivation of others, to find utility in environments over which it has little control or information, and to link this information with purposes it deliberately invents and varies. By doing so, it allows organisms to cope with novel, unpredictable situations for which routine or dedicated responses produced by if-then algorithms would fail.

The generative brain has one further function. It provides the coherence, the "theme" for the assembly of individual traits into complex living forms. Internal selection is a process analogous to artificial selection: the place of the (external) preferences of the breeder is now taken by internal performance expectations of the organism. Like artificial selection, they drastically accelerate the speed of evolution and become an important source of evolutionary direction and design. No need to climb Mount Improbable (Dawkins, 1996) when we have a simpler, more economical explanation for the emergence of complex evolutionary forms.

Both brain functions are the product of evolution. Both are present in different degrees in all life-forms. The continuing treatment of "inheritance" and "blank slate" views of the brain as contrasting and incompatible (Pinker, 2002) is therefore misplaced. Human behavior that cannot be accounted for by the effects of genes is neither a residual category nor a uniquely human property. Modular and generative brain functions deal with very different problems. Agency and redundancy, the products of the generative brain, are integral aspects of the lived part of evolution. *The adaptive benefit of agency comes not from any particular action but from the overall gain in added value derived from the flexible exploration and exploitation of environmental resources.* Our emergence and success as a species, at least until now, has been the combined result of our inherited algorithmic rules of behavior and our generative ability to solve the problems of survival during our lifetime.

Toward an Evolutionary Sociology of Human Culture

For the sociologist skeptical of evolutionary analyses of human culture, the reintegration of the lived, experienced part of selection into the theory of evolution opens some surprising perspectives. We no longer have to look for cultural analogs to genes or try to determine the reproductive effects of cultural traits. Nor are we forced to relegate agency, redundancy, and innovation to the periphery of the process of natural selection. Agency now appears as our evolved ability to cope with the problems of living by creatively probing changing environments for opportunities that meet our highly variable goals, and thus to extract as much utility from them as we can.

Pre-human and human culture have always been the product of lived *and* inherited adaptation. Experimentation, evaluation, and choice underpin both the protoculture of animals and the culture of human societies. That is the basis for the continuity that Darwin postulated in the *Descent*. Cultural variability and redundancy are an *integral*, not a residual, aspect of evolution. By the same token, human evolution continues to work under environmental constraints, and what we do can have disastrous consequences for our reproductive success (Diamond, 1995). Human culture is the combined result of long-term genetic adaptation, which provided us with fixed behavioral responses to relatively stable aspects of our environment, and of a generative brain, which allows us to react creatively during our lifetime to those parts of our environments that we can neither control nor predict. As the complexity of environments grows, especially with the emergence of dense demographic and social networks, selection pressure shifts the balance of culture from its inherited toward its lived component. The adaptive gain drawn from trial and error and internal selection during one's lifetime outpaces the specific gains derived from inherited behavior patterns. The generative brain pulls away from the modular one and increasingly dominates the evolution of culture. Culture always reflects genetic and internal adaptation, but with the branching of humans from their primate ancestors, it is more and more shaped by our generative brain.

This view of evolution suggests a solution for the twin obstacles to an evolutionary analysis of human culture: agency and redundancy. It brings agency back into the process of evolution. Like all life-forms, human actors are opportunists. They respond with creative variety to unpredictable environments in order to derive from them as much utility for their own ends as possible. Those choices that they *think* beneficial (though their actual consequences may turn out to be very different) are used and eventually retained in the long-term behavior patterns that constitute culture. A small portion of these will affect fitness and, therefore, human beings as a species.

Human agency and internal selection remain Darwinian in two important respects. First, they draw on *blind* sources. Human creativity and innovation always involves random behavior or thought trials (Campbell, 1974) and always modifies already-existing ideas and materials; "any new thing that appears in the made world is based on some object already there" (Basalla, 1988, p. 45). Inventions respond not to need but to want and to perceived shortcomings of already existing materials, artifacts, or actions (Petroski, 1992, p. 22). The accumulated knowledge of past generations (Pacey, 1990) or the windfall advantages of everyday environments (Baldus, 1977) do not appear *because* they are useful for an individual's plans. Cultural artifacts and knowledge always include the pre-done work of others whose initial appearance is unrelated to the purpose of later users. This fact is overlooked only because we tend to see invention not as incremental, endemic, and pervasive but as the discontinuous product of exceptional individuals, because we disregard the vital contributions of helpers and assistants (deSolla Price, 1984), and because we attribute only an anecdotal role to chance, neglect the role of predone work, and simplify the connection between technological and social change (Basalla, 1988, p. 57).

Second, the human ability to make selective choices is far from perfect. Complex social environments make predictions beyond the short term highly unreliable and prone to error. Human control over the evolution of culture must thus by necessity remain partial. Culture is the work of human tinkerers who pursue their individual or collective goals by muddling through and making do inventively with opportunities that happen to come their way. Internal selection is error-prone, wasteful, and imperfect. Culture therefore often strays far from the neat functional solutions and the long-term path of progressive societal development charted by so many sociological theories.

An evolutionary sociology of human culture thus provides an ontological basis for the fact that structure and agency are joint forces in evolution. The structural, objective parameters of human life are inextricably interwoven with human perception. External reality intrudes continually into the behavior of living organisms, most notably by creating the thresholds for individual and species survival. But how reality acquires utility or "sense" depends on its perceived relevance for the individual's internal preferences. Social actors always face more options than they can use. They read their external reality therefore always selectively. Objective limits and constraints define, from the organism's point of view, the range of what is possible. The objective, external and subjective, internal sides of evolution are two faces of the same coin.

An evolutionary sociology also follows Darwin in assuming that a single theory should explain all evolution, including that of human beings and their culture. But compared to the Comtian vision of a "science of society," its program of causal explanation and prediction is considerably more modest. The basic flaw of the deterministic view was that the very act of "explaining and predicting" a social system in terms of a mechanical causality forced the researcher to exclude the microdiversity and the nonaverage behavior that gave rise to social change and evolution. Sociologists consequently saw the functionally redundant and unpredictable features of the social world as a threat to the status of their discipline as an exact science. Much of their methodological effort was devoted to reducing artificially the spacial and temporal complexity of the social world in order to create idealized, quasi-experimental datasets that were immune to the "messiness of time" (Griffin, 1992, p. 403) and supported the epistemological fiction of an orderly social universe.

By contrast, indeterminacy is a feature of all evolution. The complex relationship between external reality and internal evaluation adds an element of unpredictability to evolutionary outcomes. Adaptive dilemmas often have multiple solutions, and materials, ideas, and technical or cultural artifacts can be put to multiple uses. What is an error in one goal context may become an innovation in another. There is no telling which current cultural element will be drawn upon for future purposes, when, and with what effect (Basalla, 1988; Pacey, 1990).

This suggests that Durkheim's "social facts"—those permanent, decontextualized components with inherent, finite causal attributes, do not exist. Instead, they are the warp and woof of a tapestry whose patterns are constantly remade. Tracing the descent of similar effects may not lead us to the same causes, and the same causes may have altogether different effects. Like all evolution, social processes tend to be irreversible and unrepeatable. They can be neither reduced to universal causes nor predicted by invariant laws. The evolution of human culture, like all evolution, is permanently poised between order and contingency, temporary stability and unpredictable change.

An evolutionary sociology is therefore a probabilistic, nondeterministic science. Its main focus is to reconstruct the evolutionary descent lines of social events by analyzing the blind material: the behavioral and intellectual antecedents with which such sequences begin, the social construction of relevance, the social forces that decide which of them are retained and which rejected, and the long-term consequences of the selection process. Its "laws" are like Parkinson's, not like Newton's: temporary social order emerges around selectors such as institutional constraints, religious interests, power, or wealth, but the resulting patterns will not acquire the status of laws. Sociology can model future evolution as counterfactuals or possibility spaces (Allen, 1992) but knows that its power to predict diminishes rapidly beyond the very short term.

Theories tell us what questions to ask of our data. If sociology has lately appeared to some of its practitioners to be an "impossible science" (Turner & Turner, 1990), that is perhaps because for decades the theoretical ideas that guided it have been at odds with the natural properties of social life. The complexity of human culture can neither be forced into the Procrustean bed of positivist "social laws" or functional/rational choice nor put into the straightjacket of genetic adaptationism. An evolutionary view of social life deprives sociologists of hopes for a deterministic "science of society." In exchange, it brings to sociology the most compelling of Darwin's arguments: that an unbroken line links prehuman and human evolution and that we must therefore look for the common natural principles of all life, including that of human beings and their culture.

Notes

1. Giddens's critique of evolutionary theory is symptomatic of the confusion in this area. First he discusses three examples of "evolutionism" which bear little or no resemblance to Darwin's theory of evolution, namely developmental stage models of history, Freud's thesis that the mental development of European children recapitulates the progression of human history from "savages" to European "civilization," and Parsons's evolutionary functionalism. He then blames these theories for disregarding the reflexive nature of social life, for confusion about the unit of evolution, for unilineal compression and temporal distortion, and for positing a correspondence between social evolution and personality development. Now hopelessly lost in the thicket of sociological evolutionisms, Giddens not surprisingly concludes that biological theory has nothing to tell us about culture, and that its "dangers . . . are best avoided by breaking with it in a radical way" (1984, p. 239).

2. Sociologists are beginning to notice the methodological consequences of this fact (Lieberson & Lynn, 2002).

References

Alexander, R. D. (1979). *Darwinism and Human Affairs.* Seattle: University of Washington Press.

Alexander, R. D. (1989). The Evolution of the Human Psyche. In P. Mellars & C. Stringer (Eds.), *The Human Revolution* (pp. 455–513). Edinburgh: Edinburgh University Press.

Allen, P. M. (1992). Modelling Evolution and Creativity in Complex Systems. *World Futures, 34*, 105–123.

Baldus, B. (1977). Social Control in Capitalist Societies: An Examination of the Problem of Order in Liberal Democracies. *Canadian Journal of Sociology, 2*(3), 247–262.

Baldus, B. (1990). Positivism's Twilight? *Canadian Journal of Sociology 15*(2), 149–163.

Barash, D. (1979). *The Whisperings Within*. Harmondsworth: Penguin.

Barkow, J. H. (1989). *Darwin, Sex, and Status*. Toronto: University of Toronto Press.

Barkow, J. H., Cosmides, L., & Tooby, J. (Eds). (1992). *The Adapted Mind: Evolutionary Psychology and the Generation of Culture*. New York: Oxford University Press.

Basalla, G. (1988). *The Evolution of Technology*. Cambridge: Cambridge University Press.

Beck, U. (1992). *Risk Society: Towards a New Modernity*. London: Sage.

Bernard, P. (1993). Cause perdue? Le pouvoir heuristique de l'analyse causale. *Sociologie et sociétés, 25*(2), 171–189.

Blackmore, S. (1999). *The Meme Machine*. Oxford: Oxford University Press.

Blackmore, S. (2000). The Power of Memes. *Scientific American*, October, 64–73.

Bourdieu, P. (1977). *Outline of a Theory of Practice*. Cambridge: Cambridge University Press.

Bourdieu, P. (1992). *An Invitation to Reflexive Sociology*. Chicago: University of Chicago Press.

Boyd, R., & Richerson, P. J. (1985). *Culture and the Evolutionary Process*. Chicago: University of Chicago Press.

Boyd, R., & Richerson, P. J. (2000). Evolution: The Darwinian Theory of Social Change. An Homage to Donald T. Campbell. Paper presented at "Paradigms of Social Change" conference, Berlin-Brandenburgische Akademie der Wissenschaften, January. Draft 2.2.

Bryant, J. M. (1992). Positivism Redivivus? A Critique of Recent Uncritical Proposals for Reforming Sociological Theory. *Canadian Journal of Sociology, 17*(1), 29–53.

Campbell, D. T. (1970). Natural Selection as an Epistemological Model. In R. Naroll & R. Cohen (Eds.), *A Handbook of Methods in Cultural Anthropology* (pp. 51–85). Garden City, NY: Natural History Press.

Campbell, D. T. (1974). Unjustified Variation and Selective Retention in Scientific Discovery. In F. J. Ayala & T. Dobzhansky (Eds.), *Studies in the Philosophy of Biology* (pp. 139–161). Berkeley: University of California Press.

Cavalli-Sforza, L. L., & Feldman, M. W. (1981). *Cultural Transmission and Evolution: A Quantitative Approach*. Princeton, NJ: Princeton University Press.

Collins, R. (1986). Is 1980s Sociology in the Doldrums? *American Journal of Sociology, 91*(5), 1336–1355.

Collins, R. (1989). Sociology: Proscience or Antiscience? *American Sociological Review, 54,* 124–139.

Cronin, H. (1991). *The Ant and the Peacock.* Cambridge: Cambridge University Press.

Darwin, C. (1958/1872). *The Origin of Species* (6th ed.). New York: New American Library.

Darwin, C. (1965/1872). *On the Expression of Emotions in Man and Animals.* Chicago: University of Chicago Press.

Darwin, C. (1981/1871). *The Descent of Man.* Princeton, NJ: Princeton University Press.

Dawkins, R. (1976). *The Selfish Gene.* Oxford: Oxford University Press.

Dawkins, R. (1986). *The Blind Watchmaker.* New York: Norton.

Dawkins, R. (1996). *Climbing Mount Improbable.* New York: Norton.

Dennett, D. (1991). *Consciousness Explained.* Boston: Little, Brown.

Desmond, A., & Moore, J. (1991). *Darwin: The Life of a Tormented Evolutionist.* New York: Norton.

deSolla Price, D. (1984). Of Sealing Wax and Strings. *Natural History, 1,* 49–56.

Diamond, J. (1995). Easter's End. *Discover,* August, 63–69.

Giddens, A. (1984). *The Constitution of Society: Outline of the Theory of Structuration.* Cambridge: Polity Press.

Gould, S. J. (1981). *The Mismeasure of Man.* New York: W. W. Norton.

Griffin, D. R. (1984). *Animal Thinking.* Cambridge, MA: Harvard University Press.

Griffin, L. J. (1992). Temporality, Events, and Explanation in Historical Sociology: An Introduction. *Sociological Methods and Research, 20,* 403–427.

Gruber, H. E. (1981). *Darwin on Man: A Psychological Study of Scientific Creativity.* Chicago: University of Chicago Press.

Hallpike, C. R. (1986). *The Principles of Social Evolution.* Oxford: Clarendon.

Hull, D. (1990). *Science as a Process.* Chicago: University of Chicago Press.

Humphrey, N. (1976). The Social Function of Intellect. In P. P. G. Bateson & R. A. Hinde (Eds.), *Growing Points in Ethology* (pp. 303–317). Cambridge: Cambridge University Press.

Lieberson, S., & Lynn, F. (2002). Barking Up the Wrong Branch: Scientific Alternatives to the Current Model of Sociological Science. *Annual Review of Sociology, 28,* 1–19.

Lopreato, J. (1984). *Human Nature and Biocultural Evolution.* Boston: Allen and Unwin.

Luhmann, N. (1995/1984). *Social Systems.* Stanford: Stanford University Press.

Luhmann, N. (1997). *Die Gesellschaft der Gesellschaft.* 2 Vols. Frankfurt: Suhrkamp.

Lumsden, C. J., & Wilson, E. O. (1981). *Genes, Mind and Culture.* Cambridge, MA: Harvard University Press.

Miller, G. (2000). *The Mating Mind.* New York: Doubleday.

Moore, J. R. (1985). Darwin of Down: The Evolutionist as a Squarson-Naturalist. In D. Kohn (Ed.), *The Darwinian Heritage* (pp. 435–481). Princeton, NJ: Princeton University Press.

Pacey, A. (1990). *Technology in World Civilization*. Cambridge: MIT Press.

Petroski, H. (1992). *The Evolution of Useful Things*. New York: Knopf.

Pinker, S. (1997). *How the Mind Works*. New York: W. W. Norton.

Pinker, S. (2002). *The Blank Slate: The Modern Denial of Human Nature*. New York: Viking.

Quadagno, J., & Knapp, S. J. (1992). Have Historical Sociologists Forsaken Theory? *Sociological Methods and Research, 20*(4), 481–507.

Richards, R. J. (1987). *Darwin and the Emergence of Evolutionary Theories of Mind and Behaviour*. Chicago: University of Chicago Press.

Ruse, M. (1979). *The Darwinian Revolution*. Chicago: University of Chicago Press.

Skinner, B. F. (1971). *Beyond Freedom and Dignity*. New York: Knopf.

Smith, C. U. M. (1978). Charles Darwin, the Origin of Consciousness, and Panpsychism. *Journal of the History of Biology, 11*(2), 245–267.

Tooby, J., & Cosmides, L. (1989). Evolutionary Psychology and the Generation of Culture. *Ethology and Sociobiology, 10*, 29–49.

Turner, S. P. (1987). Cause, Law, and Probability. *Sociological Theory, 5*, 15–40.

Turner, S. P., & Turner, J. H. (1990). *The Impossible Science: An Institutional Analysis of American Sociology*. Newbury Park: Sage.

Whiten, A., & Byrne, R. (1997). *Machiavellian Intelligence II: Extension and Evaluations*. Cambridge: Cambridge University Press.

Wilson, E. O. (1978). *On Human Nature*. Cambridge, MA: Harvard University Press.

Wilson, E. O. (1998). *Consilience: The Unity of Knowledge*. New York: Knopf.

Wrangham, R. (1980). Sociobiology: Modification without Dissent. *Biological Journal of the Linnean Society, 13*, 171–177.

Index

Abu-Lughod, Lila, 23
Ache, 178, 251
adaptation
  and behavior, 26–27
  and criminal behavior, 229
  and culture, 26–27
  defined, 90, 229
  and evolutionary psychology,
    90–91
  executors vs. fitness maximizers,
    259n.3
  and genes, 87–91
  and "hyperadaptationism,"
    153–54
  internal adaptation, 271
agency, 17, 222–23, 271, 279–80,
  283–88
  and genetic determinism, 283–84
aggression, and testosterone,
  237–38
Agta, 235
Alexander, Richard D., 5, 45n.10,
  48n.28, 168
Alkon, Amy, 39, 40, 48n.29
Allman, W., 229
Alternative Adaptation Theory
  (AAT), 251–52

altruism, 47–48n.27, 123, 140n.1,
  229–30
  defined, 229
Anderson, Elijah, 108
anger, and violent response, 102–03
anisogamy, 70, 80
Arapaho, 111
Arapesh, 81–82
Aristotle, 189–90
Ardrey, Robert, 128
Arnhart, Larry, 10, 45n.10
Atran, Scott, 12, 41
Aunger, Robert, 23, 46n.21
Ayoreo, 174

Bailey, F. G., 170
Bailey, K. G., 9
Baldus, Bernd, 11, 222–23, 223n.1
Baldwin, J. M., 222
band-and-bond model, 189–99, 209
  and residence rules, 190–93,
    200–02
Barkow, Jerome H., 46n.21, 47n.26,
  48n.28, 141–42n.12, 152, 170,
  176–77, 228, 249, 258
Barnard, A., 200
Barth, Fredrik, 170